Lecture Notes in Computer Sc

T0238395

Commenced Publication in 1973
Founding and Former Series Editors:
Gerhard Goos, Juris Hartmanis, and Jan van Leeuwen

Bernt Schiele   Anind K. Dey
Hans Gellersen   Boris de Ruyter
Manfred Tscheligi   Reiner Wichert
Emile Aarts   Alejandro Buchmann (Eds.)

Ambient Intelligence

European Conference, AmI 2007
Darmstadt, Germany, November 7-10, 2007
Proceedings

 Springer

Volume Editors

Bernt Schiele
Alejandro Buchmann
TU Darmstadt, Germany
E-mail: {schiele, buchmann}@informatik.tu-darmstadt.de

Anind K. Dey
Carnegie Mellon University, Pittsburgh, PA, USA
E-mail: anind@cs.cmu.edu

Hans Gellersen
Lancaster University, UK
E-mail: hwg@comp.lancs.ac.uk

Boris de Ruyter
Emile Aarts
Philips Research Europe, Eindhoven, The Netherlands
E-mail: {boris.de.ruyter, emile.aarts}@philips.com

Manfred Tscheligi
University of Salzburg, Austria
E-mail: manfred.tscheligi@sbg.ac.at

Reiner Wichert
Fraunhofer-IGD, Darmstadt, Germany
E-mail: reiner.wichert@igd.fraunhofer.de

Library of Congress Control Number: 2007938404

CR Subject Classification (1998): H.4, C.2, D.4.6, H.5, I.2, K.4

LNCS Sublibrary: SL 3 – Information Systems and Application, incl. Internet/Web and HCI

ISSN   0302-9743
ISBN-10   3-540-76651-0 Springer Berlin Heidelberg New York
ISBN-13   978-3-540-76651-3 Springer Berlin Heidelberg New York

Springer is a part of Springer Science+Business Media

springer.com

© Springer-Verlag Berlin Heidelberg 2007
Printed in Germany

Typesetting: Camera-ready by author, data conversion by Scientific Publishing Services, Chennai, India
Printed on acid-free paper   SPIN: 12187645   06/3180   5 4 3 2 1 0

Preface

Ambient Intelligence (AmI) was introduced in the late 1990s as a novel paradigm for electronic environments for the years 2010–2020. The concept builds on the early ideas of Weiser, who was aiming at a novel mobile computing infrastructure integrated into the networked environment of people. AmI takes the embedding of computing devices one step ahead by integrating computational intelligence into the entire surrounding of people, thus moving technology fully to the background and the user into the foreground by supporting him or her with intuitive and natural interaction concepts. According to the definition, AmI refers to smart electronic environments that are sensitive and responsive to the presence of people. Since its introduction the vision has grown mature, so as to become quite influential in the development of new concepts for information processing, combining multi-disciplinary fields including electrical engineering, computer science, industrial design, user interfaces, and cognitive sciences.

The AmI paradigm provides a basis for new models of technological innovation within a multi-dimensional society. The added value of the AmI vision lies in the fact that the large-scale integration of electronics into the environment enables the actors, i.e., people and objects, to interact with their surrounding in a seamless, trustworthy, and natural manner. This is directly connected to the growing societal need for communication and the exchange of information. AmI environments will therefore not only support peoples lives with the purpose of increasing their productivity, but they will also serve the largely unmet need of people for self-expression, personalized health-care, and social connectedness. A major issue in this respect is given by the growing awareness that novel concepts should meet elementary user requirements such as usefulness and simplicity. Hence, it is generally believed that novel AmI technologies should not aim at increasing functional complexity in the first place, but they particularly should contribute to the development of easy-to-use and simple-to-experience products and services. Obviously, this statement has a broad endorsement by a wide community of both designers and engineers, but reality reveals that it is hard to achieve in practise, and that novel approaches, as may be provided by the AmI vision, are needed to make it work.

Since the introduction of AmI in the beginning of this decade much research effort has been invested in the development of the concept. As a direct result of the large European investment made in the area through the Framework Program 6 (FP6) of the European Commission, there are many interesting developments that provide first proof points of the realization of the AmI vision. AmI 2007 is a conference that serves the scientific community with a platform to present research results and discuss progress in the field made so far. AmI 2007 can be seen as the continuation of a sequence of AmI symposiums and conferences in Europe. It builds on EUSAI the European Symposium on Ambient

Intelligence. EUSAI 2003 and EUSAI 2004 can be seen as the first two scientific symposiums ever held on AmI. In 2005 EUSAI was organized as a joint activity with sOc (Smart Objects Conference) and presented as the sOc-EUSAI conference. Last year we decided to drop the European flavor a to fully join the activities of the two research communities to continue as the AmI conference of which AmI 2007 was the first edition.

AmI 2007 put much emphasis on the desire to combine both scientific research and practical evaluation of novel concepts. Therefore, the conference was organized along the lines of two tracks named as Research Track and Experience Track. The current LNCS volume, which is the formal proceedings of AmI 2007, is structured along the lines of these two tracks. AmI 2007 furthermore provided the research community in AmI with a venue to discuss in an informal setting preliminary results and upcoming ideas through a number of workshops. We felt that we should not hold back the results obtained in these workshops as they are in many cases quite intriguing and therefore may be stimulating in the development of novel ideas. Therefore, we decided to publish these results in a separate Springer volume under the title *Constructing Ambient Intelligence AmI 2007 Workshop Proceedings.*

The material contained in the present volume reveals that the realization and implementation of the AmI vision in its relative short period of time of existence is rapidly gaining traction, and that some of the early ideas following from the vision are growing mature. Examples are the use of context-aware services in smart environments and the high level of personalization that is attained in ambient-assisted living environments. Also the experience design results indicate that there is a growing awareness of the fact that the success of the AmI paradigm heavily depends on the social acceptance of the newly proposed AmI technology and that we need to look carefully at the human factors side of the vision to study the relation between AmI technology and the behavior of people, thus revealing the true added value of AmI in the everyday-life of people.

In view of this, the AmI 2007 proceedings can be considered as a timely document that provides many new results and insights in the development of AmI. We are fairly confident that it provides a meaningful contribution to the dissemination of the AmI vision and we would like to thank all those who have contributed. We hope that you as a reader will have many pleasant and fruitful reading hours.

September 2007   Emile Aarts
                                                              Alex Buchmann

Message from the Program Chairs Research Papers

On behalf of the Program Committee for the Research Papers, we would like to welcome you to AmI 2007 - European Conference on Ambient Intelligence. We received 48 research paper submissions, with authors from 22 countries, and we accepted 17 papers.

Each paper was assigned to three Program Committee members for review (resulting in a total of 46.000 words). The reviewing phase was followed by a discussion phase among the respective Program Committee members in order to suggest papers for acceptance. The three PC Chairs then met in Darmstadt to make final decisions about acceptance based on all reviews, the discussion results and, if necessary, additional reviewing. We would like to thank all members of the Program Committee for their most valuable and highly appreciated contribution to the community by reading submissions, writing reviews, and participating in the discussion phase.

The range of topics evident in the selected papers covers many important topics in ambient intelligence: from sensors and mobile devices, over localization, context awareness and middleware to interfaces and applications of ambient intelligence.

We hope that you find the papers to be interesting, informative, and thought-provoking.

September 2007

Anind K. Dey
Hans Gellersen
Bernt Schiele

Message from the Program Chairs Case Studies and Lessons Learned Papers

The introduction of Ambient Intelligence (AmI) has shifted the focus from system-centric interactions towards user-centric experiences with intelligent environments. Such a shift did not only bring forward new requirements for technologies but has also created the need for innovative research methods and tools. The main goals of user-centric experiences with environments are to investigate how technology can deliver positive experiences into every day life environments, to consider people's social, creative and cognitive skills and to face the users' acceptance of the system, their privacy and trust concern.

A lot of research groups in universities, research institutes and in the industry have applied this way of technology development in the past few years. Many research labs have been funded and were built that offer a daily life ambience to support the testing and evaluation of technology prototypes under real life conditions. This kind of living and early involvement laboratories will dramatically increase the social acceptance of technology. First products are already on the market that support this kind of ambient experience as well as accomplish assistive function for health and security. Thus, this paradigm chance of developing technology proofs its advantages and has started a success story that will dominate the way research will be conducted and developments will be implemented in at least the next decade.

The conference track case studies and lessons learned introduces high-level reports of researchers relating to this AmI core. The following papers introduce first hand reports from AmI laboratories and thus highlight innovative and novel results that deal with experience prototyping and user-centered design. End user insights into current AmI development are given. The Program Committee is proud to present a high level selection of current research reports and papers that reflect the most important activities of current AmI research.

In this special track of AmI 2007, the European Conference on Ambient Intelligence, we present five selected papers discussing the experiences and lessons learned in the area of research and application development for AmI environments. These papers touch upon methodological, infrastructural and technical issues involved in AmI research.

Although any paper focusing on AmI application and experience research will bring forward methodological, infrastructural and technical challenges, the papers in this special track present a more elaborate discussion of these issues rather than on only the research findings. By making explicit the lessons learned and experiences of AmI research we bring forward the way of working in AmI-related research.

AmI environments do not only offer supporting and comforting experiences to its end users, but these environments can also become socially connected spaces that provide a sense of presence with, for example, remote family and friends. In the paper "Expected Information Needs of Parents for Pervasive Awareness Systems," Kahn et al present their experiences with using an on-online survey technique to gather end user requirements for an intelligent awareness system that connects parents with their children. This paper taps into the problem of suitable user requirements gathering techniques for designing AmI services.

AmI research has introduced the concept of Experience and Application Research Centers (EARC). These EARCs offer realistic testing environments for end users to experience innovative concepts while researchers have advanced instruments in place to learn more about, for example, the usability and acceptability of the proposed solutions. In their paper "User-Centered Research in ExperienceLab," de Ruyter et al. present their lessons learned in deploying three EARCs in the context of AmI application development. Highlighting both the infrastructural and the methodological aspects of using EARCs this paper aims at providing the AmI researcher with some valuable insights into the role of EARCs.

In the paper "Assemblies of Heterogeneous Technologies at the Neonatal Intensive Care Unit," Grönvall et al. share their experience in designing an AmI environment for a demanding and dynamic context as found in a neonatal intensive care unit. Specifically, the authors discuss their lessons learned with solutions that enable end user composition and control of AmI assemblies of technologies.

Besides experiences with methodologies and testing environments, this track presents a paper focusing on the lessons learned for using a specific technology in AmI application development. In their paper "Improving Mobile Solution Workflows and Usability Using Near Field Communication Technology," Jaring et al. share their lessons learned for deploying near field communication (NFC) technology in solutions to improve workflows in mobile situations. The experience presented in this paper is of high value for researchers and application developers in the area of AmI for mobile contexts.

To conclude, this track presents a paper discussing the lessons learned in developing and testing AmI scenarios for a public environment such as the retail environment. In their paper "Enhancing the Shopping Experience with Ambient Displays: A Field Study in a Retail Store," Reitberger et al. discuss their experiences in designing and evaluating a system for creating a sense of shared awareness between shop visitors. Such applications illustrate the potential role of AmI technology as a social mediator.

September 2007

Boris de Ruyter
Manfred Tscheligi
Reiner Wichert

Organization

Program Committee

Jakob Bardram	IT University of Copenhagen
James Begole	PARC
Michael Beigl	TU Braunschweig
Andreas Butz	University of Munich
Siobhán Clarke	Trinity College Dublin
Jolle Coutaz	Université Joseph Fourier
James Crowley	INRIA Rhone Alpes
José Encarnação	IGD
Geraldine Fitzpatrick	University of Sussex
James Fogarty	University of Washington
Tom Gross	Bauhaus University Weimar
Beverly Harrison	Intel Research Seattle
Stephen Intille	Massachusetts Institute of Technology
Antonio Krüger	University of Münster
Spyros Lalis	University of Thessaly
Anthony LaMarca	Intel Research Seattle
Marc Langheinrich	ETH Zurich
Paul Lukowicz	University of Passau
Panos Markopoulos	Eindhoven University of Technology
Rene Mayrhofer	Lancaster University
Henk Muller	University of Bristol
Tom Pfeifer	Waterford Institute of Technology, TSSG
Aaron Quigley	University College Dublin
Kurt Rothermel	University of Stuttgart, Germany
Khai Truong	University of Toronto
Kay Roemer	ETH Zurich
Chris Schmandt	Massachusetts Institute of Technology
Albrecht Schmidt	Fraunhofer IAIS and b-it University of Bonn
Kristof Van Laerhoven	TU Darmstadt

Table of Contents

AmI and Artifiial Intelligence

AmI Middleware and Infrastructure

Interaction with the Environment

Case Studies and Lessons Learned

Mobile Interaction with the Real World: An Evaluation and Comparison of Physical Mobile Interaction Techniques

Enrico Rukzio[1], Gregor Broll[2], Karin Leichtenstern[3], and Albrecht Schmidt[4]

[1] Computing Department, Lancaster University, UK
rukzio@comp.lancs.ac.uk
[2] Media Informatics Group, University of Munich, Germany
gregor.broll@ifi.lmu.de
[3] Multimedia Concepts and Applications Group, University of Ausgburg, Germany
karin.leichtenstern@informatik.uni-augsburg.de
[4] Fraunhofer IAIS, Sankt Augustin and B-IT, University of Bonn, Germany
albrecht.schmidt@iais.fraunhofer.de

Abstract. Mobile devices are more and more used for mobile interactions with things, places and people in the real world. However, so far no studies have discussed which interaction techniques are preferred by users in different contexts. This paper presents an experimental comparison of four different physical mobile interaction techniques: touching, pointing, scanning and user-mediated object interaction. To evaluate these techniques across different scenarios and to collect real usage data, four prototypes were implemented: a system for mobile interaction in smart environments, a mobile tourist guide, a mobile museum guide and a prototype for mobile interaction with advertisement posters. In each setting an experimental comparison was performed. Based on the results of these studies, which involved over 60 participants in total, advantages and disadvantages of these interaction techniques are described. Context-specific user preferences are presented for the interaction techniques, to help application designers and developers decide which interaction technique(s) to integrate into their application and which consequences this decision has.

Keywords: Physical mobile interaction, touching, pointing, scanning, user-mediated object interaction, evaluation, comparison.

1 Introduction

An important step towards implementing the vision of ubiquitous computing is the use of mobile devices, which are the first truly pervasive computers and interaction devices. So far, most mobile devices, applications and services mainly focus on the interaction between the user, the mobile device and available services. The context of use is often not considered at all or only marginally. This does not conform to our everyday life and behaviour in which context plays a central role. However, in the last few years, a huge interest in industry and academia in using mobile devices for interactions with people, places and things can be observed [1, 2, 3].

B. Schiele et al. (Eds.): AmI 2007, LNCS 4794, pp. 1–18, 2007.

This paper coins the term *physical mobile interactions* to describe such interaction styles in which the user interacts with a mobile device and the mobile device interacts with objects in the real world. They enable the nearly ubiquitous use of mobile services that are connected with smart objects. In the used terminology, a smart object can be a real world object, a person or even a location.

The usage of physical mobile interactions simplifies the discovery and use of mobile services, enables new kinds of object-, person- or location-based applications and removes several limitations of mobile devices. The most important and widespread physical mobile interaction techniques are identified to be touching, pointing, scanning and user-mediated object interaction [4].

But so far very little research is reported that has analyzed which interaction technique should be provided by an application and which interaction technique is preferred by which users in which situation. Because of this, it is very complicated for application designers to decide which physical mobile interaction technique to support within a new application or service. The application context, the location of the object, the distance between object and user, the service related to the object and the capabilities of the mobile device for instance are important factors that influence the preference of a user for a specific type of interaction technique. Therefore a study-based comparison of several types of physical mobile interaction techniques was conducted, with the main focus on an evaluation of which type of interaction technique fits best in which situations, applications and scenarios. Touching, pointing, scanning and user-mediated object interaction were used in four different prototypes and analysed in four different user studies. The results reflect the advantages and disadvantages of these interaction techniques as seen by potential users.

The paper is organized as follows. The next section gives an overview about physical mobile interactions whereby the focus lies on the interaction techniques touching, pointing, scanning and user-mediated object interaction. Next, the prototypes used for the user studies and their implementations are described. We then present the four user studies and the corresponding results. Based on this we summarize the results and discuss the advantages and disadvantages of the different physical mobile interaction techniques in the different contexts. The paper is completed by a discussion and outline of our further work.

2 Physical Mobile Interactions

A detailed overview and discussion of physical mobile interaction techniques can be found in [4, 5]. The aim of this section is primarily to give an introduction into the interaction techniques touching, pointing, scanning and user-mediated object interaction that is needed for the understanding for the following text.

By means of the interaction technique touching the user can select a real world object by touching it with a mobile device or by bringing them close together (e.g. 0 - 5 cm). Want et al. were one of the first who presented a prototype for this interaction technique which incorporates RFID tags and an RFID reader connected to a mobile device, in this case a tablet computer [6]. For instance, they used this prototype to interact with augmented books, documents and business cards to establish links to corresponding services like ordering a book or picking up an email address. In [7] this interaction technique is called TouchMe which is realized via proximity sensors that sense the distance between the augmented object and the mobile device.

By means of the interaction technique pointing the user can select or control a smart object by pointing at it with the mobile device. Fitzmaurice was one of the first who described the concept of using mobile devices for pointing based interactions with smart objects to interact with related services [8]. He described a map on which the user can point to get information about a specific area and an augmented library as a potential application area for this interaction technology. The NaviCam, a mobile device with an attached camera that interprets visual markers on physical objects, was one of the first implementations of this interaction technique [9].

The interaction technique scanning is based on the proximity of mobile device and smart object which can be a real world object as well as a location in general. The mobile device scans the environment for nearby smart objects. This action can be triggered by the user or the environment is permanently scanned by the mobile device. The result is a list of nearby smart objects. The corresponding implementations are also known as location based mobile services. Examples for this are Bluetooth, i-area [10] or the Lancaster Guide project [11].

By means of the interaction technique user-mediated object interaction the user types in information provided by the object to establish a link between them. No special technology is needed to establish a link between the smart object and the mobile device because the user is responsible for this. Examples are portable museum guides where the visitor has to type in a number to get information about an exhibit or a URL printed on an advertisement poster to get access to the corresponding services.

A first analysis of mobile interaction techniques was done by [5]. They focused on the classification of interaction techniques based on previous work and personal experience. In comparison to our work they did not experientially evaluate these techniques, nor did they use questionnaires or user studies to compare the mobile interaction techniques under investigation. Our experience gained with comparing interaction techniques however suggests this is very important to evaluate them with users even if it requires a significant investment in creating prototypes. This is very much in line with the statement reported in [12]: *the ultimate test of a product's usability is based on measurements of user's experience with it.*

3 Prototypes

As already mentioned four prototypes were developed and evaluated. The first subsection describes their purpose and their usage in the user studies. The following subsection then discusses how these prototypes were implemented with different technology.

3.1 Purpose and Usage of the Prototypes

The first prototype *mobile interaction in smart environments* focuses on the usage of mobile devices for interactions with objects in smart environments [13]. Mobile devices are often seen as control point for smart devices and environments. Similarly mobile devices are regarded in many scenarios as a terminal to access information that is related to real world objects. This includes the provision of additional services, e.g. when the TV is touched the mobile device provides an overview of the programs currently available. A further domain is adding interaction capabilities to devices and things that do not have a user interface, hence acting as a remote control for objects. With this prototype it is possible to use the interaction techniques touching, pointing and scanning to interact with smart objects like a CD player, a radio, heating or a laptop which were augmented by Mifare RFID tags and light sensors. Through this the user is able to receive status information about and to control the devices via the mobile devices. The first row of Table 1 shows how a user touches an augmented CD player. It also presents the hardware used for the implementation of the interaction technique pointing.

The second prototype *mobile tourist guide* is a mobile guide application through which users can get additional information about exhibits in an art park. This prototype supports the interaction techniques pointing, scanning and user-mediated object interaction for the selection of points of interests. User-mediated object interaction and scanning are interaction techniques that are often used as part of existing mobile outdoor guides. Therefore, the prototype supports these two interaction techniques as well. In addition to those, pointing as a novel interaction technique that requires a short distance to the exhibit is integrated. The exhibits in the park were augmented with information signs showing a number for user-mediated object interaction and a visual code [15] for the interaction technique pointing as can be seen in the first picture of the second row of Table 1.

The third prototype *mobile museum guide* supports touching, pointing and user-mediated object interaction and can be used to get additional information about objects of an exhibition in a museum. User-mediated object interaction is the most typical interaction technique used in such guides and is therefore also supported by this prototype. In addition, touching and pointing are integrated as novel interaction techniques that require a shorter distance to the exhibit. The corresponding user study was conducted in a university building in which part of a train museum was simulated. Therefore several posters showing the name of the exhibit, a picture of it and some textual information were attached to different walls. These posters were augmented with ISO 15693-3 RFID tags, visual codes and numbers. The third row of Table 1 shows how a user touches and points onto the simulated exhibits and a visitor who interacts primarily with the phone when using user-mediated object interaction.

The forth prototype *mobile interaction with advertisement posters* can be used to order cinema tickets trough the interaction with corresponding augmented advertisement posters [14]. The idea behind this prototype is similar to the previously discussed *mobile museum guide*. The big difference is that the poster is not just augmented with one link to one service. In this prototype the poster is augmented with multiple tags. There is a visual code beside every Near Field Communication (NFC) sign and on the position of every NFC sign there is a Mifare RFID tag attached to the back of the poster. The user can physically click on each of these markers by pointing at or touching them. To buy a movie ticket, for instance, the user has to select the movie, the cinema, the number of persons as well as the desired time slot through touching or pointing at the corresponding parts of the poster.

Table 1. Usage of the interactions techniques provided by the four prototypes

Usage of touching and the hardware for pointing (mobile phone with attached laser pointer, light sensor attached to smart object, USB bridge for receiving the pointing signals) in the first prototype *mobile interaction in smart environments*

Pictures taking during the user study evaluating the second *prototype mobile tourist guide*

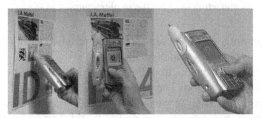

Usage of touching and pointing and user-mediated object interaction the third prototype *mobile museum guide*

Usage of touching and pointing and user-mediated object interaction in the fourth prototype *mobile interaction with advertisement posters*

3.2 Implementation

This section discusses the implementation of the four prototypes and the used hardware. Figure 1 shows the underlying basic architecture in which all elements involved in the interaction are depicted: the mobile device, the smart object and

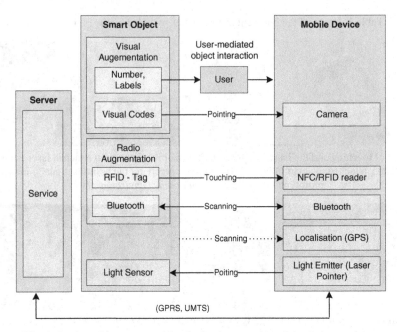

Fig. 1. Basic architecture used for the implementation of the four prototypes

related services running on a server. This figure also shows which interaction technique is implemented using which technologies.

Within a physical mobile interaction, the mobile device acts as a mediator between the physical and the digital world. The server represents the digital world which offers information and services related to the smart object. The latter represents the physical world and provides entry points into the digital world. Generally, it can be seen that the smart object provides a link to associated services that are made available by a corresponding server. In all prototypes a person can use her mobile device to interact with a smart object and thus use the service related to the smart object.

Table 2 shows the different prototypes, the types of the smart objects, the supported interaction techniques and the used hardware. The table also shows how many persons participated in the user studies, what their average age was and in which month the user study was conducted.

The software running on the mobile device was implemented using Java ME, MIDP 2.0 and CLDC 1.0/1.1. The services running on the server were implemented in Java as well, e.g. using the Java Servlet API and Apache Tomcat.

Two different devices were used for the implementation of the interaction technique touching. The first implementation is based on a Nokia 3220 with an attached Nokia NFC shell that was used to read Mifare RFID tags. The second one is on the IDBlue RFID pen which was stuck on a Nokia N70 and used to read ISO 15693-3 RFID tags. In this case the smart objects are augmented with RFID tags that can be sensed by mobile devices. Through this the application on a mobile device can read the information stored on the tag and can identify the touched object and the related services.

Two implementations of the interaction technique pointing were used; one was based on a laser pointer and the other on visual codes. The first implementation provides feedback in the real world by using a laser pointer [13] that is physically attached to a mobile phone. The objects which are controlled recognise the beam with light sensors (FW 300) built into the smart object. The recognition algorithm that detects the beam on the light sensor is implemented in a micro-controller that is wirelessly connected to the system. The second implementation uses the built-in cameras of mobile phones to take pictures of visual codes [15]. These are then analyzed and the deciphered information is used to establish a link to the object and the related services.

Table 2. Prototypes, supported interaction techniques, used hardware and information regarding the conducted user studies

	Mobile Interaction in Smart Environments	Mobile Tourist Guide	Mobile Museum Guide	Mobile Interaction with Advertisement Posters
Smart object	CD player, radio, heating and laptop	exhibits in an art park	simulated exhibits in a museum	advertisement poster
Tested physical mobile interaction technique and used hardware respective implementation				
Touching	Nokia 3220, Nokia NFC shell, Mifare RFID tags		Nokia 6630 IDBlue RFID pen, ISO 15693-3 tags	Nokia 3220, Nokia NFC shell, Mifare RFID tags
Pointing	Nokia N70, Laser pointer, light sensors	Nokia 6600, Visual Codes	Nokia N70, Visual Codes	Nokia 6630, Visual Codes
Scanning	Nokia N70 (Bluetooth)	Nokia 6600, BlueGPS RBT-3000		
User-mediated		Nokia 6600, numbers	Nokia N70, numbers	Nokia 6630, labels on the poster
Participants				
Number	20 (35% male)	17 (77% male)	8 (88% male)	17 (77% male)
Average age	28	24	28	29
Conducted	03 / 2006	11 / 2005	05 / 2006	06 / 2006

For the implementation of the interaction technique scanning, the built-in Bluetooth capabilities of mobile phones or external GPS devices were used. The Java ME APIs for Bluetooth (JSR 82) were used to scan for and to connect to other devices. For that purpose, the Bluetooth Serial Port Profile (SPP) of JSR82 which is based on the Bluetooth protocol RFCOMM was used. The GPS-based implementation of scanning used an external GPS device, the BlueGPS RBT-3000 from Royaltek, that can be connected via Bluetooth to a mobile device.

User-mediated object interaction is already available on nearly every mobile phone as it was implemented with standard Java ME interface widgets. The application running on the mobile device simply provides a corresponding input field in which the user types the number or URL she sees on the smart object.

4 Selected Results of the User Studies

This section discusses the methodology that was used within all four user studies. After this, every following subsection discusses the results of the evaluation of one prototype and its supported interaction techniques. Only the most relevant, interesting and unexpected results are presented.

4.1 Methodology

Each of the following four studies is different regarding the used prototype, the application scenarios and the evaluated interaction techniques. But all of them consisted of three basic steps: a preliminary interview, the use of the prototype and a final interview. The participants were also observed during the study and they were asked to talk about their impressions and experiences while using the prototype. The latter is known as the Thinking Aloud method [16]. Both interviews before and after the study were based on questionnaires including qualitative and quantitative questions. Questions that lead to qualitative results were mostly open questions asking for a general assessment of the interaction techniques or the prototypes itself. Quantitative results are based on predefined answers using a Likert scale. Some questions could also simply be answered with yes or no. The sequence of the usage of the interaction techniques was alternated from user to user to avoid undesired side effects. In some of the following studies the users were asked to rate the interaction technique according to different attributes. At this they could choose between the following possible answers: completely agree (4), partly agree (3), do not know (2), partly disagree (1) and disagree (0). Most of the participants of the user studies were people you often come across in a university building: students, researchers, secretaries, technical staff and visitors.

4.2 Mobile Interaction in Smart Environment

The study took place in a domestic home and a smart environment lab, which is a small flat with a bedroom, kitchen, living room and bathroom. During the study the participants were sitting in the living room and were asked to accomplish a set of tasks using the prototype. At the beginning of the study the three different interaction techniques were explained to the participants. The users were told that for each task they should select and use the interaction techniques they prefer in the given context.

The first scenario was to operate a CD player. The distance between the user and the device was 3 meters. There were no obstacles between the user and the CD player. 19 of the 20 participants preferred and therefore used pointing. One person used the interaction technique scanning.

In the second scenario the task was to open a webpage that is related to a radio program. The link to the website could be retrieved by selecting the radio. The radio was in close proximity to the user. All participants used the interaction technique touching to retrieve the link. Several users characterized the situation as very convenient for touching. It appeared to most of them that touching is the fastest technique in the setting and physical effort is low because they were in range for touching.

In the third scenario the participants had to operate a device in a different room. They were asked to switch the heating in the bathroom to 25 degree Celsius. All 20 participants in the study used the interaction technique scanning. As going to another room requires significant effort, none of the participant was motivated to move to the other room in order to use pointing or touching.

The last scenario was to access a Wikipedia web page to be displayed on a computer screen that was not in direct reach for the user. There was also no line of sight from the users starting position. In order to use the interaction technique pointing users had to move about one meter. To touch the device the users had to walk about four meters. All of the participants used scanning to select the device.

Overall the experiment showed that the relative location of the user with regard to the device that should be operated is the single most important factor for selecting an interaction technique.

In interviews we confirmed that besides the need for physical activity and interaction speed further factors play a role, most importantly security issues and intuitiveness. It can be summarized that people prefer to touch things that are near and accessible without physical effort. If they are further away and the user has a free line of sight, pointing is the preferred interaction technique. Scanning is used only if the other techniques would require physical effort.

4.3 Mobile Tourist Guide

A two-day user-study, in which 17 persons participated, was conducted in the Petuelpark in Munich (Germany) in November 2005. Mostly two participants used the prototype at the same time to simulate the more realistic situation that a small group or a couple is jointly walking through a park and not just a single person on its own. The two participants were asked to interact with six exhibits whereby the prototype was given to the other person after every interaction and every person had to use each of the three supported interaction techniques. After having used the prototype we asked the participants to rate the interaction techniques regarding the attributes simple, enjoyable, innovative and reliable. The corresponding results are depicted in the following Figure 2.

The participants saw user-mediated object interaction as the simplest interaction technique. Furthermore they saw pointing and scanning as the interaction techniques that were most fun to use whereas user-mediated object interaction with an average rating of 1.3 was seen as the least enjoyable one. This also corresponds to the results regarding the innovativeness of the interaction techniques where the participants equally preferred pointing and scanning to user-mediated object interaction. When looking at the results of the reliability of the interaction techniques then it can be seen that the participants preferred user-mediated object interaction over pointing and scanning.

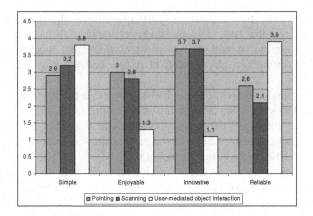

Fig. 2. Average rating regarding the attributes simple, enjoyable, innovative and reliable

Furthermore we asked them which interaction technique they prefer, they would continuously use and which one they judged to be the most enjoyable, innovative and reliable one. The corresponding results can be seen in Figure 3.

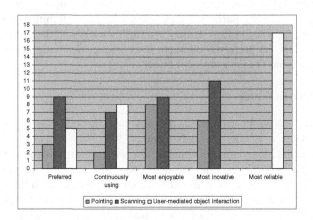

Fig. 3. Preferred ratings of the interaction techniques

9 of 17 (53%) favoured scanning over user-mediated object interaction (5 of 17, 29%) and pointing (3 of 17, 18%). These results change a little bit when asking about the interaction technique they would use continuously. Here, user-mediated object interaction and scanning were preferred most often whereas pointing was just mentioned by 2 participants. Scanning and pointing were seen as enjoyable and innovative interaction techniques whereas none of the participants connected these attributes with user-mediated object interaction. User-mediated object interaction was unanimously mentioned to be the most reliable technology when comparing it to the others. The reliability results may have been influenced by the problems the participants had with the usage of the implementations of pointing and scanning. The external GPS device sometimes had problems to receive sufficient satellite

signals and the accuracy of the identified position of the user was also sometimes not satisfying. When using pointing, some participants had problems to have the marker completely focussed with the built-in camera. Therefore, some of them needed more than one try to successfully use this interaction technique.

4.4 Mobile Museum Guide

8 participants used this prototype in order to interact with simulated exhibits in a museum. Every participant used each interaction technique twice whereby the sequence of the used interaction techniques was randomized. After having used the prototype we asked the participants to rate the interaction techniques regarding the attributes simple, enjoyable, innovative and reliable. The corresponding results are depicted in the following Figure 4.

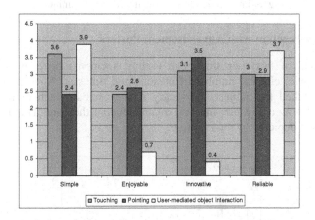

Fig. 4. Average rating regarding the simple, enjoyable, innovative and reliable

In addition to that, we asked the users what they would rate to be the preferred, most enjoyable, most innovative and most reliable interaction technique. Furthermore, we asked them which interaction technique they would continuously use. The corresponding results are depicted in the following Figure 5.

As one can see when looking at the two figures, pointing and touching are seen as enjoyable and innovative interaction techniques. In contrast to that, user-mediated object interaction and touching are seen as reliable interaction techniques whereby this is not the case when looking at the results of pointing. Furthermore, most participants would prefer the interaction technique touching when continuously using such a system. The reason for that is that a person in a museum is already close to an object to perform touching. The most noticeable disadvantage of touching, that the user must be nearby the object, has no impact in this context. Even if the context of a museum was just simulated this study shows the preference of people for touching, their interest in pointing and their trust in user-mediated object interaction.

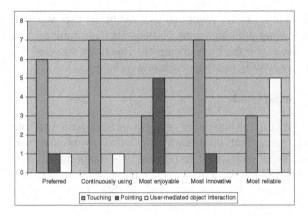

Fig. 5. Preferred ratings of the interaction techniques

4.5 Mobile Interaction with Advertisement Posters

The participants of this user study had to buy a cinema ticket using predefined settings for movie, cinema, number of persons and timeslot. After the usage of the prototype we asked the subjects how easy it is to handle each of the interaction techniques and how enjoyable, innovative and reliable they are. The average of the given answers is depicted by the Figure 6.

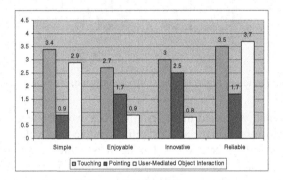

Fig. 6. Average rating of touching, pointing and user-mediated object interaction

Pointing was not seen as a simple interaction technique because the testers had problems to take a picture of the entire visual code in a sufficient resolution. The results for pointing were in general negatively affected by its implementation that needs a few seconds till the user knows whether she has successfully captured the visual code or not. Most testers said that user-mediated object interaction is not an enjoyable or innovative interaction technique. This is probably because people already knew and have already used this interaction technique.

After the user study the participants were asked which interaction technique they preferred and which of the three is the fastest. 13 participants preferred touching and 4 user-mediated object interaction. 12 persons mentioned that touching was the fastest technique whereas 5 mentioned user-mediated object interaction.

When looking at the overall result, touching is seen as the best interaction technique when taking the four analyzed attributes and the questions regarding the preferred and fastest interaction technique into account. Touching was highly ranked in all questions regarding the four attributes easy handling, enjoyable, innovative and reliable. User-mediated object interaction is seen as a reliable interaction technique that is easy to handle but is not enjoyable or innovative. Pointing received the worst marks but is seen as more innovative and enjoyable than user-mediated object interaction.

5   Advantages and Disadvantages of the Different Physical Mobile Interaction Techniques

This section summarises the results of the four studies described in the previous section. These results can help application designers and developers when deciding which physical mobile interaction technique should be supported within their application and which consequences a corresponding decision has. In the following, the properties of each interaction technique under evaluation are recapitulated and a set of findings is derived suggesting the use of specific techniques under specific circumstances.

5.1 Touching

Touching is regarded as an intuitive, very quick, enjoyable, reliable, unambiguous, innovative, simple and secure interaction technique which potentially requires physical effort but requires only little cognitive load.

It is seen as an intuitive interaction technique because of its directness and the similarity to real world activities such as pressing a button on the microwave. The interaction consists mostly of touching the smart object, waiting for feedback that the touching was successful and recognising the feedback provided by the mobile device.

This interaction technique is also very error resistant when compared to pointing or scanning. The studies have shown that people can learn touching very fast and that they make very few errors after they are used to it. It would be an error, for instance, if the NFC/RFID tag is touched too briefly so that the mobile device can not read it.

It is also an unambiguous interaction technique because first of all, it is technically impossible to read two tags at the same time in the described prototypes and second, because of the directness it is hardly possible to select a wrong tag or smart object.

Touching is typically preferred when the smart device is in reach of the user. Touching often requires the users' motivation to approach the smart device. But people try to avoid this physical effort, especially when being at home. The user studies based on prototypes of a mobile museum guide and mobile interaction with advertisement posters shows that in these cases touching is the preferred interaction technique. In these situations the user is anyway interested in being near the smart object and in this situation many of them prefer touching because of the previously mentioned advantages.

5.2 Pointing

Pointing is seen as an innovative, enjoyable and intuitive technique that requires some cognitive effort to point at the smart device and needs line of sight. It is typically preferred when the smart device and its tag are in line of sight of the user and the smart device cannot be accessed directly by the user. In the users' minds, pointing makes most sense because it combines an intuitive interaction with less physical effort (no need to actually approach the object in question).

It is also seen as an intuitive interaction technique, because it corresponds to our everyday behaviour to point at things when talking about them. Furthermore, it is an example of direct interaction techniques; these are generally seen as simpler as indirect interaction techniques.

When being at interaction distance, pointing is seen as the quicker interaction technique when comparing it to scanning but it is considered to be slower than touching. Fastness, error resistance and required physical effort of the interaction technique pointing depend heavily on its implementation. Both implementations discussed previously have in common that they require some dexterity to correctly point at the light sensor or the visual marker.

When using a laser pointer, as in the study described in subsection 4.2, it can be seen as a fast and simple type of interaction that consists only of the pointing task, waiting for the confirmation of the interaction and getting. The error resistance of this implementation is also high because the user gets direct feedback whether the interaction was recognized and whether the correct object was selected.

In all other studies, described in subsections 4.3, 4.4 and 4.5, a Java-based implementation using visual markers was used. Here the testers did not get a rapid feedback. First they had to take a picture of the marker, then this had to be analyzed by the Java version of the visual code software and then the user gets a feedback about its success or failure. Because of this, it takes several seconds until the user knows whether the visual code was recognized or not. Therefore, this implementation of the interaction technique pointing is not fast and also not error resistant. The latter especially results from the delay between taking a picture and getting the information that the image of the marker was not recognized.

Furthermore the used mobile phones and the size of the used marker also limited the distance in which an interaction was possible. This will change in the future, as mobile phones will have cameras with a high resolution and an optical zoom. The allowed distance is also based on the size of visual markers which was relatively small in presented prototypes.

A disadvantage of this interaction technique is the coordinative effort and cognitive load to point the mobile device to the marker or light sensor on the smart object. Pointing with the laser on a sensor and taking a picture of a visual marker needs considerable concentration and physical skills, especially from inexperienced users.

5.3 Scanning

Scanning is seen as an innovative, somewhat enjoyable and very technical interaction technique which is more complex to use because of its indirectness. Therefore the indirect mobile interaction technique scanning is avoided in many cases. If there is line of sight, the user normally switches to a direct mobile interaction technique such as touching or pointing.

Indirect interaction is mainly used to bridge a physical distance and to avoid physical effort. Scanning is seen as the technique with the least physical effort. Users tend to switch to scanning if a movement would be necessary to use a direct interaction technique.

A disadvantage is, that the user has to select the intended device when using for instance a Bluetooth based implementation of this interaction technique; this process is more time-consuming than directly interacting when standing close to a smart object. Furthermore the cognitive effort is higher compared to pointing or touching. It is typically used when the smart device and its tag can not be seen by the user and when the smart device is in scanning range.

A further advantage of scanning is the possibility to get a list of all smart objects in the vicinity. Thus it can be avoided to miss one. Additionally, no visual augmentation to attract the attention of the user is needed.

A disadvantage of scanning is that the user has to establish the mapping between an item on the list or map presented by the mobile device and the objects in the environment for which a high cognitive effort is required. This might sometimes lead to frustration or the interaction of the wrong object.

The study described in subsection 4.3 showed, that many testers saw the interaction technique scanning as a technique which they would prefer when using a mobile tourist guide. One important reason for this was that they like to get proactively informed when a sight is nearby.

The presented studies were conducted using on two different implementations of the interaction technique. One was based on Bluetooth and one on GPS. When using Bluetooth then the users did not like the time which is needed to show a list of nearby objects. The disadvantage of GPS - which was seen by the testers - was that the GPS device had sometimes problems to deliver the exact position on time.

5.4 User-Mediated Object Interaction

User-mediated object interaction is seen as a very reliable and simple interaction technique. The user has to establish a link between a smart object and a mobile service. In the previously discussed user studies (e.g. section 4.2 and 4.3) this merely meant typing in a simple number.

This view on simplicity and reliability might change when the user has to copy a URL using T9. This is much more cumbersome and the possibility of typing in a wrong URL is much higher. The performance of this interaction technique depends also on length of the information which has to be typed in. User-mediated object interaction is relative fast when the user has to type in for instance a three digit number and is relative slow when the user has to type in a long URL.

User-mediated object interaction is well known because it is, in contrast to the others, already used in mobile guides and many people already have experiences with its usage. Mainly because of this it is not seen as a enjoyable or innovative interaction technique.

5.5 Summary

The following Table 3 shows the advantages and disadvantages of the analyzed physical mobile interaction techniques based on the findings discussed in the previous subsections. This table also discusses attributes like fun factor or innovativeness which might be a reason for a potential costumer to buy or use a mobile service or application.

Table 3. Comparison of properties of the touching, pointing and scanning

	Touching	Pointing	Scanning	User-mediated
Rating: Good, Average, Bad				
Felt error resistance, reliability	Good	Good (laser pointer) - Bad (visual marker)	Average	Good (short number) - Average (long number)
Performance, speed (within interaction distance)	Good	Average	Bad (Bluetooth) - Good (GPS)	Average (short number) - Bad (long number)
Simplicity, Intuitiveness	Good	Good (laser pointer) - Bad (visual marker)	Average (GPS) - Average (Bluetooth)	Good (short number) – Average (long number)
Rating: High, Medium, Low				
Cognitive load	Low	Medium (laser pointer) - High (visual marker)	High (Bluetooth) - Medium (GPS)	Medium (short number) - High (long number)
Physical effort	High	Medium	Low	Low
Fun factor	High	High	High (GPS) - Medium (Bluetooth)	Low
Innovativeness	High	High	High	Low

6 Conclusion

In this paper we have presented a comprehensive experimental evaluation and comparison of the physical mobile interaction techniques touching, pointing, scanning and user-mediated object interaction. Therefore four different user studies were conducted in which the interaction techniques were evaluated in the context of mobile interaction in smart environments, a mobile tourist guide, a mobile museum guide and mobile interaction with advertisement posters.

The results show that in a smart environment the distance between the user and the smart object is an important factor for the preference of an interaction technique. If the object is within grasp, users prefer touching, if the user is too far away for touching but there is a line of sight, users prefer pointing, and in all other cases they prefer scanning. This is not true for the context of a mobile museum and tourist guide in which the user is interested in a nearby exhibit or sight anyway. Therefore, the distance between object and user does not play an important role. In this setting, factors like proactive behaviour of the application supported by scanning, simplicity and reliability provided by user-mediated object interaction, innovativeness and fun aspects related with touching, pointing and scanning or simplicity provided by touching and user-mediated object interaction can lead to user preference in a given context. The results presented here regarding the advantages and disadvantages seen by the users can be used by application designers when deciding which interaction technique(s) should be provided by their mobile application.

In our future work we will investigate further interaction techniques, other implementations of them and more applications contexts. We also plan to conduct long term studies in practical contexts to learn more whether and how the preferences of the users for the interaction techniques change over time. The findings provide grounding for creating adaptive user interfaces, that take location and activity into account. In further research we investigate how such adaptive user interfaces can be designed to enable efficient and effective interaction.

Acknowledgement

Important parts of the presented research (especially the prototype about mobile interaction with advertisement posters) were performed in the context of the Perci (PERvasive serviCe Interaction) project [17] which was funded by DoCoMo Euro-Labs.

References

[1] Kindberg, T., Barton, J., Morgan, J., Becker, G., Caswell, D., Debaty, P., Gopal, G., Frid, M., Krishnan, V., Morris, H., Schettino, J., Serra, B., Spasojevic, M.: People, places, things: web presence for the real world. Mobile Networks and Applications 7(5), 365–376 (2002)

[2] Boyd, J.: Here Comes The Wallet Phone. IEEE Spektrum 42(11), 12–13 (2005)

[3] Fowler, G.A.: QR codes: In Japan, Billboards Take Code-Crazy Ads to New Heights. Wall Street Journal (October 2005)

[4] Rukzio, E.: Physical Mobile Interactions: Mobile Devices as Pervasive Mediators for Interactions with the Real World. PhD Dissertation. Faculty for Mathematics, Computer Sience and Statistics. University of Munich (2006)

[5] Ballagas, R., Rohs, M., Sheridan, J., Borchers, J.: The Smart Phone: A Ubiquitous Input Device. IEEE Pervasive Computing 5(1), 70–77 (2006)

[6] Want, R., Fishkin, K.P., Gujar, A., Harrison, B.L.: Bridging physical and virtual worlds with electronic tags. In: Proceedings of the SIGCHI conference on Human factors in computing systems: the CHI is the limit, ACM Press, Pittsburgh (1999)

[7] Välkkynen, P., Korhonen, I., Plomp, J., Tuomisto, T., Cluitmans, L., Ailisto, H., Seppä, H.: A user interaction paradigm for physical browsing and near-object control based on tags. In: PI 2003. Workshop on Real World User Interfaces in conjunction with Mobile HCI 2003, Udine, Italy (2003)

[8] Fitzmaurice, G.W.: Situated information spaces and spatially aware palmtop computers. Communications of the ACM 36(7), 39–49 (1993)

[9] Rekimoto, J., Nagao, K.: The World Through the Computer: Computer Augmented Interaction with Real World Environments. In: UIST 1995. Proceedings of the 8th ACM Symposium on User Interface Software and Technology, Pittsburgh, PA, USA, pp. 29–36 (1995)

[10] NTT DoCoMo i-area: Location Based Services, http://www.nttdocomo.co.jp/english/service/imode/site/i_area.html

[11] Cheverst, K., Davies, N., Mitchell, K., Friday, A., Efstratiou, C.: Developing a context-aware electronic tourist guide: some issues and experiences. In: Proceedings of the SIGCHI conference on Human factors in computing systems, ACM Press, The Hague, The Netherlands (2000)

[12] Dix, A., Finlay, J., Abowd, G.D., Beale, R.: Human Computer Interaction, 3rd edn. Prentice Hall, Englewood Cliffs (2003)

[13] Rukzio, E., Leichtenstern, K., Callaghan, V., Holleis, P., Schmidt, A., Chin, J.: An Experimental Comparison of Physical Mobile Interaction Techniques: Touching, Pointing and Scanning. In: Dourish, P., Friday, A. (eds.) UbiComp 2006. LNCS, vol. 4206, Springer, Heidelberg (2006)

[14] Broll, G., Siorpaes, S., Rukzio, E., Paolucci, M., Hamard, J., Wagner, M., Schmidt, A.: Supporting Mobile Service Usage through Physical Mobile Interaction. In: PerCom 2007. Fifth Annual IEEE International Conference on Pervasive Computing and Communication, White Plains, NY, USA (2007)

[15] Rohs, M., Gfeller, B.: Using Camera-Equipped Mobile Phones for Interacting with Real-World Objects. In: Advances in Pervasive Computing, pp. 265–271, Austrian Computer Society (OCG) (2004) ISSN 3-85403-176-9

[16] Lewis, C., Rieman, J.: Task-Centered User Interface Design: A Practical Introduction (1994), http://www.hcibib.org/tcuid/

[17] Perci project, http://www.hcilab.org/projects/perci/

Portable Wireless Sensors for Object Usage Sensing in the Home: Challenges and Practicalities

Emmanuel Munguia Tapia, Stephen S. Intille, and Kent Larson

House_n, Massachusetts Institute of Technology
1 Cambridge Center, 4FL
Cambridge, MA, 02142 USA
{emunguia,intille}@mit

Abstract. A low-cost kit of stick-on wireless sensors that transmit data indicating whenever various objects are being touched or used might aid ubiquitous computing research efforts on rapid prototyping, context-aware computing, and ultra-dense object sensing, among others. Ideally, the sensors would be small, easy-to-install, and affordable. The sensors would reliably recognize when specific objects are manipulated, despite vibrations produced by the usage of nearby objects and environmental noise. Finally, the sensors would operate continuously for several months, or longer. In this paper, we discuss the challenges and practical aspects associated with creating such "object usage" sensors. We describe the existing technologies used to recognize object usage and then present the design and evaluation of a new stick-on, wireless object usage sensor. The device uses (1) a simple classification rule tuned to differentiate real object usage from adjacent vibrations and noise in real-time based on data collected from a real home, and (2) two complimentary sensors to obtain good battery performance. Results of testing 168 of the sensors in an instrumented home for one month of normal usage are reported as well as results from a 4-hour session of a person busily cooking and cleaning in the home, where every object usage interaction was annotated and analyzed.

1 Introduction

Many ubiquitous computing researchers desire a low-cost kit of stick-on wireless sensors that transmit data indicating whenever various objects in the environment are being touched or used. Availability of such a kit might aid ubiquitous computing and ambient intelligence research efforts on rapid prototyping, context-aware computing, and ultra-dense object sensing, among others. For example, prior work has demonstrated that sensors such as magnetic reed switches [1-3] and RFID tags [4] unobtrusively attached to many objects in an environment can enable a computer system to infer contextual information about the home occupant's movement and everyday activities such as "cooking," "making tea," "vacuuming," and others. Furthermore, the same types of sensors may be useful for studying behavior in non-laboratory environments, providing designers and ethnographers with new data gathering tools [5]. Sensors that can recognize object usage in everyday environments would also foster the development of embedded health assessment applications where

B. Schiele et al. (Eds.): AmI 2007, LNCS 4794, pp. 19–37, 2007.
© Springer-Verlag Berlin Heidelberg 2007

the well-being of individuals living alone in their own homes might be assessed in real-time, providing peace of mind to relatives and loved ones.

But first, in order to collect the necessary data for developing these applications, researchers require an object usage sensing technology that allows them to easily enter an existing home, unobtrusively attach sensors to as many objects as they wish (possibly hundreds), and to leave those sensors deployed for studies that might last months. For this to happen, the object usage sensing technology needs to be wireless, small, easy to install and remove, affordable, robust (electronically and physically) and not necessarily dependent upon a person wearing a tag or reader. People may be unwilling or unable to wear any technology in their homes (e.g. those suffering from medical conditions). These same sensor characteristics will also be desirable once the sensor technology migrates from use in research to use in commercial ubiquitous computing applications.

At first glance, the problem of recognizing object usage from object motion might appear trivial. One might think that a wireless object usage sensor could be designed by simply attaching a low-power, low sampling rate (e.g. 0.5Hz) motion, vibration, tilt, or accelerometer sensor to a wireless node. The device would transmit an object ID wirelessly when significant movement is observed by simply thresholding the motion, vibration, tilt, or acceleration signal, where the threshold is determined in an object independent manner (since setting object-dependent thresholds in the field increases installation complexity). We thought this would be the case.

However, when we deployed such a system in a real home, we observed some challenges that we did not initially fully appreciate. For example, the manipulation of an object can induce vibrations and movement in nearby objects that can cause false positive activations. This happens, for example, when someone forcefully closes a drawer or drops heavy objects on a surface supporting other objects that also have sensors. We refer to this problem as "the adjacency problem". While we realized adjacency activations would occur, the extent to which the problem was experienced in a real home was surprising. These false positive activations not only reduce the battery life of the sensor nodes (due to unnecessary wireless broadcasts) but also may negatively affect the performance of ubiquitous computing applications that depend upon the sensor data.

The second anticipated but underestimated challenge is that the magnitude and temporal characteristics of the motion, acceleration, vibration, or tilt/rotation generated by household objects is dramatically different among objects. Many of these motions are difficult to detect from vibration and tilt switches with low sensitivity and orientation dependencies (blind spots), and even from accelerometers sampling at less than 10Hz. For example, the motion patterns generated by an electric can-opener are different from those generated by closing a drawer on a smooth sliding mechanism, and even though a low sampling rate accelerometer will detect the can opener reliably, we found that sampling rates of at least 20Hz are required to reliably detect the "instantaneous" start and stop of smooth drawers, which dampen the motion to a surprising degree. The typical amount of motion observed when a person sits on a couch is another example of a subtle motion signal that requires a sensitive threshold and high sampling rate. Unfortunately, these relatively high sampling rates substantially impact battery life.

A third challenge we encountered is that many objects in the home, such as the telephone book and the first-aid kit, are seldom used (probably a couple of times a year). Therefore, to be useful, object usage sensors on these devices must have a very low false positive rate due to adjacent object usage or environmental noise (e.g. truck passing by). In our initial tests using simple acceleration thresholding to detect object usage, we found that random internal noise from the accelerometers, which were always sampling, would eventually (after days of use) trigger false positive activations when thresholds were set sufficiently low to capture real object usage.

Dealing with each of these three challenges impacts the fourth challenge: balancing good battery performance with robust object usage detection.

In this paper, we describe the practical issues we have encountered while trying to recognize object usage in real homes. We describe the advantages and disadvantages of existing sensing technologies used to recognize object usage, and present the design and evaluation of a specialized wireless sensor to detect object usage in existing homes. The sensor hardware and software was tuned based on our experience installing hundreds of sensors in real homes. Our two key design insights were to (1) minimize false positive activations due to adjacencies by implementing a classification rule tuned to differentiate real object usage from adjacent vibrations and noise in real-time and (2) extend battery life without sacrificing performance by combining two types of sensors with different strengths: a low-power piezofilm sensor with high sensitivity to external motion/vibration used for waking up a more energy costly accelerometer sampling at 20Hz used to differentiate between real and adjacent object usage. All technical specifications and microcode for the object usage devices developed in this work are available online [8].

2 Existing Approaches to Sense Object Usage

Previous ubiquitous computing and ambient intelligence studies where sensors have been installed in real homes for research (e.g., [1-3]) have often relied on the complex installation of reed switch sensors. A reed switch sensor typically installed in a volunteer's home consists of a data collection unit, a reed switch, and a magnet. All three components must be carefully aligned on an object (e.g. door, window or cabinet) in a way that properly activates the reed switch when the object is used. A single sensor of this type takes 5-10 minutes to install and test, and the installation of 200 of such sensors could require 16-32 man-hours of effort. This is a tremendous inconvenience to both the researchers and the subject in an experiment. The main advantage of using reed switches is good battery lifetime (possibly years, depending on object usage) that can be achieved even from small batteries since their associated circuitry can be kept in sleep mode until the reed switch is activated. However, reed switches only detect opening and closing events of objects such as doors, windows, cabinets, and drawers and are not well-suited for measuring other types of motion, such as the use of a table, chair, or appliance.

Object usage generally causes object movement or changes in object vibration, tilt, or acceleration. Therefore power efficient sensors such as vibration and tilt switches (e.g. mercury and ball switches) can be used to recognize object motion and to wake up external circuitry whenever vibration or tilt changes are detected. Unfortunately, these sensors are often uniaxial and orientation dependent, and their sensitivity to vibration or tilt is set during manufacturing. The ability to modify the sensor's sensitivity is important for detecting object usage since household objects exhibit very different motion characteristics, as previously discussed.

Another alternative for measuring object usage in a power efficient way is to use a piezoelectric film sensor. The use of piezoelectric films as a low-cost and power efficient method to measure hand jerk motions (over 2.5G) in group interactions during collective events was proposed in [9]. Piezofilm sensors can be extremely sensitive to motion, detecting even tiny vibrations in the environment; however, they do not measure static acceleration (orientation with respect to ground) that is important for detecting slow tilt/rotation movements.

Accelerometers based on micro-electro-mechanical systems (MEMs) can also be used to detect object usage by measuring changes in object static and dynamic acceleration. MEMs accelerometers can be very small and self contained so that they can be placed on nearly any household object, and installation can require no more than simply throwing a sensor in a drawer or using putty (adhesive material) to stick it in to a cabinet door. No multi-point alignment is required, so sensors that can be simply stuck on objects quickly, reducing installation time to as little as 36s per sensor, as reported in [10]. Installing 200 single-point-of-contact sensors in a home may take as little as 2 man-hours of effort, a tolerable amount of time not only for researchers but even possibly for end-users. The main disadvantage of using MEMs accelerometers to detect object usage is their relatively high energy consumption. For example, continuous sampling of the popular ADXL202 biaxial accelerometer (~500µA@3V) at 10Hz using a 3mA microcontroller results in a theoretical battery life of only 46 days from a CR2032 coin cell battery (220mA). Newer versions of the accelerometer such as the triaxial ADXL330 (~400µA@3V) can also be used, however, improvements in battery life are minimal. An obvious way to increase battery life would be to increase battery size; however, this would make the sensor nodes larger and therefore less flexible and easier to dislodge.

A promising alternative to detect object usage is to use touch, or hand-to-object proximity. Battery-less passive radio frequency identification (RFID) tags are a cost effective way to measure object touch if a person is willing to wear a reader on or near the hands, embedded in bracelets or gloves [4, 6, 7]. RFID tags cost less than $1 US, and are small enough to be installed on tiny low-value objects such as office supplies. However, end users may be unwilling or unable to constantly wear a device on the hand. In addition, existing wearable RFID readers must be frequently recharged (e.g. every 2-10 hours [4, 11]) which could be potentially more annoying than replacing sensor batteries once or twice a year. Until wearable RFID readers are improved, passive RFID tags also require a good alignment and short distances (e.g. 10cm) to the wearable reader to be read [4, 6, 7]. The reader range could be extended, but this is at the expense of battery life and an increased number of false positives due to tags in the vicinity of objects being manipulated [4, 6, 7]. Passive RFIDs can also suffer from severe interference caused by metal objects and water-rich materials [12], sometimes negatively impacting performance on common objects such as food cans, silverware, door knobs, and liquid containers.

Table 1. Advantages and disadvantages of existing sensing technologies to detect object-usage

Technology	Assumptions	Advantages	Disadvantages
Magnetic reed switches	Object has a distinct open or closed state, with change indicating usage	Low power; relatively robust to adjacent object motion; relatively inexpensive $2-5 (compared to MEMs accelerometers)	Difficult to install (3 contact points); sensitive to alignment; only senses opening and closing events
Vibration and tilt switches	Object usage will result in object vibration or tilt.	Low power; self-contained single point of contact to object; easy to install. Wide price range depending on size and type ($1-10)	Sensitivity is orientation dependent (sensitivity for some orientations is zero); Cannot change sensitivity threshold; may trigger from adjacent vibration
Piezoelectric films	Object usage will result in object's dynamic acceleration change.	Low power; high sensitivity to external acceleration/vibration relatively inexpensive <$1.5 (compared to accelerometers); easy to install	Only senses dynamic acceleration (not static); may trigger from adjacent motion; usually uniaxial and with existing form factors, it would result in a cumbersome triaxial sensor since 3 films are required
MEMs accelerometers	Object usage will result in object acceleration (static or dynamic) change above accelerometer noise	Triggered by vibration, motion, and rotation of an object; single point of contact to object; easy to install; signal can be used to discern adjacent object motion	Power hungry (400-600μA@3V); relatively expensive ($7-12); internal sensor noise may result in false positives
RFIDs	Touch or proximity of object indicates use	Small; no battery; easy to install (a sticker); very inexpensive (<$1); single point of contact to object	Requires wearable or environmental reader; trade-off between reader's range and objects detected nearby (false positives); interference from metal or water; only indicates if object is present
WISP Intel	Object usage will result in object tilt	Single point of contact to object; easy to install; no battery; potentially same advantages as passive RFIDs and accelerometers	Requires environmental readers (~$1500 each); prototype stage (not yet extensively tested in homes); same disadvantages as RFIDs; susceptible to adjacent motion since simple thresholding is used to detect usage

The wireless identification and sensing platform (WISP) [12] combines passive RFID tags and accelerometery. Readers distributed throughout a space constantly power the devices and motion sensing on the tags via a 1-bit accelerometer (mercury switch) is used to detect object usage. This approach is promising, since no battery replacement or wearable readers are required. However, the same challenges associated with passive RFIDs need to be overcome and since simple acceleration thresholding is used to detect object usage, false positives due to adjacent object manipulation remain a challenge. Consequently, the results presented in this work are also relevant in this setting.

Table 1 presents a summary of the assumptions, advantages, and disadvantages of the existing technologies available for sensing object usage.

3 Object Usage Sensor Design

Our goals when creating the object usage sensor were to create a sensor that: (1) can be installed quickly by a non-expert, (2) can accurately detect object-usage in the wide variety of everyday objects with different motion patterns (vibration, tilt, rotation) and intensities without object specific thresholds, (3) minimizes the number of false positive activations due to adjacent motion and noise, and (4) extends the node's battery life by only processing the acceleration signal when meaningful motion is detected. In this section, we describe the hardware and software design inspired from our experiences installing hundreds of sensors in real homes.

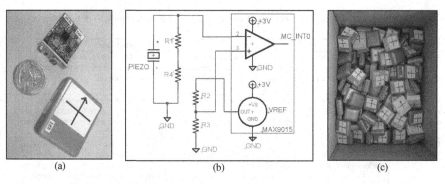

Fig. 1. (a) Image of the object-usage sensor board and casing, (b) Schematic of the object-usage sensor wake-up circuitry, (c) Box of 243 sensors for collisions test

3.1 Hardware Design

The object usage sensor nodes developed in this work are built upon an existing wireless sensing infrastructure [10]. This sensing platform uses a featherweight MAC protocol in combination with a star network topology to save energy, simplify usage, and permit simultaneous reception from high and low sampling rate sensors. More details can be found in [10]. Even though the topology and communication protocols utilized in this platform are simple, they allowed us to easily test the performance of 168 newly developed object usage sensors in a real home (see Section 4.6). Moreover, the hardware and software principles on which the object usage sensors are based and presented in this work could also be used to improve sensor performance and battery life for sensor nodes using state-of-the-art mesh networking protocols.

The basic sensor board of the adopted wireless platform consists of a 3.2x2.5x0.6cm and 8.1g (including battery) stick-on wireless node that includes a 16Mhz 8051 microcontroller (μC), a wireless 2.4GHz transceiver, a 2-axis ±2G accelerometer (ADXL202, $12 US), and a MOSFET switch to power cycle the accelerometer from a CR2032 coin cell battery. Consequently, the new object usage sensor presented in this work is limited to this 2-axis accelerometer due to the unavailability of power efficient 3-axis accelerometers (e.g. ADXL330) at the time of development of the adopted sensing infrastructure. However, as described later, the 2-axis version is sufficient to achieve good performance in recognizing object usage in practice, although newer designs could utilize the new ADXL330 3-axis accelerometer without significant cost change. This basic sensor node was designed to recognize object usage by simply thresholding the 2-axis acceleration signal sampled at 10Hz against a predefined acceleration value [10]. The sensor broadcasts its ID whenever usage is detected. Using this simple thresholding approach to recognize object usage, the battery life of the sensor is about 46 days. This battery life may be sufficient for some ubiquitous computing test deployments, but the battery life is dependent upon the assumption that a sampling rate of 10Hz is sufficient to detect tasks with "instantaneous" stops such as shutting a drawer. When we deployed these sensors in a home, however, we ultimately determined that for some types of objects such as drawers and couches, the sampling rate of 10Hz was too low to consistently detect object usage

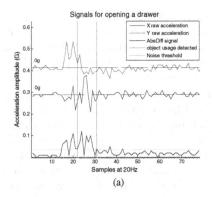
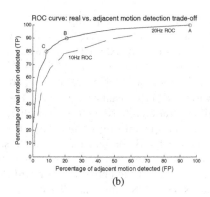

Fig. 2. (a) Raw and preprocessed acceleration signals (XY AbsDiff) for an opening a drawer event sampled at 20Hz. (b) ROC curve showing the percentage of real vs. adjacent motion detected resulting from the brute-force search of the parameters at 20Hz and 10Hz.

when it occurred. We found that doubling the sampling rate to 20Hz improved object usage detection in these objects. Unfortunately, this new sampling rate reduces the battery life to less than a month. Therefore, we sought a way to improve the battery life of the sensor node. We chose to modify the hardware to use a sensor with high sensitivity to motion/vibration to wake up the 2-axis accelerometer and associated circuitry whenever meaningful external motion is detected for a short time interval. Consequently, energy use is preserved by keeping all circuitry in power down mode ($2\mu A$) until meaningful motion is detected by the wake-up sensor.

An obvious method to increase battery life without increasing the node complexity is to simply increase the battery size. For example, coin cells such as the CR2477 (10.5g) provide 1000mA of power, 4.5 times more power than the CR2032 used by the nodes. Nevertheless, this modification more than doubles the node weight and size, increasing installation complexity and probability of dislodgement, particularly in small objects. Furthermore, the better the sensor's power efficiency, the more useful the sensors will be in any application, no matter what battery type is used.

We considered three power-efficient sensor options to wake-up the circuitry: (1) tilt switches, (2) vibration switches, and (3) cantilever-beam piezoelectric films. Tests run to determine the sensors' sensitivity to external motion (see Section 4.1) indicated that the piezoelectric film was the best option to use. The piezoelectric film sensor (Minisense100 by MSI Inc.) works as a low-cost ($1.2 in qty of 50) accelerometer (1G) that measures dynamic acceleration without requiring external power. As a result, it can be used with auxiliary electronics to wake up the μC whenever the sensor node experiences an acceleration that exceeds a predefined fixed threshold V_{TH}. The hardware for the new object usage sensor board shown in Figure 1a consists of the basic sensor node board with an additional daughter board containing the circuitry shown in Figure 1b. As shown in Figure 1b, the output of the piezoelectric film is connected to the input of a nanopower comparator (MAX9015) that compares its generated voltage with a fixed voltage threshold V_{TH}. V_{TH} is obtained from a 1.236V voltage reference (MAX9015) and a voltage divider (R2, R3) to prevent variations in V_{TH} due to battery discharge over time. The output of the comparator is connected to the μC external interrupt input to wake it up whenever the voltage generated by the piezoelectric film is greater than V_{TH}. V_{TH} was set in practice to maximize the sensor's response to external movement/vibration while preventing self-triggering by installing a variable resistor at R2 and R3. V_{TH} was finally set to 12.5mV, an acceleration threshold of 0.025g. The comparator and voltage reference (MAX9015) are always on but consume only 1μA. The production cost for the entire ad-on board (administration and NRE cost not included) is $3.9 US and was calculated assuming a production quantity of 50 and a two-month lead-time, as quoted by a U.S company (including PWB tooling, masks, stencils, soldering, and no electrical testing). This adds only 13% to the cost of the entire sensor board but substantially improves battery life. The cost of the entire sensor board (Figure 1a) under the same previous assumptions is $32.3 US. Note that 37% of the cost comes from the cost of the accelerometer ($12 US).

3.2 Object-Usage Detection Algorithm

By adding the piezo-based wake-up circuit, the sampling rate can be increased without reducing battery life. However, adjacent motion still has to be differentiated from real motion to minimize false positive activations. The main purpose of the object-usage detection algorithm that runs on the sensor node is to recognize when an object is being used by analyzing the object's acceleration signal while minimizing false positives due to adjacent object manipulation and noise. Minimizing the number of false positives helps by (1) extending battery life because each wireless transmission consumes power, (2) simplifying raw data analysis and visualization for researchers (e.g. ethnographers), and (3) minimizing potential problems when pattern classification or machine learning algorithms are used to infer context from object usage.

The first step of the object usage detection algorithm consists of preprocessing the acceleration signals over each axis (X, Y) by computing the absolute value of the difference between adjacent samples to achieve orientation invariance.

$$AbsDiff = |current\_sample - last\_sample|$$

This step eliminates the DC component of the static acceleration that appears whenever the sensor is rotated with respect to ground. Orientation invariance is important because a person installing the sensors should not be required to orient them in a particular way, increasing installation complexity. Note that even though the DC signal component over each axis is eliminated, changes in rotation are still detected.

The second step consists of creating a new signal XY generated by selecting the preprocessed signal sample with the maximum value for both axes at each given instant in time (sample). This composite XY AbsDiff signal represents the overall motion experienced by the sensor in all axes. This step reduces complexity, since any processing performed on the accelerometer signals is performed only once over the composite signal instead of two times over each individual axis. Figure 2a shows an example of the 20Hz raw acceleration (X, Y) and the XY AbsDiff composite signal, and two object usage detections for an "opening a drawer" event. The third step is to differentiate meaningful acceleration samples due to true external motion from the oscillations generated by internal sensor noise. To achieve this, the maximum noise over the XY AbsDiff signal was measured from 3 sensor nodes sitting undisturbed

Table 2. Fifty training examples were collected from each of these objects (or adjacent objects) to determine an algorithm that could discriminate real object usage motion from adjacent

Drawer	Cabinet adjacent	Couch adjacent	Cup	Faucet
Drawer adjacent	Door	Chair	Remote Control	Bed/pillow
Cabinet	Couch	Table	Toilet cover	

Table 3. Features extracted that can be computed efficiently by a low-cost low-processing power microcontroller

Feature	Description
Min value	Min value above noise level of the XY AbsDiff signal
Max value	Max value above noise level of the XY AbsDiff signal
Area under curve	Sum of all values of XY AbsDiff signal
Duration of motion	Number of samples greater than the noise level in XY AbsDiff signal
Mean	Mean of the AbsDiff signal computed sample-by-sample
Variance	Variance of the AbsDiff signal computed sample-by-sample

on a table overnight (without the piezofilm add-on, so that the sensors were sampling the accelerometer continuously). The maximum amplitude, or worse case internal noise level found was 14 (35mG). Thus, when accelerometer readings above this threshold are obtained, the signal is assumed to be from actual motion.

In the forth step, real motion is differentiated from adjacent motion in real-time using the composite XY AbsDiff signal and a simple classification rule. To generate the classification rule, we collected 50 examples of the usage of each of the objects shown in Table 2 from a real home using a wired biaxial accelerometer sampling at 20Hz. In total we collected 550 examples of real object usage and 150 examples of adjacent object usage. The objects considered had a wide range of observed motion patterns, such as vibration (table, faucet), fast opening/closing motion (cabinets), smooth one-axis motion with rapid start/stops (drawers), rotation/tilt (toilet cover), extended motion (e.g. remote control) and combinations of these. After analyzing the adjacent object usage examples, we found that 96% (144) of them had XY AbsDiff signals greater than the noise threshold. Thus, if simple thresholding were used to detect object usage, 96% of adjacent object usage would be detected as real usage.

The features shown in Table 3 were computed over the XY AbsDiff signal of the segmented examples (max length of 4s). We used these features and the 700 examples to evaluate the performance of algorithms that generate classification rules implementable as *if-then* clauses. These *if-then* clauses and the features shown in Table 3 can be computed efficiently in a low-cost low-processing-power microcontroller. Obviously, more complex algorithms such as Hidden Markov Models (HMMs) that take into account temporal information could also be used. However, their computational requirements are too high to be implemented in most low-cost microcontrollers (<$5) currently available with real-time performance.

The WEKA toolkit [13] was used to evaluate the performance of the rule-generating algorithms shown in the first column of Table 4 over subsets of the features in Table 3 using 10-fold cross validation. The number of *if-then* clauses required to implement the resulting rules in C code was also defined as a complexity measure. Table 4 presents a summary of the performance results. The performance of the Naïve

Table 4. Classification performance using 10-fold crossvalidation over the 700 examples collected. The complexity of the classification rules produced is shown in parenthesis.

Algorithm	All features	Duration + Area + Variance	Duration	Area
Naïve Bayes Classifier	81.2 (NA)	83.1 (NA)	86.1 (NA)	77.0 (NA)
Rules PART	90.0 (21)	89.2 (9)	87.8 (3)	88.7 (3)
Ripper down rule learner (Ridor)	89.6 (12)	89.3 (4)	87.9 (5)	88.3 (7)
Ripper (JRip)	90.1 (8)	89.4 (8)	**88.7 (2)**	88. 9 (4)
C4.5 decision tree (J48)	90.3 (24)	89.6 (10)	87.8 (4)	89.0 (4)

Bayes classifier was also investigated as a comparison baseline. Table 4 shows the results for the two single best discriminant features: *duration of motion* and *area under curve*. From Table 4, we observe that the rules generated by Ripper using only the duration of motion feature achieve the best compromise between classification performance (88.7%) and complexity (2). The performance is slightly higher (~1.3%) when using all the features; however, the complexity involved in computing the features and implementing the decision rules increases substantially.

The classification rule generated by Ripper is: *If duration>7 then motion=real; Else motion=adjacent.* Using this simple rule, real motion is detected whenever 7 samples (at 20Hz) over the noise threshold are observed in the combined XY AbsDiff signal within a 2-4-s window length (or length of usage example). To better understand the trade-off between *real* vs. *adjacent* detections (TPs and FPs), we performed a brute-force search over the parameter space (duration, window length) to generate an ROC curve. This was achieved by simultaneously varying the window length from 1 to 60 samples (.05s to 3s at 20Hz), varying the *duration of motion* threshold from 1 to 10 samples, and measuring the classification rule performance on the example set. Figure 2b presents the ROC curves (at 10 and 20Hz sampling rates) where each point in the plot represents a parameter setting. Not surprisingly, point A in Figure 2b (*duration*=1, window=1) is the most sensitive parameter setting offering near 100% detection accuracy for real motion but results in too many false positives for adjacent motion. The final parameters selected were *duration*=7, and window=29 (1.45s) or point B in Figure 2b. This corresponds to a real motion detection of 90% and adjacent motion detection of 21.5%. A lower FP detection of ~8% can be obtained using the settings of point C (*duration*=10, and window=29) but decreases real motion accuracy to ~80%. The ROC curves can be used during data collection deployments to trade detection performance with battery life depending on the application. Finally, these results were obtained by weighing the importance of all objects equally.

In summary, the object usage detection algorithm simply counts the number of times the XY AbsDiff acceleration signal samples gathered at 20Hz rise above the noise level threshold (35mG). If the count reaches 7 samples, the device "detects" real motion and will transmit a sensor ID to a nearby receiver. The count is reset each time 29 samples (1.45s) are observed without any samples above the threshold.

In field deployments, we noticed that it is not unusual for sensors to be placed on or near objects that move for very long periods of time continuously (e.g., a phone, running dishwasher, coffee maker, favorite chair, or leaking toilet). We therefore added a continuous usage/motion filter to minimize energy consumption whenever an object is moved for prolonged periods of time. From column 3 of Table 6 (discussed later), we observed that number of sensor firings for objects normally not used

Table 5. Sensitivity (%) of tilt, vibration, and piezoelectric film sensors to minimal external motion in all directions (X, Y, and Z) for four household objects when manipulated 10 times

Sensor	Main Axis	Drawer (%)			Cabinet (%)			Toaster (%)			Toilet (%)			Total (%)
		X	Y	Z	X	Y	Z	X	Y	Z	X	Y	Z	
Tilt	X	80	20	60	90	100	40	40	40	10	60	70	10	51.6
Vibration	Z	90	60	50	90	100	10	100	40	40	80	100	30	65.8
Piezofilm	X	90	80	80	90	100	80	70	60	70	70	90	70	79.1

continuously was between 1 and 4. Consequently, the filter activates whenever the sensor has detected real object usage 4 consecutive times (within 1.4s of each other). While the filter is on, no ID broadcasts are made, and the filter turns itself off after no movement is detected for 2s. When the filter turns off, a special code is broadcast to the receiver.

4 Evaluation

This section describes the tests performed during the development of the object usage sensor and its evaluation in a real home during realistic and worse case conditions.

4.1 Sensitivity to Installation Orientation

The sensitivity of a ball tilt switch (107-2006-EV by Mountain Switch), a miniature ball vibration switch (UBALL0100 by Particle Computer), and a piezoelectric film (Minisense100 by MSI Inc) were measured to determine their ability to rapidly wake-up the accelerometer and detect object usage accurately in any orientation (X, Y, and Z). All these sensors are uniaxial and therefore they become less sensitive as they are turned away from their main sensitivity axis (i.e. are sensitive to installation orientation). Ball-based tilt and vibration switches were preferred over mercury based switches, because they are usually more sensitive. This test was performed by comparing three sensor nodes sampling at 20 Hz each using a different sensor type as wake-up option and one sensor without the wake-up circuit (accelerometer continuously powered up). All used simple acceleration thresholding to detect object usage. These sensor nodes were placed in a drawer and cabinet (motion), a toilet cover (tilt), and on a toaster (vibration). Each object was manipulated 10 times in a worse-case scenario of minimal slow motion in each orientation (X, Y, and Z): the drawer and cabinet were opened, the toilet seat was raised, and the toaster activated. The results of comparing each sensor type are shown in Table 5. Note that wireless signal loss and lack of synchronization between the acceleration sampling between the sensors have a slight influence on the results. Overall, the piezofilm is the sensor with highest sensitivity to external motion in any direction. Consequently, only one piezofilm is required to act as a wake-up sensor. Orientation sensitivity problems with the tilt and vibration sensors could be overcome by using three sensors oriented along the X, Y, and Z axes. However, at current costs for the vibration switch at low quantities ($10 each), this solution would double the cost of the entire sensor node (~$59). For the tilt switch, its current size (16x4x4mm) would result in a sensor node with a cumbersome form factor that would increase installation complexity.

4.2 False Positives from Internal Sensor Noise

Recognizing object usage by simple thresholding of acceleration generates a large number of false positives due to (1) variations in the accelerometer internal noise amplitude due to fluctuations in the battery voltage while transmitting and (2) errors generated while reading the accelerometer values. Even when accelerometer values are read reliably 99% of the time, sampling over a day sometimes generates sufficient erroneous readings to produce several false activations. In the new object usage sensor, the problem is addressed by only sampling the acceleration when necessary (when external motion is detected). To evaluate the FP activations generated due to internal sensor noise, 12 object usage sensors were left sitting undisturbed over a table in an office space for 24 days. The number of false positives found was zero.

4.3 Wireless Link Performance and Percentage of Collisions

To evaluate the performance of the object usage sensor wireless link to interference caused by nearby metal objects and surfaces (a problem in RFIDs), we installed the sensors on a metal tuna can, a metal doorknob, and a metal spoon. A computer with a receiver was placed a few meters away. The objects were picked up and put down or used normally 10 times each. All 30 of the usages were detected. The objects were placed on many metal objects in the realistic home test reported shortly.

A concern when using simple MAC protocols and a star network topology, such as the ones used by the sensor nodes, is collisions. Therefore, we placed 243 object usage sensors in a large box, as shown in Figure 1c to measure collisions due to simultaneous activation of sensors in a real-world worse-case scenario. A computer with a receiver was placed a few meters away. The box was kicked hard 7 times (with a few seconds of no motion in between each kick) and then moved from one part of a room to another (taking exactly 5s per movement) five times. Each of these actions is very likely to activate each of the sensors in the box simultaneously. In practice, 33.7% (82) of the sensors wireless ID transmissions were detected in the kick experiment (the 66.3% not detected were lost due to collisions). We think that it is unlikely in a home environment that any typical "instantaneous" activity will result in 80+ sensors firing at the exact moment. In the 5s carry event, only 26.4% of the sensors transmissions were lost due to collisions. Consequently, the simple MAC protocol and network topology utilized is capable of detecting the simultaneous transmission of a large number of sensors and appropriate for the tests performed in this work. Collisions could be further minimized using a more sophisticated wireless protocol, as the expense of possibly requiring more costly electronics per sensor node. More details on theoretical collision tests based on number of nodes, transmission rate and time can be found in [10].

4.4 Battery Life

The battery life of the object usage sensors is dependent upon the usage of the object on which the sensor is placed. At one extreme is a sensor that is never moved. The idle theoretical battery lifetime of our new object usage sensor when it undergoes no motion and consumes 4μA in sleep mode is approximately 6.3 years from a CR2032

Table 6. Accuracy (ACC) [TP/(TP+FN)], TPs, FNs, and FPs (of nearby sensors) in a controlled test where 3 subjects used 10 home objects 30 times each. The number of average activations reported during each object usage is shown in parenthesis. The column CF shows the number of motion events for which the continuous motion filter was activated.

Object	ACC	TP	FN	FP	CF	Brief explanation (*)
Cabinet (open)	100	30 (1.8)	0	0	0	-
Cabinet (close)	100	30 (2.2)	0	2*	0	Cabinets slammed 2 times
Drawer (open)	96.6	29 (1.3)	1*	0	0	Drawer opened slowly
Drawer (close)	100	30 (1.8)	0	3*	0	Drawer slammed 3 times
Front door (open)	100	30 (3.3)	0	0	0	-
Front door (close)	100	30 (2.4)	0	3*	0	Door slammed 3 times
Wood chair on wood floor (sit down)	100	30 (2.3)	0	0	0	-
Wood chair on wood floor (get up)	100	30 (2.8)	0	1*	0	Table moved while sitting
Upholstered couch (sit down)	86.6	26 (1.2)	4	5*	0	Adjacent cushions activated
Upholstered couch (get up)	63.3	19 (1.1)	11*	2	0	Less motion than sit down
Coffee mug (sip drink)	100	30 (4.9)	0	1*	0	Dropping mug on table
Computer keyboard (typing)	100	30 (6.8)	0	0	18	-
Electric can opener (open a can)	100	30 (4.9)	0	3*	27	Spice rack beside can opener
Remote control (change channel)	100	30 (5.4)	0	0	24	-
Table (put full mug down)	20.0	6 (1)	24*	0	0	Similar to adjacent motion
Table (sign paper)	53.3	16 (1)	14*	0	0	Not enough vibration/motion

coin battery (220mAh).). In practice, we tested the idle battery life (self discharge) of 12 sensors by leaving them sitting undisturbed on a table in an office space for 9.5months. The sensors were still functional and with approximately 80% battery charge after the end of this time period. This gives us a more realistic idle battery life upper-bound estimate of roughly 4 years. At the other extreme is a sensor that is moving continuously, where the extended movement filter is disabled. In that condition, the sensor will sample from the accelerometer and transmit continuously. Three such sensors were installed on a rotating arm. The battery was measured to last 7 days and broadcast a total of 15.4 million sensor activations. If the motion filter is on, the sensors can run continuously for approximately one month and a half because the device is not transmitting continuously. To estimate the typical lifetime of a sensor installed in a home, we assume that the sensor activates 20 times a day for 3s (average motion duration for opening/closing a drawer). In that case, based up on the measured power consumption of the accelerometers and wireless transmission, the node's battery life is estimated to be 1.1 years.

4.5   False Positives from Movement of Nearby Objects

As part of a controlled test, three subjects were asked to each use 10 home objects (with sensors attached) normally 30 times. Table 6 shows the true positive (TP), false negative (FN), and false positive (FP) activations for the total of 480 object usages. The FPs correspond to sensor firings of nearby objects. The table also indicates, in parenthesis, the average number of activations reported by the sensor during each object interaction. From this number, we can see that opening events in cabinets and drawers are more difficult to recognize than closing events. Interactions that take longer clearly generate more activations, such as use of the keyboard. We can also observe that the number of FNs is near zero for most objects (8.9% overall) except for extremely low magnitude usage events such as signing a paper on a table (sensor under table) and getting up from a couch (sensor underneath center cushion). Getting up from the couch is also difficult to recognize because of wireless signal loss due to body blocking. Putting down a mug on a table was difficult to recognize because it generates short duration signals similar to the ones generated by adjacencies. Finally, the number of FPs is high for worse-case conditions such as slamming events or inevitable adjacent motion. For example, sitting on the center cushion of a three-seat couch induced significant motion on the two adjacent cushions. FPs are also slightly higher by design since we decided to err on the side of being too sensitive rather than not sensitive enough, given that higher level inference algorithms may be able to further filter FPs. This relatively controlled test suggests that the sensors are able to detect object usage well in a variety of everyday objects.

4.6   Realistic Performance in an Instrumented Residential Home

We wanted to be certain that the sensors would function well when deployed in a real home when people use objects normally. To test this, we used an instrumented condominium that has hard-wired reed switches in all the cabinetry (cabinets, drawers, doors, and appliance doors) and a comprehensive audio-visual recording system for analysis of activity and sensor firings by researchers [14].

As a first test, two volunteers (a young married couple) not affiliated with our research group were recruited and asked to live at the condominium for a period of 2.5 months. The volunteers performed their normal daily activities while video was being recorded and 168 object usage sensors were attached to objects in the environment. Sixty-six object usage sensors had hard-wired reed switch equivalents and 102 were installed on objects that had no wired equivalent (e.g. sofa, appliances, chairs, etc).

The second month of data were used to compare the wired switch sensor activations to the wireless sensor activations. We experimentally confirmed that the detection accuracy for a wired switch sensor is 99% for opening/closing events by opening and closing every cabinet and drawer at the condominium ten times. For the remainder of this analysis, we assume the wired switches accurately detect open/close events.

The overall accuracy for detecting opening-closing events of the wireless sensors with respect to the wired switches was 86.6%±16.0. An object usage sensor was considered to correctly detect a wired switch opening-closing event whenever it fired within ±5s of the wired switch activation. This ±5s window was selected to permit a temporal comparison due to delays observed in practice in the switch sensor network. After building a 1s resolution histogram over the activation time differences between wired and wireless sensors over the ±5s windows, we determined that 77.8% of the activations fire within ±1s of each other, 91.4% within ±2s, 95.8% within ±3 and 99.3% within ±3s. Delays greater than +2s represent cases where the object usage sensor does not fire instantly when an object is used (e.g. a cabinet door is opened), but instead fires sometimes during the fluid motion. Negative delays indicate that the wireless sensor fired before the wired switch due to delays in the wired sensor networks (worse case is 2s).

There were a total of 124,064 total sensor activations where 12,099 were generated by the wired switch sensors and 111,965 by the object usage sensors. Note that there are more object usage activations because each wired switch event generates varying

Table 7. Summary of the comparison results for all the three object types (cabinets, drawers and doors) that had equivalent wired switch sensors and some particular examples of the two objects with best and worse performance. True positives (TP), false negatives (FN), and other object usage activations are also shown.

Overall summary statistics				
Object	TP ($\mu \pm \sigma$)	FN ($\mu \pm \sigma$)	Other	Brief explanation (*)
Cabinets	85.6 ± 17.6	14.3 ± 17.6	53,323*	Doors swung but not closed
Drawers	87.5 ± 12.3	12.4 ± 12.3	1,037*	Drawer contents manipulated
Doors	93.6 ± 4.0	6.3 ± 4.0	33,341*	Dishwasher motor vibration
Example results for some individual objects from good (top) to worse (bottom) performance				
Object (sensor ID)	TP (%)	FN (%)	Other	Brief explanation (*)
Cabinet door hallway pantry (738)	36 (100)	0 (0)	57*	Cabinet's content manipulated
Cabinet door dining room (1009)	44 (97.7)	1 (2.3)	36*	Cabinet's content manipulated
Drawer office desk (767)	32 (96.9)	1 (3.1)	57	Drawer's content manipulated
Cabinet door master bathroom (611)	27 (87)	4 (13)	47	Cabinet's content manipulated
Drawer office desk (762)	12 (70.5)	5 (29.5)	23*	Drawer's content manipulated
Drawer utensils kitchen (530)	81 (72.9)	30 (27.1)	95*	Drawer's content manipulated
Cabinet door hallway pantry (979)	94 (80.3)	23 (19.7)	106*	Vibration induced by washer
Drawer kitchen (963)	45 (95.7)	2 (4.3)	247*	Cabinet's content manipulated
Master bathroom door (623)	700 (97.7)	16 (2.3)	2,004*	Door swung but not closed
Apartment front door (594)	507 (90)	52 (10)	1,249*	Hydraulic holder at door
Dishwasher door (792)	180 (90)	18 (10)	29,030*	Dishwasher motor vibration
Refrigerator door (996)	12 (20)	47 (80)*	143	Wireless signal loss on metal

Table 8. Examples of the number of object usage sensor activations during one month for some objects that did not have a wired switch equivalent

Object	Activations	Object	Activations
Computer keyboard	7,765	Wood chair	321
Remote control	3,519	Toilet flush	301
Upholstered couch	451	Toilet dispenser	255
Table	587	Can opener	68

numbers of wireless sensor activations (e.g. 1-4) depending on the object type, as shown in parenthesis in column 3 of Table 6. Table 7 summarizes the comparison results for the three object types (cabinets, drawers and doors) that had equivalent wired switches. The table also shows the performance for some individual objects (results located at the bottom of Table 7 are worse-case scenarios). The TPs shown in the table are the number of detected wired switch activations, FNs are the wired switch activations not detected, and 'other' is the number of times the object usage sensors fired when no equivalent wired switch activation was found. This happens while manipulating the contents of drawers and cabinets after they have been opened, or when doors are swung without being fully opened or closed (e.g. holding door to let someone in). Note that 'Other' activations are not directly comparable to TPs and TNs since reed switches generate one activation per opening/closing event and object usage sensors generate multiple. The dishwasher door (as show in Table 7) is an example when the number of 'other' activations is high because intermittent vibration of the motor constantly triggers the object usage sensor while the wired switch is only activated during the dishwasher door opening and closing. It is unfair to consider these activations as FPs since vibration is induced at the sensor by real object usage. On the other hand, the refrigerator door is an example of a high number of FNs produced because of wireless signal loss due to a large metal surface area on the refrigerator's door. Note that this is the only case where we experienced problems due to surrounding metal surfaces/objects Table 8 shows examples of the number of activations for object usage sensors that did not have wired switch equivalents over one month of data. For some objects that are continuously manipulated, such as the remote control and the computer keyboard, the number of activations is high, despite the use of the continuous motion filter. Among the most activated sensors we find the master bathroom door, the half bathroom door, the dishwasher, computer keyboard, laptop, remote control, and kitchen faucet. Among the least activated sensors we find the backyard sliding door, coffee table and some kitchen cabinets and drawers.

Finally, during the 2.5 month data collection, 23 of the most used sensors (e.g. remote control, computer keyboard, laptop, telephone, office chair, toilet flush, eyeglasses case, and coffee mug) required battery replacement after two months. The battery drain results because the continuous filter only saves energy by preventing wireless broadcasts but still wastes energy by keeping the accelerometer on. This problem and our decision to err on the side of sensitivity are the reason why the battery life observed in practice for heavily used objects differs from the battery life estimated for a typical object in the home (1.1 years). Future versions of the continuous filter might reduce the sampling rate of the accelerometer dynamically when continuous usage is detected to further improve battery life. In addition, future versions could increase the sample rate of the accelerometer after recognition of the first activation to raise the detection ratio and noise rejection at the expense of battery life.

From the previous evaluation comparing wired switches and wireless object usage sensors, it was clear that we required another test that allowed us to evaluate the performance of wireless sensors with no wired switch equivalents in more detail. Consequently, we performed a second test where a person busily cooks a pancake recipe and cleans the house (sweeping, vacuuming, doing laundry, doing dishes, wiping a surface, etc.) for a period of four hours while video was being recorded. These activities can be considered a worse case scenario to measure object usage because the kitchen has the largest sensor density and a large number of objects are manipulated or accidentally bumped into during cleaning activities (e.g. putting away things, wiping a surface, and mopping). The person was affiliated with our research group but not knowledgeable about the technical operation of the object usage sensors. A trained annotator (meticulously) labeled all object usage events (object touches >2s) from the four-hour dataset and video. We then computed the TP, FN, and FP detection rates for each object that had an object usage sensor placed on it. A sensor was marked as correctly detecting an object usage event if it activated at least once when the object was being manipulated. For example, a drawer manipulation that is a quick open and shut would be counted as one movement while manipulation consisting of an open, release, pause, and then grab and close would be counted as two usage events. The number of FP activations induced in sensors by the usage of objects nearby the object being used was also computed.

Over the course of the four hours, the annotator found 327 distinct object manipulations. The wireless sensors detected 276 of the 327 object manipulations giving a recognition accuracy of 84.4%. The number of FNs found was 51 (15.6%). Table 9 shows the break down of the FNs and FPs and provides a brief explanation for their generation. Note that the FPs shown in Table 9 are given in sensor activations while

Table 9. Explaination of FNs (given in object usages) and FPs (given in sensor activations) in the four hour test. The % column shows the percentage with respect to the total number of FNs and FPs.

	Num	% FN	Reason for generation
FN	17	33.3	Sink faucets not fired while opened or closed slowly
	15	29.4	Wireless signal loss in 2 sensors due to large metallic surface of refrigerator's doors
	7	13.7	Drawers and cabinets misses due to slow opening/closing events
	6	11.7	Checking on meal status events where oven's door was not fully opened or closed
	5	9.8	Swinging doors without closing them completely
	1	1.9	Touch of upper part of rotating chair with no movement of base (sensor location)

	Num	% FP	Reason for generation
FP	121	46.8	Industrial power mixing machine (KitchenAid 325W, 12.6kg) on at kitchen island
	56	21.7	Vibration propagated to objects located on top of sink (e.g. dishwashing liquid, liquid hand soap, and faucets) through metal surface while washing dishes
	35	13.5	Slamming drawers and cabinets (including kicking drawers to close them)
	34	13.1	Dropping heavy objects (flour, mixer, stove burners) on surfaces
	4	1.5	Bumping objects unintentionally while cleaning a surface or manipulating an object
	4	1.5	Bumping sensors installed at cabinetry (bottom) while vacuuming and mopping
	2	0.7	Kicking sensors with feet while standing in front of cabinets or drawers
	2	0.7	Firing of sensors located at the bottom drawer inside refrigerator when refrigerator turned on cooling mechanism

FNs are given in object usages. As a result, since each object usage generates several (1-7) sensor activations depending on object type, it is not possible to directly compare FPs and FNs. From Table 8, we can observe again that most FNs generated are either due to very slow motions or wireless signal loss due to metal surface on fridge's door. We can also see that the main sources of FPs are worse-case scenarios of vibration traveling through surfaces such as slamming events, constant vibration in kitchen island due to usage of a 12kg mixing machine, and vibration traveling through sink's metal surface to objects on the sink while washing dishes. This test shows how surprisingly difficult is to create an object usage sensor that works in a real environment. Application designers must be wary, for example, of using single activations to trigger events. That said, we think these results show that our sensors provide a nice compromise: good battery life and good object-usage detection with what may be an acceptable level of FNs and FPs for real-world situations. Furthermore, a portion of the FPs generated result from our decision to err on the side of higher sensitivity. FPs could be reduced by using other parameter setting from the ROC curve (Figure 2b) at the expense of lower real object usage recognition.

An interesting path for future research might be to combine proximity sensing [4, 6, 7] and motion sensing to partially mitigate the adjacency problem in some applications. In this approach, hand proximity to an object could be measured by the use of a wearable technology (e.g. RFID enabled wristwatch) and direct manipulation by object movement.

5   Conclusions

In this work we have described the challenges and practical issues involved in recognizing object usage from object motion in everyday environments -- a problem that appears trivial at first glance but turns out to be surprisingly difficult. We have presented a portable wireless sensor to detect object usage in existing homes that (1) is easy to use and easy to install, (2) extends battery life for longitudinal deployments by combining two sensing modalities, and (3) minimizes false positives due to adjacent movement of objects and environmental noise. The sensor parameters suggested err on the side of sensitivity to object usage to minimize false negatives because offline filtering could further reduce false positives. However, the sensor parameters can be modified allowing researchers to trade real vs. adjacent object usage recognition accuracy and battery life depending on the application and duration of sensor deployments. We evaluated the object usage sensors in a non-laboratory setting and showed that they can detect object usage with an accuracy of 86.6% when compared with wired reed switches over one month of data and with an accuracy of 84.4% in difficult scenario where a person is busily cooking and cleaning in a cluttered kitchen. Finally, we also characterized the situations where the sensors have failed and suggested possible paths of future improvement.

Acknowledgments. This work was supported by National Science Foundation grant #0313065 and the MIT House_n Consortium.

References

[1] Munguia Tapia, E., Intille, S.S., Larson, K.: Activity Recognition in the Home Setting Using Simple and Ubiquitous Sensors. In: Ferscha, A., Mattern, F. (eds.) PERVASIVE 2004. LNCS, vol. 3001, pp. 158–175. Springer, Heidelberg (2004)

[2] Wilson, D.: Simultaneous Tracking and Activity Recognition (STAR) Using Many Anonymous, Binary Sensors. In: Gellersen, H.-W., Want, R., Schmidt, A. (eds.) PERVASIVE 2005. LNCS, vol. 3468, pp. 62–83. Springer, Heidelberg (2005)

[3] Barger, T., Brown, D., Alwan, M.: Health Status Monitoring Through Analysis of Behavioral Patterns. Proceedings of IEEE Transactions on Systems, Man and Cybernetics Part A 35, 22–27 (2005)

[4] Philipose, M., Fishkin, K.P., Perkowitz, M., Patterson, D.J., Hahnel, D., Fox, D., Kautz, H.: Inferring Activities from Interactions with Objects. IEEE Pervasive Computing Magazine 3, 50–57 (2004)

[5] Beaudin, J.S.: From Personal Experience to Design: Externalizing the Homeowner's Needs and Assessment Process, M.S. Thesis, The Media Laboratory. MIT, Cambridge, MA (2003)

[6] Philipose, M., Fishkin, K., Fox, D., Kautz, H., Patterson, D., Perkowitz, M.: Guide: Towards Understanding Daily Life Via Auto-Identification and Statistical Analysis. In: UbiHealth 2003 (2003)

[7] Fishkin, K., Philipose, M., Rea, A.: Hands-On RFID: Wireless Wearables for Detecting Use of Objects. In: ISWC 2005, pp. 38–41. IEEE Press, Los Alamitos (2005)

[8] Munguia Tapia, E., Intille, S.S.: Environmental Sensors Hardware and Software Resources, [cited August 28th, 2007], available from http://architecture.mit.edu/house_n/MITes

[9] Feldmeier, M., Paradiso, J.A.: Giveaway Wireless Sensors for Large-Group Interaction. In: CHI 2004. Proceedings of The ACM Conference on Human Factors and Computing Systems, pp. 1291–1292. ACM Press, New York (2004)

[10] Munguia Tapia, E., Intille, S.S., Lopez, L., Larson, K.: The Design of a Portable Kit of Wireless Sensors for Naturalistic Data Collection. In: Fishkin, K.P., Schiele, B., Nixon, P., Quigley, A. (eds.) PERVASIVE 2006. LNCS, vol. 3968, pp. 117–134. Springer, Heidelberg (2006)

[11] Philipose, M.: Large-Scale Human Activity Recognition Using Ultra-Dense Sensing. The Bridge, National Academy of Engineering 35(4) (2005)

[12] Philipose, M., Smith, J.R., Jiang, B., Mamishev, A., Roy, S., Sundara-Rajan, K.: Battery-Free Wireless Identification and Sensing. IEEE Pervasive Computing 4, 37–45 (2005)

[13] Witten, I.H., Frank, E.: Data Mining: Practical Machine Learning Tools and Techniques, 2nd edn. Morgan Kaufmann, San Francisco (2005)

[14] Intille, S.S., Larson, K., Munguia Tapia, E., Beaudin, J.S., Kaushik, P., Nawyn, J., Rockinson, R.: Using a Live-In Laboratory for Ubiquitous Computing Research. In: Fishkin, K.P., Schiele, B., Nixon, P., Quigley, A. (eds.) PERVASIVE 2006. LNCS, vol. 3968, pp. 349–365. Springer, Heidelberg (2006)

Role Assignment
Via Physical Mobile Interaction Techniques
in Mobile Multi-user Applications for Children

Karin Leichtenstern, Elisabeth André, and Thurid Vogt

Institute of Computer Science
Multimedia Concepts and Applications
Eichleitnerstr. 30
D-86135 Augsburg
{Leichtenstern,Andre,Vogt}@informatik.uni-augsburg.de

Abstract. The development of engaging user interfaces that support collaboration is a great challenge – in particular if users are children. We consider mobile phones as appropriate devices for multi-user interactions with a system because novel forms of physical mobile interaction techniques with smart objects yield lots of benefits, such as being intuitive and playful to use, but also addressing children's needs for curiosity. In this paper, we introduce our approach to multi-user game-like scenarios within an ambient intelligence context which are controlled via different mobile phones and their supported interaction techniques. By providing children with multiple mobile phones we structure interactions in multi-user settings and prevent undesirable situations, such as dominant users or off-topic actions. Children get access to various physical mobile interaction techniques for interactions with smart objects which are all required to fulfill one common goal. In this way, social interaction arises in a natural manner. In order to motivate and evaluate our approach, we developed two ambient intelligence applications called *The World Explorer* and *The Escape*. Results of a user study showed that children liked working in a group and that physical mobile interaction techniques are a promising approach to increase engagement and foster social interactions but also to prevent chaotic situations by balancing the distribution of activities in multi-user settings.

Keywords: Physical mobile interaction, novel mobile user interfaces, social interaction and collaboration, multi-user application, mobile application, evaluation.

1 Introduction

Mobile phones have successfully become part of our everyday life and are the first pervasively available interaction device. Almost everybody owns a mobile phone and primarily uses it as a channel for human-human communication, such as exchanging text messages or making phone calls. Nevertheless, we see lots of unused potential of mobile phones for human communication and social interactions especially in context of ambient intelligence applications.

B. Schiele et al. (Eds.): AmI 2007, LNCS 4794, pp. 38–54, 2007.

Recent mobile phone technologies facilitate the development of user interfaces that offer more natural interaction styles, such as *pointing*, *touching* or *tilting*, based on a growing number of built-in sensors. The objective of this paper is to explore the potential of multiple physical mobile interaction techniques as a means to stimulate face-to-face collaboration between children and give developers the posibility to balance distribution of activities within multi-user settings. As Druin points out in [1], children want to use technologies which support their curiosity, their love of repetition and their need for control. The new physical mobile interaction techniques address several requirements for children because they are intuitive and playful to use but also less obstructive for real world interactions [2]. Children may freely move around in the physical environment with their mobile phones, interact with real instrumented objects, for example, by *touching* them with their mobile phone, and engage in face-to-face conversation with other children.

Zagal et al. [3] distinguish between spontaneous and a stimulated social interaction in multi-player games. Spontaneous interaction occurs naturally and is not forced through the game arrangement whereas stimulated social interaction is mandated by the game. In our case, we aim at stimulating social interactions by distributing several mobile phones with different technical features. That is not all children will have the same interaction possibilities. As a consequence, they will only be able to accomplish a task, such as solving a puzzle, if the technical features of all available mobile phones are combined. We defined role assignment via physical mobile interaction as follows. A task is split to more elementary actions. These elementary actions are assigned to several users. Thus, we force children to collaborate because only by working together they can successfully complete a task which is their common goal. As a consequence we assume that by forcing children to share resources and to arrange and agree on actions, collaboration should occur in a natural manner. The distribution of mobile phones directly corresponds to an assignment of roles which makes children aware of the overall performance as a team and each individual's contribution. In addition, mobile phones may be handed around in order to involve other members of the group in a decision and re-assign roles in a spontaneous manner.

To study the impact of multi-user applications controlled via mobile phones, we implemented two ambient intelligence indoor scenarios: *The World Explorer* and *The Escape*. *The World Explorer* is a computer-based quiz where children may collaboratively acquire knowledge through interactions with their environment and answer questions on different countries. *The Escape* is an interactive story telling environment where children jointly watch a scene on a public display and collaboratively decide on the continuation of the story. Both applications are pervasive multi-user games which enable interactions with real instrumented objects in the children's physical environment as well as virtual characters on public displays. In both scenarios, children may take on certain roles which are reflected by the use of a specific mobile phone that enables certain forms of interaction. The children only succeed in the two games if they are willing to collaborate.

In the next section, we first discuss interaction styles for ambient intelligence environments that may be easily realized by making use of novel mobile phone technology. After that, we report on earlier studies that investigate how to foster multi-user interactions by appropriate interaction techniques. We then describe the typical technical implementation of a multi-user application based on role assignment.

In particular, we discuss how different roles can be assigned by making use of multiple mobile phones' technologies. Finally, we report on an empirical study that has been conducted with the aim to explore the potential benefits of our interaction techniques for social interactions between children but also usability issues and engagement of children.

2 Physical Mobile Interaction

Recent mobile phones support several network interfaces as access to infrastructure-based networks (GSM/GPRS/UMTS) or ad-hoc-based networks (Bluetooth/Infrared/NFC). These network capabilities and a growing number of built-in sensors such as cameras, accelerometers and temperature sensors support novel forms of mobile interaction techniques. These progresses in technology are the basis to build novel mobile interaction techniques [2. 4]. One example is called *touching* which uses the mobile phones network interface NFC (Near Field Communication). NFC enables selections of instrumented RFID-objects. There are several further physical interaction techniques such as *scanning* and *pointing* [2, 4]. Ballagas et al. give a comprehensive overview on various possibilities to use a smart phone as a ubiquitous input device [5].

These new forms of mobile interactions can address some usability problems of mobile phones, such as the reduced amount of information that can be displayed on miniaturized screens and the limited input functionalities of a mobile phone's keyboard. The benefit is that interactions with the mobile phone are directly mapped onto interactions with the physical world surrounding users. Thus, interactions with the real world are called *physical mobile interaction techniques.*

Until now, research with physical mobile interaction has mainly concentrated on the development of new interaction techniques and their comparison, but did not use several phones and their supported physical mobile interaction techniques as interfaces to multi-user applications for children. Ballagas et al. [6] used a mobile phone and its built-in camera as an input sensor to control a mouse pointer on a public display, a technique which is called *sweep*. Another technique called *point&shoot* enables a selection of widgets [6]. We describe in [2, 20] techniques called *scanning*, *pointing* and *touching* which can be used to select objects in a smart environment. They used these techniques in user experiments to analyze in which context which interaction technique is preferred by the user [2, 7, 20]. This paper extends our previous work by not only concentrating on single-user interactions with smart objects. We decided to use existing physical mobile interaction techniques and investigate multi-user settings for children. Moreover, we want to find out whether children have any preferences for a mobile interaction technique represented by a role and finally if children feel engaged when interacting in our application settings. Thus, our three main research goals were to investigate the children's level of engagement and their social behaviour when interacting with different physical mobile interaction techniques as well as usability issues.

A significant amount of work has been devoted to location-aware applications until now. In these applications mobile phones and information about users' location are used in multi-user settings. Examples include pervasive games, such as *Savannah* [8],

Can you Hear me now [9] or *Paper Chase* [10]. In contrast to our work, these examples only used the users' location as real-world input, but did not include physical mobile interaction techniques which must be performed explicitly. Moreover, they did not assign user roles via different mobile phone technologies.

Beale [11] described different multi-user applications for human-human communication using mobile phones, such as a Bluetooth dating service or a bogging service. In contrast to our work they did not use mobile phones to allow for interactions with the physical world and their applications were not directed to children.

We see benefits in combining different physical mobile interaction techniques as a basis to create hands-on to use, curious and playful user interfaces for children. In particular, we expect that multiple physical interaction techniques increase fun and enhance the children's willingness to interact with a computer system through their ambient intelligence world but also prevent dominant users and decrease off topic tasks by balancing the activity level of all involved children in a multi-user application.

3 Multi-user Interaction

CSCW researchers regard the assignment of roles as an important means to structure collaboration between the single members of a team. We consider role assignment via physical mobile interaction techniques a promising way to foster social interactions between children. Kirschner and Van Bruggen argue that social relationships can be built if children establish a joint understanding, trust, and responsibility [12]. We suppose real world roles can address these three requirements. Children need to agree on the distribution of roles and the responsibilities associated with them. They need to trust each other because each child is required to achieve a common objective and finally all children are responsible to make best use of their roles for group success. Apart from supporting the establishment of social relationships, role play might enhance the attractiveness of the software since children can swap their roles when applications are played more than once.

A number of collaborative interfaces for children have been developed, such as *KidPad* [13] and *Teatrix* [14], that allow children to collaboratively create stories on a virtual stage. These applications make use of multiple mice or tangible interfaces, but in contrast to our work, role assignment is not based on the distribution of interaction devices. For instance, in *Teatrix* [14] children may select the roles of characters that they control in a story, such as the role of a hero or that of a villain, but role assignment is done via a GUI. There are also a number of game-like environments which make use of role assignment. Savannah [8] is a pervasive game where children take on the role of lions. Other examples are the pervasive games *Paranoia syndrome* [15] and *Virus* [16]. *Paranoia syndrome* defines three different kinds of role. Children can take on the roles and skills of a technician, doctor and scientist, but these definitions are not based on physical mobile interaction techniques as in our case. In *Virus*, children take on the role of a virus and transmit it via their mobile devices by getting within proximity of other users. In this way, complex algorithms can be learnt in a simulation. These three examples provide evidence of the fact that children like role playing games.

Of particular interest to our own research are studies that investigate how collaboration between group members may be supported by appropriate use of interaction devices. There is empirical evidence that children seem to be more engaged and more active when playing on a computer with multiple input devices and cursors than when using a computer by themselves. Inkpen and colleagues [17] observed that giving each child an input device had a positive effect on collaboration even if only one child could interact at a time. Mandryk and colleagues [18] investigated the use of handheld devices to foster collaboration between children in a game. A study revealed that children preferred to play the game with friends than by themselves and that the children spent a great deal of time interacting with each other. We assume that similar effects will be achieved if children are equipped with various mobile phones to interact with an application. That is several mobile phones are distributed and used as interaction devices within their ambient intelligence world. In our case, interaction devices are, however, used in an asymmetrical manner. That is not all users are able to accomplish the all steps of a task to complete a goal because the phone that is assigned to them might not support a specific activity.

Based on this research, we came up with the following idea. We decided to create multi-user applications controlled by mobile phones and their supported physical mobile interaction techniques. To prevent dominant users and chaotic interactions in multi-user applications we decided to split a task in more elementary user interactions and assign these different interactions to different user roles. We use a simple task to illustrate role assignment: A user first wants to request information and therefore selects an object, then he interprets the received information about the object by evaluating it on several aspects and finally reacts to the interpreted information by executing an option. The example illustrates that the task requires three basic actions of the user: Initiation, Evaluation and Execution. Our idea of role assignment is using these three required actions to successfully complete a task and assign the three actions as user roles to children. In the example we have the role called *initiator* who is the requester of the information, the *evaluator* who receives and interprets information and finally the *executor* who is selecting an option. These roles can be mapped to physical mobile interactions techniques in several ways. We decided to map the role of the initiator to the physical mobile interaction technique called *touching*, the role of the evaluator to *scanning* and the executor to *tilting*.

4   Multi-user Applications

Based on our ideas about role assignment in multi-user applications within an ambient intelligence world, we have implemented two prototypes: (1) *The World Explorer*, a mobile Computer Supported Collaborative Learning (mCSCL) application and (2) *The Escape*, an interactive storytelling system. We implemented two types of applications that address different content, but employ similar interaction techniques to realize the role concept in order to investigate whether the type of the applications has any impact on social behavior, children's engagement for a physical mobile interaction technique and usability issues. In the following we describe the basic concept, the mapping between roles and physical mobile interaction techniques and an abstract description of the architectural implementation of our two applications.

4.1 Applications

The World Explorer is a mobile and pervasive learning software that supports multi-user interactions for children by combining several physical mobile interaction techniques. We assigned the role of the initiator, evaluator and executor via the techniques *touching*, scanning and *tilting*. The objective of this application is to enhance learning about aspects of different cultures in a playful and entertaining manner by a virtual journey around the world. In *The World Explorer*, different physical locations in the classroom represent different countries in the world. Thus, children can move in their physical environment which corresponds to a virtual travel to a certain country. Once children have moved to one of these countries, they can find different physical objects representing several themes, such as music or geography (see Figure 1).

Fig. 1. Smart Objects as Interaction Target for Physical Mobile Interaction *touching*

Children can select a topic and ask for information related to the topic in terms of a multimedia presentation or they can directly request a question related to the topic and try to answer it. We expected *The World Explorer* to support collaboration between children by defining different fields of activities that correspond to a particular role (initiator, evaluator and executor). The distribution of roles was supposed to stimulate social interactions because each role and the associated skills are required to fulfill a team's common objective, namely to answer as many questions correctly as possible. Figure 2 shows the role assignment of the initiator, evaluator and executor in *The World Explorer*. The initiator selects a country and its topic by interacting with smart objects in the ambient world via the technique *touching* which initiates a request for information about that topic. The evaluator receives information via the technique *scanning* which can help answering the question and the executer can answer the question displayed on the public display via the technique *tilting* (see Figure 3).

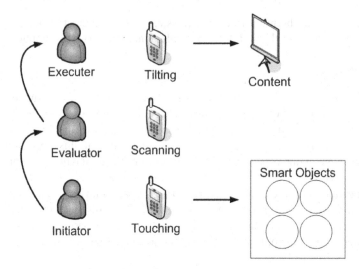

Fig. 2. Role Assignment of The World Explorer

Questions and answers are presented by a team of virtual reporters on the public display. These reporters guide the children during their world travel by introducing countries, themes and questions, but also by providing help during the game itself. For example, they inform the children if one role has not yet been occupied.

Fig. 3. Virtual Conference with Reporters

We can use our approach of role assignment for other applications as well. To illustrate the generic approach we developed another application called *The Escape*. It is a story telling software which automatically generates interactive 3D animated stories. This story is told from the perspective of a dwarf who is held prisoner by the orcs. Apart from the dwarf, there are two further virtual characters: an elb and an orc. In our stories, the dwarf wants to escape and asks at certain decision points the children what strategy to follow. In particular, the dwarf can choose out of three different options which are represented as smart objects. The common goal for children playing *The Escape* is helping the dwarf to successfully escape.

Children can decide on the progress of the story by selecting one of the smart objects, but they do not know exactly which actions are associated with them and the resulting consequences for the story, because the usage of the objects depends on the current story context. Thus, children first select one of the supported smart objects to request hints and interpret its usage for continuing the story on the consequence for the dwarf. Thus, children can jointly discuss the single options and hints to agree on which option to select. Finally, an object can be selected and the story goes on. For *The Escape* we defined two real world roles to take on the initiator and the combined role of the evaluator and executor.

The initiator can apply the physical mobile interaction technique *touching* and pick up one of the offered real world objects, which are physical objects augmented with RFID-tags. We used several smart objects such as a stone, a sword or a key representing progress of the story. The combined role of evaluator and executor automatically receives hints from the oracle regarding the smart objects in the current context of the story because of her physical mobile interaction technique *scanning*. Thus, she gets an idea about the consequences of the different options.

Overall, *The Escape* is a storytelling application that aims at encouraging social interactions between children, because children have to collaboratively decide on the best strategy for the dwarf.

4.2 Architecture

In the following, an abstract architecture for applications, such as *The World Explorer* or *The Escape*, is described to provide a better understanding of the general concepts underlying our implementation (see Figure 4). For user interaction, we deploy several mobile phones, each of them requiring different physical mobile interaction techniques that correspond to the roles of the initiator, the evaluator and the executor.

The initiator requires a mobile phone which enables him to initiate a request. In case of *The World Explorer* the initiation is done by selecting a smart object in the physical environment via the technique *touching* which requires a mobile phone with a built-in RFID reader. We used the Nokia 3220, its NFC shell and the Nokia NFC & RFID SDK.

The evaluator uses a mobile phone that enables him to receive information. We used the interaction technique called *scanning* on the mobile phone of the evaluator and pushed information (text, image, audio or video) via Bluetooth to the phone.

The executor requires a mobile phone that enables him to trigger an event. In our case the executor selects an option via scrolling through options and selecting one of them. We used the technique called *tilting* to scroll through options via *tilting* the phone to the right and to the left or up and down. The Samsung SGH E760 supports a built-in accelerometer and an API to receive such *tilting* events.

Apart from the mobile phones and the smart objects a GUI on a public display is required to present the virtual world and a file server is required to support the evaluator with the relevant information. Moreover, a server is needed to control the logic of the application which particularly includes the coordination of the different user roles.

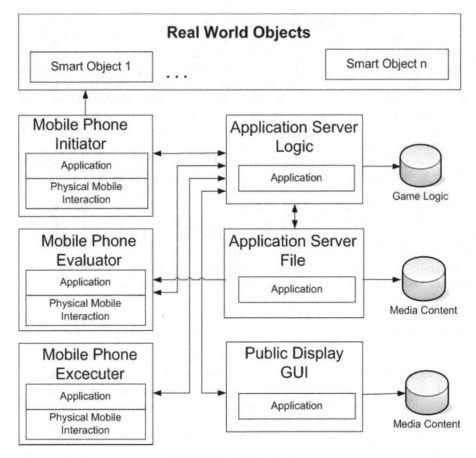

Fig. 4. Abstract Architecture

5 Evaluation

We evaluate our approach to multi-user mobile interaction by means of the two applications: *The World Explorer* and *The Escape*. In particular, we conducted a user study with 48 children at the age of 9-15 years with an average age of 12.43. 11 of the subjects were male and 37 female. We used two applications for our evaluation in order to investigate in how far our findings may be generalized. In the following, we outline the experimental setting and discuss our results.

5.1 Experimental Setting

First of all, we were interested in the children's attitude towards multi-user applications that are controlled via different mobile phones and their physical mobile interaction techniques.

Via questionnaires and video observation, we investigated whether children found find it curious and engaging to use mobile phones and mobile interaction techniques or not and if there are any preferences for specific physical mobile interaction techniques. We compared these results to former results of a studies described in [2, 20].

Moreover, we hoped that the results of the analyzed video recordings would help us to identify potential usability issues regarding the different physical mobile interaction techniques.

Finally, we aimed at investigating the social behavior of children when roles are assigned to them via physical mobile interaction techniques. In this vein, we captured videos of the tests and analyzed them focusing on on- and off-topic communication, social interactions as well as the distribution of user activities. In sum, our user study addressed the following three goals:

- Engagement in form of preferences for a physical mobile interaction technique which is evaluated via a questionnaire and video observation
- Usability issues for children when using physical mobile interaction techniques which is evaluated via video observation
- Social interactions in form of group activities and the influence of role assignment via physical mobile interaction which is evaluated via video observation

Each test was structured in four phases. First, we asked children general questions about mobile phones, computer games and their media usage in general. Before starting the tests, we showed and explained the two applications, the mobile phones, and the corresponding physical mobile interaction techniques. Then, the children tested in groups of three or two both applications and each role of *The World Explorer* and *The Escape*. Children could freely use the applications. We only switched the roles after some interactions. We alternately started with *The World Explorer* or with *The Escape* for the different groups to prevent any biases. After the children had finished their tests, we asked them specific questions about the two applications to investigate their level of engagement for a physical mobile interaction technique and for the single applications

5.2 Results of Questionnaire

In the general part of our questionnaire we asked children for their background in mobile phone and media usage. Only 12 out of the 48 children did not own a mobile phone, but all of them had already played games on mobile phones or on a computer. They spent at least two hours per day alone watching television or sitting in front of a desktop PC playing games. As we were highly interested in social interactions and group activities, we first asked the children rate on a scale from one to five how much they like group activities for problem solving where one means not at all and five means very much. The average value of the result is 4.58 which was significantly above the average value of three ($t(47)=17.892$, $p<0.001$).

Figure 6 and 7 present the results of the questionnaire we gave the children after performing the tests to determine their level of engagement and their preferences regarding a specific mobile interaction technique.

Touching. The results illustrate that most children liked best *touching* in *The World Explorer* (27 children) and in *The Escape* (31) which was represented by the role of the initiator. Some of them told us that they preferred *touching* over other physical mobile techniques because it is easy to use, highly active and curious which is in line with the results we obtained in an earlier evaluation [2, 20]. Children liked to easily pick up real world objects.

Tilting. 7 children liked *tilting* represented by the role of the executor most in *The World Explorer* and pointed out two reasons. On the one hand they liked the special usage of the mobile phone and on the other hand they liked the ability to interact with the public display and log in answers.

Scanning. Finally, in *The World Explorer* 9 (11 in *The Escape*) children liked *scanning* represented by the role of the evaluator. They preferred the role of an evaluator because they considered it as advantageous to get hints from the system and thus acquire more knowledge which they can give to other children.

Overall, we can say, that children liked *touching* most as an interaction technique which is independent of the specific application. We interpret the results as follow. Children want to take over a highly active part in games which includes innovative interactions with mobile phones, but the interaction technique should still be quick and easy to use. In comparison to the results, we reported on in [2, 20], we identified an additional factor that determines a user's preference for a specific mobile interaction technique. Not only a user's physical location and current activity is important, but also the novelty of a mobile phone must be considered. Curiosity and the level of activity can increase or decrease the motivation of users and consequently their preference for a physical mobile interaction technique and its associated role. Table 1 shows overall children's attitude towards the three physical mobile interaction techniques regarding usability, activity level and innovation. The table is based on the verbal feedback we got from the children.

We also compared the children's preferences regarding the two applications. We asked them to rate several catchwords between one and five where five represents the best rating. The averaged results showed that the children considered the *The World Explorer* and *The Escape* as fun (*The World Explorer*: 3.98 / *The Escape*: 4.15), cool (3.92 / 4.25) and exiting (3.42 / 4.08). t-tests for one sample revealed that all values were significantly above the average value of 3.0 ($p<0.015$ for exiting in the case of the *The World Explorer*, $p<0.001$ in all other cases). A paired samples t-test revealed that the differences were significant for exiting ($df(47)=-4.363$, $p<0.001$) and cool ($df(47)=-2,141$, $p<0.037$). These results were also confirmed when asking the children for their preferences. Overall, 55 % children preferred *The Escape* whereas only 21 % preferred *The World Explorer* and 24 % liked both applications at the same level.

Table 1. Children's classification of the different Physical Mobile Interaction Techniques

	Usability	Usability	Innovation
Touching	Easy to Use	Highly active	Curious
Tilting	Difficult to Use	Active	Curious
Scanning	Easy to Use	Very Passive	Ordinary

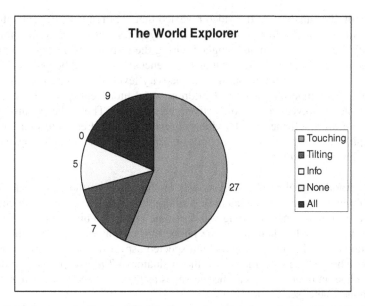

Fig. 5. Preferences for Physical Mobile Interaction Techniques in The World Explorer

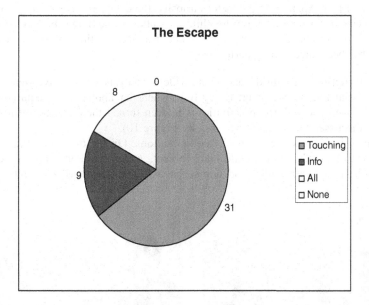

Fig. 6. Preferences for Physical Mobile Interaction Techniques in The World Explorer

5.2 Results of Observations

During the tests we captured the children and afterwards analyzed the videos to investigate the children's level of engagement and social interactions as well as to detect potential usability problems.

Engagement. The analysis of the video revealed that children were very attentive and engaged. Almost all children watched the displayed content of our applications very observantly, but also had fun and laughed during the tests and were eager to play our games again (see Figure 7). Regarding preferences for a specific physical mobile interaction technique we found out that the activity level of the supported interaction technique is an important aspect. Children were more engaged whenever their assigned role involved a lot of active interactions. Thus, the results of the questionnaire are confirmed by the video observation. Children were more attentive when employing the techniques *touching* or *tilting* than when employing the more passive technique *scanning*.

Usability. Another goal of the analysis was to shed light on the children's usage of physical mobile interaction techniques. Children did not have any problems with *touching* or *scanning* whereas *tilting* was for some children a bit tricky (see Figure 8). It was not very easy for them to tilt the phone in the right way to scroll through the single options. Another interesting and unexpected aspect was the children's usage of the mobile when taking over the role of the evaluator in *The Escape*. They intuitively held the phone on their ear to hear the messages as they are used to it from traditional mobile phone usage (see Figure 9).

Furthermore, an important aspect we observed is that children liked visual, auditory and haptic cues. Using these cues involves different senses of the children: see, hear and feel. Apart from the factor curiosity, the cues also provide a system with feedback which helps to increase the children's attentiveness and decrease off-topic activities. Children have a direct feedback about actions of the system, such as that *touching* has been successfully performed.

Social Interaction. The third goal of our videos analysis was to investigate which kinds of social interaction occur. Every time when our applications required a user interaction, we observed group activities. Children turned their bodies towards each other and discussed the different options (see Figure 10).

Overall we observed two forms of collaborations. On the one hand, the children helped each other whenever a child had problems using the phone and on the other hand children had both verbal and non-verbal social interactions when interpreting

Fig. 7. Children are interacting with our Application

Fig. 8. Children are using the Physical Mobile Interaction Technique *Touching* and *Tilting*

Fig. 9. Child is getting information in *The Escape*

Fig. 10. Social Interactions

hints and answering questions. At each point children had to select an option, they were very attentive and discussed intensively the single options before executing a selection to prevent failures in the game. We also achieved a balanced level of activity and attentiveness. Obviously, the application setting helped to avoid that some users took on a very dominant behavior. Moreover, we observed hardly any off-topic activities. Overall, the video recordings provide evidence that role assignment via physical mobile interaction may help to ensure that all users in a multi-user application will be involved actively. Furthermore, role assignment gives an interaction structure to the game. Each child knows about its role within the game which prevents chaotic situations.

6 Conclusion and Discussion

We presented a concept of multi-user applications for children in an ambient intelligence environment which can be controlled via different mobile phones and their supported physical mobile interaction techniques. We assigned different user roles via these physical mobile interaction techniques namely: the initiator, the evaluator and the executor. Each of these roles is required to fulfill a common objective and we expected that the associated physical mobile interaction techniques help to structure the interaction and prevent dominant users. In order to provide evidence for this assumption, we developed and evaluated two applications: *The World Explorer* and *The Escape*.

Our user study showed that children enjoyed group activities and the usage of different physical mobile interaction techniques. Children found our applications curious and engaging, in particular they liked the application *The Escape*. Our user study also identified the children's preferences for specific physical mobile interaction techniques and provides further evidence for the results of the study conducted by Rukzio and colleagues [2, 20]. Most children preferred *touching* over other mobile interaction techniques which was independent of the used application. Children liked having an active role in a game. In particular, they enjoyed performing different physical interactions with real world objects and at the same time doing it quick and easy. We consider physical mobile interaction techniques as feasible interaction techniques for children when supporting a high activity level and being intuitive and quick to use.

Our user study also showed that social interactions arise in forms of group activities. Our applications stimulated social interactions such as discussing and agreeing on the choice of different options but also helping each other. Moreover, observations showed that role assignment via physical mobile interaction techniques can help to structure interactions within a game. Children are assigned a clear role by giving them a specific mobile phone which helps to avoid chaotic multi-user interactions. The distribution of different roles to children can prevent dominant users and balance the level of activity between the involved children.

Overall, our results showed that different mobile phones enable promising new interaction techniques in multi-user applications for children. On the one hand they address the children's needs for fun, curiosity and control which is important for children's willingness to interact with a system and on the other hand they also stimulate social interactions.

In our future work, we plan to conduct further experiments to find out how specific role assignments support group activities. Therefore we plan to conduct tests that evaluate role assignments in different combinations to find out how they influence the distribution of interactions, on- or off-topic activities, social interactions and engagement.

Moreover, we plan to develop further prototypical multi-user applications that combine embodied conversational agents with physical mobile interaction techniques in the context of the eCircus project [19]. These different mobile multi-user applications are planned for different age groups including adults.

Apart from that, we recognized a need to simplify design and evaluation processes of applications, such as *The World Explorer* and *The Escape* and see benefits in automatically annotate and analyze captured user tests. Thus, we are currently specifying an adapted design process and a tool addressing these issues to make evaluations of such application more efficient.

Acknowledgments. We are grateful to all the students who participated in our practical course. We like to thank Sebastian Thomas, Christian Pratsch, Michael Ailinger, Robert Mysliwiec and Lars Müller for their work on *The World Explorer* and Tobias Lüßmann, Thilo Grashei, Michale Kutsch and Georg Döhring for their work on *The Escape*.

This work was partially supported by European Community (EC) and is currently funded by the eCIRCUS project [19] IST-4-027656-STP. The authors are solely responsible for the content of this publication. It does not represent the opinion of the EC, and the EC is not responsible for any use that might be made of data appearing therein.

References

1. Druin, A.: The Design of Children's Technology. Morgan Kaufmann Publishers, San Francisco (1999)
2. Rukzio, E., Leichtenstern, K., Callaghan, V., Holleis, P., Schmidt, A., Chin, J.S.-Y.: An experimental comparison of physical mobile interaction techniques: Touching, pointing and scanning. In: Dourish, P., Friday, A. (eds.) UbiComp 2006. LNCS, vol. 4206, pp. 87–104. Springer, Heidelberg (2006)
3. Zagal, J.P., Nussbaum, M., Rosas, R.: A Model to Support the Design of Multi Player Games. Presence: Teleoperators and Virtual Environments 9(5), 448–462 (2000)
4. Välkkynen, P., Korhonen, I., Plomp, J., Tuomisto, T., Cluitmans, L., Ailisto, H., Seppä, H.: A user interaction paradigm for physical browsing and near-object control based on tags. In: Chittaro, L. (ed.) Mobile HCI 2003. LNCS, vol. 2795, Springer, Heidelberg (2003)
5. Ballagas, R., Borchers, J., Rohs, M., Sheridan, J.G.: The Smart Phone: A Ubiquitous Input Device. IEEE Pervasive Computing 5(1), 70–77 (2006)
6. Ballagas, R., Rohs, M., Sheridan, J.G.: Sweep and point and shoot: phonecam-based interactions for large public displays. In: Conference on Human Factors in Computing Systems CHI 2005 extended abstracts on Human factors in computing systems, Portland, USA (April 2005)
7. Leichtenstern, K., Rukzio, E., Callaghan, V., Schmidt, A.: Mobile Interaction in Smart Environments. In: Fishkin, K.P., Schiele, B., Nixon, P., Quigley, A. (eds.) PERVASIVE 2006. LNCS, vol. 3968, Springer, Heidelberg (2006)

8. Benford, S., Rowlanda, D., Flintham, M., Hull, R., Reid, J., Morrison, J., Facer, K., Clayton, B.: Savannah: Designing a location-based game simulating lion behaviour. In: International Conference on Advances in Computer Entertainment Technology, Singapore (June 2004)
9. Can You See Me Now? http://www.blasttheory.co.uk/bt/work_cysmn.html
10. Boll, S., Krösche, J., Wegener, C.: Paper chase revisited – a real world game meets hypermedia. In: The fourteenth conference on Hypertext and Hypermedia, Nottingham, UK (2003)
11. Beale, R.: Supporting Social Interaction with Smart Phones. IEEE Pervasive Computing 4(2), 35–41 (2005)
12. Kirschner, P., Van Bruggen, J.: Learning and Understanding in Virtual Teams. CyberPsychology & Behavior 7, 135–139 (2004)
13. Stanton, D., Bayon, V., Neale, H., Ghali, A., Benford, S., Cobb, H., Ingram, R., O'Malley, C., Wilson, J., Pridmore, T.: Classroom collaboration in the design of tangible interfaces for storytelling. In: CHI 2001. Proceedings of the SIGCHI conference on Human factors in computing systems, New York, USA (2001)
14. Machado, I., Paiva, A., Prada, R.: Is the wolf angry or...just hungry? In: AGENTS 2001. Proceedings of the fifth international conference on Autonomous agents, New York, USA (2001)
15. Heumer, G., Carlson, D., Kaligiri, S., Maheshwari, S., Hasan, W., Jung, B., Schrader, A.: Paranoia Syndrome – A Pervasive Multiplayer Game using PDAs, RFID, and Tangible Objects. In: Third International Workshop on Pervasive Gaming Applications on Pervasive Computing 2006, Dublin, Ireland (May 2006)
16. Collella, V., Bororvoy, R., Resnick, M.: Participatory Simulations: Using Computational Objects to Learn about Dynamic Systems. In: CHI 1998. Proceedings of the SIGCHI conference on Human factors in computing systems, Los Angeles, USA (April 1998)
17. Inkpen, K., Ho-Ching, W., Kuederle, O., Scott, S., Shoemaker, G.: This is fun! We're all best friends and we're all playing: supporting children's synchronous collaboration. In: CSCL 1999. Proceedings of the 1999 conference on Computer support for collaborative learning, International Society of the Learning Sciences (1999)
18. Mandryk, R., Inkpen, K., Bilezikjian, M., Klemmer, S., Landay, J.: Supporting children's collaboration across handheld computers. In: CHI 2001. Proceedings of the SIGCHI conference on Human factors in computing systems, New York, USA (2001)
19. eCircus-Project: http://www.e-circus.org
20. Leichtenstern, K.: Mobile Interaction in Smart Envionments. Diploma thesis at Media Informatics, Ludwig-Maximilians-Universität, Munich, Germany

Context-Sensitive Microlearning of Foreign Language Vocabulary on a Mobile Device

Jennifer S. Beaudin[1], Stephen S. Intille[1], Emmanuel Munguia Tapia[1],
Randy Rockinson[1], and Margaret E. Morris[2]

[1] House_n, Massachusetts Institute of Technology
One Cambridge Center, 4FL, Cambridge, MA 02142 USA
{Jbeaudin,intille}@mit.edu
[2] Digital Health Group, Intel Corporation,
20270 NW AmberGlen Court; AG1-102, Beaverton OR 97006 USA
Margaret.Morris@intel.com

Abstract. We explore the use of ubiquitous sensing in the home for context-sensitive microlearning. To assess how users would respond to frequent and brief learning interactions tied to context, a sensor-triggered mobile phone application was developed, with foreign language vocabulary as the learning domain. A married couple used the system in a home environment, during the course of everyday activities, for a four-week study period. Built-in and stick-on multi-modal sensors detected the participants' interactions with hundreds of objects, furniture, and appliances. Sensor activations triggered the audio presentation of English and Spanish phrases associated with object use. Phrases were presented on average 57 times an hour; this intense interaction was found to be acceptable even after extended use. Based on interview feedback, we consider design attributes that may have reduced the interruption burden and helped sustain user interest, and which may be applicable to other context-sensitive, always-on systems.

Keywords: microlearning, language learning, context-sensitive, context-triggered, mobile phone, sensors, home, deployments.

1 Introduction

In this work we explore the use of context-sensitive ubiquitous computing for learning. Although many applications have been proposed that use ubiquitous computing and context-aware sensing for reminders, entertainment, medical monitoring, and communication systems, relatively little work has been reported on how context-aware systems might be exploited to build applications that help people incrementally learn new things. Yet, automatic detection of context may enable learning tools that present information and interactions to people at appropriate moments as they engage in their everyday lives. We describe our experience building and testing such a system, and we report some observations that may be relevant to those interested in creating other types of "always-on" applications that use ubiquitous computing and automatic context detection.

B. Schiele et al. (Eds.): AmI 2007, LNCS 4794, pp. 55–72, 2007.

The inspiration for this work was an eLearning technique called "microlearning," where a difficult learning task is broken into a series of very quick learning interactions, distributed over time [1]. Rather than having to learn or practice everything at once, the learner is presented with a small, manageable chunk of information at regular intervals. Researchers in previous work have explored how to deliver learning interactions using technology during moments when the user may be more receptive, in idle moments such as during the start-up period of computing devices and when computer screen-savers are automatically initiated [2].

The brief interactions used by microlearning systems may not be appropriate for in depth learning, but they may allow users to chip away at a larger learning goal. Moreover, temporally-spaced presentation has been shown to yield higher learning rates than massed presentation (i.e., "cramming") [3]. Microlearning interactions may also serve a "priming" role by repeatedly bringing the learning task to the user's attention; users may then be more mentally prepared to take advantage of richer learning opportunities, such as those that occur in classrooms and in natural domain-interaction contexts.

Ubiquitous technology can be usefully applied for microlearning because it can reach users throughout the day, when they have idle time, and in contexts that are related to the information being learned. Research on "encoding specificity" has suggested that information is memorized in combination with contextual cues that facilitate retrieval in matching contexts ([4, 5]). A person is more likely to recall something if it was learned in association with cues that will be available at the time of retrieval. For example, if a person learns information when she is in a specific physical context (e.g., underwater [6]), she is better able to recall that information later when in that same context. While factors such as task attention requirements affect the extent to which context acts as a retrieval cue [7], these findings suggest that learning information in contexts similar to those where the information will be needed (exploiting ubiquitous computing) may aid later retrieval.

Additionally, learning that occurs without formal instruction, such as first language acquisition, seems to be based on *meaningful* exposure and interaction [8]. That is, learners are most receptive to information, ideas, and skills that are relevant to their current needs and actions. Context detection may provide the opportunity to deliver learning interactions at times when users can immediately apply what they learn.

1.1 Acceptance and Usability of an Always-On Application

We developed this language learning system to explore how ubiquitous technology may enable users to chip away at a larger learning task in a non time-intensive way and during periods when they are better able and more motivated to do so.

The real benefit to users of systems such as these would likely come from frequent engagement over an extended time period. However, data about how such systems, once deployed, are used over time are as yet underreported. Questions that are difficult to answer in the absence of usage data and user feedback include whether acceptance would wane after a period of novelty, what types of impromptu interactions would result, and to what extent users would perceive such a system as valuable, given the sensing requirements and interruption burden. These questions apply to a variety of ubiquitous systems that present information in context.

To begin to address these questions, we conducted a study in which a microlearning prototype was deployed in a real-life context for an extended time. Participants lived with the application as part of their day-to-day home life, and after the study period, they were interviewed. We use this case study to show proof of concept that a ubiquitous system that presents information to users in context at rates as high as 142 times per hour might be tolerable for several weeks of intense use. We also use the case study to gather information about how to improve a system that presents continuous microlearning feedback.

1.2 Learning Domain: Second Language Vocabulary

Second language learning was chosen as our application domain because it affords a straightforward mapping between content and context (i.e., foreign language labels that relate to objects and events), it is a learning task of interest to many people at different stages of life, and it is not easily sustained by learners through other means for an extended period of time.

Bilingualism is essential for many people in the world today and even in countries where citizens do not need to learn more than their native language, it is recognized that learning a second language is valuable for economic and social mobility [9]. For those interested in language learning, however, the challenges of becoming proficient, particularly when not immersed in a culture speaking the language, can be daunting. The Foreign Service Institute estimates that it takes approximately 480 classroom hours to become minimally proficient in a second language that has a similar structure and phoneme system (e.g. English speakers learning Spanish) [10]. It is estimated that a vocabulary of 6,000 to 7,000 words is required for unassisted comprehension of spoken language (analysis for English [11]). While a smaller vocabulary may be sufficient for a traveler's needs, even learning 100 spoken words and being able to recognize them in context represents a significant memorization task.

Adults approach this task using a variety of formal and informal methods, including classroom instruction, books, audio CDs, and multimedia software. These methods can be difficult to sustain, particularly given their time requirements and the motivation issues related to being a novice speaker (i.e., social inhibition). There is a need for methods and technologies that reinforce these more intensive efforts.

A few notable applications of ubiquitous technology for language learning have been proposed and prototyped, including a common-sense language translation application for mobile phones [12] and presentation of foreign language vocabulary incrementally via a screen-saver application [2] and SMS messaging to mobile phones [13]. To our knowledge, using detected context to trigger language-learning interactions has not yet been studied, and we are not aware of any extended deployments of such systems outside of lab settings.

1.3 Context Detection

Context detection for ubiquitous computing is an active area of research, with proposed strategies ranging from using RFID tags on objects to using computer vision for image analysis. Recent work in ubiquitous computing suggests that object-based dense sensing can be used to recognize context, even in complex, real-world settings such as homes (e.g., [14-16]). When using this approach for context detection, miniature sensors are attached directly onto many objects in the environment and can enable a computer system to infer contextual information about the home occupant's movement and everyday activities such as "cooking", "making tea," "vacuuming", and others. These sensors are small and inconspicuous. Further, when mass-produced, they should be possible to manufacture at a low cost. Although other types of context detection could also be used to build context-sensitive microlearning applications, object-based dense sensing was the approach used in the case study we present here. Context was detected by using motion sensors and RFID tags to detect object usage and object touch. Although not used in this experiment, more advanced inference of activity type could also be used in an extension of the proposed system.

One criticism of object-based dense sensing is that the infrastructure, which could consist of tens to hundreds of small sensors stuck on objects, may be too difficult to install and maintain over time. We later address how ubiquitous computing applications that provide immediate value to the end user, such as just-in-time microlearning, might be useful in addressing this concern.

2 System Design

The system was designed to mimic informal strategies that beginning learners of a second language often employ. These include placing vocabulary labels on objects in their home (e.g., taping the word "puerta" to the door), asking friends who are native speakers for words that reference objects or situations in the immediate context (e.g., "How would I ask for a cup of coffee?" while getting coffee), and practicing L1-L2 translation pairs (e.g., "milk - leche").

We wanted to take advantage of the consistency and ubiquity afforded by the sensing and mobile technology - learning can take place anytime and everywhere - while giving the user control over the level of attention and engagement he or she would give to any interaction, including having the option of ignoring it. To do this, we designed the system to be "always on," but to be hands-free with short interactions. To enable users to make progress on a microlearning task, we expected that the application would be run for several weeks or more, yet it needed to sustain interest. The system was designed, therefore, to provide some variability on repeat interactions and to be scalable to exploit improvements in the sensing and inference algorithms.

2.1 Scenario

Here we describe the operation of the system from the user's perspective. Stacy has just arrived home and is wearing her mobile phone at her belt. When she opens the door, she hears "door" (in English) and then the Spanish translation "puerta." She puts her coat in the closet and hears "closet - armario." She sits down on the couch and hears "couch - sofá," followed by "cushion - cojín." "Cojín" is repeated again. She watches television for about 30 minutes, without hearing any phrases. She then gets up to make a snack in the kitchen. She opens the refrigerator and hears "refrigerator - refrigerador." She grabs a container of milk, and hears "milk - leche." That is a word she hasn't heard before, so she pulls out the phone and presses a button to have the phrase repeated. As the phrase is played, she looks at the screen on the phone to see the word. She tries pronouncing the word and then sets the phone on the counter while she continues preparing her meal.

2.2 System Design

The prototype system employed ubiquitous sensing to detect context and a mobile phone for audio and visual presentation. Built-in and wireless stick-on multi-modal sensors detected the participants' interactions with objects, furniture, and appliances and sent signals to a server in real-time. The mobile phone application polled the server using a GPRS connection and responded to sensor activations by showing and audio playing English and Spanish phrases associated with the moved object.

Although the system can be deployed solely with portable sensors, for the purposes of the work reported here, it was deployed in a highly-instrumented home. The live-in home was designed to support the collection of rich, multi-modal sensor datasets of domestic activities and to provide a naturalistic environment for the evaluation of novel ubiquitous computing technologies that use house-wide sensor systems [17]. Volunteers are recruited to move into the instrumented home and treat it as their own home as much as possible during their stay. They often provide explicit feedback during or after the study, which supplements the rich record of their activities and interactions with technologies that is collected using the home's infrastructure. The couple who used the system described here lived in the home for ten weeks and used the language learning tool for the last four.

In this work, four types of sensors were used. The 1000 sq. ft. apartment has eighty small, wired switches embedded discretely in all cabinetry and appliances that were used in this work. The home also has water flow sensors on all hot and cold taps in the unit. In addition, a portable kit of "object usage" wireless sensors was deployed on furniture and other objects in the home (Figure 1a). These sensors contain a sensitive piezo trigger that wakes up an accelerometer when the sensor the object is attached to (or placed in) is moved. The sensors are small and can be attached to most objects with adhesive putty or simply placed in drawers or pockets or under cushions. A sensor ID is transmitted wirelessly to a receiver in the home when the sensor moves.

Fig. 1. a) A stuck-on wireless object usage sensor detects movement of the TV remote control; b) the RFID bracelet worn by the user senses "near touch" events, such as when this salt container is retrieved from the pantry; c) A simple UI: the Spanish phrase "lavaplatos" is displayed and played on the mobile phone when the dishwasher door is opened

The fourth class of sensors used were radio frequency ID (RFID) stickers, cards, and buttons that were placed throughout the home, on cabinet and appliance surfaces, as well as movable objects, such as cooking utensils, cleaning equipment, food containers (Figure 1b), portable electronics, and books or magazines. In this study, the male volunteer wore an RFID reader built into a bracelet form factor [18]. Whenever the user's wrist comes within a few inches of an RFID tag, the bracelet wirelessly sends the tag ID to a receiver connected to the home's infrastructure, and the "near touch" event is recorded. The bracelet was taken off each night and when the volunteer left the apartment and plugged in to charge. Although the bracelet is a bit bulky at first, the volunteer was able to adjust to it and wear it continuously while in the unit for 10 weeks.

Computers in the home, enclosed out of view from the inhabitants, receive data from the sensors. The data are time-stamped and stored locally to disk. Identification numbers from selected sensors are then transmitted to a secure server that can be polled by client applications to trigger sensor-activated interactions.

Identification numbers for the sensors were associated with phrases that describe the object the sensor was stuck on or placed in (i.e., "refrigerator") and objects typically contained within, if any (i.e., "eggs," "milk"). In a few cases, simple words that may be related to the sensor-tagged object (i.e., "exit, entrance" for door, "science" for a science textbook) were also associated with a sensor ID. These sensor-phrase associations were stored in XML format on the server and were assembled by both the participants and the researchers.

The participants, as part of a concurrent protocol investigating self-installation of home sensors for context-detection, were asked at the beginning of the study period to place the wireless object usage sensors on furniture, objects, appliances, cabinetry, and other movable parts in the home and to label their placement of the sensors using an application on the mobile phone. The participants entered the room location and selected a label for the host object from a list of 1949 items for each placed sensor. Researchers placed additional object usage sensors and RFID sensors on all objects that were untagged and that could robustly accommodate a sensor without impacting object usability and provided object labels for the wired sensors, RFID sensors, and researcher-placed object motion sensors.

Four hundred phrases were selected from this combined inventory to be used by the language application. The selected phrases were nouns and were translated by a research team member into Spanish (Mexican dialect). Spanish was chosen based on the travel interests of the participants, the availability of a Spanish translator, and the prevalence of Spanish as a language in North America. Examples of English-Spanish pairs that were used include "keyboard - teclado" and "aftershave - loción para afeitar." Eighty-five wired switch sensors, 170 wireless object motion sensors, 431 RFID tags, and 14 wired flow sensors had labels with matching vocabulary.

The language learning software was written in C# for phones with the Windows Mobile operating system. For this study, an AudioVox SMT5600 mobile phone was used. The software application polls the server for sensor activations every second. These activations are mapped to any associated words, which are returned to the phone. If no sensor activity is detected for more than 5 minutes, the software polls the server less frequently (once a minute), to save battery. Due primarily to GPRS connection time, there is a latency of 5-15 seconds between action and word presentation on the mobile phone, although a near instantaneous presentation speed can be achieved on a PC. GPRS was selected over WLAN or Bluetooth to maximize battery life (~6 hours versus ~2 hours of active polling on the mobile phone).

When the phone receives phrases corresponding to a recent action within the home, the software filters the list to reduce repetition: a phrase cannot be played more than 2 times in a minute or 6 times in an hour. This decision was made to reduce the interruption burden and to allow a greater variety of phrases to be played during any given period. A phrase is randomly selected from those that remain. The English phrase is displayed on the mobile phone screen while a sound file of the phrase spoken in English is played. Then the Spanish translation is displayed and played (Figure 1c). The application then visually presents an option to repeat the phrase. The only other interface element is a 30-minute mute option.

The application starts automatically when the phone is turned on and does not require user interaction for normal use. For this study, the mobile phone was used only for this application and not for communication purposes. It was expected that the phone would be carried at the belt or in a pocket or purse some of the time. Given that previous research has shown that people do not necessarily carry their phones with them while at home [19], sound play was made loud enough to be heard within a room and adjacent spaces if the phone was set down.

3 Exploratory Study

The exploratory case study was designed to assess the acceptability and perceived value of the system. To this end, we sought to provide a study context that would be similar to a real-world scenario. Participants (who were not aware they would be testing a language application when they signed up for the study) were provided with vocabulary for a language that they were motivated to learn. In order to avoid introducing undue stress or artificial motivators, we did not set an expectation that they would be tested or have them complete comparison learning tasks. As a result, however, we were only able to conduct a limited evaluation of learning performance.

The participants were recruited from a pool of individuals who had responded to postering, electronic mailing lists, and press articles announcing that subjects were needed to study how to make technology easier to use in the home. The participants were a married couple: a woman, age 31, working in the publishing industry, and a man, age 29, a high school science teacher. Although they both worked in science-related fields, they did not have advanced knowledge of computer science or sensor technology. They were recruited for a primary study to investigate personal health monitoring and were asked to try out several mobile-phone applications during their 10-week stay, but they were not given details about these applications beforehand. Among the reasons they provided for their interest in participating was to *"see how we can use technology to simplify our life, not complicate it."*

Before the study, they were asked to describe their foreign language backgrounds, travel history, and countries where they would like to travel. They both had taken a few years of Spanish in high school (10+ years earlier), but admitted that they were very rusty. They listed 13 countries that they would like to visit, and Spanish is the primary language in three.

For the first six weeks of the study, the couple participated in other protocols. At the beginning of the study, they were asked to place wireless sensors throughout the home using a mobile phone application to register and label their locations. They field tested two other mobile phone applications: a names and faces microlearning application [20] and a brief cognitive assessment game. These applications prompted brief interactions on a timed schedule. Over the entire study, data about their daily activities were recorded by the home's sensing infrastructure. The participants were encouraged to maintain as normal a routine as possible. They went to work, had visitors over, cooked meals, attended to sleep and personal needs, and worked on projects and leisure activities according to their own preferences.

The male participant was asked to carry the phone with him whenever he was at home. He was instructed to turn off the application and plug the phone into a charger near the door whenever he left. It was noted from the collected data that on weekdays, the participants were only running the application in the evening. For the final week of the study, the participants were encouraged to try it in the morning as well. Even though the male participant was the primary user, the female participant could also hear words when she was in the unit. Further, sensors activated by both individuals were triggering the word selection.

Our primary goal was to obtain qualitative feedback on the experience of using the context-sensitive microlearning application in the home for four weeks. The male participant provided feedback about how the application was working four times during the study by email. Both participants were interviewed together after the study in a 90-minute session; the interview was audio recorded and transcribed (identity-masked email feedback and interview transcripts are available at http://architecture.mit.edu/house_n/data/languagelearning/).

Both participants were given a post-study quiz on their aural comprehension of the presented vocabulary. The male participant was initially quizzed alone. After each phrase was played, he verbally provided the English translation. He could ask that a phrase be repeated up to two times. In this session, he was quizzed on 130 of the phrases. However, it was determined that the extended quizzing was logistically and mentally taxing, so the quiz was broken into two sessions. In the second session, both participants were quizzed at the same time and wrote down their responses. The male participant was quizzed on all 400 phrases. The female participant was only quizzed on the second day, on a subset (270) of the phrases.

4 Results

The participants used the application on 26 different days between October 5-November 1, 2006, for a total of 120.9 hours. The mean daily run time was 4.6 hours (SD=2.0). The longest consecutive run time was 6.67 hours. The participant muted the application 13 times on 5 evenings (for an average of 78 minutes).

The male participant reported that he turned on the phone and application as soon as he remembered after getting home from work. He initially did not run the application in the morning because he was in rush (*"I burst out of the house so quickly"*) and because he did not want to disturb his wife, who was still sleeping while he was getting ready. On weekends, the participants woke up later and were often at home for a longer period of the day. On these days, they turned on the phone when they got up and turned it off when they went to sleep.

With the settings used during the study, the application could run for about 5 hours before the phone ran low on battery power. The phone dipped to ≤10% battery charge five times, after the application was run for between 4.8 to 6.1 hours. The male participant reported that the battery power usually was sufficient and that on the few occasions when it was running low, it was easy to charge the phone wherever he was.

The male participant typically set the phone on a surface near to where he was doing an activity and left it unplugged. He identified the study area near the computer, the countertop between the kitchen and living room, and the living room couch area as common places where he would leave the phone. If the phone was left in the study area, the audio play was still loud enough to hear in most parts of the apartment.

Phrases were played 6,926 times during the study period, on average 57.3 times per hour and up to 142 times in one hour. While the application was running, activations were detected from 70 wireless object usage sensors, 80 RFID tags, 22 switch sensors, and 6 flow sensors. A subset of these activations triggered phrase play. Up to 400 different phrases were available to the application, but only 274 were actually presented. If multiple words were activated within a narrow time window, only one was randomly selected to play. Additionally, some objects in the home were not interacted with or not in a way to trigger sensor activation. Phrases for particular objects were played between 1 and 578 times, with a mean of 25.3 (SD=63.9). Frequently played phrases included toilet (578 times, see note later), computer keyboard (530), computer (447), sink (292), chair (274), and faucet (212). When asked to estimate the total number of different phrases that they heard, the male participant guessed 100 and the female participant guessed 75.

4.1 Pilot Learning Performance Results

Both participants performed better on audio comprehension of phrases that were presented during the study than on those they had not heard during the study. The 126 phrases that were not played during the study were used as "control phrases" when evaluating performance. The male participant guessed correctly on 57.7% of the presented phrases (158/274) and 51.6% of the control phrases (65/126). The female participant guessed correctly on 39.9% of the presented phrases (71/178) and 28.3% of the control phrases (26/92).

Table 1 presents pilot performance data for each participant grouped by frequency category. These data suggest that the more highly played words or phrases were learned better than phrases played less frequently. A point biserial correlation coefficient of r=0.19 (p < 0.01) was computed for the combined performance data for the participants with respect to the raw number of times each phrase was played. This suggests a weak, but statistically significant relationship between the frequency with which each phrase was played and whether the participants recalled the correct translation. It should be noted however, that both participants recognized several of the control phrases, which were not played during the study; in some cases, these phrases were cognates of phrases that were played, but in other cases, the participants likely knew the phrases beforehand.

Table 1. Pilot performance data for each participant; scores reflect percentage correct for the subset of phrases tested for different frequency of play categories

Times Played	Male's Scores		Female's Scores	
20+	54/68	79.4%	28/45	62.2%
8-19	40/63	63.5%	19/42	45.2%
4-7	30/64	46.9%	15/45	33.3%
1-3	34/79	43.0%	9/46	19.6%
0 (control)	65/126	51.6%	26/92	28.3%

4.2 Usability and Acceptability

The male participant's initial reaction to the language tool, provided via email, was surprise at its accuracy and the eerie quality of having a system sensing one's actions, *"it's almost creepy, like the phone knows what you're doing! But it seems like an awesome way to learn a language."* At first, it seemed to present phrases too frequently, *"the phone might speak a bit too often, it was almost constant (well, not quite, but it seemed it) at a few points."* After 10 days, the participant concluded *"most of the time though, it's a welcome interruption. Every now and then I wish I could bring it along with me somewhere just to hear it say different words!"*

The participants noted that the phrases seemed to get into a kind of queue at times, with a noticeable delay between an action and a stream of phrases related to that action. This resulted from the pilot application's phone network latency. They estimated that most of the time, though, the pairing was *"pretty fast,"* with a phrase playing within 10-15 seconds following an action, although it was difficult for them to judge. At times, the participants would wonder why there was a burst of phrases, corresponding with their actions, followed by a relative silence for a period of time (a likely result of the filtering heuristics, limiting repeated phrase play).

The participants were asked to describe situations when phrase play was irritating. The male participant noted that he had muted the application a few times when watching movies or on the phone. However, having the application on in the morning was the most difficult, *"I guess because I was in the shower, and trying to relax, and still waking up, the phone kind of got to me."* The female participant described a day working at home and listening to audio transcripts; the language tool, using an auditory medium, disrupted her focus on work, *"it would drive me nuts."*

However, the participants noted for the most part, the "background" quality of the application made it easier to selectively attend to or ignore. The male participant commented, *"it was nice that you can do it while you are doing other things. You can kind of choose your level of attention. If you thought you were busy or stressed, then you could kind of ignore it, but if you were relaxed, you could kind of listen to it more. So it seemed very flexible to me in that sense. Whereas I got a language CD once and played it in the car, I was driving, but I felt like I was forcing it on myself."*

The female participant noted that the idea of having an always-on application sounds like it should be burdensome, but the four-week experience convinced her otherwise, *"I think that if someone had said, outside of this experiment, 'you're going to have this phone ... and the language is going to be based on things that you move and it's going to say the words,' I would think, well, this time and this time during the day, I don't have much going on, and I can concentrate. But now that, since we've had it running in the background, I found no problem with that."*

Given that the application had this "background" quality, the participants were asked what determined their level of attention to phrase presentation. The male participant described that he would ignore the phrases, *"when I was mentally engaged, like reading or when I was writing stuff, then I would miss words."* He would attend to the phrases when he was active, but doing more physical tasks, *"I actually found, when it was in my pocket, and I was moving around doing things, I felt like my attention was pretty high then, mostly."* Both participants felt that being the subject of the phrase aided learning and comprehension, *"I definitely would hear words better if it was something that I was using, as opposed to when it was something that [my spouse] was using."* Sometimes the application was easy to ignore; when they had a visitor over, he didn't seem to notice, instead quickly settling in to watch a movie with the participants. The researchers noticed a similar phenomenon in pilot testing, when bystanders seemed oblivious to the phrase play.

The participants indicated that the application was not disruptive to their conversations. They often took a playful approach, repeating phrases they liked, such as "fregadero" (sink), and teasing each other when a phrase revealed something one person was doing, out of sight of the other. *"I would get a glass of water and [my spouse] would be like 'can I have some water too?' (laughs)."* The English phrase was presented first, making it possible for the female participant to try to *"beat the machine"* by speaking the translation before it was played.

Because the male participant was carrying the phone, the female participant typically did not have the opportunity to see the phrase or ask for it to be repeated. In the last week, she had the application running in the morning after her husband had left for work. *"That's when I realized, I'm much more of a visual learner, because if I can see the word, I can remember it, a lot better than when I just heard it."* The male participant agreed, *"it's almost like when I see the word, then it would sound different the next time. But generally, when I would see it just one time, it would kind of click."* He primarily used the "repeat" option to see the phrase, if it was unfamiliar.

4.3 Mental Model of the Sensing System

The participants reported that they rethought their understanding of the sensing system after the application was introduced. Played phrases led them to question where sensors were placed, what the sensors "knew" about their actions, and the range of data transmission.

When they installed the wireless object usage sensors at the beginning of the study, they were given instructions that described how the sensors worked and provided recommendations on how to optimize detection through careful placement. They lived with the sensors for six weeks before running the language-learning tool, but once they were able to hear words play in correspondence with their actions, they were able to investigate how sensitive the sensors actually were. For example, the male participant described experimenting with jostling the toilet paper to determine what degree of movement would trigger phrase play. *"Because it [the sensor] wasn't on something that was moving, and I didn't think it would get anything. But ...it wasn't just random – and I tested it out a few times, because I kept hearing it."*

For the first few days with the language application, the participants reported that they moved more objects, such as the broom, just to discover which objects had sensors and labels. They discovered RFID tags that they didn't know were there or had forgotten about. *"I think I noticed the ones on the shelves in the kitchen earlier, but I totally forgot about them until the language program, because I think they said bowls, and we were looking at the bowls, and there's nothing on the bowls! Then we noticed the RFIDs underneath."*

The participants were not sure whether the RFID-tagged objects were also contributing to phrase play. They realized that some objects with wireless object usage sensors triggered multiple phrases, including those referencing objects inside or related to the primary object. In one case, the phrase "egg - huevos" was played when the female participant was actually getting eggs from the refrigerator. After a careful inspection, she determined it wasn't a case of a "hidden" sensor, but rather a coincidental pairing of phrase and action. They also discovered that interaction with an object might also trigger a nearby object, presumably due to bumping or vibrations. *"I would open a cabinet and it would say 'cabinet,' but it would also say 'sink' or something. It felt like that area [the kitchen island] was all interconnected."*

The participants also discovered situations where labels were not correct or sensors were not functioning. For example, the phrase for "antiseptic" was played when accessing the medicine cabinet, but no antiseptic was contained within. All chairs but one in the dining room triggered "chair - silla," due to a failed sensory battery. On the night when they left the application on for a while, they were surprised not to hear "bed" (again, likely due to a failed battery).

The language tool also gave the participants a greater awareness of the apartment and each other's routines. Typically, the participants would turn off the application just before going to bed. One night, they left it on as an experiment. They continued to hear phrases, which they presumed were being activated due to vibrations in the house. *"It was interesting, it kind of gave you a feel for how many things are in motion, realizing that the shelves are vibrating and the toilet's vibrating."*

They frequently heard a stream of translations for "cup, saucer, placemat," which helped them locate the source of a funny vibration sound in a cabinet, perhaps related to the under-cabinet lighting. The participants determined that the toilet had a leak, and was continually running, because they heard "toilet - taza del baño" more than any other phrase. The female participant described one incident where the language tool made her more aware of something she had forgotten to do. *"It was actually helpful one time when I left the burner on, and it would say burner every once and a while, so we'd gone to sit down for dinner, and I said, 'why's it doing that?' and the burner was on (laughs) so I turned it off."*

The introduction of the language tool reminded them that their activities were being recorded. *"I definitely became more conscious of being recorded again when the language phone came into play. It was making it very obvious, you lifted your glass and it said 'glass.'"* The male participant described how having the objects he was using echoed back, and knowing that his spouse was possibly hearing those phrases too, made him more self-conscious of his routine in the bathroom. *"I might have been a little bit conscious about that a few times, like making sure I'm shaking the soap so it's clear that I'm washing my hands. It definitely reminds you of things."*

The female participant reported that she became more aware of some of her husband's routines that normally she did not observe first hand. In the morning, when she is still resting, her husband is getting ready for work. *"I got more aware of [my spouse]'s morning routine, when [he] had it on in the morning. I hear the movement around in the morning, but I don't know what he's doing, but when that was on, 'oh, he did this, and then he did this.'"* She described how she assumed that when he was working in the afternoon and evening in the office, that he stayed in one place at the computer. While she was in the kitchen or living room, however, she could hear phrases that indicated he was going into the bedroom or interacting with the stereo.

The participants reported that they were comfortable with having this new awareness of their home and each other's routines, and even found humor in some of the situations that arose, but when asked to describe what it would be like to have phrases corresponding with their actions transmitted to relatives or vice-versa, they had mixed feelings. Both participants imagined that it would be fun for kids to know a little bit about what their relatives were doing and the female participant imagined that it would be a good way to informally monitor older adults or kids at home alone. *"It would be good in one way, because you would be thinking about them, like 'Why are they using the water heater again?' (laughs)... I could see it as an interesting way to keep tabs on them in a non-conscious way, learning the vocab. But then also like, 'it sounds like their stove is on...'"* The male participant, however, worried that it might lead family members to judge each other; *"I could see myself saying to my mom, 'you were reading that book for 13 hours,' and she could say 'you were on the computer for 14 hours'."* He also noted that it would remove plausible deniability with respect to not answering the phone; *'how come you didn't answer your phone the other day? I know you're at home, because you were on the computer' (laughs)".*

4.4 Ideas for Re-design

During the study, the male participant suggested that he would like to be able review phrases that had been played on a given day, *"if I'm in the middle of doing things, I don't see the screen, so it's hard to know exactly how things are said correctly without seeing the word in print. When possible, I press the button to have a word repeated, but sometimes I can't (when my hands are full), so I'd like to be able to review them later."* After the study, he decided that it would be something he would do once or twice a day, when he had a spare moment working at the computer or at dinnertime. The female participant suggested that, *"I feel like it would be useful, since it's a program that's on the phone, if you could take the phone with you and review the words that happened, riding [public transit]."*

Both participants liked the diversity of phrases, even though they felt there were many that they didn't hear frequently enough to learn. They did wish that the vocabulary set had gradually shifted to include verbs and phrases. They noted that some phrases, such as computer keyboard, became boring, because even though they had learned them, they were frequently repeated. The male participant suggested being able to indicate that a phrase was learned so that a new phrase (e.g., "typing") could be introduced. The old phrase could then be played again every so often to help them retain what they had learned.

As an added challenge, the female participant suggested that hearing multiple speakers say the phrase would be helpful, *"because then you could pay more attention to what the word is supposed to be."* The participants were asked if they would be willing to grade other people's pronunciations, if they could have that service done for them in return. The male participant suggested instead that the application should *"have you pronounce the words and record them, and then maybe if it mixed your pronunciations in with the other person's,"* and that would be helpful for gradually correcting pronunciation without feeling threatened.

The participants had commented that the act of taking the quiz forced them to listen more closely to the phrases than the more passive exposure they had received during the study. They were asked about a possible interactive feature, where a Spanish phrase would be played, relating to a nearby object, that they would then have to interact with or move to "guess" the answer. The male participant had some reservations about the application having an interactive component, *"What I like about it now is that it doesn't involve much from you... it is kind of background, you can carry it your pocket and set it down somewhere and still hear it. And if I had to actually like do something, because a lot of times your hands are occupied or your mind's occupied and it would be kind of disruptive to get up and shake the chair."*

However, the female participant proposed that a game-like mode would be acceptable if it could be deliberately (not automatically) initiated and in particular, if used when playing with younger members of the family. The male participant agreed, suggesting that if a prompt to initiate a game was ignorable, as it was with the mobile phone cognitive game that he tried out in the earlier part of the study, that it would be acceptable; *"like once or twice a day, I could choose the time or if it buzzed me. If it said 'alright, now it's time to play.' If I had a few minutes from what I'm doing, and then go and do it."* The female participant noted that an interactive mode would probably be more vulnerable to a novelty effect, and would be best employed when the user was actively preparing for a trip.

The participants noted that the installation of the wireless object usage sensors at the beginning of the study was a tedious task, *"that was pretty intense, all those sensors. I don't know how to make it faster, because it seemed like it was as fast as it could go, but ... It was just a lot of time to spend."* When asked what it would be like to tie the language application more closely to the sensor installation, the female participant felt that it would provide a needed motivation to complete sensor setup, *"here we were just putting it on and there wasn't an immediate ... knowledge of how the [sensors] were going to be useful, but maybe if we had [something that said] 'tomorrow, if you have all these [sensors] up, you are going to start learning these words."* The male participant commented, *"I could see having the language program working and I guess placing the [sensors] more strategically or even adding RFIDs to some things... if there were things you wanted to learn, put the [sensors] right on there. And I could see doing it gradually... but it might not seem so bad - not going around the house searching for things, but as we used them."*

The participants concluded that they would like to have this kind of application in their own home. They envisioned using the application for two months prior to traveling to a foreign country, at about the time when they usually book their flights. During that two-month period, they would see themselves running the application continuously. The male participant commented, *"Even at four weeks, it wasn't getting that old. And that was, even with one set of words, so I imagine if the vocabulary evolved over time, it could stay fresh for a while."* When asked how many words they would expect to learn during that period, the male participant described spending two months in Greece and estimating afterward that he had learned about 500 words. Correspondingly, he would want the language tool to help them be ready for a vacation, with two months of prep time, by learning about 500 words, and ideally up to 800-1000 words, in order to function well as travelers in the culture.

5 Discussion

Ubiquitous sensing systems are becoming sufficiently robust and flexible to support the prototyping of context-sensitive applications. Live-in laboratories and portable research kits provide the opportunity to test out these applications in real life situations for an extended period of time. However, these studies are necessarily limited in the number of participants, and therefore results must be interpreted as exploratory. The participants in this study were optimistic about possible uses of technology, though they were not experts. By agreeing to participate in a study where their everyday routines were recorded for research, they demonstrated a comfort with ubiquitous sensing that may not be shared by most individuals.

Several design decisions were made to focus on exploring the usability and acceptability of an always-on microlearning application. The vocabulary set was limited and was presented simply, as L1-L2 pairs. Spanish was chosen as the second language despite the participants having some previous knowledge of it and its closeness, through its phoneme system, cognates, and loanwords, to English. Comparison conditions, with learning out of context, were not available. The learning performance quiz was conducted out of context and with a less formal procedure than would be used in a large-n experimental study.

Given these study attributes and design decisions, we were able to investigate how a young couple, who would be likely to consider purchasing ubiquitous technology as it becomes available, would respond to an always-on interface designed to help them with the task of learning vocabulary in preparation for travel. Because they were able to live with the application for a one-month period, having it run for over 120 hours and hearing almost 7000 phrases, they experienced a variety of situations where the interface was either compelling or irritating, accurate or unexpected. The application became part of their everyday life and featured in their conversations and activities.

Other protocols were run simultaneously during this study, which inevitably affected the participants' evaluation of the prototype. For example, the participants took it as a given that their activities were being sensed. However, they also had a more comprehensive experience of the system. Having placed and labeled many sensors themselves, and with a greater understanding of what exactly was being detected in their daily routines, they were able to weigh the benefits of the application with the burdens of setup and being monitored. Having tried out mobile applications earlier in the study, they were able to compare the "background" aspect of the application with more interactive interfaces. After four weeks, the participants had more expertise on the use of the system than the researchers and were able to provide articulate feedback and ideas for extensions.

The learning performance gains evidenced by the quiz suggest what we would expect – that more exposure to words would lead to more learning. They also show, however, that a phone-based interface may be able to support learning, even for the difficult task of aural comprehension of foreign language vocabulary. However, the gains, especially when factoring in the participants' previous knowledge of Spanish, were relatively small, and certainly below the participant's learning expectation of 250 words per month. This may be attributable to both the simplistic heuristics used to determine phrase presentation and the passive quality of the interactions.

Several techniques may make phrase presentation more effective. Using the principle of spaced repetition, phrases could be played very frequently at first, at every interaction with an object, and then increasingly less often as the phrase becomes familiar. As the participants suggested, aural presentation could be reinforced with more opportunities for reviewing information visually. This could occur in periodic prompted review sessions, such as while riding the bus; through subtle placement in other media, such as having presented words automatically translated on viewed web pages; or with novel display techniques [21]. The elimination of the latency introduced by the current phone implementation might also allow a higher density of words to be presented at the same level of user burden, potentially increasing learning effectiveness. Moreover, near zero latency creates new interface opportunities, such as double tapping an object to hear a word again.

Although the non-demanding background quality of the interface was viewed as a benefit, adding more interactive features, such as giving the user the ability to review phrases or to specify when a phrase has been learned, as well as periodic quizzes or games, might aid learning. Applications that are delivered on the PC or phone typically receive explicit user input and usage pattern data that can help determine content and interaction pacing to match the learner's needs. A ubiquitous interface such as the one described in this work must find new ways to obtain this information without tipping the scale back to burdening the user with forced interactions.

Applications that employ immediate context-sensitive feedback may provide a motivation to purchase, train, and maintain ubiquitous sensing systems, even those that use dense-object sensing consisting of hundreds of miniature sensors placed on objects throughout a home. The participants demonstrated more insight and interest in the working of the sensing system after the language tool was introduced, and through playful interaction they were learning about the strengths and limitations of the sensor system, as well as information that would be helpful to maintain it over time (e.g., strategies to identify if and when something is not working). Future work needs to explore how the immediate rewards of an application such as this can be leveraged to help enable installation, use, and maintenance of other sensor-enabled applications with delayed return-on-investment, such as longitudinal personal health monitoring.

The observations from this study suggest that, at least for some people, it may be possible to layer context-sensitive interactions onto everyday routines without them being perceived as burdensome. Although it seems like the high density of messages (up to 142 audio-clips in one hour) would be disruptive, the participants in this study found it possible, for the most part, to choose their level of attention to the always-on interactions. It may be that the repeated exposure, which appeared to be associated with learning rates, also lessened the demand quality of the interactions. The congruence between the message and the participants' immediate context may have also reduced the perceived disruption. The participants liked the "background" quality of the interface and considered what they were doing "learning a language." This suggests that the non-demanding aspects of always-on microlearning applications may be valuable for introducing users to involved tasks, without risking burnout.

We have used the interview feedback from this study to consider design attributes that may be applicable to other context-sensitive, always-on systems that need to sustain user interest, while avoiding unnecessary disruption. These attributes include "background" audio presentation with optional, visual feedback; preferential presentation when users are engaged in physical tasks or are moving through a space; repetition and context congruence to support selective attention; and built-in opportunities for review, quizzing, and signaling readiness for new information, perhaps in idle moments, such as during a commute. Always-on systems that encourage the users to experiment, to care about correct mappings, and to get new content in exchange for extending or elaborating a ubiquitous system may be easier to maintain. Finally, systems that provide simple and playful interactions, encourage self-awareness of personal routines, and give users extended, non-demanding exposure to a more complicated task may be perceived as having immediate value and may justify the introduction of novel ubiquitous computing in the home.

Acknowledgments. This work was supported by Intel Corporation. We thank our participants for the generous contribution of their time and feedback, and TIAX LLC for collaboration on the PlaceLab. The sensors used were developed with support from National Science Foundation grant #0313065. The PlaceLab stay was funded by Microsoft Research.

References

1. Hug, T., Gassler, G., Glahn, C.: Integrated micro learning - an outline of the basic method and first results. In: Proceedings of Interactive Computer Aided Learning, pp. 1–7. Kassel Univeristy Press (2004)
2. Hug, T.: Micro Learning and narration. In: Fourth Media and Transition Conference, Cambridge, MA (2005)
3. Dempster, F.N.: Effects of variable encoding and spaced presentations on vocabulary learning. Journal of Educational Psychology 79(2), 162–170 (1987)
4. Tulving, E., Thompson, D.M.: Encoding specificity and retrieval processes in episodic memory. Psychological Review 80(5), 352–373 (1973)
5. Davies, G., Thomson, D.M.: Memory in context: Context in memory, vol. ix, p. 359. J. Wiley, Chichester (1988)
6. Godden, D.R., Baddeley, A.D.: Context-dependent memory in two natural environments: On land and underwater. British Journal of Psychology 66(3), 325–331 (1975)
7. Smith, S.M., Vela, E.: Environmental context-dependent memory: A review and meta-analysis. Psychonomic Bulletin & Review 8, 203–220 (2001)
8. Brown, H.D.: Principles of Language Learning and Teaching, 2nd edn., vol. xvi, p. 285. Prentice-Hall, Englewood Cliffs, N.J. (1987)
9. Importance of learning a second language survey, in Gallup Poll (2001)
10. McGinnis, S.: The less common alternative: A report from the task force for teacher training for the less commonly taught languages. ADFL Bulletin 25(2), 17–22 (1994)

11. Nation, I.S.P.: How large a vocabulary is needed for reading and listening? The Canadian Modern Language Review 63(1), 59–82 (2006)
12. Faaborg, A., Espinosa, J.: Using common sense reasoning to enhance language translation with mobile devices. Last accessed (March 2007), http://agents.media.mit.edu/ projects/ globuddy2/
13. Thorton, P., Houser, C.: Using mobile phones in English education in Japan. Journal of Computer Assisted Learning 21(3), 217–228 (2005)
14. Wilson, D.H., Atkeson, C.: Simultaneous tracking & activity recognition (STAR) using many anonymous, binary sensors. In: Gellersen, H.-W., Want, R., Schmidt, A. (eds.) PERVASIVE 2005. LNCS, vol. 3468, pp. 62–79. Springer, Heidelberg (2005)
15. Philipose, M., Smith, J.R., Jiang, B., Mamishev, A., Roy, S., Sundara-Rajan, K.: Battery-free wireless identification and sensing. IEEE Pervasive Computing 4(1), 37–45 (2005)
16. Tapia, E.M., Intille, S.S., Larson, K.: Activity recognition in the home setting using simple and ubiquitous sensors. In: Ferscha, A., Mattern, F. (eds.) PERVASIVE 2004. LNCS, vol. 3001, pp. 158–175. Springer, Heidelberg (2004)
17. Intille, S.S., Larson, K., Tapia, E.M., Beaudin, J., Kaushik, P., Nawyn, J., Rockinson, R.: Using a live-in laboratory for ubiquitous computing research. In: Fishkin, K.P., Schiele, B., Nixon, P., Quigley, A. (eds.) PERVASIVE 2006. LNCS, vol. 3968, pp. 349–365. Springer, Heidelberg (2006)
18. Fishkin, K.P., Philipose, M.: Hands-on RFID: Wireless wearables for detecting use of objects. In: ISWC 2005, pp. 38–43 (2005)
19. Patel, S.N., Kientz, J.A., Hayes, G.R., Bhat, S., Abowd, G.D.: Farther than you may think: An empirical investigation of the proximity of users to their mobile phones. In: Dourish, P., Friday, A. (eds.) UbiComp 2006. LNCS, vol. 4206, pp. 123–140. Springer, Heidelberg (2006)
20. Beaudin, J.S., Intille, S.S., Morris, M.: MicroLearning on a mobile device. In: Dourish, P., Friday, A. (eds.) UbiComp 2006. LNCS, vol. 4206, Springer, Heidelberg (2006)
21. Intille, S.S., Lee, V., Pinhanez, C.: Ubiquitous computing in the living room: Concept sketches and an implementation of a persistent user interface. In: Dey, A.K., Schmidt, A., McCarthy, J.F. (eds.) UbiComp 2003. LNCS, vol. 2864, Springer, Heidelberg (2003)

Ambient Intelligence for Decision Making in Fire Service Organizations

Ralph Bergmann

University of Trier
Department of Business Information Systems II
54286 Trier, Germany
bergmann@uni-trier.de
www.wi2.uni-trier.de

Abstract. This paper describes the results of the European Project AMIRA (Advanced Multimodal Intelligence for Remote Assistance) which deals with the support of emergency services (in particular fire services) by Ambient Intelligence. We address the problem of mobile decision support by providing mobile multi-modal access to mission-critical knowledge from different heterogeneous knowledge sources. For this purpose, we analyzed the requirements of fire service organizations as part of a socio-technical study. Further, the AMIRA system was designed based on methods from Artificial Intelligence. It implements domain specific search strategies to identify decision relevant knowledge from available knowledge sources. The developed system has been implemented as prototype and successfully evaluated in a comprehensive evaluation based on user trials.

1 Introduction

Ambient Intelligence (AmI) [1,2] is the vision of our future environment being surrounded by various kinds of interfaces, supported by computing and networking technology providing an intelligent, seamless and non-obtrusive assistance to the humans. This broad vision addresses all areas of human life, such as home, work, health care, and leisure activities. To approach this vision, it is very important to study concrete scenarios in which AmI can provide useful support to the people acting in the respective environment. The development of prototypical AmI systems and their systematic trial in a real environment leads to new results about the technologies involved and their integration, as well as to results on the acceptance of the AmI technology by its users.

This paper describes the results of the European FP6 Project AMIRA[1] (Advanced Multimodal Intelligence for Remote Assistance) which deals with support of emergency services (in particular fire services) by AmI. In recent years, the demand for support systems for emergency services, has increased significantly in order to improve methods for all types of protection. In particular in fire service organizations, there is a demand for supporting inexperienced incident commanders (ICs). As first attendance at incident

---

[1] AMIRA was funded by the European Commission's 6th Framework Programme (IST-2003-511740). The partners of AMIRA are: Kaidara (France), Fast (Norway), DaimlerChrysler (Germany), Fire Service College (U.K.), University of Trier (Germany).

B. Schiele et al. (Eds.): AmI 2007, LNCS 4794, pp. 73–90, 2007.

grounds, ICs are in charge of the fire crew and are required to make dynamic decisions in a safety and risk critical environment, utilizing a range of skills in a time critical manner. This decision making process can be improved by providing knowledge of different kinds, for different purposes, and from different sources, according to the particular emergency situation. This knowledge provision must be embedded in the working environment, i.e. at the fire service ground in various modalities via mobile devices. Within the AMIRA project, we analyzed the requirements of fire service organizations as part of a socio-technical study that has been conducted in close collaboration with the Fire Services College (FSC), which is the UK governmental training and research center establishment for UK fire services (see Sect. 2). Based on this requirements analysis, the AMIRA system has been designed and implemented. It supports knowledge access through multimodal mobile and stationary clients in the working environment of the fire service (see Sect. 3). Finally, the system has been tested in several real fire fighting scenarios simulated on the training ground of the FSC (see Sect. 4).

The main focus of this paper is on how to apply methods from Artificial Intelligence (AI) such as agents, case-based reasoning (CBR), and workflow modelling in an AmI scenario. From this point of view, our work is related to the work published in collections addressing the relationship between AmI and AI [3,4]. Examples of related projects (for different application scenarios) are SmartKom[2] and SmartWeb[3].

2   Socio-technical Study

The goal of the socio-technical study was to elicit the user needs of fire service members with respect to optimizations of their current state of working. To ensure that the to be developed AmI support is designed according to the user's needs and is accepted, we

- analyzed the current state of working practices in fire services,
- elicited a set of user requirements for AmI support, and
- derived a set of use cases.

The study was also aligned to socio-technical research in information society [5,6] for ensuring a comprehensive view on user needs. In the following the main achievements of the conducted socio-technical study [7] are presented.

2.1   Current State of Working Practices

For elaborating the current state of working practices, related projects, available documents and existing studies (e.g. a study from the "Chief and Assistant Chief Fire Officers Association" (CACFOA) [8]) were analyzed. Furthermore, questionnaires were developed that were specially tailored to young ICs in order to acquire knowledge about user needs and to uncover deficiencies in terms of the required support for ICs. These questionnaires and interviews were conducted at FSC at which representatives of different UK fire services took part. Altogether 78 fire fighters and ICs were involved in the interviews and debriefings. As a major result the general working process in a fire service

---

[2] http://smartkom.dfki.de
[3] http://smartweb.dfki.de/

organization has been analyzed. In particular it has been identified, which information sources are used and which devices are used to access them during the phases of the fire service process (see Fig. 1). At the *beginning of an incident*, crews get a radio or teleprinter message that consists of an address, a map reference, the type of incident, the role (of the fire crew), and the location. Depending on the incident further information can be received by radio or pager. In order to gain information about the incident whilst *on route*, the officers, when mobilized, will listen to the radio and wait for informative messages detailing what is happening at the incident. On *arrival*, the officers put their fire kit on and book their attendance whilst capturing as much information as possible about the incident. The officer who arrives first has to view the incident to get information about it. This means walking around the incident and assessing the activities being carried out, as well understanding the requirements of the incident. Throughout the *command period until handover* the fire fighters are expected to get control of the fire or over the hazardous materials. Therefore, they need much support in analyzing and revealing unknown materials or in decision support how to extinguish the fire in the time-critical situation. In *handing over* the first officer in charge gives the subsequent officer all the important information gathered during the first phase. After leaving an incident there are different procedures or post debriefs for *review*. The formalized debriefs are for capturing what has happened at that incident and are sent round to all the crews and to all persons involved. After incorporating all the comments it is then turned into a final report that is published in the Intranet in the scope of the routine notices. Altogether about 30 knowledge sources are in use during work, e.g. operational notes, fire facts, incident information, location information. Some knowledge sources are only available on papers, other knowledge sources can be accessed via electronic devices. Colleagues or human experts can be seen as knowledge sources as well. Particularly,

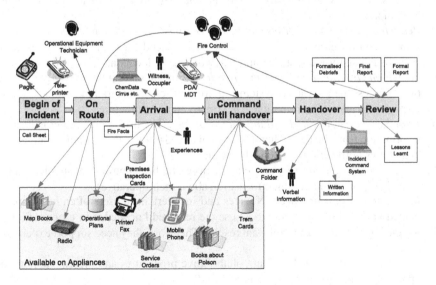

Fig. 1. Fire Service Processes and Knowledge Sources

the analysis of the interview transcripts and questionnaires highlighted the danger of information overload or overflow. Due to this overload of information, a large number of text-based documents have to be read in order to determine the specific information wanted. Usually, for ICs wearing their working clothes it is very cumbersome to access these knowledge sources and, additionally, they would have to be aware what kind of information is provided by which knowledge source.

2.2 User Requirements

To make this analysis more concrete, requirements on a future decision support system in the spirit of the AmI vision were deduced from information source interrogations and from the conducted interviews. In summary, the following requirements were identified:

1. *Information support:* ICs should be supported with information and working instruction for decision making. Only ICs demand such support because fire services are hierarchically structured, so that other fire fighters involved in the incident should get information only from the responsible IC.
2. *Mobility:* For supporting mobile workers, the envisaged information support must be able to provide information at any location the mobile worker can be: Mobile access is needed. While working in time and business critical processes, mobile workers demand short response time regarding information support.
3. *Ease of use:* The usability of the envisaged computer support has to be aligned to the requirements during work, e.g. that fire fighters wear operational kits, such as helmets, goggles or breathing apparatus and thick gloves. The information support enables users to smoothly access information by a hands-free access. One solution is the integration of a speech dialogue system for information access.
4. *Core information:* To avoid information overload, the information provided to the IC must be concise and easily understandable. Highly complex information must be avoided.
5. *Reduction of the number of systems in use:* Because of a large number of information sources and different access methods there is a need for reducing the number of systems in use for facilitating improved working on location.
6. *Search on structured and unstructured data:* For integrating the existing information sources, the envisaged system requires sufficient integration methods due to disparate formats of information, e.g. structured or unstructured.
7. *Knowledge exchange and collaborative working:* The fire control center is lacking information from the field. Therefore, an enhanced information support is demanded that allows notifications and collaboration.
8. *Pro-active information support:* Furthermore, the fire control they should be pro-actively supported in getting information about their operatives.
9. *Integration of best practices:* Novices and inexperienced users often lack sophisticated knowledge about how to assess the required knowledge in a time-efficient manner and how to avoid irrelevant results. Therefore, they need support to perform an adequate search process.
10. *Information capturing:* Efficient collaborative procedures and system support for updating the knowledge sources is required.
11. *User profiles:* User profiles are required that ensure the users' authenticity and authorization.

2.3 Use Cases

The three following use cases make the elicited requirements more concrete.

Use Case 1: IC requests Information via a Speech Dialogue System. Within the fire services the IC is the only person who is in charge and responsible for the decisions made at the incident. Consequently, there is a need to support the IC during arrival and command when he lacks information necessary for decision-making. The IC should be supported in requesting information and receiving answers by using a mobile system which can be accessed by speech or a comfortable GUI on a tablet PC/PDA. One example scenario is the situation in which the IC arrives at the incident and he does not know how to interpret the situation or how to act. For example, an inexperienced IC and his crew come to a road traffic accident where a truck is involved labeled with an emergency action code (EAC) indicating dangerous goods. The IC is not sure of the encoding, so that he uses the AMIRA system to perform a query which includes the EAC and a description of the accident like 'vehicle accident' and 'fire affecting or likely to affect load'. To articulate the information request the IC uses a speech dialogue system. After that the AMIRA system initiates a retrieval based on the information request. In the retrieval process human experts can also be involved. Finally, the retrieval response is synthesized into speech and presented to the IC. Thus, the IC receives instructions how to act and what has to be taken into consideration for further decisions.

Use Case 2: Pro-Active Information Support. By monitoring user-system interactions (Use Case 1), the AMIRA system can elicit information directly related to the operation in which the operatives are currently working. By analyzing this information, the AMIRA system is able to pro-actively support the fire control (working in the fire service headquarter) with information about the situation in the incident ground. During or after the operation this information can be used as part of the operation debrief protocol or for reproducing actions or decision made during operation.

Use Case 3: Post-Incident Analysis. Collaborative post-incident analysis of operations is managed by the AMIRA system. This encompasses pro-actively asking involved persons (control, IC and fire fighters) for information about their last actions concerning possible modifications to guidelines or work instructions.

3 The AMIRA System

The AMIRA prototype system implements the three use cases, while Use Case 1 is considered most comprehensively. Due to the space limitations of this paper, only a short technical overview on the system is given here, which is focused on this use case. For detailed descriptions of the various aspects of the system we refer to previous publications [9,10,11].

3.1 Overall Architecture

The fundamental idea of the system is to combine multimodal interaction via speech dialogs, PDAs, tablet PCs, and desktop PCs (in the headquarter) with recent approaches to knowledge management and search technology as depicted in Fig. 2.

For this purpose the Collaborative Agent-based Knowledge Engine (CAKE) has been developed. It acts as a mediator between the users' information needs and the knowledge available in knowledge sources. Users (in this case ICs) interact with CAKE either through graphical user interfaces (GUIs) provided via portable devices (PDAs or tablet PCs) or through a mobile natural language speech dialog component connected to CAKE via a wireless connection. CAKE captures the context of the emergency situation by asking specific questions. Thereby it determines the decision problem of the IC. CAKE then provides intelligent decision support by autonomously enacting a domain specific search strategy to extract relevant information from the knowledge sources. This search process simulates the behavior of an expert information seeker knowledgeable in the domain of fire fighting and knowledgeable about the competencies of the knowledge sources. The process has several variants depending on the context (see Sect. 3.4). The general flow of activities is as follows:

1. CAKE analyzes the decision problem (including contextual information),
2. it selects appropriate knowledge sources,
3. it queries them for decision relevant knowledge,
4. it ranks and aggregates the results, and
5. communicates the results back to the incident commander either via a graphical user interface or through the speech synthesizer of dialog component.

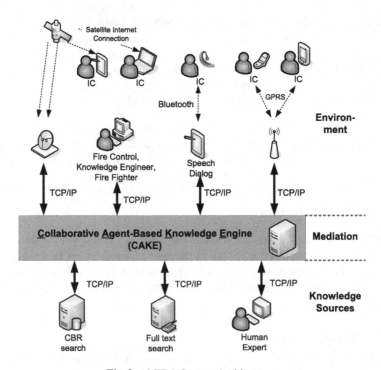

Fig. 2. AMIRA System Architecture

3.2   User Interfaces

Graphical User Interfaces. The graphical user interfaces can be used on different stationary and mobile devices and allows the ICs to interact with the system. Different GUIs have been implemented to suit the different display sizes. The user can interact with the system through a textual query typed into a single search field of the user interface or alternatively by filling a structured form (constructed dynamically) and thereby answering particular questions concerning the situation. Figure 3 shows two screenshots of the PDA GUI. The left side of this figure shows the GUI for entering the query (structured

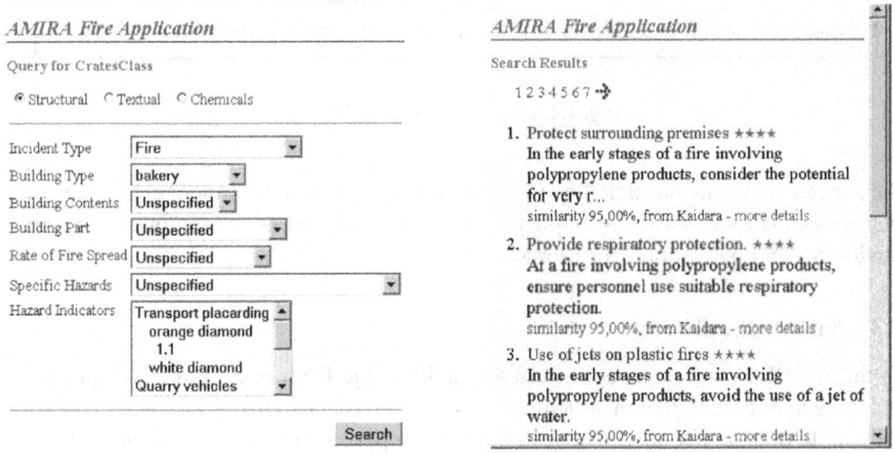

Fig. 3. Example Graphical User Interface on the PDA

mode form) and the right side shows the overview of the displayed result. The result display and navigation is similar to what is known from internet search engines. For example, the IC can click on a result item to see the details of this recommendation. As shown access to the system via a PDA is possible, however in many situations access via a tablet PC turned out to be more comfortable in case the IC is wearing gloves. The GUI for the tablet PC is similar and therefore not shown here.

Speech Dialog. The speech dialog component is responsible for executing the dialog with the user. It consists of a sequence of questions asked to the user via the speech synthesizer (see Fig. 4, left). These questions are mostly identical to the fields of the structured query form of the GUI. For each question there is a predefined limited vocabulary of possible answer terms (including synonyms). The speech analyzer examines the answers trying to identify words from the vocabulary. Given the particular noisy environment it is important to restrict the vocabulary in order to increase the recognition rate. If an answer cannot be recognize with sufficient probability, the dialog component asks a confirmatory question (to be answered by Yes or No). After results have been retrieved (right side of Fig. 4) they are presented to the user via the speech synthesizer. Using particular commands in a predefined vocabulary (like *next, details, first, exit, ...*)

System: Please describe the incident.	**[1—2 seconds later]**
User: There is a bakery burning.	System: Five result items have been found.
System: The incident type is Fire and the	Number one: In early stages of a fire
building involved is a bakery?	involving polypropylene products,
User: Yes.	consider the potential for very rapid
System: What kind of materials are involved?	spread of fire. Do you want more details
User: Plastic crates.	or got to the next item?
System: The type of material is plastic?	*User: Next*
User: Yes.	System: Number two: At a fire involving
System: Is the fire spreading rapidly?	polypropylene products, ensure
User: Yes.	personnel use suitable respiratory
	protection. Do you want more details or
	got to the next item?
	User: Details.
System: Now retrieving information.	System. Respiratory protection is mandatory ....

Fig. 4. Example of a Speech Dialog

the user can navigate through the result list. The speech dialog component has been implemented [12] with IBMs WebSphere Voice Server as well as with an internal Speech Dialog System by DaimlerChrysler Research.

3.3   Knowledge Sources

In the AMIRA context, a sophisticated search engine from Fast DataSearch provides indexing and searching of unstructured documents or data archives. Instead of indexing the whole documents only, this search engine supports the search of document fragments, called 'scope search'. This avoids the retrieving of long and verbose documents; focusing instead on the most important 'scope' of the document. Secondly, Kaidara Software provides a similarity-based search engine based on a structural case-based reasoning approach [13] and enables a search on past experiences that are represented by highly structured data in form of cases. Through these two search engines, 12 different knowledge sources are made available such as a chemical database, UN numbers on hazardous substances, procedure notes, emergency access codes, incident logs, risk assessment notes. Each knowledge source consists of a repository of text documents or is a relational database with structured information. Furthermore human experts in remote locations (e.g. in the fire service headquarter) are also accessible and can receive questions they are supposed to answer to provide help to the IC. All knowledge sources are related to special purposes and normally do not overlap each other by content, so that the competence area of each information source can be characterized differently. Consequently, the need for a meta-search process implementing efficient search strategies becomes obvious. The usage of such search processes enables novices to reuse search strategies of experienced users.

3.4   CAKE

CAKE is a generic architecture and tool implemented in the author's research group during the past four years within various research projects [9,10,11]. It is used to implement the mediation layer of the AMIRA system (see Fig. 5).

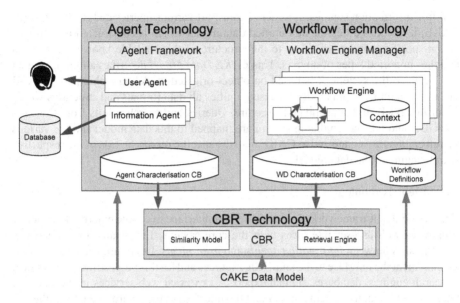

Fig. 5. CAKE System Architecture

As a key feature, CAKE offers sophisticated strategies for information access and information routing. These strategies address the challenge that in many business domains, knowledge relevant during daily work is scattered over a rich set of heterogeneous information sources. The individuals requiring the knowledge might not even be aware of these sources. Therefor, CAKE aims at providing this knowledge to the users by performing an intelligent search process enacted automatically and being invisible to the user. The following description stresses those components and features of CAKE relevant for the AMIRA application.

CAKE combines several technologies and concepts that have their origin in AI, aiming at addressing the "intelligence bit" of the AmI vision. It makes use of *agent technology* in order to integrate various interfaces with the environment (in this case stationary and mobile multimodal user interfaces) as well as interfaces to the knowledge sources. It uses *workflow technology* for representing business processes and for specifying the collaboration among agents (for example through a search strategy). Instead of supporting static and fully pre-defined processes, CAKE aims at supporting flexible and changing processes through adaptive workflow management. This flexibility is achieved by integrating a structural case-based reasoning component [13,14] able to perform similarity search on workflows, tasks, and agents. An overview of CAKE's architecture, showing the interactions of the three key technologies is shown in Fig. 5. These key technologies, which set upon an underlying common data model, are explained in the following sections.

3.5 Unified Data Model

Mediating between search components and user interface components, CAKE addresses the challenge of dealing with differently structured search queries and search results of multiple information sources. In order to transport various queries and results through CAKE, it includes a flexible and unified data model which is constructed in an application specific manner according to the structure of the available knowledge sources and the supported types of queries. This *CAKE Data Model* describes all kinds of data that occur in the system. It is based on object-oriented modeling techniques. We call this model a unified data model because it unifies all data formats and structures which occur in CAKE in a consolidated structure. Queries and search results from the various GUIs and the speech dialog system are mapped to this data model and the various search engines are connected to CAKE map the specific representation of the respective search engine to the data model.

3.6   Agent Technology

The CAKE agent framework provides a unified interface to couple external knowledge sources as well as user interfaces with the core system. Technically, the framework distinguishes between *information agents* and *user agents*. Information agents are used to implement the interface to the knowledge sources and for this purpose they can connect to search engines, databases, human experts, or external web services in the internet. On the other hand, user agents implement the interface to the environment by gathering and requesting information and by feeding back decision-relevant knowledge to the users. Each agent is composed of a *technology component*, a *wrapper*, and an *agent characterization*. The technology component is an external software component (e.g. a search engine) for accessing a knowledge source. To enable the communication between CAKE and different technology components, wrappers are used to fulfill two tasks: first, to map between the technology components' ontologies (data models) and the CAKE unified data model and second, to realize the technical interface, i.e. the communication protocol.

The agent characterization describes the agent's competencies. The characterization of information agents consist of attributes like the agent's role, the quality of data the agent provides, the area of expertise, the type of service it offers, and the data format. The characterization of user agents include a user model, e.g. representing the level of expertise of a worker.

In order to support dynamic environments, agents can be registered and deregistered in an agent repository (called *Agent Characterization CB*) and CAKE allows dynamic agent allocation during workflow enactment. For exploiting these potentials, task descriptions only contain agent roles in order to specify what kind of agent should carry out the corresponding task. Based on these roles an appropriate agent characterization can be retrieved (see Sect. 3.8) and the corresponding agent can be allocated to the task in an ad-hoc manner. Hence, the agent framework is able to manage heterogeneous agents that have completely different purposes, knowledge, and capabilities [15].

A difference to other agent-based approaches is that CAKE agents do not negotiate with each other. Instead, workflows are especially developed for organizations acting as loose contract among agents and capturing best practices about efficient cooperation. Best practices often occur as organizational norms or past experiences, e.g. about which agents are working together efficiently.

3.7   Workflow Technology

The goal of the workflow component is to model and execute various kinds of processes. CAKE distinguishes between the representations of *business processes* ("real-world processes") and internal processes called *collaboration pattern*. Both kind of processes are formally represented as *workflow definitions* that can be instantiated and executed in concrete situations at runtime. These workflow instances are in the following shortly denoted as *workflows* and the situations are represented in the so called *context* of the workflow. Each workflow definition consists of a *workflow characterization*, a set of *task descriptions*, and the *control flow relationships* among the task descriptions. The latter allows arranging the tasks in sequence, in parallel, or in loops, but does not cover data flow at all; data exchange is realized by using the context.

In the context of AMIRA, the collaboration patterns are of high importance. They are used to represent search strategies as a process. A search process can be viewed as a collaborative process conducted by several search components in order to achieve a common result set. Among other details, those search processes include information about which sources are relevant, which distribution techniques for the current query should be used, and how the result should be merged by use of well known methods from distributed information retrieval [16]. Figure 6 illustrates an example of a collaboration pattern.

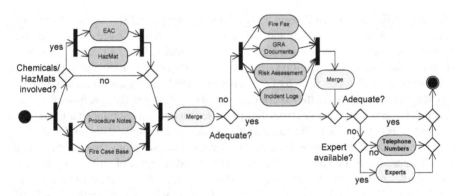

Fig. 6. Example of a Collaboration Pattern represented as UML Activity Diagram

This pattern describes a search strategy based on the available information sources for retrieving information related to burning plastic materials and how to react in this situation. This pattern involves only relevant knowledge sources in order to avoid irrelevant and bad result items. First, two parallel branches are triggered. One starts off an activity that searches the fire case base and procedure notes, the other checks if chemicals or hazardous materials are involved. If this is the case, both activities, the EAC and the Haz-Mat, initiate queries to the respective knowledge sources. Both sources contain details about plastics fires, burning bakeries or similar incidents. Next the branches run together, the retrieved information is merged into an intermediate result set. Appropriate merging methods are extensively discussed in [16]. Then the adequacy of this set is checked. If it is adequate, the final result set is achieved. Otherwise, four knowledge sources that consist of more general or verbose contents and are hence of a lower quality, are located on the second search level. Again, the results from the different knowledge sources are merged into one result set. If this result set is adequate, the collaboration is completed. If the result set is still not sufficient, the current query cannot be solved by computer support. Then it checks if a human expert is currently registered who is able to answer this query at once. Otherwise, telephone numbers of suitable experts are searched and represented to the IC. Please note that this collaboration pattern is executed by CAKE without interference with a human (except if a human expert is explicitly requested for information) within one or two seconds.

This is only one example of a collaboration pattern. According to the socio-technical study many best practices were encountered and hence several specific collaboration patterns were collected. Each pattern describes a search process for a particular kind of information request and is characterized by a meta-data description of the information requests for which it is appropriate (collaboration pattern characterization). Consequently, for each individual request it is necessary to select the best possible collaboration pattern. CAKE incorporates a case-based retrieval component (see Sect. 3.8) which automatically selects an appropriate collaboration pattern with respect to the users' information request.

3.8   Structural Case-Based Reasoning Technology

Within CAKE, Case-Based Reasoning (CBR) technology [17,13] is applied for various purposes. CBR is a methodology and technology for experience-based problem solving. Experiences are called *cases* and they are collected stored in a so called *case base*. A case contains a characterization of the situation in which a particular experience is made together with a description of the experience itself (e.g. a lesson learnt). If a new problem needs to be solved, the experiences stored in the cases of the case base are reused. Particularly, cases are retrieved from the case base that contain a similar characterization of a previous situation than the one currently under investigation. This implements the common principle that similar problems do have similar solutions. Hence, the core of a CBR approach is a component for similarity-based retrieval of cases from the case base. CAKE makes use of a *structural CBR approach* [13]. This means that cases are represented in structured object-oriented form. They are also instances of the CAKE Data Model. The case retrieval step of the CBR component makes use of an explicitly modeled similarity measure. This similarity measure is a function that compares a characterization of the current situation (context) with a characterization of a case and assesses their similarity. We do not provide a single standard similarity, but enable the system developer to model the notion of similarity according to the requirements of the domain [14].

We use this CBR component for two different purposes. First, it is used for the selection of a suitable collaboration pattern whenever a new request comes in from a user. Therefore, collaboration pattern are treated as cases representing best practice search strategies. Their characterizations are stored in the *WD Characterization Case Base* (see Fig. 5). A characterization of a particular collaboration pattern describes the situation in which this collaboration pattern can be (or has been) applied successfully. When a new similar situation occurs, the collaboration pattern is used again.

Second, CBR it is used for the selection of appropriate agents, whenever an agent communication is initiated. CAKE uses CBR for this tasks to overcome the inflexibility of static assignments of agents. Therefore, also agents are treated as cases, whose characterizations are stored in the *Agent Characterization Case Base*.

4 Evaluation

In order to assess the AMIRA system prototype against the socio-technical study, a summative evaluation has been conducted at the end of the project. The main goal of the evaluation was to assess to what degree the requirements and the overall expectations are met from the users' point of view. Therefore, several questions to be answered in the evaluation are formulated in advance. The most important questions were:

- Q1: Does the AMIRA system provide information of high quality?
- Q2: Is the AMIRA system well suited as a decision support system?
- Q3: Does the AMIRA system provide an added value to incident procedures?

Instead of relying on trials in laboratories, the evaluation was based on trials conducted in real environments. Such trials provide a realistic evaluation of the fire service application, uncovering benefits and deficiencies. Because it involved several user opinions, the evaluation would show different perspectives on the application and its usage.

4.1 Trial Participants

In order to achieve a representative sample of interviewees, 73 trial participants were selected from fire service organizations in UK (42) and Sweden (31). The participants undertook different roles within their organizations and most of them had been working as incident commanders for different periods of time, as depicted in Fig. 7.

Among the trial participants were watch managers (WM), crew managers (CM) and fire fighters (FF). A watch manager leads the work of teams or individuals to achieve their objectives. Additionally, he/she is responsible for ensuring effective performance and for leading and supporting people to resolve incidents. A crew manager educates and informs communities to improve awareness of safety matters. Beyond these roles, different characteristics are considered when selecting the participant: the degree of experience as an IC and as a fire fighter; full-time or retained fire service member; and age. The selection of interviewees tended toward focusing on those having little experience as an IC, or on fire fighters without any experiences as an IC.

4.2 Conducting the Evaluation

The performed evaluation consisted of four steps:

1. *Definition of concrete scenarios:* The scenarios devised for the trials were fire-related incidents involving plastic crates and traffic incidents resulting in a fire.
2. *Elaboration of questionnaires focused on scenarios, use cases and user requirements:* To collect information related to these criteria, the questionnaire included

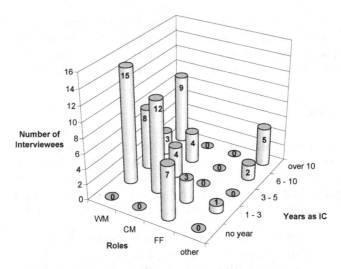

Fig. 7. Roles of Participants and Years as Incident Commander

both open and closed questions. Open questions motivate interviewees into thinking and reflecting in order to formulate their opinions and feelings. Whereas closed questions imply checking boxes for several answers and are, consequently, easier and more quickly answered. In addition, the questionnaire provided space for comments, which the respondents could add if they wished.

3. *Trial procedure:* In total 19 field trials were conducted between May and June 2006 at the Avon Fire & Rescue Service at Westmidland Fire Service and at the Swedish Fire College. The trials followed a pre-defined plan, organising how users were instructed and how to proceed. Before starting the trials, the participants were briefly introduced to the concept of knowledge management support for collaborative and mobile working. The focus on critical incident management, based on the scenarios, was also explained. The AMIRA system was then described and demonstrated to the participants. Then each participant deals with a particular scenario. He/she uses the AMIRA system in a realistic simulation of the scenario performed at the fire service grounds to get assistance in the decision-making process. Afterwards a debrief is carried out by one member of the trial team. This is done as a face-to-face structured interview using the questionnaire. In parallel, each trial phase is also observed by a senior officer. Each trial ends with an intermediate analysis.

4. *Analysis of debriefs, interviews, and questionnaires:* This final analysis is based on statistical data collected via questionnaires, and presents the conclusions drawn from the questionnaires. The analysis of questionnaires implies subjective and user-centred viewpoints. Nevertheless, the corresponding conclusions are well established, since they are based on highly experienced opinions.

4.3   Evaluation Results

We now present the evaluation results with respect to the three above mentioned questions. The first question relates to the quality of the information provided. For collecting

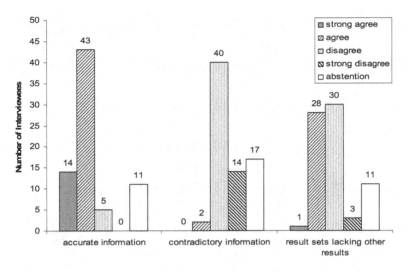

Fig. 8. Quality Criteria

opinions about the quality, questions concerning accuracy of information, contradictory information and incomplete result sets were included in the questionnaire. Figure 8 presents the questionnaire results of the quality criteria. Based on the corresponding answers, conclusions about precision and recall could be drawn. A majority of interviewees confirmed that the AMIRA system supported accurate information. This fact stresses the precision achieved by the retrieved information. Additionally, the interviewees were asked to estimate the percentage of the accurate information: 69% of all interviewees estimated the percentage between 95% - 100%. The next question related to whether contradictory information was retrieved by the AMIRA system. The main trend was to disagree that contradictory information had been retrieved, however 17 abstained from voting. At last, half of the interviewees agreed that the result sets lack other results which would be of particular importance with respect to the current information request. This indicates a deficit in terms of recall but it can be traced back to the prototypical implementation of the AMIRA system, which does not include all organizational information sources.

The second question addresses the appropriateness of AMIRA as a decision support system. Therefore, the questionnaire included questions relating to confidence in the AMIRA advice, helpfulness for decision, crew safety and consequences triggered by the advice. All questions were positively assessed as illustrated in Fig. 9. One of the most important results was that the interviewees were confident in the advice given by the AMIRA system. This confidence is fundamental for decision making. Beyond that, the advice was assessed as helpful for decision, particularly helpful for resolving the incident. Furthermore, the given advice supported crew safety which is of crucial importance for all fire services. Finally, the interviewees classified the AMIRA system as decision support system by agreeing that they had changed their tactical plans based on the advice provided.

The third question concerns the consequences triggered by the AMIRA system. The results of the questionnaire are illustrated in Fig. 10. On the one hand AMIRA advice

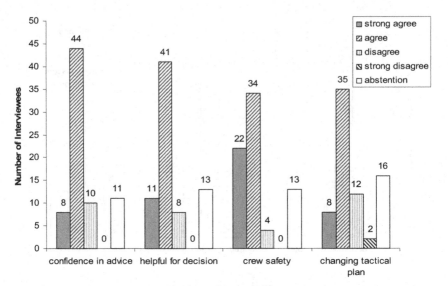

Fig. 9. Decision Making

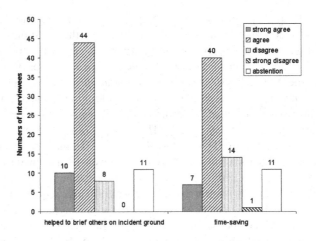

Fig. 10. Added Value for the Incident Process

helped to brief others on the incident ground and on the other hand time-saving was achieved by this system. Both perspectives are positively assessed by over half of the interviewees.

5   Conclusion

We presented the development of an AmI system for decision making in fire service organizations. Based on a socio-technical study a set of requirements from the users' point of view have been acquired. Based on these a purposive system design was made.

AMIRA uses the generic CAKE architecture and tool. CAKE is generic in the sense that many aspects of the system can be configure to suit the needs of a particular application: data models, collaboration pattern, agent descriptions, and similarity measures are defined through XML-files produced by a prototypical knowledge editing tool. This makes CAKE easily adaptable to different applications. In the context of the AMIRA project two further applications have been realized (mobile maintenance of fire engines and mobile maintenance of rescue equipment), which demonstrate this flexibility.

The work also presents a further example of successfully using AI technology to make AmI systems behave intelligently. In the case of AMIRA the intelligence lies in the conduction of a search process that simulates the search strategy of an expert information seeker knowledgeable in fire services and knowledgeable in the characteristics of the accessible knowledge sources. AMIRA provides this expertise in a transparent way to less experience ICs.

The evaluation conducted for assessing the AMIRA system against the socio-technical study demonstrated the usefulness of the approach. The evaluation process was mainly based on field trials, conducted several times, and questionnaires. Since questionnaires collect user opinion by nature, the evidence of evaluation results was achieved from a subjective point of view. This emphasizes the user-oriented approach of the AMIRA project. In summary, the usability of the system is acceptable, but to make it more easily applicable to a busy hands and busy eyes environment, the hardware used need to be developed further to provide a more compact package which is better integrated. This is a potential link to other projects addressing AmI support in emergency services such as the project wearIT@work[4].

Acknowledgement. The author acknowledges the contribution to this paper by the members of his research group, particularly by A. Freßmann and R. Maximini.

References

1. IST Advisory Group: Ambient intelligence: from vision to reality.Technical report, IST Advisory Group (2003), `ftp:// ftp.cordis.lu/pub/ist/docs/ istag-ist2003_draft_consolidated _report. pdf`
2. Ahola, J.: Ambient intelligence. ERCIM NEWS 47, 8 (2001)
3. Schmid, K.: KI — Künstliche Intelligenz. Ambient Intelligence, Schwerpunkt (2/2007)
4. Augusto, J.C., Nugent, C. (eds.): Designing Smart Homes. LNCS (LNAI), vol. 4008. Springer, Heidelberg (2006)
5. Huws, U.: Socio-economic research in the information society: a user's guide from the RESPECT project. Technical report, Institute for Employment Studies, Sussex (2004)
6. Social Research Association: Commissioning Social Research: a Good Practice Guide (2002)
7. Freßmann, A., Bendeck, F.: Socio-economic study of user needs. AMIRA Deliverable D2.1.0. Technical report, AMIRA Project (2005)
8. Chief Fire Officers Association: Cacfoa mobile data study. Technical report (2001)
9. Freßmann, A.: Knowledge Management Support for Collaborative and Mobile Working. Dr. Hut Verlag, München (2007)

---

[4] www.wearitatwork.com

10. Bergmann, R., Freßmann, A., Maximini, K., Maximini, R., Sauer, T.: Case-based support for collaborative business. In: Roth-Berghofer, T.R., Göker, M.H., Güvenir, H.A. (eds.) ECCBR 2006. LNCS (LNAI), vol. 4106, pp. 519–533. Springer, Heidelberg (2006)
11. Maximini, R.: Advanced Techniques for Complex Case-Based Reasoning Applications. Dr. Hut Verlag, München (2006)
12. Will, T.: Creating a dynamic speech dialogue — equipping cake with a standardised voicexml interface (Master's thesis)
13. Bergmann, R., Althoff, K.-D., Breen, S., Göker, M., Manago, M., Traphöner, R., Wess, S.: Developing Industrial Case-Based Reasoning Applications. LNCS (LNAI), vol. 1612. Springer, Heidelberg (1999)
14. Bergmann, R.: Experience Management. LNCS (LNAI), vol. 2432. Springer, Heidelberg (2002)
15. van Elst, L., Dignum, V., Abecker, A.: Towards agent-mediated knowledge management. In: van Elst, L., Dignum, V., Abecker, A. (eds.) AMKM 2003. LNCS (LNAI), vol. 2926, pp. 1–30. Springer, Heidelberg (2004)
16. Giese, M., Freßmann, A., Bergmann, R.: Using ontology-mapping techniques for content-based result merging. In: 4. Konferenz Professionelles Wissensmanagement — Erfahrungen und Visionen, GITO-Verlag Berlin (2007)
17. Aamodt, A., Plaza, E.: Case-based reasoning: foundational issues, methodological variations, and system approaches. AI Communications 7, 39–59 (1994)

Supporting Independent Living of the Elderly with Mobile-Centric Ambient Intelligence: User Evaluation of Three Scenarios

Marketta Niemelä[1], Rafael Gonzalez Fuentetaja[2], Eija Kaasinen[1], and Jorge Lorenzo Gallardo[3]

[1] VTT Technical Research Centre of Finland, P.O.Box 1300, 33101 Tampere, Finland
{marketta.niemela,eija.kaasinen}@vtt.fi
[2] Telefónica I+D, Madrid, 28043 Madrid, Spain
[3] Telefónica I+D, Boecillo, 47151 Boecillo, Valladolid, Spain
{rfg,jorgelg}@tid.es

Abstract. Mobile-centric ambient intelligence refers to systems, where personal mobile device is used to access ambient information and services. In this paper, we present three scenarios describing how independent living of elderly can be supported with mobile-centric ambient intelligence services. The scenarios have been prepared in the MINAmI project, which is developing an open technology platform for mobile-centric ambient intelligence. The scenarios focus on supporting self-care and safety at home. The three scenarios have been evaluated by groups of elderly people and the two self-care related scenarios also by medical experts, in both Spain and Finland. We report the results of these evaluations, and draw conclusions for user acceptance of mobile-centric ambient intelligence supporting independent living of the elderly.

Keywords: Mobile-centric ambient intelligence, mobile phone, independent living, user evaluation, focus group, elderly.

1 Introduction

Ambient intelligence (AmI) refers to a powerful, invisible computing system, embedded to our environment and everyday life to serve its users anywhere, anytime (e.g., [6][7]). In mobile-centric AmI, the personal mobile terminal of the end-user acts as a gateway and interface to ambient services. MINAmI project [13] together with the predecessor project MIMOSA have aimed to make ambient intelligence a reality by utilizing mobile phone as the platform [8].

According to Roussos and colleagues [15], mobile-phone based AmI is among the first and most realisable steps towards the world of AmI. There are over one billion mobile phones in the world, and potential services based on the personal mobile phone can be applied in several areas of life, from information access to health care. Mobile phone offers many features needed in AmI applications such as identification of the user, user interface and network connections. This facilitates AmI solutions that

B. Schiele et al. (Eds.): AmI 2007, LNCS 4794, pp. 91–107, 2007.

do not require extensive changes in the environment. These kinds of solutions will enable AmI services earlier than visions where AmI is totally embedded in the environment, requiring extensive infrastructures. Mobile phones can be used as ID tokens – secure personal devices – that can disclose personal information when needed and that the user can easily control. Finally, if mobile phones act as the visible part of AmI services, this makes them and the whole AmI system easier to conceptualize and interact with. This may ease the adoption of services and increase user acceptance of AmI.

One of the target user groups of ambient intelligence are the elderly. Ambient intelligence systems may help elders live independently at home longer as the systems enable unobtrusive monitoring for safety and health care, assistance in everyday tasks such as finding eye glasses and remembering to take medication, and contacting to friends and relatives living far away. For this purpose, ambient intelligence is often manifested as systems installed at home, "smart homes" (e.g., Aware Home [3] and the Roberta system [1]).

Mobile-centric ambient intelligence provides application possibilities for supporting independent living of the elderly. Mobile AmI systems enable different kinds of remote monitoring, automatic alerts, and assistance in everyday tasks such as reminding. Elderly people have well accepted e.g. safety bracelets connected to the mobile phone and enabling rough positioning of the person in emergency, and mobile phone based reminders to take medication in time [12].

Applying mobile AmI for the elderly also introduces challenges. The usability of the mobile phone is often experienced weak, due to the small size of the device with respect to the common weak-sightedness and physical deficiencies of elders. This and possible other reasons may complicate the social acceptance of mobile technology and AmI services among the elderly. Furthermore, cultural differences even between European nations may affect the success of mobile AmI.

In the MINAmI project [13], we prepared scenarios illustrating the use of mobile-centric ambient intelligence applications. The scenarios were evaluated with potential users in several focus groups. In this paper we describe three of those scenarios that are related to assistive living and health care. In this paper, we concentrate on the evaluation results that we got in focus groups consisting of elderly people. The results give insight to understanding the attitudes of elderly people towards AmI solutions supporting independent living, especially solutions where mobile phone is used as the platform. We also collected application-specific feedback of the three scenarios, relating to medicine taking, sleep problems, and sensored home. Two of the scenarios that were related to health care, were also evaluated by medical experts. Both user and expert evaluations were carried out in two countries, Finland and Spain.

2 Related Work

Different research activities have focused on AmI solutions targeted to elderly people. Those solutions have often been related to assistive living and health care. Several intelligent or assistive homes are in development, focusing to supporting lives of elders by facilitating their health and self-care and supporting their social relationships. For instance, The Center for Future Health [4] and Aware Home

Research Initiative (AHRI) at Georgia Tech [3] develop houses equipped with sensors, monitoring devices and biosensors to help senior inhabitants to participate in disease detection and health management by themselves. One of the AHRI projects is the Memory Mirror, which is an RFID based system that monitors taking medication. A reader placed on a shelf records picking up and returning tagged pillboxes. An image of a taken medicine appears in a time line display, thus reminding of the already taken drug.

Roberta [1] is a home system based on contemporary computer technology for supporting elders living and monitoring vital health related data. A web platform supports collecting and monitoring health data from the participants, administration of medication, communication amongst home care workers and coordination through a shared calendar system. The user interface of Roberta is a tablet PC with wireless monitors. In the evaluation of Roberta, it was however found that only a few of the elders learned to use the tablet PC despite intense and repeated training.

Mobile phone has been implemented in different kinds of automatic monitoring and alerting systems that have been created to increase the feeling of safety – both of the elderly herself and for her relatives. Miyauchi and colleagues [14] developed a system that detects an elder's fall by personal accelerometer and breathing sensors. For mobile users, the system positions the mobile phone of the elder and sends an alert and a map showing the elder's location to the family or other relevant persons. Global positioning system (GPS) enables more accurate positioning, and this is used in the monitoring system for elderly with dementia by Lin and colleagues [9]. Their system is able to track the wandering person both outdoor and indoor by utilising both GPS and mobile phone positioning. In addition, the system warns if the person leaves a predetermined area with the help of RFID technology: RFID tags can be embedded to the objects the elder often wears, and the reader at the doorway. If the reader detects the elder leaving the house with no company, the system will trigger further actions.

In Adamos project, social acceptance of proactive mobile services has been evaluated in France and Finland [2][5]. A scenario described different proactive mobile services including several health-related services, such as monitoring, reminding, informing, and supporting in regard to medication, fitness, and nutrition. For instance, the proactive service system monitored the person's heart rate and alerted if it was too high, reminded him about the medication, and suggested meals in the restaurant. The health-related mobile services were found valuable and helpful, as long as the control remains in the user's hands, in both Finland and France. Cultural differences were found in such aspects that do not directly relate to healthcare: the Finns tended to accept services that support more efficient working better than the French. Also, the Finns female users better accepted the evaluated services and were more ready to adopt and apply them in their lives than their French counterparts.

Results from previous research show that AmI solutions for the elderly seem to have potential especially in the fields of independent living and health care. Our approach differs from other research on the area because we are focused on a platform solution. The MINAmI mobile platform will serve as a platform for different AmI applications and services, thus facilitating personally selected collections of AmI services for the elderly.

3 Platform for Mobile-Centric Ambient Intelligence

The MIMOSA project [8] developed an open technology platform for ambient intelligence services, to be implemented in a mobile phone. In the vision of MIMOSA the user uses her/his mobile device to communicate with the surrounding environment by wirelessly reading close tags and sensors embedded to everyday objects. Tag and sensor data may also be redirected to relevant applications. In addition, the phone enables wireless connection to the Internet. As the communication can be tied to a specific place, object, and time, this approach enables context-related information and services. Central components of the architecture are shown in Figure 1 and described below.

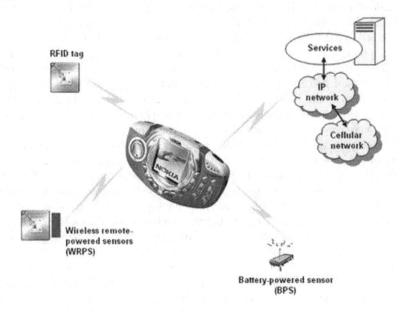

Fig. 1. The architecture for mobile-centric ambient intelligence

Personal mobile phone. The mobile phone is the user's personal trusted terminal and gateway for interaction with the ambient intelligence system. The mobile phone composes the context services and the network services into intelligent applications, and enables the user to control and interact with these applications.

RFID tags. Local connectivity to tags provides access to data and functions related to the environment and different objects in it. The communication between a tag and a reader is powered by the reader integrated in a personal mobile device, so no battery is required for this purpose. As a result, tags are short-range devices and require the reader to be close enough to enable the communication.

Sensors. Similar to tags, sensors can be battery-powered or powered by the reader. Wireless remote powered sensor (WRPS) includes a sensor and a tag for identification. With battery-powered sensors (BPS) the RF communication is powered by batteries, increasing considerably the maximum distance between the reader and the sensor node.

Context services. Getting tag and sensor data from the environment and even from the user opens possibilities for a vast amount of applications and services. .Context services take care of collecting tag and sensor data from the environment and redirecting it to relevant applications and services. Context data is stored onto a context engine that facilitates implementing context-aware features to applications.

Network services. Optional remote connectivity allows connections to the vast amount of services accessible by Internet (and other networks).

In the MINAmI project [13], this basic architecture will be extended by developing mass storage RF tags based on low power technologies. These tags enable access to much more data than just the tag ID. MINAmI project is also developing active event sensitive tag technology including wake up sensors (acceleration, shock, and temperature) and local clock for time stamping. These enable long-term logging of measurement data and logging to be activated based on a sensor reading. These technology advancements should notably increase the number and quality of potential applications, services, and user interaction methods of mobile-centric ambient intelligence systems. MINAmI project is developing several demonstrators to illustrate and test the approach. These demonstrators integrate the different technologies to be developed within the project. The scenarios illustrate the design ideas of the forthcoming demonstrators.

4 Scenarios

The MINAmI scenarios presented in this paper describe applications related to taking medication, off-line health monitoring at home, and smart home functions. The focused users of the applications generalize beyond the elderly, and indeed in two scenarios the main character is not an older person but a middle-aged man. Nevertheless, the applications and the contexts in the scenarios can be considered relevant for elders' lives so that it makes sense to use them in evaluating older people's acceptance of mobile AmI.

Fig. 2. Screenshots of the three animations: *Medication event monitoring system* on the left; *Sleep apnoea diagnosis* in the middle; and *Friendly assistance and security at home* on the right

The scenarios were first written in text together with the application field experts participating in the project. The stories were then animated to cartoons of 1-3 minutes duration (screenshots in Fig. 2). Cartoons were considered as a convenient media as they illustrated the product ideas in a way that was easy to understand but still left room for the imagination of the watcher. We utilised the animated scenarios in project presentations and in user evaluation activities, including both focus groups and web questionnaires. Cartoons worked well as a medium for the elderly and we found neither adverse reaction nor comments about the characters used.

The three scenarios are quite different from each other and the ambient intelligence in them supports people in different ways and situations. Also the mobile phone plays different roles. In the *Medication event monitoring system* scenario, the mobile phone is a gateway in automatic data transfer. In the *Sleep apnoea diagnosis* scenario, the mobile phone is a gateway in user initiated data transfer, and receives notifications from the system to the user. In the *Friendly assistance and security at home scenario*, the user receives notifications from the system to the mobile phone. We now shortly describe the scenarios.

4.1 Medication Event Monitoring System

The *Medication event monitoring system* scenario introduces a smart pillbox with a counter for openings and closings of the cap. The cap includes a clock, and is so able to count hours elapsed since the last opening. The cap is programmable and can be set to follow a certain "recipe". The pillbox collects compliance information, reflecting how well the patient takes her medicine in time.

The smart pillbox can communicate with the mobile phone by a local wireless connection (e.g., Bluetooth). The patient can see his medication information in the mobile phone display. The information can then be sent to a treating doctor via an Internet connection.

In the animated scenario, a patient Tom receives a smart pillbox from his doctor to support his medical treatment. Tom uses the pillbox to check when the time to take the next pill is. The compliance information is automatically transferred from the pillbox to Tom's mobile phone and then sent to a secure Internet database.

When the medication starts to affect positively after a few days, Tom becomes careless and forgets to take the pills for several days. In this phase, the pillbox sends the patient data via the mobile phone to a care centre, which notifies the doctor by an e-mail. The doctor makes a phone call to the patient to check the situation.

4.2 Sleep Apnoea Diagnosis

The *Sleep apnoea diagnosis* scenario demonstrates the use of a *Sleep quality logger,* which is a plaster integrated with sensors for detecting certain brain waves (electroencephalographic waves, EEG), and movements of the head (acceleration data). The sleep quality logger also includes a memory for collecting sensor data over a longer time period (approx. 10 hours). The plaster with the sensors is set to a person's forehead, allowing unobtrusive monitoring of the person's EEG and head movements, for instance, over a night. The data can be later analysed for detecting abnormalities.

The sleep quality logger can be read with the mobile phone via a local, short-range wireless connection (RFID communication). Reading happens by taking the mobile phone close to the plaster (15-30 cm). The reader on the phone then recognizes the plaster and automatically uploads the monitored measurements from the logger memory on the plaster. We call this interaction method *touching*. The information can then be sent to a healthcare centre via an Internet connection.

In the scenario, a middle-aged male patient Tom is suffering from daytime fatigue and the doctor supposes sleep apnoea. Tom is given a sleep quality logger and instructions of how to use the plaster at home. In the evening, Tom fastens the logger plaster to his forehead and goes to sleep. At the same time the sensors start automatically collecting data. In the morning, Tom touches the logger with his mobile phone to upload the data collected overnight on to the phone, and to send the data to the healthcare centre. Tom however immediately receives an SMS from the *Sleep quality analyser* system of the centre. The SMS warns about that the plaster has been badly connected, and the collected data quality is not sufficient. In the next evening, Tom takes the logger and this time fastens it better to his forehead. In the morning, the data sent to the sleep quality analyser is valid, and the system makes an appointment for Tom with the doctor.

4.3 Friendly Assistance and Security at Home

The *Friendly assistance and security at home* scenario presents ambient sensors for home, which are a set of interlinked sensors such as vision sensor able to detect persons and animals, infrared motion sensor, door opening sensor, and wearable accelerometer for detecting if the user falls down. The sensors can be clustered to offer specific functions for security, home care, and comfort, for instance. The sensor clusters are connected to a central node, which is the access and control point to the system and also the gateway to other systems external to the house. The mobile phone is connected to the home system via GSM network communicating with the central node.

In the scenario, an old lady Mrs Setford lives in a big house with her dog Norman. All rooms of the house are equipped with ambient sensors. As Mrs Setford moves in the stairs, lights go on automatically. As evening has come, Mrs Setford sets the ambient sensor system to a security mode by controlling the system with a simple remote control device. When Mrs Setford is watching TV, Norman wanders to the basement. The system detects the pet and sends a notification to the lady's mobile phone. Later, a burglar tries to enter the house through the basement, but the system detects him and starts a general alarm sound in the house. This frightens the burglar away. Mrs Setford however has startled herself and fallen down. The system detects also this and sends an alert to a home care centre. A centre officer calls Mrs Setford to her mobile phone to ask about the situation. Mrs Setford can't get up by her own, so a care centre nurse goes to the house to help her.

5 User Evaluation

The user evaluation was carried out to provide us understanding about the elderly people's attitude towards and acceptance of AmI technologies to support their independent living, especially if the mobile phone is included as an interface. Beyond that, we wanted to get application-specific feedback of the three scenarios, relating to medicine taking, sleep problems, and sensor-equipped home. The two health-care related scenarios were also evaluated by medical experts. We also made a tentative intercultural comparison between the results of the evaluations carried out in two countries, Finland and Spain.

5.1 Method

We used the *focus group* method for the user evaluation. Focus group means interviewing a collected group of volunteer persons who belong to the targeted user segment or are experts in the field under evaluation (e.g., [10]). The interview situation is quite informal and the participants are free to discuss about the topic beyond the presented material. The focus group method is usually efficient in finding different viewpoints and suggestions for improvement for the evaluated topic. Another motivation to choose this method was to facilitate elderly people's participation and to capture their attitudes, certainly difficult to achieve with web questionnaires, the other option we were considering.

In this evaluation, we had altogether five focus groups, of which three were of elderly people (two in Finland, one in Spain) and two consisted of medical experts (one in Finland, one in Spain) (see Table 1). Our goal was to organize one focus group of elderly people per scenario and country (overall 6) and one focus groups of physicians and/or nurses per scenario and country for the healthcare related scenarios (overall 4). The number of participants in each focus group should be 6-8. Due to the project's schedule constraints, it was not possible to meet this goal in the number of focus groups. The number of participants was barely met. This makes rigorous intercultural comparison not possible although some tentative differences are shown in the summary section

After agreeing a common script and schedule, these focus groups were independently organized and carried out in both countries. Preliminary conclusions gathering interviews in both countries were distributed fifteen days after the last interview to the project partners.

Table 1. The scenarios were evaluated by five focus groups

Scenario	Application field	Focus group
Medication event monitoring system	Healthcare	Elderly people and medical experts
Sleep apnoea diagnosis	Healthcare	Elderly people and medical experts
Friendly assistance and security at home	Homecare	Elderly people

The evaluations of the elders were arranged in day rooms of service centres for elderly in Finland (Fig. 3) and in Telefonica I+D premises in Spain. The medical experts were interviewed in a hospital in Finland and in a primary care centre in Spain.

Fig. 3. Participants of the second elderly group in Finland watching the animation. Discussions were held around the table behind.

Following the script, the moderator raised questions regarding technology usage (mobile phone and computer usage mainly) and life style habits related to the scenario being evaluated. Then the scenarios, illustrated as animations, were presented to the participants by projecting the animations from a laptop to a big screen. The animations were shown one at a time, after which the participants were interviewed about the scenario. The participants were encouraged to discuss about the scenario beyond the animation and interview questions. The estimated time for each scenario was 1-2 hours, to give ample time for debate. Interviews were recorded and informed consent forms were signed by participants, according to the project ethic guidelines.

5.2 The Focus Groups in Finland and Spain

In Finland, there were two elderly groups, of which one evaluated the scenario *Friendly assistance and security at home*, and the other commented the *Medication event monitoring system* and *Sleep apnoea diagnosis* scenarios. In Spain, one elderly group evaluated all three scenarios. In addition, medical experts in both Finland and Spain evaluated the two healthcare-related scenarios, *Medication event monitoring system* and *Sleep apnoea diagnosis*. Within each country, the same moderator conducted all focus groups.

The elderly groups in Finland. The two groups of elderly people in Finland were collected by contacting two service centres for aged people. The first group consisted of four people, two women and two men, with ages between 65-79 (Table 2). None of them used computers, as they were considered to be too expensive and useless. The mobile phone was used by three of the four elders, most often for phone calls but also for text messaging (SMS). The second group of elderly people consisted of 10 people, of which two were men, with ages between 65-80 (Table 3). Five of these participants used computer for different purposes such as text processing, e-mail, and Internet browsing. Eight participants used mobile phone for making phone calls, reading and sending text messages, and also as a clock.

Table 2. Composition of elderly group #1, Finland

P#	Gender	Age	Form of residence	Computer use	Mobile phone use
1	Male	65	Rental apartment	No Would like to use for it's practicality	Yes (10 yrs) Communication with relatives and important offices
2	Male	69	Apartment in nursing home	No Not interested at all	Yes (> 1 yr) Phone calls
3	Female	71	Apartment in nursing home	No Not interested	No Not interested
4	Female	79	Rental apartment	No, but has used earlier Not interested anymore	Yes (6 yrs) Communication

Table 3. Composition of elderly group #2, Finland

P#	Gender	Age	Form of residence	Computer use	Mobile phone use
1	Female	78	Apartment house	Yes (5 yrs) Text processing, e-mail	Yes (10 yrs) Phone calls, SMS
2	Male	67	Apartment house	Yes (3 yrs) E-mail, Internet	Yes (1 yr) Phone calls, SMS
3	Female	--	--	No	Yes (4 yrs) Phone calls, SMS
4	Male	80	Apartment house	No	Yes (4 yrs) Phone calls
5	Female	78	Apartment house	No	No
6	Female	76	Apartment house	No	Yes (1 yr) Phone calls, clock
7	Female	81	Apartment house	Yes (10 yrs) Text processing	Yes (15 yrs) Phone calls, SMS, for personal safety
8	Female	72	Apartment house	Yes (5 yrs) E-mail, Internet	No
9	Female	65	Apartment house	Yes (2 yrs) Text processing, E-mail, Internet	Yes (7 yrs) Phone calls, SMS, clock
10	Female	71	Apartment house	No	Yes (3 yrs) Phone calls, reading text messages, clock, alarm clock

The elderly group in Spain. The Spanish group (Table 4) consisted of five participants, two females and three males, with ages between 67-87. They reviewed all three scenarios in a single session, with a total time of 3 hours, approximately and coffee breaks in between. All but one used mobile phone for phone calls and also for SMS but mainly receiving, not sending messages. All but one often used a desktop computer at home; one of them had a laptop. The main computer usages were Internet browsing, e-mail, calendar, and playing videos and music. This group's experience of using mobile phone and computer in years was not asked.

Table 4. Composition of elderly group #3, Spain

P#	Gender	Age	Education	Form of residence
1	Female	71	Assembly specialist of telecom. company	Flat
2	Female	69	Merchant	Flat
3	Male	67	Building Worker	Flat
4	Male	87	Public Administration section responsible	Flat
5	Male	71	Sales representative	Flat

The medical experts in Finland. In spite of six medical experts' pre-acceptance to participate to the focus group, only two were able to come due to simultaneous work with patients. One of the medical experts was a doctor in child diseases (female) also diagnosing sleep apnoea of children less than 16 years old. The other was a staff nurse (male) in heart diseases with experience on tele-cardiogram research (Table 5). Both medical experts used computer extensively at their work for searching for information, storing and processing patient data, and communication.

Table 5. Composition of medical expert group #1, Finland

P#	Gender	Age	Background	Sector
1	Female	39	Paediatrics	Public
2	Male	46	Staff nurse in heart diseases	Public

Table 6. Composition of medical expert group #2, Spain

P#	Gender	Age	Background	Sector
1	Male	54	Family doctor	Public, Primary care
2	Female	48	Family doctor	Public, Primary care
3	Female	36	Paediatrician	Public, Primary care
4	Male	38	Family doctor	Private
5	Female	35	Oncologist	Public, Hospital
6	Female	41	Anatomical pathologist	Public, Hospital

The medical experts in Spain. In Spain, the National Health Service is organized in two sectors: *primary care*, dealing with routine visits to family doctors, paediatricians and general healthcare, and *hospitals*, where more specialist physicians work. The focus group included three physicians from primary care, two from hospitals, and one physician from the private sector, working for a large pharmaceutical company (Table 6). All used computer at work, most frequently to access to databases, clinic histories, bibliographic searches, and up-to-dates from papers of their scientific communities.

6 Results

6.1 Medication Event Monitoring System

The *Medication event monitoring system* scenario rose lively commenting among the elderly. It was pointed out by both Finnish and Spanish groups that older people often use a wide variety of different medicines and thus have a pill kit to arrange the drugs. Therefore, they did not find the smart pillbox useful (indeed, the real user group of the smart pillbox is rather those who take a single drug).

The participants preferred that the dosing data should not be transferred to a doctor, but either the pillbox or the mobile phone should notify the patient herself. In the scenario, the doctor has a major role in monitoring and reminding the patient, and this was associated to surveillance by the Finnish participants. These participants were in general reluctant about intelligent devices and had doubts about reliability of such monitoring. For instance, opening the pillbox cap does not ensure actually taking the medicine. Also they were concerned about intelligent devices weakening people's cognitive skills, because they won't have to strive to remember anymore.

The Finnish participants did not pay special attention to the usability of the smart pillbox. The Spanish elders however felt that using the mobile phone as an interaction device would be too difficult to manage for them, similarly to many other functions beyond ordinary phone calls and reading SMS messages.

Overall, none of the participants would use the pillbox themselves, but all they believed that the next generation, more used to and skilled with technology, will take this kind of devices and services into use.

Also the medical experts in both Finland and Spain pointed out that the alert notification should be generated in the pillbox and not be a duty of doctors (or rather nurses in Spain). Otherwise, their impression of the application was positive, because *not* taking medication regularly in time is a widespread and often critical problem in medical treatment. They even suggested that, by proper feedback, this kind of device could reinforce the motivation of some patients to comply with the treatment.

The experts noted that patients could feel being surveyed when using the application. There was also discussion about data confidentiality. All acknowledged that new technologies and services should be checked against the current data protection laws and the consequences of not protecting this kind of data. For instance, if an enterprise somehow gets the confidential info about one of its employees not strictly following a certain treatment; they could punish the employee by not funding his private medical care.

6.2 Sleep Apnoea Diagnosis

The scenario of monitoring sleep at home was perceived positively by both the Finnish and Spanish participants. They commented that a more familiar environment assures better sleep and thus more reliable data than collected in a sleep laboratory, and the elders would benefit from reduced or no waiting time in hospital.

The Finnish elders thought the device itself to be handy and easy to use. Reading the data from the logger to the mobile phone by just moving them close to each other was found to be simple. However, the Spanish interviewees perceived the same problems of using the mobile phone as in the previous scenario: using the mobile phone for interaction with an external device and for data transfer would be unmanageable. Also the Finns thought that if the interaction would require menu browsing and using the normal mobile phone interface, it would be problematic.

Transmitting EEG data over the network raised some questions related to privacy in the Finnish group. Two persons thought that no health-related information should be in the Internet at all, as the risks for misuse and uncontrolled distribution of the sensitive information are too big. Others were ready to allow Internet transmission but the patient data protection law must be followed and all transmission should be secured. The Spanish elders did not raise privacy questions.

The medical experts commented that the device would be useful for gross screening of apnoea or other sleep problems if the system was reliable enough, in terms of medical as well as use issues. The Spanish experts pointed out reliability and simplicity as key factors for success. The system should be very sensitive and resistant to false negatives, that is, the system cannot afford failing to detect a sleep apnoea in a case where using a polysomnogram could detect it. Also, repeated failures in use would make the patients refuse from using the system. Both Finnish and Spanish experts agreed that according to the scenario, the device was very easy to use. Patients would have to take care of placing the plaster correctly, but the interviewees appreciated the system being able to detect a loose contact. Again, data transmission was a sensible topic similarly to the previous scenario. The data collected by the device would be private, so transferring, storing, and handling the data should be secured.

6.3 Friendly Assistance and Security at Home

All elder participants found the Friendly home system presented in the scenario valuable and acceptable, as it would increase the feeling of safety at home. The Finnish group appreciated all the different features of the system (automatic lights, the system reporting about the pet, intruder and fall detection alarms).

The Spanish as well as Finnish participants worried about the price of the system and who could afford such systems. Other challenges were seen in how the system would be maintained and fixed, and by whom. It was wondered if dust and moisture could affect the system. Increased electromagnetic radiation at home did not worry the participants. In their words, there is so much radiation already everywhere that little more makes no harm.

There was a thread of conversation about what this kind of system means in terms of privacy. When being surveyed, it should not be done directly by somebody (either physically present or with cameras). In this respect, the system was perceived as invisible and, in the end, losing privacy was not such a big concern. The increased feeling of safety was seen more important. The Spanish group even suggested placing sensors in such intimate places as bathrooms, because these places were seen problematic for elderly people. The Spanish participants however were concerned about trusting external home care or security centres, which must get access to inside the home in case of an alarm.

6.4 Attitude and Acceptance of AmI Technologies Supporting Independent Living

Both Finnish groups of elderly people presented strong opinions about the role of technology in homecare of old people. Technology can be helpful and useful for people who are motivated and skilled enough to use it, and who live far away from city centres. There was however a fear that relying too much on technology would cause deterioration in cognitive and memory abilities. Furthermore, the participants stressed that technology should never replace human contact and relationships.

The participants saw that there is a risk that a society may embrace technology too much and too quickly and people would be alienated from each other and social relationships. Technology to some extent can support and assist but human relationship and face to face meetings are important. There is a danger of dividing people into a sort of technocracy with two classes of citizens: those who don't have access to the Internet or computer use due to their financial situation, personal cognitive or physical skills are in a risk of being categorised to a lower class of society. This was found unacceptable and should be taken into consideration in the design of technical systems.

The Spanish group of elderly people showed an ambivalent feeling of acceptance and detachment from technology. On one hand, the futuristic and optimistic scenarios that were shown made them wonder at the progress of science and technology. On the other hand, they recognized that perhaps they were not able to get benefit from it, as they considered themselves most of the time not skilled enough to use these kinds of mobile phone applications.

The medical experts thought that remote monitoring of patients and homecare/self-care enabled by technology is useful, when the patient group is carefully selected and the patient is not set in an unequal position in society if she or he does not have access to the Internet or can't use the technology.

The experts wondered if this kind of technology development will lead to a possibility to acquire better and complementary information about the patient, or to a situation where doctors are replaced by technology as the patient does not perceive the physical presence of the physician necessary. The clinical examination of the patient is crucial, because in remote reception or monitoring, only a narrow understanding of the condition of the patient can be obtained, and because at the reception the patient may reveal such seemingly unrelated but important things that would not be disclosed in remote monitoring situation.

Remote monitoring may however decrease the need to follow-up receptions and so save the scarce resources. Remote monitoring systems would require reliable, automatic collection and pre-analysis of the patient data.

7 Summary and Discussion

In this paper we have presented the results of a qualitative study where we studied the attitudes of elderly people towards some mobile-centric ambient intelligence solutions in the fields of housing and health care. The results point out issues that require attention when designing these kinds of systems for elderly users and the results also point out candidates for further intercultural user studies. To a large extent, the results can be generalised beyond the actual scenarios that were evaluated.

The friendly home monitoring system presented in the *Friendly assistance and security at home* scenario was appreciated both by Finnish and Spanish interviewees. The home system increases the feeling of security, which is important to the elderly. Also, the EEG logger application in the *Sleep apnoea diagnosis* scenario was found useful as it would save elders' time, hospital resources, and enable more convenient monitoring and perhaps more reliable diagnosis. The smart pillbox application in the *Medication event monitoring system* scenario was not found to be suitable for elders due to the variety of different medicines elders often need to take. The scenario was also associated to surveillance. That is why the interviewees would have preferred monitored data to be processed by a technical system rather than a person, even if (s)he would be in a professional role.

Overall, mobile phone was well accepted as a device for data transfer and notifications. However, usability problems with mobile phones were raised. The Spanish elders found the two applications deploying data transfer via the mobile phone, the smart pillbox and the EEG logger, difficult to use and being beyond their skills.

The Finnish elders did not perceive the applications as difficult to use but rather the opposite. In the Finnish group, eight of the ten participants had used the mobile phone more than one year for making phone calls and SMS, but also for other functions. As we don't have data regarding how long the Spanish elders had been using mobile phone and computer, it may be that the Finnish elders were more experienced with mobile phones and thus perceived the touch-based interaction only as an improvement to the current situation. In other words, the Finns compared the usability of touching to a situation in which the common mobile phone interface would be used for interaction, whilst the Spanish evaluated the usability as their general ability to use the applications.

The Finnish participants appeared to be stricter in relation to privacy and security of data transfer than the Spanish. Perhaps these issues are currently more in public discussion in Finland. Instead, the Spanish wondered whether the home care or security centres are reliable enough to be trusted to access homes in alarm situations. This question was not raised in discussions among the Finnish interviewees. This may reflect a general cultural difference: in both countries: privacy and security are important but in somewhat different contexts. The medical professionals in both countries stressed the importance of privacy and security in transferring, storing and handling medical data

In both countries the elderly accepted services and applications facilitating life, supporting health-care and improving the possibilities of living independently at home. However, the interviewees stressed that the services should be provided in such a way that elders will be capable of using them with their weakened sight and other physical, sometimes also cognitive, deficiencies. Usability and simplicity of devices and applications are crucial in this, as been stated also elsewhere [1]. As pointed out by the elders themselves, the next user generation may better accept advanced technological aids as they already have the skills and experience of using mobile phones and computers.

Medical experts raised the important ethical issue of how the technology will be utilised. Remote monitoring should not replace clinical examinations. However, with follow-up studies remote monitoring will save efforts from both the doctors and the patient and still provide good quality care. The monitored data may even be more reliable, as was stated in the case of sleep monitoring.

The elderly were worried of situations where they would feel forced to quickly adopt new technology. We agree with Aalokke and colleagues [1] as they argue that technology should evolve together with elders, transforming in time to meet their changing needs and abilities. With more advanced, perhaps context-aware and proactive applications and services, provided with very simple human-system interfaces, mobile-centric ambient intelligence may be welcomed by the elderly. Simple interaction methods such as touching with the mobile phone to read monitored data and to trigger actions may, if wisely applied, notably decrease the cognitive burden when using AmI applications and is thus one promising step to that direction.

The results of our study will be utilised in designing the actual demonstrators in MINAmI project. In addition, the results give a good basis for a qualitative user study, with which we will be able to collect more extensive feedback of user attitudes towards MINAmI AmI concept and related applications.

Acknowledgments. We want to thank our partners from the MINAmI project, especially Aardex, GE Health Care and Hager Security who have given us insight to the applications fields of housing and health care.

References

1. Aalokke Ballegaard, S., Bunde-Pedersen, J., Bardram, J.E.: Where to, Roberta?: Reflecting on the Role of Technology in Assisted Living. In: Proceedings of the NordiCHI conference, pp. 373–376 (2006)
2. Arhippainen, L., Forest, F.: Future Proactive Services for Everyday Life. In: InSciT 2006. Proceedings of the I International Conference on Multidisciplinary Information Sciences and Technologies, Mérida Spain, pp. 122–126 (2006)
3. Aware Home Research Initiative. http://www.cc.gatech.edu/fce/ahri/
4. Center for Future Health. http://www.centerforfuturehealth.org
5. Forest, F., Arhippainen, L.: Social acceptance of proactive mobile services: observing and anticipating cultural aspects by a Sociology of User Experience method. In: The Proceedings of the smart Objects and Ambient Intelligence (sOc-EUSAI), Grenoble France, pp. 117–122 (2005)
6. ISTAG: Ambient Intelligence: from vision to reality (2003), http://ica.cordis.lu/docum ents/documentlibrary/ADS0000806EN.pdf
7. ISTAG: Scenarios for Ambient Intelligence in 2010 (2001), ftp://ftp.cordis.lu/pub/ist / docs/ istagscenarios2010.pdf

8. Kaasinen, E., Tuomisto, T., Välkkynen, P.: Ambient functionality - Use cases. In: Smart Objects & Ambient Intelligence joint conference, sOc - EUSAI, Grenoble (October 12-14, 2005)

9. Lin, C.-C., Chiu, M.-J., Hsiao, C.-C., Lee, R.-G., Tsai, Y.-S.: Wireless Health Care Service System for Elderly with Dementia. IEEE Transactions on Information Technology in Biomedicine 10(4), 696–704 (2006)

10. Marshall, D.C., Rossman, D.G.B.: Designing Qualitative Research, 3rd edn. Sage Publications, London (1999)

11. Memory mirror. http://www.cc.gatech.edu/fce/ecl/projects/dejaVu/mm/index.html

12. Mikkonen, M., Väyrynen, S., Ikonen, V., Heikkilä, M.O.: User and Concept Studies as Tools in Developing Mobile Communication Services for the Elderly. Personal and Ubiquitous Computing 6, 113–124 (2002)

13. MINAmI project home page. http://www.fp6-minami.org/

14. Miyauchi, K., Yonesawa, Y., Ogawa, H., Maki, H., Caldwell, W.M.: A Mobile phone-based Safety and Life Support System for Elderly People. In: Proceedings of the Consumer Communications and Networking Conference, pp. 81–84 (2005)

15. Roussos, G., Marsh, A.J., Maglavera, S.: Enabling pervasive computing with smart phones. IEEE Pervasive Computing 4(2), 20–27 (2005)

A Study on the Suitability of GSM Signatures for Indoor Location

Carlos Bento, Teresa Soares, Marco Veloso, and Bruno Baptista

Centro de Informatica e Sistemas da Universidade de Coimbra (CISUC)
Portugal Telecom Inovação (PTI)

Abstract. Location is an important topic on Ambient Intelligence. Different techniques are used, alone or together, to determine the position of people and objects. One aspect of this problem concerns to indoor location. Various authors propose the analysis of Radio Frequency (RF) signatures as a solution for this challenge. An approach for indoor location is the use of RF signals acquired from a Global System for Mobile Communications (GSM) by Mobile Units(MU).

In this paper we make a study based on around 485.000 signatures gathered from four buildings. We present our conclusions on the suitability and limitations of this approach for indoor location.

1 Introduction

A problem of crucial importance on Ambient Intelligence is the location of people and objects. Many proactive decisions and services are mainly, or in part, dependent on position determination.

Although the problem of open air positioning is well addressed by Global Positioning System (GPS) technologies, indoor location is a much harder one and various approaches have been adopted in the past.

Some of these approaches comprise a specific infrastructure for location. It is the case of active badge systems based on infrared technology [1], or active bats supported on RF and ultrasound signals [2]. Under adequate conditions, both solutions provide good results in terms of accuracy and precision.

Another method is indoor GPS. In this approach RF emitters placed in buildings produce signals similar to GPS devices [3].

Active badges and indoor GPS have in common the need for a dedicated infrastructure which makes these systems expensive and time consuming in terms of implementation. A different approach is followed by systems that support location on the analysis of RF signatures provided by radio stations, wireless Local Area Networks (LAN), GSM infrastructures or Bluetooh ad−hoc networks.

A system that scans radio stations is RightSPOT [4]. In this program the location of a device is supported on signal strengths from FM radio stations. RADAR is another system for location based on a WiFi infrastructure [5]. In this system signals are received from various WiFi base stations. Triangulation is used to determine the user's coordinates. Other approaches comprise, for instance, the use of Bluetooth signals [6].

B. Schiele et al. (Eds.): AmI 2007, LNCS 4794, pp. 108–123, 2007.

The RF signatures produced by GSM networks can be used for indoor location [7], [8], similarly to what is performed in WiFi environments [9], [10]. Notwithstanding, it is much harder to work with GSM scenarios due to the higher complexity of the path between the Base Station and the mobile device. In general, GSM signals are affected by complex reflection mechanisms and fading resultant from weather conditions and other fluctuations in the propagation medium.

In this paper we make a study on the suitability of GSM signatures for indoor location. We analyze around 485.000 signatures collected in four buildings with different characteristics and study those signatures concerning their stability along time, weather conditions, level of occupancy of the buildings, and diversity along the space dimension. We also test various kinds of learning algorithms and compare the quality of the classifiers produced for location.

Section two presents related work on the acquisition and study of GSM signatures. The next section describes the experimental framework and data. In section four we make a first study on the GSM signatures. Section five shows the results obtained with various kinds of learning algorithms for generation of positioning classifiers, and in the last section we list the main conclusions from this study and elaborate on the suitability and limitations of GSM signatures for indoor location.

2   Related Work

The interest in studying the use of GSM signatures for indoor positioning has increased along the last years and comes in the sequence of using these kind of techniques for indoor location supported on WiFi signatures. Otsason *et al.* [7] propose the use of extended signatures comprising not only the signal level from the 6 strongest cells but also additional ones going up to 32 GSM extra channels. In their work they stress the stability of GSM signals along time, namely for the strongest cells, and show how these signals are yet more stable than the corresponding signals for WiFi systems. In their study they present a 3 hour long reading that makes evident their statements. In Otsason's work it is also shown that the signal strength of the three strongest cells varies significantly when we walk along a building [11].

GSM signatures have also been applied to detect user activity in terms of the user being stationary, walking or driving [8]. This study is also supported on the diversity of signatures along space. This kind of prediction is less demanding than location, as it is supported on the average variation of the Euclidean distance between consecutive signatures. Comparatively, for location prediction, signatures for different locations can have the same Euclidean distance. In their work they use GSM network traces collected by three members of the team in their daily lives along one month.

Another work comprising intensive use of GSM data for location is the one performed by Chen *et al.*. In their work they collected GSM signatures comprising the signal strength for up to 7 cells along 208 hours driving in the city of Seattle. Their database comprises traces from 6756 distinct cells across three network providers.

In all these works the authors collected a large number of GSM signatures indoor and outdoor, and used them for localization purposes. Studied their stability along time and diversity along space [8], [11]. In our work we make a systematic and detailed study on the qualities of GSM signals for indoor location. We use a large data set comprising more than one hundred hours of readings inside four buildings. By studying the stability of these signatures along the time dimension we conclude on the longevity of a database of signatures for inference of position. By analyzing their stability under changes in weather conditions, and degree of occupancy of buildings, we study the potential of this approach for indoor location under real situations.

3   Experimental Framework

To help us with the process of data acquisition we built a mobile station comprising a GSM modem, a computer and a UPS unit (Figure 1). The GSM modem is a Sony-Ericsson GT47 unit. The modem was attached to a pole. It is 1.7 meters high above the floor. We developed a platform for data reading and parsing, analysis and visualization, location prediction and calculation of statistical parameters.In acquisition mode signatures were collected at a rate of around 1 signature per 2 seconds. Each signature is represented by a vector of received

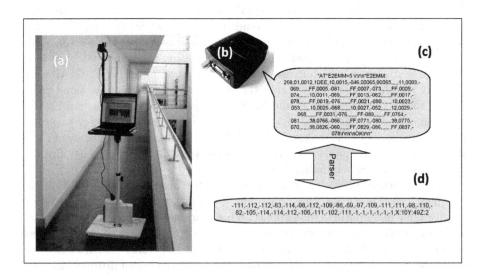

Fig. 1. (a) Mobile station, (b) GSM modem, (c) data as received from the modem, and (d) after parsing

signal strength values. This vector comprises the values for all Broadcast Channels (BCH). Each vector comprises between 16 and 32 values in dBms representing the respective BCHs received signal strengths.

Our work took place on data acquired at four buildings: Department of Informatics Engineering (DEI) in Coimbra; Escola Superior de Tecnologia e Gestão de Oliveira do Hospital (ESTGOH); family apartment at the center of a urban area in Coimbra (APA1); family apartment at the perimeter of Coimbra (APA2).

The block of the Department of Informatics Engineering is a six floor concrete building. Data acquisition took place at floors 4 and 5 at the center of contiguous rooms and along a corridor. Escola Superior de Tecnologia e Gestão de Oliveira do Hospital is also a concrete building but with a thinner structure than DEI. At ESTGOH readings were taken also at the center of rooms and in corridors along floor 2. Data acquired at APA1 and APA2 concern to small family apartments in concrete buildings and are typical living apartments in a urban area.

As we are mainly concerned with the application of GSM signatures for indoor location at room level, which is an important kind of problem for development of location based services, all the readings were taken at the center of the rooms or, if acquired along corridors, they were collected using a 5 meters step between acquisition points.

3.1   GSM Signatures

GSM signatures are saved after parsing the steams of data received from the modem in engineering mode (Figure 1). Data acquisition were performed with the goal of making two kinds of studies (stability/diversity):

1. *Stability* (independency) of the signal level along the time axis.
2. *Stability* (independency) of the signal level regarding different weather conditions.
3. *Stability* (independency) of the signal level along different degrees of occupancy of the buildings.
4. *Diversity* (dependency) of the signal level along the space dimension.

Data acquisition were performed in seven modes, with the following goals in mind:

1. *Static Short Term Reading (SSTR)* - Sequence of readings in a building, at a certain hour and day, with good weather, and low degree of occupancy of the building. Readings taken along a period of 15 or 30 minutes.

   Experimentation showed that median and standard deviation does not change significantly when we go from 15 to 30 minutes. In this way only the older readings were performed along 30 minutes, with the more recent ones being 15 minutes long, corresponds, approximately, to 450 readings per cycle.
2. *Static Long Term Reading (SLTR)* - Sequence of readings in a building, with good weather, and low degree of occupancy along all the reading period. These readings were taken, preferentially, at weekends. Readings taken along a period of 24 hours.

With a reading rate around 30 readings per minute, each SLTR comprises around 43.200 readings. In fact, the number of available readings is a little lower. Due to synchronization problems between the GSM modem and the GSMile platform, readings in a percentage between 0.2 and 0.4% are scrawled. These invalid readings are filtered before signature analysis.

3. *Static Morning/Evening/Night Reading (SMENR)* - Sequence of readings in a building, with good weather, and low degree of occupancy of the building along the entire reading period. Readings taken successively in the morning, evening, and at night along periods of 30 or 15 minutes.

4. *Static Clear/Rainy Weather Reading (SCRWR)* - Sequence of readings in a building, at about the same hour, along a clear and a rainy day. Readings are taken along two days as close as possible and by periods of 30 or 15 minutes.

5. *Static Empty/Full Reading (SEFR)* - Sequence of readings in a building, at about the same hour along two different days, one with a low degree of occupancy (people occasionally circulating along a corridor) and another with very high degree of occupancy (students leaving a crowded room) of the building. In general, readings were taken successively on a Sunday and the next Monday at an hour of the day coincident to the end of classes at DEI and ESTGOH. Readings are taken in periods of 30 or 15 minutes.

6. *Dynamic Closed Space Reading (DCSR)* - Sequence of readings along successive rooms, during a period never higher than an hour, with weather and degree of occupancy as constant as possible. Readings were taken at the center of each room. At each point of acquisition the station stopped to acquire 15 readings and then resumed its movement into the next room. The sequence of readings was repeated three times along each session.

7. *Dynamic Open Space Reading (DOSR)* - Sequence of readings along a corridor with reading points separated by 5 meters, during a period never higher than an hour, with weather and degree of occupancy as constant as possible. At each point the acquisition station stopped to acquire 15 readings (needed around 30 seconds) and then resumed its movement to the next point in the corridor. The sequence of readings was repeated three times along each session.

Table 1. Number of signatures per building and mode

	DEI	ESTGOH	APA1	APA2	TOTAL
SSTR	39600	19800	39600	39600	138600
SLTR	84000	42000	84000	84000	294000
SMENR	3960	3960	3960	3960	15840
SCRWR	3960	3960	3960	3960	15840
SEFR	3960	3960	3960	3960	15840
DOSR	1620	360	270	0	2250
DCSR	1260	720	720	450	3150
TOTAL	138360	74760	136470	135930	485520

In Table 1 we show the approximate number of readings taken at each building by mode of acquisition. These readings are the subject of study for the present paper, and are available for free use by the research community at $ftp : //dei.uc.pt/ \sim bento/45rf2387/gsmReadings/$.

4 Preliminary Results from Experimental Data

The signatures were studied concerning their stability along time, weather conditions, and degree of occupancy of the buildings, and their diversity along the different places in a building. Figure 2 presents inverted histograms representing the signal strength of the last signature for each BCH, average signal strength, and standard deviation for the sequence of readings in all the fixed point modes, except SSTR. These signatures were all gathered at the 4th floor of DEI.

At Figure 2a it is evident that for the majority of the BCHs the standard deviation of the signal strength is very small when in the SLTR mode. Looking at Figure 2b we conclude that signal strength is stable, with standard deviations similar to the ones that were found for 24 hour readings.

Comparing Figures 2b and 2c we see that for various channels the signal strength standard deviation experienced some increase on rainy conditions. This is a result that we, in general, observed along other experiments - although rain does not change the average signal strength it causes a modest increase on the signal strength standard deviation.

Figure 2d relates to readings at similar conditions as the ones in Figure 2b, but during a period in which students are leaving from classes, with crowds along the corridor where the readings are being obtained. Comparing Figures 2d and 2b we see that, for various channels, the signal strength standard deviations experienced significant to large increases. This is a result that we confirmed various times. It is evident that this perturbation is not similar for all the channels, maintaining some channels the previous stability and others becoming very unstable with the movement of crowds around the antenna. This configures effective problems for localization supported on GSM signatures.

In Figure 3 we present the same kind of graphs showed for static readings, but now using data acquired at the center of 14 rooms at floors 4 and 5 at DEI. The standard deviations presented in Figure 3a make evident a large diversity concerning the signal strength for each BCH, with the exception of three/four channels (in a total of 17 channels) not following this tendency. If we had a graph also with the readings along time we would see at the 7th room the starting of the sequence having a strong change in the values for the channel strength. This corresponds to a handover process - something that we have to take into consideration when using GSM signatures for location.

Finally, observing Figure 3b we perceive that we have a large standard deviation for the signal strength on the various BCHs, making evident the diversity of signatures received along the 18 acquisition points in the corridor.

Readings along the corridor resulted into longer signatures (vectors) than the ones at the center of rooms (21 comparing with the 17 channels at rooms).

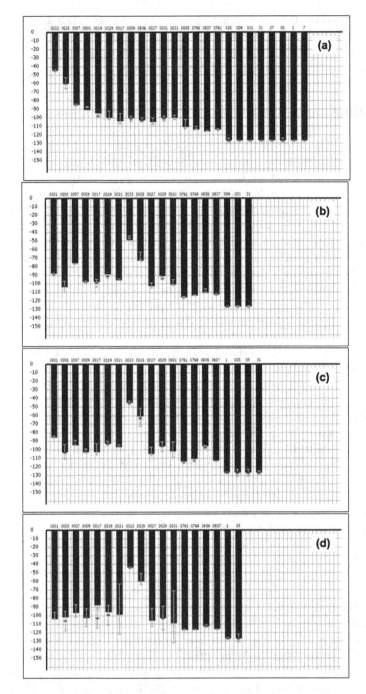

Fig. 2. Signal strength for the last signature, plus graphical representation of the average and standard deviation for each BCH in the signature for different modes of acquisition at DEI: (a) SLTR, (b) SSTR, (c) SCRWR, (d) SEFR

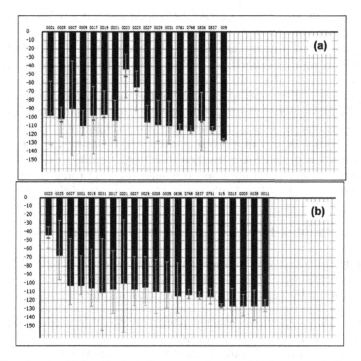

Fig. 3. Signal strength for the last signature, plus graphical representation of the average and standard deviation for each BCH in the signature for different modes of acquisition at DEI: (a) DCSR, and (b) DOSR

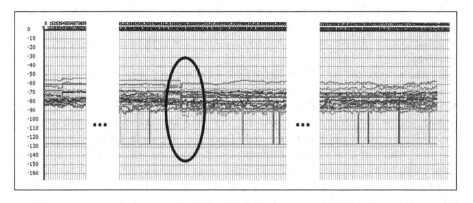

Fig. 4. Effect on the traces of opening a door in a room at APA1

Channels number 0015, 0003, 0038, and 0011 are not present in the previous readings at the center of the rooms. Notwithstanding these channels present average signal strengths bellow -120 dBm which is close to the sensibility limit of the GSM modem, making these readings insignificant and discardable.

Also concerning the analysis of the GSM signatures it is interesting to devote some attention to the graph of Figure 4.

In this Figure we present segments of the traces taken during 24 hours at the center of a room at apartment APA1. Above the aspects concerning the stability of the signal strengths along time, the interesting observation is that at a certain moment we opened the door of the room that communicates to a verandah. What happened was that this opening strongly changed the signatures - the instant is represented by the encircling oval in Figure 4.

This observation embodies a problem - the need to include, in the database, the signatures for all the configurations that have a strong possibility of happening for this room; and a promise - the opportunity of using this to perceive various kinds of modifications/activities in the room using GSM signatures.

5   Experimental Results on Indoor Location

After a preliminary study on the data concerning shape and statistical characteristics we performed experiments with various learning algorithms for prediction of indoor location. We had in mind getting conclusions on two different questions:

1. Are the GSM signatures gathered along corridors less predictive than the ones acquired at the center of rooms?
2. Can algorithms conceptually simple like k-Nearest Neighbor rival with algorithms conceptually and computationally more expensive like Bayesian Networks and Neural Networks?

The first question is obviously interesting in order to understand the limitations of this approach. The second one has special relevance when considering the implementation of location algorithms based on GSM signatures in smart phones or Personal Digital Assistants (PDA), to name devices with limited computational resources.

For these tests we organized signatures collected in mode DCSR and DOSR. Performed experiments with data gathered in each of these modes, separately for DEI, ESTGOH, APA1, and APA2. For each building we merged four sequences of readings for the points of acquisition. Then the signatures from each of these four buildings were randomly ordered. Each test for each building comprised ten runs, each one with three different configurations: 10 folds learning with cross validation; 75% of data for training and 25% for classification; 50% of data for training. We used six algorithms from Weka [13] for this experiment: Naive Bayes; Bayesian Network; Neural Network; 1-Nearest Neighbor; 3-Nearest Neighbor; and J48 (Weka implementation of C4.5 [14]).

For Naive Bayes the numeric estimator precision values were chosen based on analysis of the training data set. The Bayesian network was trained using the simple estimator with the K2 searching algorithm. For the neural network we used a multilayer perceptron with a learning rate equal to 0.3 and a momentum equal to 0.2, 500 training epochs, and a validation threshold (number of times in a row that the validation set error can get worse before training is terminated) equal to 20. The k-Nearest Neighbor run with $k = 1$ and $k = 3$, with no distance weighting, and the use of the mean absolute error. J48 was used with a confidence factor for pruning equal to 0.25, the minimum number of instances per leaf equal to 2, and the number of folds for reduced-error pruning equal to 3 (1 for pruning and 2 for growing the tree).

In Table 2 we show the number of examples per building and acquisition mode used by the learning algorithms along the training and classification phases.

Table 2. Number of examples per building and type of data partition

	10 folds	75% train 25% classif.	50% train 50% classif.	TOTAL
DEI(DCSR)	234/26	195/65	130/130	260
ESTGOH(DCSR)	288/32	240/80	160/160	320
APA1(DCSR)	72/8	60/20	40/40	80
APA2(DCSR)	180/20	150/50	100/100	200
DEI(DOSR)	162/18	135/45	90/90	180
ESTGOH(DOSR)	144/16	120/40	80/80	160
APA1(DOSR)	27/3	23/7	15/15	30

In the next subsections we present the results obtained for location at rooms (DCSR mode) and along corridors (DOSR mode).

5.1   Location at Rooms

Using the algorithms previously described and the signatures acquired at the center of the rooms - at DEI, ESTGOH, APA1 and APA2 - we obtained the results shown in Figures 5, 6, and 7. In these figures algorithm (1) is the naive Bayes, algorithm (2) the Bayesian network, algorithm (3) the multilayer perceptron, algorithm (4) the 1-Nearest Neighbor, algorithm (5) the 3-Nearest Neighbor, and algorithm (6) the J48 Tree. These figures present the percentage of correctly classified instances per algorithm and building, or by other words, the percentage of times that the classification produced by the respective learning algorithm predicted correctly the location where the GSM signature has been collected.

From the results we see that all the algorithms achieved a performance on predicting the location from moderate to very good (results between 80.46% and 100%).

In general, the results obtained at APA1 and APA2 are better than the other ones. In fact, also observing the traces for the signatures, we verified that in these buildings the changes produced by going from one room to another were stronger, although the center of the rooms are closer to each other than at DEI and ESTGOH. In terms of algorithms the ones that had higher percentages of correct results are the multilayer perceptron and the k-Nearest Neighbor (k-NN), performing the 1-NN better than the 3-NN!

```
Tester:    weka.experiment.PairedCorrectedTTester
Analysing: Percent_correct
Datasets:  4
Resultsets: 6
Confidence: 0.05 (two tailed)
Sorted by: -
Date:      23-01-2007 17:06

Datas                (1) bayes.Nai   (2) bayes.   (3) funct   (4) lazy.   (5) lazy.   (6) trees.
-----------------------------------------------------------------------------------------------
DEI                       97.88         98.42       99.15       98.85       92.85       95.12
ESTGOH                    81.50         98.13       99.38       98.78       98.59       99.13
APA1                     100.00         99.75       98.75      100.00      100.00       99.88
APA2                      99.50         99.50       99.70      100.00       99.95       99.50
-----------------------------------------------------------------------------------------------
```

Fig. 5. Percentage of correct classifications for locations at the center of rooms, using 10 folds cross-validation

```
Tester:    weka.experiment.PairedCorrectedTTester
Analysing: Percent_correct
Datasets:  4
Resultsets: 6
Confidence: 0.05 (two tailed)
Sorted by: -
Date:      23-01-2007 17:08

Datas                (1) bayes.Nai   (2) bayes.   (3) funct   (4) lazy.   (5) lazy.   (6) trees.
-----------------------------------------------------------------------------------------------
DEI                       97.85         98.16       97.70       98.01       92.19       94.02
ESTGOH                    80.46         96.52       98.51       97.38       97.26       97.76
APA1                      98.97         98.97      100.00      100.00      100.00       99.47
APA2                      99.40         99.60      100.00      100.00       99.80       98.60
-----------------------------------------------------------------------------------------------
```

Fig. 6. Percentage of correct classifications for locations at the center of rooms, using 75% of data for training and the remaining for testing

```
Tester:    weka.experiment.PairedCorrectedTTester
Analysing: Percent_correct
Datasets:  4
Resultsets: 6
Confidence: 0.05 (two tailed)
Sorted by: -
Date:      23-01-2007 17:09

Datas                (1) bayes.Nai   (2) bayes.   (3) funct   (4) lazy.   (5) lazy.   (6) trees.
-----------------------------------------------------------------------------------------------
DEI                       97.00         96.54       97.31       96.77       87.54       90.15
ESTGOH                    80.61         92.52       98.38       98.01       96.20       96.32
APA1                      99.50         99.25      100.00      100.00      100.00       97.50
APA2                      99.60         99.10       99.80       99.80       99.50       98.60
-----------------------------------------------------------------------------------------------
```

Fig. 7. Percentage of correct classifications for locations at the center of rooms, using 50% of data for training and the remaining for testing

We also find from these results that reducing the number of examples in the training data set to 50% does not degrade significantly the quality of the classification.

5.2 Location in Corridors

In this experiment we used data gathered along a corridor at DEI, ESTGOH, and APA1. We do not have data from APA2 as this apartment does not have a long open space that we can consider in this category.

The number of examples per data set for this experiment are presented in Table 2, and the results in terms of percentage of correct classifications of the locations associated to the GSM signatures are shown in Figures 8, 9, and 10.

These results show that all the algorithms, except the naive Bayes, achieved a percentage of correct classifications that goes from moderate to very good. Naive Bayes performs pretty badly at ESTGOH with results between 59.40%

```
Tester:    weka.experiment.PairedCorrectedTTester
Analysing: Percent_correct
Datasets:  3
Resultsets: 6
Confidence: 0.05 (two tailed)
Sorted by: -
Date:      22-01-2007 17:59


Datas            (1) bayes.Nai   (2) bayes.   (3) funct   (4) lazy.   (5) lazy.   (6) trees.
----------------------------------------------------------------------------------------------
DEI                    98.33        98.39       98.33       98.89       94.78        97.50
ESTGOH                 65.56        97.13       97.81       96.31       96.25        98.13
APA1                  100.00       100.00       96.67      100.00      100.00        97.00
----------------------------------------------------------------------------------------------
```

Fig. 8. Percentage of correct classifications for locations in points along a corridor with a step of 5 meters between points, using 10 folds cross-validation

```
Tester:    weka.experiment.PairedCorrectedTTester
Analysing: Percent_correct
Datasets:  3
Resultsets: 6
Confidence: 0.05 (two tailed)
Sorted by: -
Date:      22-01-2007 18:15


Datas            (1) bayes.Nai   (2) bayes.   (3) funct   (4) lazy.   (5) lazy.   (6) trees.
----------------------------------------------------------------------------------------------
DEI                    97.73        98.39       98.43       99.77       96.02        97.07
ESTGOH                 63.27        96.26       97.76       95.76       95.51        98.01
APA1                  100.00       100.00       97.32      100.00      100.00       100.00
----------------------------------------------------------------------------------------------
```

Fig. 9. Percentage of correct classifications for locations in points along a corridor with a step of 5 meters between points, using 75% of data for training and the remaining for testing

```
Tester:    weka.experiment.PairedCorrectedTTester
Analysing: Percent_correct
Datasets:  3
Resultsets: 6
Confidence: 0.05 (two tailed)
Sorted by: -
Date:      22-01-2007 18:22
```

Datas	(1) bayes.Nai	(2) bayes.	(3) funct	(4) lazy.	(5) lazy.	(6) trees.
DEI	95.89	96.33	98.00	98.33	90.89	95.00
ESTGOH	59.40	93.00	97.50	95.50	95.62	98.13
APA1	100.00	100.00	98.00	100.00	100.00	97.33

Fig. 10. Percentage of correct classifications for locations in points along a corridor with a step of 5 meters between points, using 50% of data for training and the remaining for testing

and 65.56%. Again the 1-NN performs consistently better than the 3-NN. These good results are closely followed by the ones obtained with the Bayesian network, neural networks and J48.

Again we found that the results using only 50% of the examples for training does not degrade significantly the performance of the learning algorithms, although for this experiment the initial number of examples is much lower than the ones used for the experiment at the center of rooms.

6   Conclusions and Future Work

Performing indoor location based on signatures of GSM signals is a challenging task due to the various types of perturbations that the received signal suffers along its path. Signal propagation is quite sensitive to changes due to the movement of people and objects, weather conditions, changes in the physical path from the base station to the receiver, and changes in the building landscape. In this way, although this task is similar to the one performed by other systems like RADAR, in fact, GSM systems have to deal with a much more complex RF scenario.

The study of the 485.000 signatures gathered in four buildings with different configurations enlightened some questions we had on the suitability of GSM signals for indoor location.

Firstly, and concerning the stability of the signatures along time, weather changes and modifications on the number of persons circulating on the area, we concluded that GSM signals are quite stable along time. This becomes evident from the 24 hour long readings we performed at the buildings. These long cycle readings achieved similar results at the four buildings.

The only perturbation we found from time to time was on single BCHs that for a reading changed abruptly its signal level. In general, this is something that does not affect the results on indoor location, as the algorithms that are used take into consideration all the channels and are robust to noise on an isolated channel.

Concerning to weather perturbations (like rainy days) we observed that the majority of channels increase a little their standard deviation. This is also something that does not introduce significant perturbation on the process of indoor location.

Regarding to the stability of signatures, on presence of crowds around the antenna, we observed strong changes on the signal level. Those changes affect some channels leaving others unchanged, which introduces clear difficulties for the location algorithms.

Secondly we were interested in understanding if we had a good diversity of signatures when going from one point to another. In fact, as it was shown in Figures of section 3, readings taken along a sequence of rooms or a sequence of points along a corridor at intervals of 5 meters both exhibited large standard deviation and significant change.

Another observation was that changes in the configuration of rooms like opening/closing a door results into significant changes on the GSM signatures. This is, in one way, a problem that we have to take into consideration for location purposes, but it is also an opportunity for the use of GSM signatures for inexpensive detection of activity in a room.

In this study we were also interested in understanding how well known learning algorithms deal with the problem of prediction of locations from GSM signatures. Previous studies used some of these algorithms with success [7], [8], [15] but we wanted to make an extensive comparison of them and understand if methods conceptually simple like k-NN could compete with more sophisticated ones like Bayesian networks and neural networks.

From our observations we found that algorithms like 1-NN and 3-NN performed quite well, and at a certain level with surprise, we concluded that, in general, 1-NN performed better than the more expensive 3-NN.

As we previously guessed, the learning algorithms performed better (higher percentage of correct locations) in buildings with small rooms and corridors like the family apartments than in larger ones like DEI and ESTGOH. We believe that the more intricate concrete structure of an apartment, without large open spaces, like the ones we have at DEI and ESTGOH, improves the diversity of signatures along the space dimension and so facilitates the generation of good classifiers for location.

All GSM signatures were gathered at the center of rooms or along corridors. A criticism that can be made to this option is how well the conclusions on stability and diversity on these data can be transposed to signatures gathered in other points of a room. In order to study the sensibility of the location process to the point in room used for data gathering we constructed a location based reminder using the data obtained at DEI [16] that makes location at room level. We inserted reminders in this application for various rooms at DEI. None of the rooms were contiguous. The signatures were taken at different points of the respective room, not necessary at the center. The reminders were fired all the times in the correct room or nearby. Although this experiment does not provide quantitative results, we conclude that also other points in a room, not at the center, provide data acceptable for location at room level.

A problem that has to be taken into consideration is the mechanism of handover that sometimes takes place during the process of training the system or during the location process. It is known that a handover can take place in different situations - defined by the GSM standards and operators - and this makes, sometimes, difficult the training of the learning algorithm.

Another problem concerns to changes on the plan of frequencies, and to the splitting of sectors in the Base Stations. These changes can be quite frequent in dense urban areas and imply the need to perform corresponding training operations from the side of the location system. To our understanding this is a main obstacle to the success of this kind of technologies. We think that applying some well known processes of recalibration, used in other areas, could come in help of this approach for indoor location. We intend to study this problem in the future.

References

1. Want, R., Hopper, A., Falcão, V., Gibbons, J.: The active badge location system. ACM Transaction on Information Systems 10(1), 91–102 (1992)
2. Ward, A., Jones, A., Hopper, A.: A new location technique for the active office. IEEE Personal Communications 4(5), 42–47 (1997)
3. van Diggelen, F., Abraham, C.: Indoor GPS Technology. CTIA Wireless-Agenda, Dallas (May 2001)
4. Krumm, J., Cermak, G., Horvitz, E.: RightSPOT: A Novel Sense of Location for a Smart Personal Object. In: Dey, A.K., Schmidt, A., McCarthy, J.F. (eds.) UbiComp 2003. LNCS, vol. 2864, Springer, Heidelberg (2003)
5. Bahl, P., Padmanabhan, V.N.: RADAR: An In-Building RF-based User Location and Tracking System. In: IEEE INFOCOM 2000, Tel-Aviv, Israel (2000)
6. Patil, A.P.: Performance of Bluetooth Technologies and Their Applications to Location Sensing. Master of Science Dissertation. Department of Electrical and Computer Engineering (2002)
7. Otsason, V., Varshavsky, A., LaMarca, A., de Lara, E.: Accurate GSM Indoor Localization. In: Beigl, M., Intille, S.S., Rekimoto, J., Tokuda, H. (eds.) UbiComp 2005. LNCS, vol. 3660, Springer, Heidelberg (2005)
8. Sohn, T., Varshavsky, A., LaMarca, A., Chen, M.Y., Choudhury, T., Smith, I., Consolvo, S., Hightower, J., Griswold, W.G., de Lara, E.: Mobility Detection Using Everyday GSM Traces. In: Dourish, P., Friday, A. (eds.) UbiComp 2006. LNCS, vol. 4206, Springer, Heidelberg (2006)
9. Lorincz, K., Welsh, M.: MoteTrack: A Robust, Decentralized Approach to RF-Based Location Tracking. In: Strang, T., Linnhoff-Popien, C. (eds.) LoCA 2005. LNCS, vol. 3479, Springer, Heidelberg (2005)
10. Battiti, R., Nhat, T.L., Villani, A.: Location-aware computing: a neural network model for determining location in wireless LANs, Technical Report DIT-02-0083 (2002)
11. Otsason, V.: Accurate GSM Indoor Localization Using Wide GSM Fingerprinting. Master's Thesis, University of Tartu (2005)

12. Chen, M.Y., Sohn, T., Chmelev, D., Haehnel, D., Hightower, J., Hughes, J., LaMarca, A., Potter, F., Smith, I., Varshavsky, A.: Practical Metropolitan-Scale Positioning for GSM Phones. In: Dourish, P., Friday, A. (eds.) UbiComp 2006. LNCS, vol. 4206, Springer, Heidelberg (2006)
13. Witten, I.H., Frank, E.: Data Mining: Practical machine learning tools and techniques, 2nd edn. Morgan Kaufmann, San Francisco (2005)
14. Quinlan, J.R.: C4.5: Programs for Machine Learning. Morgan Kaufmann Publishers, Inc., San Francisco (1988)
15. LaMarca, A., Chawathe, Y., Consolvo, S., Hightower, J., Smith, I., Scott, J., Sohn, T., Howard, J., Hughes, J., Potter, F., Tabert, J., Powledge, P., Borriello, G., Schilit, B.: Place Lab: Device Positioning Using Radio Beacons in the Wild. In: Gellersen, H.-W., Want, R., Schmidt, A. (eds.) PERVASIVE 2005. LNCS, vol. 3468, Springer, Heidelberg (2005)
16. Baptista, B., Bento, C.: InfoAssistant: A Personal Assistant Based on Indoor Location, Technical Specification. University of Coimbra and Portugal Telecom (March 2007)

How Computer Vision Can Help in Outdoor Positioning

Ulrich Steinhoff[1], Dušan Omerčević[2], and Roland Perko[2],
Bernt Schiele[1], and Aleš Leonardis[2]

[1] TU Darmstadt, Germany
[2] University of Ljubljana, Slovenia

Abstract. Localization technologies have been an important focus in ubiquitous computing. This paper explores an underrepresented area, namely computer vision technology, for outdoor positioning. More specifically we explore two modes of positioning in a challenging real world scenario: single snapshot based positioning, improved by a novel high-dimensional feature matching method, and continuous positioning enabled by combination of snapshot and incremental positioning. Quite interestingly, vision enables localization accuracies comparable to GPS. Furthermore the paper also analyzes and compares possibilities offered by the combination of different subsets of positioning technologies such as WiFi, GPS and dead reckoning in the same real world scenario as for vision based positioning.

Keywords: computer vision based positioning, local invariant features, sensor fusion for outdoor localization.

1 Introduction

Today, there exist a wide variety of location systems both commercial and research with different levels of accuracy, coverage, cost of installation and maintenance, and frequency of location updates [1,2]. Not surprisingly however any system has its respective strengths and weaknesses. For example standard GPS-based systems can achieve good levels of accuracy but the coverage is often limited in practice. Positioning based on WiFi (802.11 access points) is an interesting alternative but the achievable accuracy strongly depends on the density of mapped beacons [3]. Also GSM-based positioning has been advocated to achieve meaningful levels of accuracy, usable for various applications, even though not (yet?) in the range of GPS-based positioning [4].

Another far less explored alternative is computer vision-based positioning. There are several reasons why computer vision-based positioning presents an interesting alternative to more traditional positioning systems. First, the ubiquity of camera-equipped mobile devices and proliferation of high-speed wireless data connections increases the chances of acceptance of such a technology. Second, recent advances in computer vision technology suggest that vision-based positioning may enable highly accurate positioning based on single camera snapshots

B. Schiele et al. (Eds.): AmI 2007, LNCS 4794, pp. 124–141, 2007.

[5]. And third, digital map providers such as Tele Atlas, as well as Google and Microsoft, already possess and continue to record large image databases of urban areas and other environments. All these reasons, individually and taken together motivate us to explore and analyze vision-based technology for positioning, alone and in combination with other outdoor positioning methods.

This paper aims to address the following questions related to vision-based positioning: what is a realistic level of accuracy which can be obtained with current vision technology using different cameras including today's cell-phone cameras; how can snapshot based positioning be augmented to provide continuous location estimates; how does vision-based positioning compare to other technologies such as GPS, WiFi and Dead Reckoning and how may these technologies complement each other. In order to better understand the applicability of this technology, we will also discuss requirements and constrains of today's vision technology.

In this context we develop, describe and analyze two basic modes of vision-based positioning. The *first mode* uses single snapshots (called query images in the following) taken e.g. with the camera of a standard cell-phone, while the *second mode* employs additionally pedestrian dead reckoning. The first mode of operation positions the single query image w.r.t. a database of geo-referenced images and therefore allows to estimate the user's location as well as the user's orientation in world coordinates. As can be seen from the experiments presented in this paper the achievable median accuracies are comparable to or even better than standard GPS-based positioning. This first mode can be used to position oneself at the beginning of a trip e.g. after exiting a building or a subway station and to obtain directions and local map-information for further navigation. Due to the high levels of accuracies one could also use a single snapshot to correct a position-estimate obtained by another, less accurate technology such as GSM (e.g. close to the destination of a trip). This mode can be used also to support augmented reality applications where additional information is provided e.g. for a tourist site or a shopping mall. The second mode of vision-based positioning enables continuous positioning of a walking person by combining single snapshots for accurate positioning and an inertial sensor to enable incremental update of the current position estimate between single snapshots. To allow continuous position estimates we deploy a dead reckoning (DR) device. As the incremental update will obviously degrade over time we use a Kalman filter formulation to integrate multiple position estimates based on different snapshots and the DR estimate. The applicability of this mode of vision-based positioning is similar to that of other continuous positioning technologies such as GPS and WiFi. Therefore, the accuracies obtained by this mode of operation will be directly compared to these technologies.

The contributions of this paper are the following. First, we analyze the state-of-the-art in computer vision for snapshot based positioning using different types of cameras under realistic conditions. Second, we improve upon the existing vision-based position systems (e.g., [5]) by employing a novel high-dimensional feature matching method of [6]. Third, to enable continuous positioning we complement vision-based positioning with an incremental movement estimate obtained from DR. In particular we will discuss the relation of average distance between snapshots and accuracy of position estimate. Fourth, we record realistic data of pedestrians tracks in the city of Ljubljana including GPS, WiFi and DR sensor data as well as snapshots. Fifth, we analyze and compare the different technologies individually and in combination in terms of accuracy and in terms of requirements.

In the following we present related work (Sec. 2), then we give an overview and evaluation of the vision based positioning sytem (Sec. 3). Secondly (Sec. 4) we employ this system in combination with pedestrian dead reckoning to enable continuous positioning. Thirdly (Sec. 5) we evaluate the positioning by meaningful combinations of GPS, WiFi and DR in our scenario for a comparison to vision based position methods, and close with a summary and outlook (Sec. 6).

2   Related Work

Vision-based positioning recently attracted a lot of attention, especially because of the proliferation of digital cameras and camera phones. The authors of [7] and [8] were among the first to present a camera phone based prototype for personal navigation in urban environments. They first recognize the building in the query image and then estimate the geometric relation between the facade in the query image and the images or models in the database. However, they rely on the presence of dominant planes and estimation of vertical vanishing direction for alignment. In [9], the authors also use buildings as landmarks for localization in a two-stage recognition process but rely only on geometric regularities of man-made structures, such as parallel and orthogonal lines. A different approach [10] aims to recognize user location from images captured with a camera-equipped mobile device by first performing image-based search over a database that indexes a small fraction of the Web utilizing hybrid color histograms. Then, relevant keywords on these web pages are automatically identified and submitted to a text-based search engine (e.g., Google). The resulting image set is filtered to retain images close to the original query image thus enabling approximate user localization if the matching images have the location attributed or the web pages include some location information (e.g., street address).

All methods described up to now provide only very approximate positioning that is inferior compared to the accuracy of the GPS. Recent advances in computer vision algorithms and hardware performance have however enabled approaches that can provide in near real time not only similar but in many circumstances even better positioning accuracy than provided by the GPS. For example, given a database of reference images of city streets tagged by geographical position, the system of [5] computes the geographical position of a novel query image within a few meters accuracy. In their approach local visual features are used first to select the closest reference images in the database and then to estimate the camera motions between the query image and the closest reference images. The estimated camera motions are then used to position the query image by means of triangulation.

Among the systems enabling the continuous positioning, the positioning systems using WiFi access points either use "fingerprinting" [11,12] or simply the estimated positions of receivable access points from public or company owned databases [13,14,15]. While fingerprinting can obtain high levels of accuracies (close to 1m) it also requires a tedious calibration effort which seems unfeasible for large areas with dynamic changes in the access point infrastructure (often the case in outdoor scenarios). Other approaches like PlaceLab have been designed with a low barrier-of-entry and a wide availability in mind which is why we build on this framework in the paper. GSM-based positioning is not as well developed today even though network-providers and researchers are working towards better levels of accuracies [4].

In pedestrian navigation by dead reckoning (DR), the authors of [16] were one of the first to use inertial sensors, compass and fusion with GPS, which was the basis for the Pointresearch DRM Module, commercially available in the 5th generation [17]. There is also an extensive body of academic research on the subject. The work of [18] was among the first to introduce the use of additional gyroscope sensors and leading to commercially available devices [19], furthermore a range of other approaches exist [20,21,22,23,24]. Dead reckoning enables a relative or incremental position estimation due to the user's orientation and walking speed, typically using the dependency of step frequency and step length [25]. To realize an absolute position estimate this information is in most approaches fused with GPS data only.

3   Vision-Based Positioning

In the following we first give an overview of our approach to vision-based positioning. Then we present the employed algorithms in detail. Finally, we describe the setup of experiments and present the results of evaluation of our approach in a real world scenario.

Method overview. Fig. 1 illustrates our approach to vision-based positioning. In our approach, similarly as in [5], the user takes a query image (blue frame) at his current position and this image is matched to a database of reference images (green frames) by matching local visual features. Matched local visual features are further used to estimate geometric relations between the query image and the matching reference images. The estimated geometric relations are then employed to position and orient the query image (and consequently the user) w.r.t. the reference images. An important requirement for such a vision-based positioning system is that the reference images must adequately cover the area where vision-based positioning shall be performed. It is important that the query image contains sufficient overlap with at least one, but preferably more reference images. The number of reference images thus required depends on the type of the scene and can be substantial (i.e., several thousand reference images per square kilometer). While this is a significant number of images, companies such as Tele Atlas, Google and Microsoft work on such databases already today for many cities around the world. An additional requirement regarding the

Fig. 1. A query image D50-R10 (thick, blue frame) and some reference images (thin, green frames) used to position and orient the query image and consequently the user. The two reference images on the left were shot from the standpoint T14, while the two reference images on the right were shot from the standpoint T13. Some geometric relations relating the query image with one of the reference images are indicated by the dark green lines.

reference images is that the geographic positions from where the reference images were taken must be measured accurately, e.g. by GPS or by more traditional surveying techniques (e.g. theodolite), while the absolute camera orientations of the reference images can be estimated in the preprocessing stage by estimating geometric relations between reference images.

Matching image regions. The local visual features are detected independently in each image using some subregion saliency measure (e.g., specific area around corners, area of similar color, area bounded by curves) that is invariant to common image transformations such as viewpoint or photometric changes. The image subregions selected as the local visual features are then described in a compact form (typically as a feature vector) retaining only information on image structures that is independent of common image transformations. Based on recent performance evaluations [26] and [27] we have chosen Maximally Stable Extremal Regions (MSER) as local feature detector [28] and Scale Invariant Feature Transform (SIFT) as feature descriptor [29]. The SIFT descriptor describes the image subregion by a 128-dimensional vector representing a histogram of gradient orientations.

Matching images. The first step of the presented vision-based positioning system is to identify which reference images depict the same scene as the query image. For this we use a novel image matching method [6] based on the concept of meaningful nearest neighbors. A local visual feature detected in a reference image is considered a meaningful nearest neighbor if it is sufficiently close to a query feature such that it is an outlier to a background feature distribution of irrelevant match candidates. The background feature distribution is estimated from the extended neighborhood of a query feature given by its k nearest neighbors. When applied to image matching, meaningful nearest neighbors are independently weighted for each query feature. The sum of weights then defines the similarity of a reference image to the query image.

To make search for k nearest neighbors more efficient, we employ a novel approximate nearest neighbors search method of [6] that is based on sparse coding with an overcomplete basis set and provides a ten-fold speed-up over an exhaustive search even for high dimensional spaces while retaining excellent approximation to an exact nearest neighbors search.

Estimation of geometric relations. The second step of the presented vision-based positioning system is to estimate geometric relations between the query image and the matching reference images. The type of geometric relation that we employ is called epipolar geometry [30]. Epipolar geometry is independent of scene structure and only depends on the cameras' internal parameters and relative pose. If the cameras' internal parameters are known, the relative pose of the two images can be extracted from the known epipolar geometry. The most important internal parameter of the camera is the focal length that we acquire from the EXIF header of the images while we assume standard values for other internal parameters of the camera [30]. If the internal parameters of the camera are known and if at least five correspondences are established by matching image regions of the two views, the epipolar geometry relating two views can be estimated using the *five-point algorithm* [31]. Existing matching algorithms cannot guarantee that all correspondences (matching image regions) are true correspondences, i.e., that they are projections of the same structure in 3D world [9], so we resort to a hypothesize-and-test approach in order to find a subset of true correspondences among all the matching image regions. In the hypothesize-and-test approach we first construct a hypothesis by calculating the epipolar geometry from a selected five-tuple of the correspondences and then we test how many tentative correspondences are consistent with the hypothesized epipolar geometry. The hypothesized epipolar geometry consistent with most of the tentative correspondences is selected as the representative one. It is infeasible to consider all possible five-tuples of correspondences so we construct hypotheses only from a few dozen tentative correspondences with the highest weight as provided by the feature matching algorithm [6].

Positioning the query image. In the final step of our approach we use the estimated geometric relations to position and orient the query image w.r.t. the reference images. Our positioning method chooses among a set of predefined positioning strategies based on the number and the type of estimated geometric relations. The *first* strategy is used when the query image and one of the reference images are shot from locations that are very close together compared to the depicted scene. In such a case the query image is positioned at the location of the reference image, while the orientation of the query image is calculated by estimating rotation relating the query and the reference image. The *second* strategy uses triangulation to position the query image. This strategy is chosen either when we know the geometric relations of the query image with three or more reference images not shot at the same standpoint, or if we know the geometric relations of the query image with two reference images and we also know the camera orientation of at least one reference image. The *third* strategy is selected when only two geometric relations of the query and reference images are known and we do not know the camera orientations of the reference images. This strategy also uses triangulation to position the query image, but with an additional assumption that the query image was shot at the same height from the ground as the two reference images. The *fourth* strategy is chosen when only one geometric relation is known. In such a case the query image is positioned at the location of the respective reference image. If no geometric relation can be estimated, then we use the *fifth* strategy that positions the query image at the location of the most similar reference image, but only if the reference images is similar enough.

3.1 Setup and Experiments

In our experiments we used Ljubljana urban image data set[1] that consists of 612 reference images of an urban environment covering an area of 200 × 200 square meters (see Fig. 2). At each of the 34 standpoints 18 images were captured at 6 orientations and 3 tilt angles covering a field of view of 360° × 100° (see Fig. 3). All images were taken with a Nikon D50 digital SLR camera with a field of view of 88° × 52° at a resolution of 6 megapixel in November 2005 in overcast weather. The positions of the reference standpoints were measured by classical surveying techniques using a theodolite for relative measurements (with an accuracy of 10cm) and a high accurate GPS device for absolute positioning (accuracy 50cm).

The 17 query images were shot from 13 distinct positions where a user might want to position himself. The query images were captured in January 2007 in light snowfall weather. At every query location three images were shot using Nikon D50, Sony DSC-W1, and Sony Ericsson (SE) W800 cameras. Nikon D50 is a high-end digital SLR camera with 6 megapixels, Sony DSC-W1 is a standard consumer grade camera with 5 megapixels and SE W800 is a mobile phone equipped with a 2 megapixels camera. The ground truth positions were calculated by measuring the distance from each query point to two geo-referenced standpoints of the Ljubljana urban image data set. Nine query images taken by the three cameras at three different standpoints together with the most similar reference images are presented in Fig. 4.

---

[1] Available online at http://vicos.fri.uni-lj.si/LUIS34/

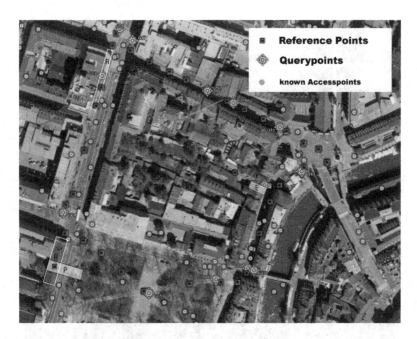

Fig. 2. Overview of the Test area. In the image the reference points, snapshot points and known access points from the wigle.net database are shown. (P) marks a pedestrian underpass, (E) a passage and (R) roofed areas.

3.2 Results

The results of the vision-based positioning system are given in Table 1. The position of the query images could be established in 14 (13 for SE W800) out of 17 cases with a median positioning error of 4.9m for Nikon D50 camera, 6.6m for Sony DSC-W1 camera and 6.2m for SE W800 camera phone. The method fails altogether if vegetation or dynamic objects compromise most of the user image.

The results of the Nikon D50 camera are discussed in more detail and these insights also hold for the other two cameras. For seven query images the first positioning strategy was selected (Q02, Q08, Q10, Q11, Q12, Q15 and Q16) so their position was set to the corresponding reference point. In the case of query image Q02 the algorithm incorrectly selected this positioning strategy, therefore the localization error is large (31.8m). For three query images (Q01, Q13 and Q14) the second positioning strategy was selected so that their positions were estimated by triangulation (an example is presented in Fig. 5). In four cases (Q04, Q07, Q09 and Q17) only one related image was found, so that their positions were set to these reference positions by choosing the fourth strategy. As seen with Q17 large errors could be produced when triangulation is not possible. The remaining three images (Q03, Q05 and Q06) were not matched at all, since any approach based on local features has problems with images holding just vegetation or if large parts of the images are occluded (examples are shown in Fig. 6).

Fig. 3. The 18 images shot from standpoint T02 are shown. Using 6 orientations and 3 tilt angles a field of view of 360° × 100° is covered.

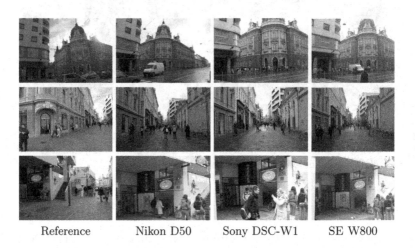

Reference   Nikon D50   Sony DSC-W1   SE W800

Fig. 4. Three out of 17 query images for Nikon D50, Sony DSC-W1 and SE W800. In the first column are the most similar reference images.

In conclusion the vision-based positioning system works quite well, however more effort should be put into improving the five positioning strategies that we use to position and orient the query image w.r.t. the reference images. The major improvement of our vision-based positioning system over the system of [5] is that we employ a novel high-dimensional feature matching method of [6]. By using this feature matching method we are able to identify with much higher accuracy than the existing methods (e.g., [32]) which reference images depict the same scene as the query image. Additionally, the weighting of correspondences provided by the method of [6] increases the probability of correct estimation of geometric relations. It is also worth to mention, that the number of reference images to be searched could be cut down substantially if a coarse initial position would be provided by non-vision sensors such as GPS, WiFi or GSM. The speed-up thus achieved would be linear with the number of reference images to be related to the query image.

Table 1. Comparison of positioning accuracy for Nikon D50, Sony DSC-W1 and SE W800 cameras. All results are presented in meters.

Image		Q01	Q02	Q03	Q04	Q05	Q06	Q07	Q08	Q09
Nikon D50		8.7	31.8	NA	8.2	NA	NA	4.3	1.7	5.0
Sony DSC-W1		9.4	31.8	NA	8.2	NA	NA	4.3	1.7	5.0
SE W800		6.1	23.8	NA	8.2	NA	NA	4.3	1.7	5.0
mean error	**median error**	Q10	Q11	Q12	Q13	Q14	Q15	Q16	Q17	
7.8	**4.9**	4.7	4.7	3.7	7.7	5.5	2.0	2.0	18.9	
11.2	**6.6**	4.7	10.4	3.7	37.7	4.6	14.7	2.0	18.9	
14.8	**6.2**	26.8	NA	3.7	50.2	6.2	36.1	2.0	18.9	

D50-Q01   T01-3U   T34-3U

Fig. 5. The query image Q01 (left) is matched to two reference images and therefore the position could be calculated by means of triangulation

Fig. 6. Query images that could not be positioned (bottom row) and the most similar, manually selected images among reference images (top row)

4 Continuous Positioning by Vision and Dead Reckoning

In the previous section we presented single snapshot based positioning. In this section we aim to combine the vision based positioning system with an incremental positioning system to allow continuous localization. This also allows the comparison to the evaluation of continuous positioning by different combinations of GPS, WiFi & DR (Sec. 5) in a real world scenario, which employs the same pedestrian dead reckoning device. In our evaluation we consider also the impact of the frequency of vision snapshots to the overall accuracy of the system.

For the fusion of vision-based snapshot positioning and relative motion estimation, whose accuracy degrade over time, we employ a Kalman filter. For the prediction of the state vector for any given timestep, the time and the estimated displacement since the last snaphot are employed, while the variance in the update by vision is considered as static value, derived from the average accuracy of the vision results.

4.1 Setup

The setup used for our experiments in this and the next section consists mainly of standard, of-the-shelf hardware. As main device for our recordings we use a tablet PC, which allows easy marking of the ground truth while walking for recording. For the experiments on multi-sensor positioning in the next Sec. 5 the computer is equipped with a suitable PCMCIA Wireless Network Card for scanning 802.11b/g networks (Prism 2 chipset) and connected via Bluetooth to a Holux GR236 GPS receiver (SiRFIII), placed on the shoulder of the user for best possible reception. For gathering relative position information we use a Dead Reckoning Compass (DRC) from Vectronix [19], which measures the displacement of the user with an electronic compass and step estimation by accelerometer and outputs an estimated position in geographic coordinates once a second over a wired connection. We decided to record the standard output of positions near the geographic point of origin in a stretch, not using the feature of setting the device to an initial position for adapted output to the current geographic height. As we're interested in the relative displacement per time interval in meters for the fusion, this allows for a more flexible evaluation. The DRC is placed on the recommended position on the back of the user, near the body's center of gravity. The so-called body height parameter, which influences the internal step length estimation, is calibrated to the user, and the magnetic offset adjusted to the local declination of the earth magnetic field. No individual optimization for the single traces or part of traces was done for a realistic setting. For the body offset angle a value of zero degree was used, as expected by the position of the sensor on the body. Good fixation of a DR sensor and a static body offset parameter can be expected to work better in realistic scenarios than current techniques for online correction [17]. For the recording we used an adopted version of the Placelab stumbler, which was extended to support the DR device and for creation of timestamped logfile entries by clicks on the map when passing ground truth points.

4.2 Experiments

For the evaluation we analyzed 7 different traces in an area of the inner city of Ljubljana. For ground truth we decided to use the 47 exactly measured points (34 reference & 13 query image points), which have a mean distance of about 20m (Fig. 2). Additional ground truth points were introduced for the pedestrian underpass (P) and behind the entry to an alleyway (E). Roofed areas with partially occluded view to the sky are marked with R. Each trace consists of a different set of these points and we recorded timestamps when passing them. The length of the traces varies from 0.6km to 1.75km, with a total length of 7.4km. These traces are outdoors, with only short parts with obstructed view to the sky. To simulate normal pedestrian behavior, we walked constantly and did not stop on each ground truth point, except for a small portion including the query points for the visual positioning. The photo shooting on query points was simulated by stopping and turning, while the actual photos were taken separately with the 3 different cameras (Fig. 4) on the same day and commonly used for all traces.

4.3   Results

As motivated earlier this second mode of vision-based positioning incorporates the relative position estimate from DRC to allow continuous positioning like typically provided by GPS devices. For this we evaluate the same traces as for the multi-sensor positioning (Sec. 5) but employ different sub-sets of image-based query points in combination with dead reckoning. A Kalman filter is used to fuse the information from the vision-based positioning and the movement estimate from the DRC device. More specifically, whenever a trace reaches one of the included query points a correction is achieved by vision-based positioning and between these points the position estimate solely relies on the DRC-estimate. Note that the correction is only available in case of a successful positioning of the query image (cf. Table 1) For traces not starting on a query point an initial error of 10m is assumed. In Table 2 we show results for the median error over all traces for the different cameras. The highest overall accuracy (9.5m to 10.3m depending on camera type) is reached when using all available query points. Reducing the number of query points results in less accurate position estimates: using (on average) only every 2nd (12.4m to 12.9m), every 3rd (12.6m to 14.4m) or every 4th query point (14.1m to 14.9m). Fig. 7 shows a representative example. This reduction in accuracy however is quite low given that the average distance between the query points is increased from about 100m to 330m. Further increasing the average distance between query points to 269m and 455m mostly results in a larger variance of the achievable accuracies (11.2m to 18.6m). In general the results show, that Kalman filter based fusion of vision-based positioning and the dead reckoning device provides the user with an accurate position

Table 2. Results of vision-based positioning with dead reckoning for different query points available on the traces and the used cameras.

Available QPs	Nikon D50	Sony DSC-W1	SE W800	avg. QP distance
All	9.5m	10.2m	10.3m	94.5m
every 2nd (avg)	12.4m	12.9m	12.5m	172.7m
every 3rd (avg)	12.6m	13.1m	14.4m	279.9m
every 4th (avg)	14.1m	14.7m	14.9m	319.3m
Q04,Q07,Q13	11.9m	13.1m	14.7m	283.6m
Q04,Q09,Q13	11.2m	12.9m	14.0m	269.0m
Q04,Q13	14.9m	18.3m	18.6m	455.3m

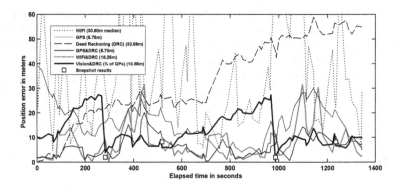

Fig. 7. Comparison of different sensors and combinations for Trace 6 (1743m). This is the longest trace and starts in the park (south) and uses reference points counterclockwise for 2 rounds (c.f. Fig. 2).

estimate even when using only few snapshots on the trace. As we will see in Sec. 5, the accuracies are often better than WiFi & DR-based positioning and in many cases comparable to or slightly worse than GPS. In Fig. 7 we show results for the longest trace with a set of every 4th querypoint available. Also included are the results from multi-sensor positioning (Sec. 5) for comparison.

5   Multi-sensor Positioning

For comparison to the vision-based positioning we evaluate the different non-vision-based positioning techniques, and combinations thereof in the same scenario. In our experiments we employ location information from GPS, WiFi and DR and combine them in different combinations to a single position estimate. We decided to build on the open source Placelab framework [13] for our experiments, as it offers a flexible basis with built-in WiFi positioning and fusion of location information of different sensors with a particle filter [33]. As an important aspect the framework aims less for precision than on coverage for the WiFi part. Instead of tedious reference measurements, which are unrealistic for a greater outdoor area, it makes use of public available maps of access point, to which users can easily contribute by wardriving/warwalking.

5.1   Setup and Experiments

As introduced in Sec. 4, we use for the recording mostly of-the-shelf hardware and an adopted version of the placelab stumbler, which was extended to support the dead reckoning device as additional sensor and to support marking of the ground truth points with timestamped log entries. As a database for access points maps we used the freely available and growing *wigle.net* database with currently over 9 million mapped access points.

For the evaluation of positioning by different combinations of GPS, WiFi and Dead Reckoning we extended the Placelab framework [13] to fuse the relative

Table 3. Comparison of positioning accuracy for Multi-Sensor based positioning. All results are presented in meters.

| | Length (m) | Single Sensors | | | | | | | | |
| | | WiFi | | | GPS | | | Dead Reckoning | | |
		mean	med	max	mean	med	max	mean	med	max
1	866.2	30.0	22.3	88.0	11.7	10.4	29.4	19.9	21.6	35.7
2	828.5	36.5	29.5	124.6	12.5	11.1	33.9	15.2	14.8	26.2
3	598.4	56.2	48.1	117.8	9.1	6.2	53.2	13.1	13.6	18.5
4	689.9	39.3	33.1	93.0	10.4	8.4	29.0	26.6	29.6	37.9
5	999.2	57.7	50.2	154.3	10.2	7.3	28.6	20.2	24.2	29.7
6	1743.8	36.3	30.6	122.9	7.8	5.7	31.5	32.6	26.9	58.8
7	1647.7	51.5	38.6	211.9	8.2	6.7	21.2	16.4	13.0	40.7
		43.9	**36.1**	**211.9**	**10.0**	**8.0**	**53.2**	**20.6**	**20.5**	**58.8**

| | Length (m) | Particle Filter | | | | | | | | |
| | | GPS&WiFi&DRC | | | GPS&DRC | | | WiFi&DRC | | |
		mean	med	max	mean	med	max	mean	med	max
1	866.2	10.1	10.1	27.4	10.0	8.9	25.9	19.0	13.1	56.3
2	828.5	11.2	9.5	28.2	11.2	9.8	27.7	18.6	18.6	27.8
3	598.4	7.3	4.6	23.5	7.1	4.8	23.5	23.6	23.8	39.1
4	689.9	10.3	7.6	31.3	10.1	7.2	32.2	12.6	7.8	47.1
5	999.2	7.4	6.2	21.1	7.6	6.5	23.1	9.9	9.1	20.1
6	1743.8	7.1	5.9	20.8	6.1	5.7	20.2	16.2	15.4	39.0
7	1647.7	5.8	4.9	15.0	5.6	5.0	14.7	16.0	15.1	30.2
		8.5	**7.0**	**31.3**	**8.2**	**6.9**	**32.2**	**16.6**	**14.7**	**56.3**

motion estimate of the dead reckoning device with the absolute position estimate of WiFi and GPS. The GPS and WiFi measurements are used in the sensor model of the particle filter to update the weight of the particles. From the dead reckoning device we extract the relative displacement per interval, and use this information in a specially built motion model for the particle filter, to take motion information of the user and the typical error of the dead reckoning device into account.

5.2   Results

In our evaluation we analyze the achievable accuracies of GPS, WiFi and DR in our scenario, alone and in meaningful combinations. Detailed results on the different traces are given in Table 3. GPS and WiFi-based positioning enable the user to determine absolute position, while DR can only determine relative position of the user.

GPS. As our traces are situated outdoors with a view to the sky, a valid GPS signal is available throughout the entire traces, with some short exceptions in a pedestrian underpass. Positioning by GPS alone performs well in this setting with an average median error of 8m over the 7 traces and median maximum error of 29.4m.

It has to be considered for these results, that the position of the GPS device on the shoulder of the user was a best case scenario, and obviously not common in daily use. Additionally, the used GPS device based on a SiRF III chipset, has shown an explicitly higher sensitivity than devices based on earlier chipsets and semi-professional GPS device for surveying. Signal loss was encountered only shortly in traces that include a pedestrian underpass, but in this situation the measured error increased to a maximum of 53.2m.

WiFi. For the positioning by WiFi the test area had not the best premises, due to an uneven distribution of the access points or even areas with no active access points at all (e.g. shopping street in the north), as shown in Fig. 2. In the case-study we used the freely available beacon databases of the wigle.net community after recording and adding separately gathered warwalking data of approximately 2h in the test area and neighboring areas. Thus, for a realistic scenario, the employed beacon database is fully independent from the traces used in evaluation.

In our traces we reached an average reception of 3.57 known access points on the ground truth points, varying between 3.05 to 3.92. Positioning based on triangulation of the available beacons yielded an average median error of 36.1m over the 7 traces, varying from 22.3m to 50.2m. The maximum error encountered, which has to be taken into account when using only WiFi for priming of e.g. vision-based positioning, varies for the traces between 81m and 210m, with a median of 122m.

Dead Reckoning. The DRC device was fixed on the belt at the recommended position on the back of the user and adjusted to the user (see Sec. 4.1). No individual optimization for the single traces or part of traces was done for a realistic setting. For the evaluation of DR alone we determined the error which would occur in the traces of our scenario, given a perfect positioning in the beginning. For a more general accuracy estimation of the positioning by DR in our scenario we look how the accumulated error changes over distance. For the evaluation of DR alone the DRC output of absolute coordinates was transformed to the local coordinates of the test area, while for the fusion with other sensor data only the relative translation per interval was used in the motion model of the particle filter.

When assuming a perfect initial positioning and continuation by DR alone, we determined that for our traces the smallest maximum error was 18m on the shortest trace (598m), while the biggest error was 58m was on the longest trace(1743m). For all traces the maximum error encountered was less than 5.5% of trace length with a median of 3.2%. Trace 6 (Fig. 7) shows a typical error accumulation. In some of the other traces, e.g. 1 and 2, the accumulated error decreases strongly at some points of time by chance due to counteracting errors. While this decreases the overall error of DR for this approach to evaluation, it is no advantage for the fusion with other sensors, which need an accurate estimate of the users displacement over shorter time periods.

GPS & Dead Reckoning. The fusion of GPS and DR shows the best accuracy, further improving the accuracy of GPS. For the fusion of GPS and DR device data we employ an adopted particle filter, which uses the relative position information in the motion model. On average we reach median error of

6.9m in 7 traces, an improvement of 1.1m over positioning with GPS only, and all traces show a better accuracy than 10m in median. Also the maximum error of GPS is significantly reduced due to the position updates by DR. For example Trace 3 encountered a short phase of difficult reception in a roofed area and signal loss in a pedestrian underpass. In this case, using GPS alone results in a maximum error of 53.2m due to holding of the last known position, whereas the combination with DR shows only a maximum error of only 23.5m. In Fig. 7 the resulting error over time for Trace 6 is shown, including also GPS and DR error over time. In this trace the maximum error is decreased from 31.5m to 20.2m in a difficult reception situation in roofed area, while the median error is only slightly improved.

While already improving the accuracy and maximum error in an outdoor setting with only short phases of reception outage, the biggest advantage could be seen in scenarios mixed with longer indoor periods, e.g. shopping malls. The use of the DR additionally to GPS is able to reduce the average error to less than 50% from 46.5m to 21.5m for a mixed inner city/shopping mall example, and has reduced the maximum error from 138.3m to 39.0m in a different scenario not shown in this paper.

WiFi & Dead Reckoning. The combination of WiFi positioning and DR yields a significant improvement in our experiments. With a median error of 14.7m this combination is in the range of twice the error of GPS and combinations including GPS. Also the maximum error is heavily reduced compared to WiFi-positioning, with a maximum of 56.3m and median of 39.0m. This is even comparable to results of GPS positioning, and could represent a sound basis for the priming of vision-based technologies without the use of GPS.

GPS & WiFi & Dead Reckoning. The combination of all 3 sensors did not yield further improvements over the use of GPS and DR in our scenario. This can be explained by the high accuracy of the latter position methods, which results in slightly lower accuracy when using also the less accurate WiFi positioning in the particle filter. Due to the high weight of GPS and DR in the Particle Filter the error is only 0.1m higher and shows a similar characteristic to the GPS&DR, and could offer extended availability when the reception of GPS cannot be guaranteed for longer periods.

6   Conclusion and Outlook

This paper analyzed and extended the current state of the art in vision-based positioning for outdoor positioning and provided a comparison to other positioning technologies such as GPS and WiFi on a large and challenging image data set. Accuracies obtained for single snapshot based positioning are in the order of 5-6.5m depending on the employed camera. By extending single snapshot based positioning with a dead reckoning compass, continuous localization is possible with accuracies in the order of 10-15m which is only slightly worse than standard GPS and better than typical WiFi-based positioning. We also described various novel combinations for multi-sensor-based positioning such as WiFi & Dead Reckoning which significantly improve accuracies w.r.t. WiFi alone.

Vision-based positioning has gained interest not only in the research community but also for commercial application. Even though the obtained accuracies are promising there are several issues to be solved before vision-based positioning will be a commodity service available on any camera-equipped hand-held device. Current devices have neither the processing nor the storage capabilities to perform vision-based positioning on the device, therefore the query images have to be sent for remote processing. Also the amount of images that need to be considered depends on the size of the uncertainty in the position before vision-based positioning. In that sense it is advantageous to possess a rough first position estimate to reduce processing time. Nevertheless due to the high commercial interest (e.g. from digital map providers) and with further improvement in fast image database indexing, vision-based positioning may soon become a reality.

Acknowledgements. This research has been supported in part by: Research program Computer Vision P2-0214 (RS), EU FP6-004250-IP project CoSy, EU MRTN-CT-2004-005439 project VISIONTRAIN, and EU FP6-511051 project MOBVIS.

References

1. Hightower, J., Borriello, G.: Location Systems for Ubiquitous Computing. Computer 34(8), 57–66 (2001)
2. Hazas, M., Scott, J., Krumm, J.: Location-Aware Computing Comes of Age. Computer 37(2), 95–97 (2004)
3. Cheng, Y.C., Chawathe, Y., LaMarca, A., Krumm, J.: Accuracy Characterization for Metropolitan-scale Wi-Fi Localization. In: MobiSys (2005)
4. Varshavsky, A., Chen, M.Y., de Lara, E., Froehlich, J., Haehnel, D., Hightower, J., LaMarca, A., Potter, F., Sohn, T., Tang, K., Smith, I.: Are GSM Phones THE Solution for Localization? In: WMCSA 2006 (2006)
5. Zhang, W., Košecká, J.: Image based localization in urban environments. In: International Symposium on 3D Data Processing, Visualization and Transmission, pp. 33–40 (2006)
6. Omerčević, D., Drbohlav, O., Leonardis, A.: High-Dimensional Feature Matching: Employing the Concept of Meaningful Nearest Neighbors. In: ICCV (2007)
7. Johansson, B., Cipolla, R.: A system for automatic pose-estimation from a single image in a city scene. In: Proc. of International Conference on Signal Processing, Pattern Recognition, and Applications (2002)
8. Robertson, D., Cipolla, R.: An image-based system for urban navigation. In: BMVC, pp. 819–828 (2004)
9. Zhang, W., Košecká, J.: Hierarchical building recognition. Image and Vision Computing 25(5), 704–716 (2007)
10. Yeh, T., Tollmar, K., Darrell, T.: Searching the web with mobile images for location recognition. In: CVPR, vol. 2, pp. 76–81 (2004)
11. Bahl, P., Padmanabhan, V.N.: RADAR: An In-Building RF-based User Location and Tracking System. In: IEEE Infocom 2000, IEEE Computer Society Press, Los Alamitos (2000)

12. Ekahau. Online http://www.ekahau.com
13. LaMarca, A., Chawathe, Y., Consolvo, S., Hightower, J., Smith, I., Scott, J., Sohn, T., Howard, J., Hughes, J., Potter, F., Tabert, J., Powledge, P., Borriello, G., Schilit, B.: Place Lab: Device Positioning Using Radio Beacons in the Wild. In: Gellersen, H.-W., Want, R., Schmidt, A. (eds.) PERVASIVE 2005. LNCS, vol. 3468, Springer, Heidelberg (2005)
14. Skyhook Wireless. Online http://www.skyhookwireless.com/
15. Navizon: Peer-to-Peer Wireless Positioning. Online http://www.navizon.com/
16. Judd, T.: A Personal Dead Reckoning Module. In: ION GPS 1997 (1997)
17. Macheiner, K.: Performance Analysis of a Commercial Multi-Sensor Pedestrian Navigation System. Master's thesis, IGMS, Graz University of Technology (September 2004)
18. Ladetto, Q., Merminod, B.: Digital Magnetic Compass and Gyroscope Integration for Pedestrian Navigation. In: 9th Saint Petersburg International Conference on Integrated Navigation Systems (2002)
19. Vectronix. Online http://www.vectronix.ch/
20. Randell, C., Djiallis, C., Muller, H.L.: Personal Position Measurement Using Dead Reckoning. In: Fensel, D., Sycara, K.P., Mylopoulos, J. (eds.) ISWC 2003. LNCS, vol. 2870, Springer, Heidelberg (2003)
21. Gabaglio, V.: GPS/INS Integration for Pedestrian Navigation. Astronomisch-geodätische Arbeiten in der Schweiz, vol. 64 (2003) ISBN 3-908440-07-6
22. Jirawimut, R., Ptasinski, P., Garaj, V., Cecelja, F., Balachandran, W.: A Method for Dead Reckoning Parameter Correction in Pedestrian Navigation system. Instrumentation and Measurement 52(1), 209–215 (2003)
23. Kourogi, M., Kurata, T.: Personal Positioning based on Walking Locomotion Analysis with Self-Contained Sensors and a Wearable Camera. In: ISMAR 2003 (2003)
24. Beauregard, S., Haas, H.: Pedestrian Dead Reckoning: A Basis for Personal Positioning. In: WPNC 2006 (2006)
25. Bertram, J.E.A., Ruina, A.: Multiple Walking Speed-Frequency Relations are Predicted by Constrained Optimization. Journal of Theoretical Biology 209(4) (2001)
26. Mikolajczyk, K., Tuytelaars, T., Schmid, C., Zisserman, A., Matas, J., Schaffalitzky, F., Kadir, T., Van Gool, L.: A Comparison of Affine Region Detectors. IJCV 65(1-2), 43–72 (2005)
27. Mikolajczyk, K., Schmid, C.: A Performance Evaluation of Local Descriptors. PAMI 27(10), 1615–1630 (2005)
28. Matas, J., Chum, O., Urban, M., Pajdla, T.: Robust wide-baseline stereo from maximally stable extremal regions. Image and Vision Computing 22(10), 761–767 (2004)
29. Lowe, D.G.: Distinctive image features from scale-invariant keypoints. IJCV 60(2), 91–110 (2004)
30. Hartley, R., Zisserman, A.: Multiple View Geometry in Computer Vision, 2nd edn. Cambridge University Press, Cambridge (2004)
31. Nister, D.: An efficient solution to the five-point relative pose problem. IEEE PAMI 26(6), 756–777 (2004)
32. Tuytelaars, T., Van Gool, L.: Content-based image retrieval based on local affinely invariant regions. In: Huijsmans, D.P., Smeulders, A.W.M. (eds.) VISUAL 1999. LNCS, vol. 1614, pp. 493–500. Springer, Heidelberg (1999)
33. Hightower, J., Borriello, G.: Particle Filters for Location Estimation in Ubiquitous Computing: A Case Study. In: Davies, N., Mynatt, E.D., Siio, I. (eds.) UbiComp 2004. LNCS, vol. 3205, Springer, Heidelberg (2004)

Toward Recognition of Short and Non-repetitive Activities from Wearable Sensors

Andreas Zinnen, Kristof van Laerhoven, and Bernt Schiele

Computer Science Department, TU Darmstadt,
Hochschulstr. 10, 64289 Darmstadt, Germany
{zinnen,kristof,schiele}@informatik.tu-darmstadt.de

Abstract. Activity recognition has gained a lot of interest in recent years due to its potential and usefulness for context-aware computing. Most approaches for activity recognition focus on repetitive or long time patterns within the data. There is however high interest in recognizing very short activities as well, such as pushing and pulling an oil stick or opening an oil container as sub-tasks of checking the oil level in a car. This paper presents a method for the latter type of activity recognition using start and end postures (short fixed positions of the wrist) in order to identify segments of interest in a continuous data stream. Experiments show high discriminative power for using postures to recognize short activities in continuous recordings. Additionally, classifications using postures and HMMs for recognition are combined.

Keywords: activity recognition, postures, HMMs.

1 Introduction

Context awareness is a central issue in ubiquitous and wearable computing. The opportunity to perceive the world from a user's perspective is a key benefit of wearable systems compared to stationary, desktop-centered computers. While context information can consist of any information describing the situation of the user, for many applications the current activity of the user is considered to be of particular importance. There has been much research in recognition of repetitive and long time activities such as walking or running. Today's approaches already recognize diverse low-level activities such as hammering, screwing or running.

Many interesting activities, e.g. those in the maintenance domain, are non-repetitive and happen in a very short time frame. To give a reasonable estimation of whether the maintenance worker has finished a task such as performing an oil check, the system needs to identify sub-activities like opening the oil container, pushing or pulling the oil stick and opening or closing the hood. Many of those activities happen within a time frame of less than 1 second. The activities may only occur occasionally in between long periods of unrelated, arbitrary events. Both the shortness and the individual performance of the activities make the recognition a highly challenging task.

B. Schiele et al. (Eds.): AmI 2007, LNCS 4794, pp. 142–158, 2007.

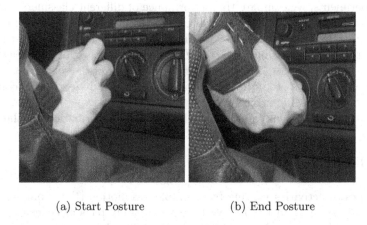

(a) Start Posture   (b) End Posture

Fig. 1. Postures surrounding the activity *turning on the heating*

The activities that we aim to recognize are defined by short sequences of arm movements amid irrelevant data. This paper focuses on spotting a subset of activities that require interaction with objects, for instance the knob when turning on the heating. We have observed that such activities can be separated into three segments: First, the user keeps the arm fixed for a very short time when grabbing the object. Second, the user moves the arm and therefore changes the position of his arm while performing the activity. Third, the user's arm has reached an end position for a short time due to the affordances of the respective object. It can be observed that the fixed positions before and after the movement are similar for several users. For recognition, one sensor placed at the dominant wrist is used. Since acceleration sensors and gyroscopes are small, they can easily be integrated into wrist watches that the user may strap on in the future.

Example: Figures 1(a) and 1(b) illustrate the short fixed positions of the arm before and after turning on the heating of a car.

The rest of the paper is organized as follows. Section 2 summarizes related work in activity spotting and recognition, especially using Hidden Markov Models. Section 3 describes the experimental setup including the used data sets and sensors.

In section 4 , existing approaches using HMMs for spotting relatively short activities are applied. Fully-connected as well as left-right Hidden Markov Models are trained for ten activities on hand segmented training data. Whereas HMMs achieve high recognition rates on hand segmented test data, the models cannot easily be transferred to the continuous test data for short activity recognition.

The main contribution of this paper is introduced in section 5. A new classification method uses short fixed positions of the subject's body parts (*postures*) to segment and identify possible parts for a specific activity in the continuous data stream. We will show that the subjects' fixed arm positions before and after performing an activity can differentiate the short activities from the rest of the data surprisingly well. Classifiers are defined using features based on the start postures, on the end postures as well as on the difference between both.

In experiments, we compare the performance of different classifiers and show that fusing several features on postures attains the best recognition results. Since many segments of the data can be discarded by calculating the low-cost posture features, the approach reduces the computing requirements over the data stream. Therefore it will allow for a more costly classification over the segmented parts in the future. In the last step, the classification using posture features is combined with the trained HMM activity models.

Sections 6 and 7 discuss and summarize the main contributions of the paper.

2   Related Work

Many types of activities varying from simple locomotion [1] to complex every-day [2] and assembly tasks [3] have been successfully recognized using sensors. Minnen et al. [4] approach the discovery of activities by identifying reoccurring motifs in multivariate time series using unsupervised algorithms to identify the motifs. By training HMMs on the motifs, the authors achieve a recall rate of 96,3% with a precision of 88,4%.

Clarkson and Pentland [5] developed an algorithm for unsupervised clustering of audio and video data. They capture a person's visual and aural environment and use high level HMMs to classify scenes like being at a supermarket or in a video store. Oliver et al. [6] discover that HMMs have the ability to capture different levels of abstraction with respect to the time granularity. The authors use layered HMMs on acoustic and visual information to annotate keyboard and mouse events. HMMs have been used in experiments for gesture and speech recognition [8]. Acceleration sensor-based gesture recognition using HMMs have been studied in [8,9,10]. Kela et al. [7] propose a system offering freely trainable gesture commands. Using those gestures, users can control external devices with a hand held wireless sensor unit.

Most of the approaches described above have been successful either for seg-mented recognition, or for scenarios in which the irrelevant data for arbitrary activities was easy to model. The following groups concentrate on recognizing ac-tivities in a longer data stream including non relevant data: Stiefmeier et al.[14] present a method for continuous activity recognition based on ultrasonic hand tracking and motion sensors. The sensors are attached to the user's arms. The authors describe a segmentation based on hand tracking, show how classification is done on both the ultrasonic and the motion data and finally discuss several classifier fusion methods. [11] performs continuous activity recognition combin-ing a wrist-worn acceleration sensor with a microphone. Their approach is built on the observation that two different kinds of sensors are unlikely to agree in classification of a false positive. Considering those classifications, the authors are able to reliably segment activities of interest from a longer data stream. In [12], the authors present a technique to automatically track the progress of maintenance or assembly tasks using body worn sensors. They combine data from accelerometers with frequency sound classification. On a simulated assem-bly task, most activities in a continuous data stream are classified with zero false positives and 84.4% accuracy. Situation analysis based on sound has been investigated by Clarkson and Pentland [15].

3 Experiment Setup

3.1 Data Set

For the initial experiments reported in this paper, a data set of 10 different activities performed by one subject was recorded. The test and training data were recorded on two different days. While recording the test data, the subject was given a script containing 10 very short activities in a car context: Turning the heating on/off, pulling and releasing the handbrake, opening and closing the sun shield, hood and oil container. The subject recorded these activities in a car during driving and while performing an oil check. Later, the data was annotated using recorded audio data. The data was recorded with one XSens MTx sensor at the subject's right wrist. The 10 activities were repeated 15 times in different sequences, and interrupted by unrelated activities such as reading a map, driving or browsing the glove locker and trunk. The overall test data set has a length of about 18 minutes with a sample frequency of 100 Hz. The longest activities were opening and closing the hood with a maximum length of 2.5 seconds. Opening the sun shield was the shortest activity with a maximum length of 0.5 seconds. Since most considered activities take less than one second to perform, the data of interest makes up less than 2 minutes of the overall data. The training data was recorded on a different day, and the subject performed all activities ten times. Using the training data, a minimum and maximum length of the recognized activities was defined. The values can be seen in table 1.

Table 1. Minimum and maximum times for the considered activities

Activity	Minimum Length[s]	Maximum Length[s]
Open Hood	0.6	2.5
Close Hood	0.8	2.2
Open Oil container	0.2	0.6
Close Oil container	0.2	0.6
Open Sun shield	0.2	0.5
Close Sun shield	0.2	0.7
Pulling Handbrake	0.2	0.6
Releasing Handbrake	0.2	0.6
Heating on	0.2	0.7
Heating of	0.5	1.2

3.2 Sensor and Annotation

The MTx [16] is an inertial measurement unit that integrates a 3-dimensional magnetometer as well as calibrated 3-dimensional linear acceleration, rate of turn and magnetic field data. A sensor fusion algorithm is used which allows the MTx to accurately calculate absolute orientation in three-dimensional space by integrating gyroscopes, accelerometers and magnetometers in real-time. The orientation as calculated by the MTx is the orientation of the sensor-fixed co-ordinate system with respect to a Cartesian earth-fixed co-ordinate system. Because of magnetic disturbances in our car scenario, any data from the magnetometers is completely disregarded. Therefore, we do not obtain an absolute orientation towards the magnetic north. The provided orientation data can still be used to reliably calculate the position of the sensor towards the gravity giving a strong feature for the position and posture of the user's arm. This orientation is used to transform the gravity vector of the global system into the sensor coordinate system.

4   Activity Recognition with Hidden Markov Models on Segmented and Continuous Data

Hidden Markov Models (HMM) [17] are widely adopted for gesture and speech recognition. HMMs have intrinsic properties which make them attractive for gesture recognition. An HMM is a statistical model in which the modeled data is assumed to be a Markov process with unknown parameters. During learning, the parameters are estimated from the observations.

Continuous activity recognition is difficult, especially when looking at relatively short activities in longer recording. In this section, HMMs are applied to relatively short activities in a longer recording.

In a first step, HMMs trained on segmented data are applied to hand-segmented test data. The trained models are applied to each of the segmented activity sequences of the test data set. Whereas the results using fully-connected HMMs were not sufficient (see 4.1), the performance of left-right HMMs demonstrates the suitability of HMMs for our segmented activities resulting in high recognition rates (see 4.2) for the considered segmented activities. HMMs seem to be adequate models for segmented activities.

After training, we apply the HMMs trained on hand-segmented data directly to sliding windows over the continuous data. As the activities are very short, we observe a low precision when aiming for a high recall (see 4.3).

4.1   Fully-Connected HMMs on Hand Segmented Activities

Each model is trained on ten hand-segmented instances of one activity using the Hidden Markov Model Toolbox for Matlab written by Kevin Murphy [13]. In the first experiment, we train one fully-connected HMM for each activity with three states and single gaussian distribution. Features of the models are the three dimensional acceleration values. We apply them to all activity segments of the test data. Each HMM returns the probability of the model given the segment. Maximum Likelihood classification returns the most probable model for the segment. The overall recognition rate of the activities is 80%. The activities *open hood and open oil container* have a low recall under 50%. Furthermore, *close*

Table 2. Confusion Matrix on hand segmented data using fully conntected HMMs - overall recognition rate: 80%

	OH	CH	COC	OOC	HON	HOFF	BON	BOFF	OSS	CSS	Rec	Prec
Open Hood:OH	7	7	0	0	0	0	0	1	0	0	0.47	0.88
Close Hood:CH	0	15	0	0	0	0	0	0	0	0	1	0.68
Close Oil Cont:COC	0	0	13	2	0	0	0	0	0	0	0.87	0.5
Open Oil Cont:OOC	0	0	12	3	0	0	0	0	0	0	0.2	0.6
Heating On:HON	1	0	0	0	14	0	0	0	0	0	0.93	1
Heating Off:HOFF	0	0	1	0	0	14	0	0	0	0	0.93	1
Brake On:BON	0	0	0	0	0	0	15	0	0	0	1	0.71
Brake Off:BOFF	0	0	0	0	0	0	0	15	0	0	1	0.94
Open Sun Shield:OSS	0	0	0	0	0	0	2	0	13	0	0.87	1
Close Sun Shield:CSS	0	0	0	0	0	0	4	0	0	11	0.73	1

hood and close/open oilcontainer have a precision under 70%. Good results can be obtained for *releasing the handbrake and turning the heating on/off*. Both recall and precision are over 93% with fully connected HMMs. *Open the hood and opening the oil container* are confused often: 7 out of 15 times, the system recognizes close hood instead of open hood. 12 out of 15 times, the system recognizes close oil container instead of opening it. Table 2 summarizes the confusion of the activities. In the next paragraph, we discuss left right HMMs which reduce the confusion.

4.2   Left-Right HMMs on Hand Segmented Activities

Left-right models perform better than fully-connected models on the data in the segmented case. To improve the recognition rate of the approach in 4.1, we train left-right HMMs for each activity. Again, the three dimensional acceleration values are the features. On average, the recognition of all 10 activities improves (see table 3). The recognition rate for all activities is 88%. The recall increases or stays at the same level except for *close sun shield*. Especially for *open hood and open oil container*, a higher recall can be observed. *Close hood and close/open oil container* have a higher precision compared with the fully connected results. It can be noticed that apart from minor exceptions, both the precision and the recall are better for left-right HMMs. In the following, we apply the same models to the continuous data.

4.3   Left-Right HMMs on Continuous Data

The following experiment applies the trained models from the segmented case to continuous training data. Although our experiments with the left-right models on segments have led to good results, HMMs applied to the continuous data do not provide sufficient recognition. In the following paragraphs, we explain how we evaluate the performance of left-right HMMs on continuous data. Furthermore, we summarize the results.

Table 3. Confusion Matrix on hand segmented data using left-right HMMs - overall recognition rate: 88%

	OH	CH	COC	OOC	HON	HOFF	BON	BOFF	OSS	CSS	Rec	Prec
Open Hood:OH	10	3	0	0	0	0	1	1	0	0	0.67	0.77
Close Hood:CH	0	15	0	0	0	0	0	0	0	0	1	0.83
Close Oil Cont:COC	0	0	15	0	0	0	0	0	0	0	1	0.83
Open Oil Cont:OOC	3	0	3	9	0	0	0	0	0	0	0.6	1
Heating On:HON	0	0	0	0	14	0	0	1	0	0	0.93	1
Heating Off:HOFF	0	0	0	0	0	15	0	0	0	0	1	1
Brake On:BON	0	0	0	0	0	0	15	0	0	0	1	0.71
Brake Off:BOFF	0	0	0	0	0	0	0	15	0	0	1	0.83
Open Sun shield:OSS	0	0	0	0	0	0	0	0	15	0	1	1
Close Sun shield:CSS	0	0	0	0	0	0	5	1	0	9	0.6	1

Evaluation Criteria. In the following, the applied method for evaluation of a continuous activity recognition system is described.

First, the Log-Likelihood of each point in time of the data is calculated for the trained HMMs. Here, a sliding window with the specific point in time as a center is used. The window length is different for each activity. In the analysis, the maximum length of each activity (see table 1) is taken as window width.

The second step smooths the Log-Likelihood curve with a smoothing window length equal to the maximum activity length. Furthermore, the *tolerance* length of the evaluation is set to the same value.

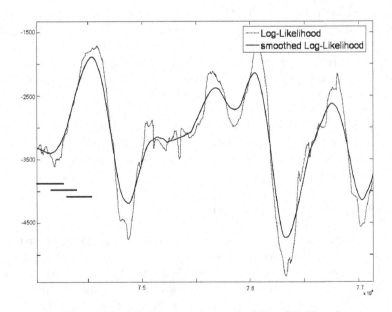

Fig. 2. Log-Likelihood and smoothed Log-Likelihood

The third step counts the activities' detections for a specific threshold. An evaluation window of *tolerance* length slides over the smoothed data. The sliding step size is half of the *tolerance* length. Figure 2 illustrates the Log-Likelihood (dashed curve), the smoothed Log-Likelihood (solid curve) and three example evaluation windows. If the current evaluation window contains a smoothed value higher than the threshold, we count it as detection. If, for a detection, the center of the evaluation window and the center of an annotation are closer to each other than half the *tolerance*, the detection will be counted as a *true positive*. Otherwise, we count the detection as a *false positive*. For a varying threshold and for each activity, the *true* and *false positives* are analyzed and evaluated in precision-recall characteristics.

Results. In this experiment, the left-right HMMs trained on labeled data are applied to fixed sliding windows. The HMMs do not yield high recognition rates on the data set. Contrary to the segmented case where the HMMs were able to classify the activities in a satisfying manner, the number of false positives in the continuous case increases tremendously. For all activities, the precision drops when increasing the threshold for detections. *Closing the sun shield* performs best among all activities. Nevertheless, for a recall of 0.1, the precision is already less than 10% and even drops for a higher recall. For activities with a high acceleration variance like *pulling or releasing the hand brake*, the precision even drops and stays under a value of 0.01 for a recall higher than 0. Tuning of the parameters for modeling of states, transitions or distribution as well as an extension of the features would probably lead to slightly better results. However there still remains a high modeling effort since the shortness and variance of the activities require different parameters for each activity. In the next section, we will introduce a new method using postures with the ability to identify short activities in longer recordings.

5   Segmentation and Classification Using Postures

As expected and as shown in the previous section, HMMs alone applied to sliding windows are not sufficient for the recognition of short activities. This section introduces a new approach using users' *postures* as short fixed positions of the body or of body parts to differentiate short activities from unimportant data in a continuous data stream. As mentioned before, in many cases the user keeps the arm still for a very short time before and after performing activities.

On the one side, we use postures to extract data segments from the continuous data (see section 5.1). On the other side, we illustrate for those segments that postures themselves can be used to discriminate short activities from unrelated data (see section 5.2). A first experiment compares the distinctiveness of the posture before and after the activity as well as the difference in orientation of both posture vectors for ten activities. Each of the classifiers using the postures and the difference in orientation performs on average better than the approach applying HMMs to a sliding window. The difference in orientation between the end and start posture as feature works best. Subsequently, the results are improved by combining the three classifiers. Stability of the classifier is of high importance since the thresholds have to be learned from the training data. Additionally, we show that the classifier still remains stable if we gradually increase the thresholds. Finally, we show that the classification using HMMs on top of the classification using the posture and distance feature can improve the recognition rate for a subset of the activities, but not necessarily on average.

5.1   Segmentation of the Continuous Data Stream

This paragraph describes how fixed postures can be used for a reliable segmentation of the activity sections. As mentioned before, many human short term activities are characterized by movements which start and end by very brief fixed positions of the body or of body parts. We call these fixed positions at the beginning and the end of a movement *postures*. In a first step, the data is grouped in regions where the user either moves the arm (movement) or keeps the arm position still (posture). The grouping is based on the variance of the current sensor orientation. If the sensor's orientation changes quickly, the variance is high and a movement will be recognized. If the sensor is kept still, low variance indicates a posture. Using those regions of movements and postures, we build data segments that are enclosed by two separate postures. The classification can be performed on those segments. Before, overlapping segments have to be discarded to ensure a correct recognition evaluation. The following paragraphs go into more detail regarding the segmentation algorithm and elimination of overlapping segments. Section 5.2 describes in detail how the classification is done using postures.

Grouping of the data in regions. At each point in time and for each sensor position, the gravity in the sensor's coordinate system points to a specific direction. For a user keeping his/her arm in almost the same position for a short period of time, this direction will not change. A user performing a movement, e.g. when pulling the hand brake, will cause a significant change of this direction. Using the rotation matrix provided by the MTx (see 3.2), the gravity vector $(0 \quad 0 \quad 9.81)\,m/s^2$ is transfered into the sensor coordinate system. The upper figure in 3(a) illustrates the transformed components of the gravity vector in the sensor coordinate system while performing the activity *turning the heating on*. The crosses illustrate the annotated activity. In the first part, the values stay nearly constant. Between samples 100 and 120, there is a high variance in the data which settles again in the remainder of the displayed data. The variance is calculated over a sliding window of 10 samples of each curve. Accordingly, those three values are added to obtain the magnitude of the variance. A high variance indicates a fast change of the arm's position which can be seen between samples 100 and 120 in Figure 3(b). A low variance acts as an indicator for a posture. Clearly identifiable is that the variance curve remains low at the beginning (start posture) and the end (end posture) of the annotated activity. A defined threshold for the variance separates phases of postures from those moving the arm. The lower figure in 3(b) contains the mentioned variance (dashed) and a

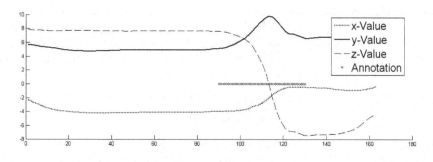

(a) Annotation and Direction of Gravity

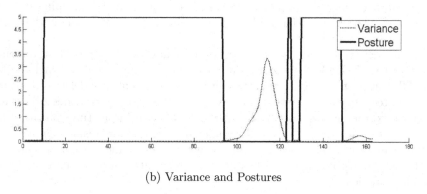

(b) Variance and Postures

Fig. 3. Segmentation on the activity *turning on the heating*

visualization of the grouped regions (solid). If a region is a posture, the posture value is increased to 5 for visualization.

The experiments show that a threshold for the variance of 0.01 for opening and closing the hood and a threshold of 0.03 for all other activities results in a sufficient segmentation. The threshold for opening/closing the hood has to be lower since the hood's pneumatic closing mechanism prevents the user from changing the arm's position very fast. A higher threshold would classify the slow movement between the start and end posture as a posture as well.

Segmenting the data. By means of the detected posture areas, the segments are built. Later, the activity classification will be performed on those segments. A segment starts at the end of one posture and ends at the beginning of another. Furthermore, segments for a specific activity have a restricted length defined in table 1. A minimum length of 0.2 seconds and a maximum length of 0.7 for turning the heating on will lead to two segments in the illustrated example in figure 3(b), one ranging from sample 94 to 123 and the other from 94 to 129. It is obvious that both segments in the example contain the movement of the activity *heating on* motivating the necessity for a handling overlapping segments. The next paragraph explains how to address overlapping segments.

Discarding overlapping segments. The example in figure 3(b) illustrates that overlapping segments can both contain the same activity. Before evaluating the performance of our method for activity detection in section 5.2, it is helpful to keep only one of those overlapping segments. For this we define the overlap between two segments S_1 and S_2 if equation 1 holds true:

$$\frac{length(S_1 \cap S_2)}{length(S_1 \cup S_2)} > 0.5 \tag{1}$$

$S_1 \cap S_2$ stands for the common region of S_1 and S_2. $S_1 \cup S_2$ means the conjunct region of S_1 and S_2. This equation ensures that not only segments with a high common region overlap. Furthermore, the regions have to be of similar size.

If two segments overlap, the distance between the segments' postures and the according learned postures of the specific activity in the training data is calculated. The segment that is closer to the training data will remain; the other one will be discarded.

In this section, we discussed the grouping of data into regions of movements and postures. Using those regions, data segments are built that are enclosed by two different postures. Subsequently, overlapping segments are deleted to ensure a correct recognition evaluation in a later stage. This section provides a basis for the next experiments where we show that classifiers using features on the start and end posture of the segments obtain high recognition results for activity spotting in continuous data. In the following, the distinctive performance of start posture, end posture and the difference in orientation of both are analyzed for our activities.

5.2   Classification Using Postures

The following experiments show that separate features built on top of start and end posture as well as the orientation difference between both lead to high recognition rates. Classifiers using those features are applied on the segments as extracted in section 5.1. The obtained results are better for each separate classifier compared to the classification using HMMs. We will show that a classifier combining the features obtains the hightest recognition rates.

Classification using separate postures. This experiment evaluates three single classifiers using three different distance vectors:

- Posture 1: Distance of the segment's start posture to a mean start posture of the training data of each activity
- Posture 2: Distance of the segment's end posture to a mean end posture of the training data of each activity
- Diff Pos 1 & Pos 2: Distance of the segment's difference vector to a mean difference vector of the training data of each activity

A segment is accepted as detection if the considered distance is lower than a predefined threshold. To evaluate a classifier, the according threshold for the distance is increased stepwise. Figure 4 illustrates the average precision-recall for the three single classifiers Posture 1, Posture 2 and Diff Pos 1 & 2 over all activities. The precision plot shows a clear difference between classifier 3 and the other two. Up to a recall of almost 0.9, classifier 3 has a precision of more than 0.6. Classifier 1 and 2 perform slightly worse. Compared to the Hidden Markov Models, the results are still good. We notice that each classifier models a different subset of activities in a sufficient way.

The strongest results for classifier 1 could be observed for the activities *open and close sun shield and close hood*. In contrast, the precision of *brake on/off, heating on and open hood* is low.

Classifier 2 recognizes the activities *close hood or sun shield and open oil container* with a high precision in average. Even for a quite high recall of almost 0.7, the precision is still 1. The precision drops to a minimum of 0.5 for complete recall.

Classifier 3 is selective for more activities: 6 out of 10 activities have a higher precision than 0.5 for a recall between 0.1 and 1. For *heating on and close sun shield*, the precision remains higher than 0.9 for a recall between 0 and 1. Obviously, classifier 3 depends on the start and end posture. In the case that either the start or end posture has a high variance, the difference will not perform as good anymore. *Heating off* is an example where this effect occurs. Both classifiers 2 and 3 do not score a high precision when increasing the recall for classifier 2 and 3.

The experiments show that postures and the difference between postures already qualify as features for a good classifier. Almost all activities in our set are modeled very well by at least one classifier. In the following paragraph, a classifier will fuse the three features and obtain better recognition results than classifiers using the single features.

Classification with combined postures. The previous experiments demonstrated features on single postures and the difference of two postures as a strong feature to reduce the number of *false positives* in a continuous data stream. All three postures individually perform on average much better than the approach using HMMs on the segments or on a sliding window. Also, one can observe that dependent from the activity, different postures can classify better than others. In the following, we demonstrate that a combination of the three features can improve the recognition significantly.

On average, the combined classifier performs better than the three classifiers on single features. Figure 4 includes the precision-recall curve of this classifier ("Combination of all"). The classifier has a high precision of 0.8 on average for a recall between 0 and 1. Only for *open hood, turning the heating off, pulling and releasing the handbrake* we do not find an optimal value. *Opening the hood* performs worst. The precision is still higher than 0.5 for a recall between 0.2 and 0.9.

The observations in this section confirm that a combination of the three features defined on the postures results in a high recognition rate. For manually-chosen thresholds, a recall of 1 with a 100% precision can be noted. As the thresholds have to be learned in future experiments, an interesting question is how the choice of threshold values changes the performance of the classifier. Therefore, we decrease the accuracy of the optimal thresholds for the three

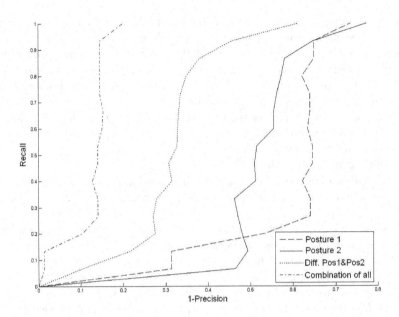

Fig. 4. Precision-Recall: average for (Posture 1), (Posture 2), (Diff Pos 1 & Pos 2) and fusion

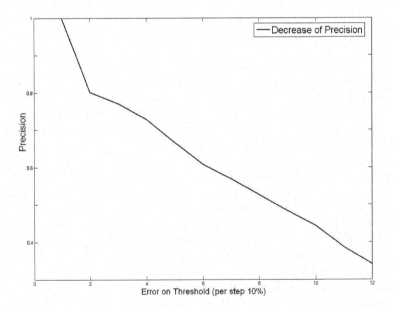

Fig. 5. Average decrease of the precision increasing the thresholds (per step 10%)

distances with 10% each step. Each step, more false positives will be detected. Figure 5 shows how the precision goes down. Nevertheless, this experiment indicates the robustness of the fused approach since for thresholds that are chosen 50% higher than the manually-chosen value, the average precision still remains above 0.6.

5.3 Classification with Postures and HMMs

We have obtained good average recognition rate of the fused postures' classifiers so far. Nevertheless, the average performances for *open hood, turning the heating off, pulling and releasing the handbrake* are not satisfying. In the next section, we briefly describe the potential of fusing the classifiers using postures with the ones using HMMs. In addition to the classifier fusing the features, the trained HMMs are applied on the resulting segments to further restrict false positives. For three out of those four activities, the recognition did not improve significantly. Only for *turning the heating off*, we obtained better results when including the HMM for activity recognition. Figure 6 shows the improvement of the integrated approach (dashed line) against the one fusing the postures (solid line). Whereas the posture approach's precision drops and stabilizes on a precision value around 0.4, the inclusion of the HMM Log-Likelihood leads to a precision of 0.9 for a recall of 0.9. The precision for a maximal recall drops to an adequate precision of 0.7. This example motivates the potential of a better movement model between the two postures.

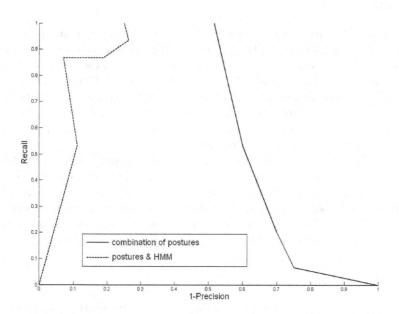

Fig. 6. Precision-Recall for turning the heating off with combination of postures and HMMs

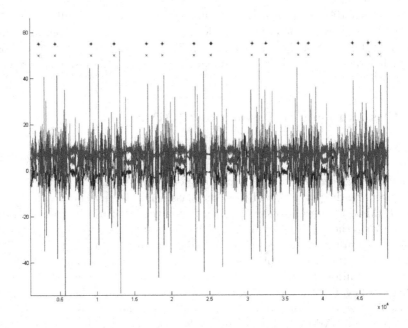

Fig. 7. 18 minutes data stream with annotations (x) and detections (*) for turning the heating on: classifier fusing posture features

6   Discussion

Especially in the area of wearable computing, the reduction of the computation effort is of high importance. The proposed method is able to reduce the calculation and evaluation effort with low-cost features. Many of the suitable segments can be discarded if the postures do not fit any activity. Activities that are composed of two postures and an activity segment with varying sensor position will be segmented in a reliable way. The experiments with HMMs have illustrated that there is still a need and potential for better modeling of the data between postures to increase the distinctive power.

Figure 7 displays the data stream of 18 minutes recorded data. Annotations for the activity *heating on* are signed with a cross. Detections of the classifier fusing the start and end posture as well as the difference are marked with an asterisk. For the specific activity, the system detects all activity instances without detecting a wrong segment. Six out of ten types of activities can be classified with a similar precision, for the other four, the precision is not much lower.

7   Conclusion

This paper has analyzed different methods for activity spotting in continuous data. A first experiment demonstrates that left-right HMMs trained on segmented training data model the segmented activity test sequences sufficiently.

For the continuous case, we note that Hidden Markov Models cannot easily be transferred from a segmented to a continuous recognition. The experiment's results show that the models cannot discriminate the short activities from irrelevant data. More specifically, the number of false positives is too high.

The proposed approach using postures to segment and classify the data obtains good results. Three different features and fusion of them have been evaluated. In particular, the postures already classify the regarded activities to a high degree. Postures seem to be a good feature both for segmenting the data stream in smaller segments as well to reduce the number of segments to analyze in more detail. A classifier fusing the distance features of the start and end posture, as well as the distance between both, performs best in average. At the end, it is shown that a further combination with the HMMs does not always lead to better results yet. Just for one out of four examples, the recognition rate increases. However, the results show the potential of combining the fused features with a better and more distinctive model of the movement sequence between the start and end posture.

This work evaluates and motivates the feasibility of postures for activity recognition with one user. In future work, the feasibility evaluation has to be pursued with different users. Eventually, more general features have to be defined in that case. As mentioned before, the modeling of the movement part between the postures has to be enhanced. The integration of higher level context, e.g. the task order of a specific activity is also a promising approach to increase the recognition rate.

References

1. Huynh, T., Schiele, B.: Analyzing features for activity recognition. In: Proceedings of the 2005 joint conference on Smart objects and ambient intelligence: innovative context-aware services, ACM Press, New York, USA (2005)
2. Lukowicz, P., Ward, J., Junker, H., Staeger, M., Troester, G., Atrash, A., Starner, S.: Recognizing workshop activity using body worn microphones and accelerometers. In: Pervasive Computing (2005)
3. Bao, L., Intille, S.: Activity recognition from user-annotated acceleration data. In: Mattern, F. (ed.) Pervasive Computing (2004)
4. Minnen, D., Starner, T., Essa, I., Isbell, C.: Discovering Characteristic Actions from On-Body Sensor Data. In: Proceedings of the Tenth IEEE International Symposium on Wearable Computers (ISWC), IEEE Computer Society Press, Los Alamitos (2006)
5. Clarkson, B., Pentland, A.: Unsupervised clustering of ambulatory audio and video. In: Icassp (1999)
6. Oliver, N., Horvitz, E., Garg, A.: Layered representations for human activity recognition. In: Proceedings of the Fourth IEEE Int. Conf. on Multimodal Interfaces, IEEE Computer Society Press, Los Alamitos (2002)
7. Kela, J., Korpipää, P., Mäntyjärvi, J., Kallio, S., Savino, G., Jozzo, L., Marca, D.: Accelerometer-based gesture control for a design environment. Personal Ubiquitous Comput. (2006)

8. Mäntylaä, Mäntyjärvi, Seppänen, Tuulari: Hand gesture recognition of a mobile device user. In: The Proceedings of the international IEEE conference on multimedia and expo (2000)
9. Hoffman, F., Heyer, P., Hommel, G.: Velocity profile based recognition of dynamic gestures with discrete hidden markov models. In: Proceedings of gesture workshop (1997)
10. Iacucci, G., Kela, J., Pehkonen, P.: Computational support to record and re-experience visits. Personal and ubiquitous computing 8(2) (2004)
11. Ward, J., Lukowicz, P., Tröster, G.: Gesture spotting using wrist worn microphone and 3-axis accelerometer. In: Proceedings of the 2005 joint conference on Smart objects and ambient intelligence: innovative context-aware services: usages and technologies (2005)
12. Lukowicz, P., Ward, J., Junker, H., Stäger, M., Tröster, G., Atrash, A., Starner, T.: Recognizing Workshop Activity Using Body Worn Microphones and Accelerometers. LNCS (2004)
13. Murphy, K.: Hidden Markov Model (HMM) Toolbox for Matlab, http://www.cs.ubc.ca/murphyk/Software/HMM/hmm.html
14. Stiefmeier, T., Ogris, G., Junker, H., Lukowicz, P., Tröster, G.: Combining Motion Sensors and Ultrasonic Hands Tracking for Continuous Activity Recognition in a Maintenance Scenario. In: 10th IEEE International Symposium on Wearable Computers (2006)
15. Clarkson, B., Sawhney, N., Pentland, A.: Auditory context awareness in wearable computing. In: Workshop on Perceptual User Interfaces (1998)
16. http://xsens.com/
17. Rabiner, L.: A Tutorial On Hidden Markov Models. Proceedings of the IEEE (1989)

Distributed AI for Ambient Intelligence: Issues and Approaches

Theodore Patkos, Antonis Bikakis, Grigoris Antoniou, Maria Papadopouli, and Dimitris Plexousakis

Institute of Computer Science, FO.R.T.H.
Vassilika Vouton, P.O. Box 1385, GR 71110, Heraklion, Greece
{patkos,bikakis,antoniou,mgp,dp}@ics.forth.gr

Abstract. Research in many fields of AI, such as distributed planning and reasoning, agent teamwork and coalition formation, cooperative problem solving and action theory has advanced significantly over the last years, both from a theoretical and a practical perspective. In the light of the development towards ambient, pervasive and ubiquitous computing, this research will be tested under new, more demanding realistic conditions, stimulating the emergence of novel approaches to handle the challenges that these open, dynamic environments introduce. This paper identifies shortcomings of state-of-the-art techniques in handling the complexity of the Ambient Intelligence vision, motivated by the experience gained during the development and usage of a context-aware platform for mobile devices in dynamic environments. The paper raises research issues and discusses promising directions for realizing the objectives of near-future pervasive information systems.

Keywords: Ambient Intelligence, Distributed AI, Context Awareness, Action Theories, Multi-agent Cooperation.

1 Introduction

The vision of Ambient Intelligence assumes a shift in computing towards a multiplicity of communicating devices disappearing into the background, providing an intelligent, augmented environment, where the emphasis is on the human factor. Realizing this vision requires the integration of expertise from a multitude of disciplines; distributed intelligence, dynamic networks and ubiquitous communications, human-computer interaction and intuitive user-friendly interfacing, robotics, and hardware design are embraced under the influence of the Ambient Intelligence paradigm. This paradigm implies a seamless medium of interaction, advanced networking technology and efficient knowledge management, in order to deploy an environment, where entities describe themselves, are aware of each other and can figure out ways to interoperate at syntactic and semantic levels.

Arranging a physical environment, where mobile and stationary devices communicate and cooperate to achieve common objectives, has proven to be a laborious task for the research community. Although much success has been achieved in

B. Schiele et al. (Eds.): AmI 2007, LNCS 4794, pp. 159–176, 2007.

defining theoretical frameworks for the fields of distributed AI, agent teamwork and coalition formation, planning and reasoning about actions and cooperative problem solving over the last years, the advent of ubiquitous and context-aware computing has produced new challenges, pushing research in these fields to its limit. Existing approaches have difficulty in meeting the real-world challenges imposed by developing ambient information systems, since they typically rely on restricted models and simplifying assumptions, which do not hold in realistic conditions. Already works are being published that question the logic and rational behind some of our larger expectations; Rogers, for instance, in [1] argues that the progress in Ubiquitous Computing research has been hampered by intractable computational and ethical problems and that the field needs to broaden its scope, setting and addressing other goals that are more attainable.

It is our intention in this paper to investigate the challenging new issues that emerge from this domain and focus on research in the field of Distributed Artificial Intelligence under the context of symbolic planning. In particular, we identify and describe three general classes of problems: (a) the challenge of handling the complexity of generating and executing planning tasks in a dynamic and uncertain environment; (b) the challenge of cooperation between devices that have varied skills, but pursue common goals, distributing their resources and capabilities accordingly; and (c) the challenge of sharing enhanced plan representations among participating entities and evaluating their execution. Our selection of this subfield of AI is justified by its high relevance to the distributed nature and goal-directed behavior of ambient computing environments, and also by its significance in the research towards ambient computing engineering. Table 1 summarizes the requirements of each subject and the techniques that are studied in the rest of this analysis. Although, there are previous works that reflect on limitations of each individual approach under various conditions, to the best of our knowledge, this is the first attempt to frame a range of problems under the Ambient Intelligence domain assessing techniques towards this near-future reality, while at the same time proposing enabling directions of research.

The motivation behind this problem statement paper has been our involvement in a running project that concerns the development of a context-aware platform. The paper is more of a survey and analysis of existing methodologies that have been studied as potential integrals of our platform, rather than a focused evaluation report on a specific implementation. Our objective is to identify gaps in the capabilities of current AI techniques and to suggest the most productive lines of research. As such, the contribution is of both theoretical and practical significance; from a theoretical standpoint we raise numerous research issues and challenges that need to be addressed for understanding the domain and enabling ambient computing systems to operate effectively, while from a practical perspective, we discuss shortcomings of state-of-the-art techniques when applied to real-world conditions and suggest ways to overcome their restrictions.

The rest of this paper is organized as follows. We first briefly present our ongoing work in developing a semantics-based framework that supports services for mobile users in a dynamic environment. The next three sections deal with

Table 1. Overview of Problem Analysis

Domain	Requirements	Methods
Dynamic and Uncertain Environment	Time and Concurrency Continuous Change Non-Determinism Sensing, Knowledge and Belief Natural and Exogenous Actions	STRIPS Situation Calculus Fluent Calculus Event Calculus Action Languages MDPs
Distributed Planning and Coalition Formation	Coordination Cooperation Commitment	GPGP CPS POCL Planning Logic-based Approaches
Plan Representation and Monitoring	Common Plan Interpretation Profile Modelling Online Plan Refinement	HTNs Skeletal Plans Model-based Diagnosis

each of the three problem classes mentioned above. Each section reveals problems that emerge during the development of our platform, projects them to more generic ambient computing requirements and overviews related state-of-the-art research. We conclude in Section 6 with a discussion on enabling research directions towards a pragmatic Ambient Intelligence implementation.

2   Contextual Pedestrian Guide

To motivate the need for a theoretical consideration of the field, we concentrate on the design and analysis phases of a running project that involves the development of semantics-based context-aware services utilizing technologies and formalisms from the Semantic Web and Ambient Intelligence domains. The objective of the project is to explore the intelligent pedestrian navigation by implementing a Context Pedestrian Guiding platform (CG) [2] for users in indoor environments. We focus on modelling and representing context for efficient processing and dissemination of context-based knowledge, in order to develop services for mobile users. A working prototype of the system has been installed in the premises of our research facilities.

2.1   System Design

The platform's architecture, depicted in Figure 1, is designed to support user-centered and device-independent functionality, in order to provide the technical feasibility for building a multitude of context-based services. The framework, intended for indoor environments, is based on a centralized configuration and achieves a high level of transparency in inter-device communication, context management and service deployment.

An RDF-based context model has been designed for use in the CG platform, aiming at addressing issues concerning semantic context representation,

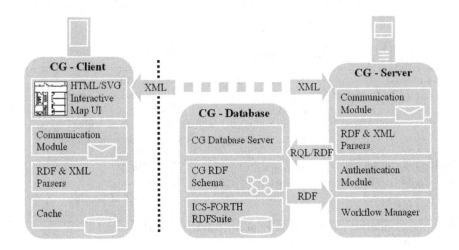

Fig. 1. The CG platform architecture

knowledge sharing and context classification. The ontology captures the relevant notions of physical and semantic entities situated in the system and provides a formal vocabulary for structuring location and other context-aware services. The generic CG RDF Schema follows the abstract design principles of other large-scale pervasive computing ontology frameworks, such as the SOUPA project [3], and defines the high-level concepts of Person, Geographical Space, Location Co-ordinates, CG-Client and Event, as well as the relations among them. The model captures static information (i.e., device ID for CG-Client devices) and dynamic contextual data (events) that have both spatial and temporal extensions, such as user login, change of location in the building and others.

A CG-Client module characterizes the devices with which a user can experience services provided by the CG platform. Different mobile devices can connect as CG-Clients in the system, such as PDAs or laptops, taking advantage of the flexible and portable Web-based model used for its development. CG-Clients connect with the CG-Server, a core component of our centralized architecture that acts as a middleware for processing, managing and transforming stored and inferred knowledge preserved in the CG-Database, while also offering the medium for synthesizing and publishing the desired services. The CG-Server queries the RDF database using the RQL query language.

2.2   CG Services

The system currently supports several services that enable users to obtain and superimpose context-related information on maps, while additional services are in the process of deployment on top of the framework, as will be described next. Our first concern was to implement a number of semantics-based services, such as personal/room information retrieval, room reservation and note keeping, for which a number of automatically generated RQL queries assist users in retrieving relevant RDF-annotated information. A newly published note, for instance, is semantically matched with the preferences of other users, in order to recognize whether its content is of interest to them.

Our present focus concerns the development of personalized, navigational and groupware services. In particular, we wish to enhance the platform with semantic profiles for purposes of context-awareness, privacy and customization of service provisioning depending on the device used. The use of a standardized semantic profile format will provide a unified and secure interface that is not going to be just a repository of static knowledge, but also a semantic directory of dynamic and context specific information. It will encapsulate personal rule definitions about users preferences, device specifications, service invocation and privacy policies. Moreover, we study semantics-based path planning algorithms that, in collaboration with the context ontology and the user's profile information, will assist users in navigating in the premises, considering not only ground plans and landmarks, but also the state of the user's context. Finally, we design and develop groupware services, such as group-calendars, information sharing applications, group notifications, bulletin boards etc., exploiting Semantic Web technologies to support the definition of associations with the context model and user profiles.

3   Complex, Dynamic and Uncertain Environments

Based on the identification of the requirements that a context-based platform, such as the one briefly described above, introduces and the experience gained with its deployment, we conduct a problem statement on the generic challenges of the Ambient Intelligence field and an evaluation of current research solutions.

3.1   Domain-Specific Challenges

The majority of services provided by our platform requires a certain degree of reasoning and plan management skills by the participating agents[1]. For instance, an agent wishing to print a document must deliberate on whether to use the slow inkjet printer located near the user or the faster high resolution laser printer of the adjacent room. It is our intention to enhance our platform with an increasing number of context dimensions and, therefore, the computational complexity of the planning tasks is a reality that we cannot afford to overlook. This challenge motivated us to consider mathematical methods for addressing aspects related to planning, actions and causality. Reasoning about action is a well-formalized and well-characterized subfield of AI, but has not yet been fully integrated in the ambient computing domain. When research on planning within the AI community established the *classical planning problem* for the development of techniques for agents to generate courses of action in order to reach a desirable world state,

---

[1] It is common trend in ambient computing system engineering to have devices participate in communication and negotiation tasks represented by some notion of intelligent software agents. In the rest of the paper we often interchange the terms device and agent, according to context.

it adopted a number of simplifying assumptions to delimit the domain. Some of them were very restrictive; the planning agent was considered omniscient, its actions deterministic, atomic and simultaneous, the environment static and the only source of change in the environment was the agent itself, while no other exogenous event occurred. Of course, these simplifications do not persist in realistic planning situations and must be relaxed or completely eliminated when adapting planners to Ambient Intelligence systems.

3.2 Problem Statement

While studying the Ambient Intelligence domain under the planning context, it is important to understand the class of problems that planning methods face and the challenges that these problems introduce. The ambient environment is an open and highly dynamic environment. Mobile devices connect and disconnect to the network, contributing services with durations that vary according to their expected presence in the environment and the availability of their resources. In fact, even actions, goals and sensor observations have a temporal dimension, whose duration may only be partially known in advance. The assumption of complete world knowledge can no longer persist; agents do not know *a priori* all other entities that are present at a specific time instance nor can they communicate directly with all of them. As a consequence, they have limited perception to acquire knowledge about the world they live in and have to generate plans preserving a level of uncertainty on both the state of the world, the available actions to achieve certain state of affairs and the outcome of those actions. Even the fact of committing different agents to certain tasks cannot be guaranteed to hold, since agents might disconnect before plan generation completes or new and more beneficial opportunities might arise, underscoring the importance of monitoring plan execution and replanning in opportunistic ways. The non-deterministic nature of the environment is emphasized by the recognition that not only agents, but also exogenous events occur, in unpredictable and concurrent manner, affecting the state of the world.

These observations essentially sketch a very challenging dynamic and uncertain environment with increased planning complexity. The question is whether current efforts can attack this problem and provide computationally efficient and scalable solutions under these conditions.

3.3 State-of-the-Art Approaches on Acting in Complex Domains

The AI research community has made significant progress on exploring techniques for extending the classical planning paradigm, relaxing some of its assumptions and much success has been achieved in defining theoretical foundations for modelling more complex domains. Reasoning about action and planning is a fundamental area of research within AI that studies the logical characterization of the concepts of action, change and planning of action sequences to accomplish a given task. Knowledge representation and reasoning has resulted in various formalisms, motivated by theorem proving, state space search and associated logic techniques.

The first effort towards an axiomatization of domains using action theories was accomplished by the STRIPS [4] action representation language that, despite being very restrictive in terms of expressivity, the simplicity of its semantics resulted in a quick and wide adoption. This simplicity justifies the fact that STRIPS now constitutes the core of PDDL (Planning Domain Description Language), the standardized syntax used in the International Planning Competitions, and is also utilized in a multitude of planning formulations.

The Situation Calculus [5], a second-order language designed for representing dynamically changing worlds, is the most influential formalism for reasoning about action and change. All changes are the result of named *actions* performed by agents, while a sequence of actions, denoting a possible world history, is represented by a first-order term called *situation*. Relations and functions whose truth values vary from situation to situation are called *relational* and *functional fluents*, respectively. Actions, situations and fluents are the main ingredients of the Situation Calculus formalism that give a complete treatment of reasoning about action, proposing solutions to many fundamental problems, such as the frame problem. The pure Situation Calculus has been extended to accommodate time [6] and concurrent actions [7], indeterminism and actions with uncertain effects [8], sensing and knowledge-producing actions [9], that is actions whose effects are to change a state of knowledge, ramifications [10] and other parameters.

Although the Situation Calculus suffices to solve the representational frame problem, concerning the efforts to specify the non-effects of actions, it fails to address the inferential frame problem for actually computing these non-effects. The Fluent Calculus [11] that extends the Situation Calculus by the notion of *state*, expressing the fluents that hold in a situation, proposes a more general solution and is more expressive under certain circumstances. For instance, apart from solutions to concurrent, continuous [12] and non-deterministic actions [13], the Fluent Calculus has recently been shown to provide the desired expressivity to solve the frame problem in the context of belief and belief revision [14]. Both calculi have well-established programming languages based on Prolog for cognitive agents to perform automated reasoning (Golog and Flux), their implementations though do not scale well to long action sequences and are restricted to small-scale applications with moderate computational effort.

The Event Calculus is also a widely adopted formalism for reasoning about action and change that addresses more naturally certain phenomena, such as continuous time, concurrent, partially-ordered and triggered events. A number of different dialects have been proposed that are summarized in [15] and [16]. The basic idea of the Event Calculus is to state that fluents are true at particular time-points if they have been initiated by an action occurrence at some earlier-time point and not terminated by another action occurrence in the meantime. The calculus supports default reasoning, i.e., reasoning in which a conclusion is reached based on limited information and later retracted when new information is available, using circumscription.

In addition to these calculi, a family of action theories have been developed that are independent of a specific axiomatization, by attempting formal validation methods for assessing correctness and ensuring that the encoding of any domain will yield correct results. Their semantics are based on the theory of causal explanation, which distinguishes between the claim that a formula is true and the stronger claim that there is a *cause* for it to be true, leading to "causal rules". Gelfond and Lifschitz [17] give an overview of such causal languages, such as action languages $\mathcal{A}$ and $\mathcal{C}$ [18]. The action language $\mathcal{C}+$ [19] that has evolved from $\mathcal{C}$, in an important recent formalism that provides a uniform model for supporting, in addition to conditionals and concurrent actions, also indirect effects and non-deterministic actions. Other similar languages are being proposed (i.e., $G\mathcal{C}+$ [20]) and, although this collection of languages had initially established results for a restricted class of domains, it is now characterized by its high expressivity, natural language-like syntax and clear formal semantics.

Furthermore, when discussing planning in dynamic, stochastic environments, we must not neglect decision-theoretic planning tools that extend the classical AI planning paradigm by modelling problems, in which actions have uncertain effects, agents have incomplete information about the world and solutions are of varying quality. Much recent research on decision-theoretic planning has explicitly adopted the Markov Decision Process (MDP) framework as an underlying model. MDPs have two general impediments that make AI researchers skeptical; how they can model a wide range of planning problems and if they can scale to solve planning problems of reasonable size. This is because the generality of the framework comes at a high price in terms of space for storing the transition matrices and policies, in terms of time required to generate a solution policy and in terms of ease of specification. To obviate the need for explicit state space and action enumeration, certain recent works focus on representing the dynamics of first-order MDPs using stochastic actions and objective functions of generalizations of the Situation Calculus [21] and the Fluent Calculus [22].

The above mentioned formalisms are prominent in handling certain aspects of the planning challenges given the demands raised by ambient computing. The literature is rich with notable related surveys and comparative analyses (i.e., [23,24,25,26]). Still, a common conclusion inferred by studying these formalisms and confirmed by different sources is that combining separate phenomena, such as non-determinism, natural actions or continuous change, in a unified model is no trivial task. It is a fact that most extensions to the problem have been investigated in isolation and combining co-existing models has proven to be very challenging [13]. Moreover, we lack a rich set of good heuristic techniques for generating effective contingent plans and it seems unlikely to find optimal solutions to non-trivial problems; new and dramatically different approaches are needed to deal with them [24]. This conclusion justifies the fact that, despite the rapid progress accomplished on reasoning about actions and planning, researchers have delayed applying theory to practice, when confronting the complexity of realistic domains. To our opinion, although Situation Calculus guided research in the field for years and still is the origin for novel ideas since many inspiring researchers work with it, its reasoning capabilities are limited to short action sequences, thus reducing its applicability for real-life large-scale implementations. We trust the Event Calculus to present the most complete solution for addressing key issues of commonsense reasoning for Ambient Intelligence. It is highly usable, comprehensive and handles inherently most of the important aspects of reasoning about actions, as shown in recent studies (i.e., [27]).

4   Distributed Planning and Multi-agent Coordination

4.1   Domain-Specific Challenges

Extending our platform with new services has made evident the importance of seamless collaboration between numerous devices that must work together to achieve common objectives. Even the more ordinary services like the management of a presentation in a meeting room may involve continuous cooperation between devices, as diverse as the room's projector, the lighting dimmer, the lecturer's laptop and many others. Complicated services require more sophisticated models of teamwork between devices, which differ in capabilities, characteristics and resource limitations. The establishment of common objectives among them entails a comprehensive understanding of the problem domain between participating entities and a confirmed desire to distribute their knowledge and to contribute their capabilities, in order to generate plans for achieving these objectives. Moreover, the assumption that the availability of devices is known beforehand is not valid in our platform, and, therefore, we have to come up with ways to arrange the formation of coalitions at execution time.

4.2   Problem Statement

The Ambient Intelligence domain is frequently characterized as a sensor and device-rich environment supported by software capable of fully leveraging its capacity and providing distributed services. A multitude of appliances, however diverse in capabilities and characteristics, needs to be seamlessly integrated into the users' everyday lives, placing them and their tasks on the center of attention. This scheme requires devices to coordinate their actions, cooperate in generating plans and collaborate during their execution.

If all agents in a system were omniscient of the goals, actions and interaction of their fellow community members and could also have unlimited computational resources, it would be possible to know exactly the present and future actions and intentions of each. Obviously, this in not the case in most real-world systems and in ambient computing structures, in particular. Despite the fact that our platform currently utilizes a centralized knowledge base, there are many situations where services would benefit by distributing reasoning tasks among different devices. A typical example is when a user's connectivity with the network is undermined due to coverage range or bandwidth restrictions, while he can still engage in ad hoc communication with other mobile devices in its vicinity, which contribute resources and services. This decentralized self-organizing infrastructure is a nontrivial challenge for the realization of the AmI vision.

4.3   State-of-the-Art Approaches on Teamwork in Cooperative Problem Solving

Coordination does not imply either cooperation or reciprocation; appliances in a smart space, though, are expected to collaborate in achieving common objectives, after a particular level of trustfulness has been established. Therefore, agents in AmI environments are designed to engage in Cooperative Distributed Planning [28], according to which they are endowed with shared objectives and representations, with the purpose to jointly develop and execute a plan in a coherent and effective manner.

Of the most prominent approaches for multi-agent action coordination is Durfee and Lesser's Partial Global Planning (PGP) framework [29] and its extension Generalized PGP [30]. According to this framework, each agent is not aware of the presence of other agents or their capabilities at the start of the plan generation process, but incrementally obtains a partial conception of their plans. Agents dynamically determine sets of long-term and short-term decisions for achieving their objectives, evaluating a number of predictions and ratings. In GPGP, coordination and task assignment are achieved by negotiation using a family of domain-independent coordination algorithms, while planning is based on a set of heuristics. The framework focuses on dynamically revising plans in cost-effective ways given an uncertain world, rather than optimizing plans for static and predictable environments and can lead to sub-optimal results with reduced costs. Despite its advantages, the framework is restricted to domains where temporary incoherence among agents is affordable as information about unanticipated changes to plans is propagated. Therefore, it is inappropriate for domains with irreversible actions where guarantees about coordination must be made prior to any execution [31]. In addition, PGP assumes explicit communication between agents in order to achieve coordination and is not scalable when agents' commitments to partial subgoals are not highly persistent.

In fact, this notion of commitment is essential when attempting to coordinate multi-agent interactions and has been given much importance in the Joint Intention model developed by Cohen and Levesque [32], influencing many works since. This model specifies how a group of agents can act together by sharing certain mental beliefs about the cooperative behavior and forming individual and joint commitments for pursuing goals. The Cooperative Problem Solving (CPS) abstract formal model of [33] is based on the Joint Intention theory and is the first comprehensive attempt to formalize intentions by making a distinction between commitments and conventions (a means for monitoring a commitment) in a mathematical framework. CPS describes a teamwork process evolving in 4 stages, namely recognition, team formation, plan formation, and team action. Although structured around some restricting assumptions, the framework provides principles, which lay a solid ground for designing models that face challenges of teamwork formation in more complicated systems.

Many researchers explore the multi-agent plan coordination problem by extending the partial-order, causal-link (POCL) definition of a plan described in [34]. According to this definition, a plan has temporal and causal partial order constraints on plan steps and as new steps are added (i.e., when loosely-coupled agents attempt to combine their plans) these constraints might get violated and inconsistencies or plan flaws might arise. There are works that investigate ways to transform inconsistent plans into consistent. In [35] a general plan-space search algorithm is described that repairs flaws by exploiting a hierarchical plan representation to reduce the complexity of the plan coordination problem. The same type of flaws, namely causal link threatening and parallel action interference, as well as redundant actions between agents that coordinate their plans, are handled in [36] using the propositional satisfiability approach. There, the authors have developed branch and bound algorithms for multi-agent coordination and cooperation scenarios, where actions have time extents and individual plans are iteratively expanded to an optimal, with respect to length, joint plan. A different approach is followed in [37] that casts the multi-agent plan coordination problem as a type of Distributed Constraint Optimization Problem and examines the efficiency of applying techniques from this domain for solving the problem, such as ADOPT, an algorithm that exploits local communication and parallel computations. Still, this problem is shown to be NP-Hard [38] and attempts to develop computationally-efficient algorithms that produce optimally-coordinated plans are limited, focusing mostly on restricted forms of it (see for example [39]).

Other efforts logically analyze the ability of agents to cooperate in executing complex actions for reaching certain states of affairs. In [40] a complete axiomatization for a dynamic logic that models agent capabilities in executing collective plans in environments that require concurrent actions of several agents is presented. Such formalisms, which are based on cooperation logics, such as Coalition Logic [41] and Coalition Logic for Propositional Control [42], represent important tools not only for verification purposes by proving that a desired goal of a system can be achieved, but also for explicitly capturing how a plan can be executed. Still, they require the designer to sacrifice expressivity, in order to handle the complexity of real-world dynamic and multidimensional problems.

As the previous discussion has shown, despite the well-studied tools and techniques in the repertoire of distributed AI, many of its accomplishments fail to function efficiently when applied to real-world conditions, a conclusion confirmed by many recent studies as well ([31,43,44]). However interesting the existing approaches on distributed planning and coalition formation may be, the common feeling is that they are not mature enough to guarantee successful teamwork in a pragmatic context-aware environment. It is anticipated that more comprehensive methods for coordination and distributed planning in open and dynamic environments must arise that will overcome issues mentioned above.

5   Plan Representation and Monitoring

5.1   Domain-Specific Challenges

The overall implementation of our context-aware platform was structured around a number of observations that specify the basic motivations of the domain, such as the desire to provide context-aware services to users that operate on a variety of mobile devices. In order for our architecture to support this scheme, we seek ways to represent the capabilities of these devices so that services can be adapted according to them. Profiles of devices must be flexible enough to capture both the complex actions that they can perform, but also decompositions of them to more low-level actions, so that planning agents can understand and combine these actions to distribute responsibilities during service execution. There are obstacles that we need to overcome for achieving this type of interactions in our framework, since we assume that the existence of visitors possessing partially unknown mobile devices is going to be a common situation for the system.

5.2   Problem Statement

In order for any Ambient Intelligence framework to support the challenges discussed so far, we also need to seek ways to represent device and service profiles, plans and goals in a manner that is mutually apprehended and correctly interpreted by all participating entities. Instead of exclusively focussing on improving our planners, other facets of the problem should also come into consideration that can refine the planning task. Autonomous agents need to recognize which planning problems and opportunities to consider in the first place. They need to be able to weight alternative incomplete plans and to decide among competing alternatives on execution time. They need to be able to function intelligently in an ambient environment in a way that comports with the inherent bounds on their computational resources. They need to share a common plan representation or a common ontology for describing their plans, goals and actions. And they need to be able to exchange freely their plans and describe their action behaviors, privacy policies and authenticity certificates, in terms of expressive planning languages.

5.3   State-of-the-Art Approaches on Plan Representation and Monitoring

Much of the research has been focusing on representing plans using some form of abstraction and decomposition, with hierarchical task networks (HTN) [45] being the most notable approach. HTN plan representations allow a distributed planning agent to successively refine its planning decisions as it learns more about other agents' plans. This abstraction-based methodology has been widely used in a variety of domains, and attempts have also been presented to adapt it to the Ambient Intelligence domain (see [46] for an illustrative example). An interesting application of HTN-like action representation is demonstrated in [47], where the intention is to model joint complex actions of multi-agent partially ordered plans under temporal and precedence constraints in dynamic environments. Compared with classical planners, HTN planners have more sophisticated knowledge representation and reasoning capabilities and are more expressive, because they can even be used to encode undecidable problems. Logics-based formalisms are evenly expressive and is hard to say which formalism is more effective. Both types are suitable in different situations, as illustrated in [23], and combining them is a useful topic for future research.

A rather similar approach, originally proposed in [48], is representing procedural knowledge in a library of skeletal plans. Skeletal plans are plan schemata at various levels of detail, which capture the essence of the procedure, but leave room for execution-time flexibility in the achievement of particular goals and are also being tested in real-world systems, such as [49]. Although being reusable in various contexts and able to capture in restricted form both complex and primitive actions, skeletal plan representations are domain-specific and it is questionable if they can confront the openness of ubiquitous systems.

In fact, there is a significant gap in the field for methods and tools capable of representing both complex and primitive actions in an expressive manner and with formal semantics, with only few exceptions being present (i.e., McIlraith et. al in [50,51]). Attention should be given in representations that allow a system to capture and share the capabilities of the diverse devices that operate in it and permit them to distribute common plan configurations.

Creating a conflict-free plan for a multi-agent system in a dynamic and unpredictable environment that will remain conflict free during execution, is a laborious task. As agents execute their plans, they monitor their execution by making partial observations that are used to detect plan deviations. Part of related work concentrates on how to explain such erroneous actions by applying *Model-based Diagnosis* [52]. This technique is used to infer abnormalities of internal components of a given system from its input-output behavior and studies, such as [53] and [54], adapt and extend Model-based Diagnosis to multi-agent planning systems. Each component has several health modes; a normal mode and several fault modes. Once the health mode for each component is specified, the behavior of the total system is defined and the output can be inferred. In fact, since in a plan several instances of the same action might occur, an error occurring in one instance might be used to predict the occurrence of the same error in an action instance to be executed later on. The result of Model-based Diagnosis is a suitable assignment of health modes to the components, called a *diagnosis*, such that the actually observed output is consistent with this health mode qualification or can be *explained* by this qualification. Using this technique we can adjust the plan execution within the margins of the plan by determining events that cause constraint violation, thus avoiding replanning the tasks. In [53], in particular, actions are described in an object-oriented manner, rather than the traditional state-based approach. This view of actions as components, and preconditions and effects of actions as objects, allows the plan itself to be viewed as the structural description of a system.

6   Conclusions and Future Lines of Research

As research in AI is oriented towards addressing real-world problems, exploring relaxations of the simplifying assumptions, the efficiency and viability of existing methods will be tested. We have attempted an assessment of state-of-the-art approaches and principles to determine where there is room for improvement and where a different research perspective is necessary, in the context of ambient computing systems. It is indeed evident that there are still serious obstacles that have not been hurdled. Nevertheless, in this paper we argue that regression steps are not justified. To pursue the vision of intelligent environments we need to rethink about the capabilities of our existing tools and focus on those fields that seem more prominent in meeting the new challenges and ideas that the main tenet of Ambient Intelligence introduces. As a starting point, two abstract research directions are presented next that, although being moderately novel in classical AI, are highly relevant in the cross section of Ambient Intelligence and AI research. Departing from the typical planning picture, we attempt to contrast the state-of-the-art in symbolic planning with requirements imposed by ambient computing scenarios, citing also initial attempts that follow these directions.

6.1   The Continual Planning Paradigm

Our remarks concerning a highly dynamic, uncertain environment, where planning and reasoning tasks are performed by devices that may have limited resources available and where knowledge concerning world state is dynamically acquired, have led us to abandon traditional multi-agent planning approaches. As argued in [25], autonomous agents in dynamic environments need to be able to form incomplete plans now, adding detail later and deciding upon the amount of detail to include at each time instance. A new paradigm has been proposed that interleaves plan generation and execution and adopts strategies that allow agents not to plan too much detail too far into the future so that they can confront with the diversity of upcoming events. This technique of performing a tightly coupled control loop between plan generation and execution, first proposed in [28], is called *Continual Planning* and requires an iterative collaboration of the tasks of environment monitoring, plan adaptation and replanning.

More specifically, [28] suggests that an agent should plan continually when aspects of the world can change dynamically beyond the control of the agent, when aspects of the world are revealed incrementally, when time pressures require execution to begin before a complete plan can be generated or when objectives can evolve over time. Continual planning suggests having a single plan and continuously monitor its execution, in contrast to the traditional approach of handling uncertainty by planning for all the contingencies that might arise. Since this approach views planning as an ongoing, dynamic process it can benefit the system not only by reacting to unhealthy situations, but also by adapting to opportunities to improve the plan, repairing it when necessary. Only recently have frameworks started adapting to this real-time planning and execution approach ([47,55]), while the need to explore this direction of research in ambient applications has also been underscored by many recent reports (i.e., [43,44]).

6.2   Context-Aware Planning Paradigm

We have already stressed the fact that in order to attain the goal of planning in dynamic and partially known environments we have to endow agents with cognitive capabilities. When agents weight alternative subplans to reach a certain state of affairs or even when they consider the most profitable next step to a plan, it is often useful to interleave reasoning in the process. Until recently, most approaches only modelled conventional aspects, such as precedence constraints or plan length, relying on replanning techniques to deal with plan failure, when new constraints were added. Nonetheless, the impact of planning can be increased if we consider a richer set of aspects that are truly related to the domain we model. Temporal constraints, such as action durations and temporal instantiation of action are a common alternative for accomplishing scheduling tasks in real time, while a number of studies deliberate on action durations and deadlines of goals. This is a more pragmatic approach requiring reasoning about whether or not goals can be achieved by their deadlines and leads in associating priority values to goals and to the actions which contribute to those goals.

Reasoning over a richer collection of metrics and focusing on the most relevant ones might prove an essential aid in improving planning, both from the computational standpoint, by reducing the search space, and from the perspective of efficiency, since more accurate plans will be generated. Indeed, we believe that the Ambient Intelligence domain raises many opportunities for exploiting reasoning to influence the efficiency of planning. The most important leverage is to exploit the context in which an agent is situated, affecting its plan-generation capabilities. Context awareness has become a hot topic in recent computing research and reasoning on context can be an important source of information both for allowing agents to determine the current state of the world and for restricting possible future states, enabling them to constraint and better prioritize their goals. Moreover, it is anticipated that privacy and trust issues are going to be of utmost importance in designing Ambient Intelligence systems, strengthening the need to include trustfulness values, along with importance values, to actions and subplans. This will enrich the plan evaluation process by allowing users to prioritize goals not only by their significance and success probability, but also by taking into account preference and privacy profiles. We expect this new paradigm of *context-aware planning* to play a determinant role in ambient IS, guiding computationally efficient planning solutions in realistic conditions. Studies, such as [55] and [56] adopt this new trend, incorporating resource allocation and user preference metrics in plan refinement and execution.

References

1. Rogers, Y.: Moving on from Weiser's Vision of Calm Computing: Engaging Ubi-Comp Experiences. In: Dourish, P., Friday, A. (eds.) UbiComp 2006. LNCS, vol. 4206, pp. 404–421. Springer, Heidelberg (2006)
2. Patkos, T., Bikakis, A., Antoniou, G., Papadopouli, M., Plexousakis, D.: A Semantics-based Framework for Context-Aware Services: Lessons Learned and Challenges. In: UIC 2007, pp. 839–848 (2007)
3. Chen, H., Finin, T., Joshi, A.: The SOUPA Ontology for Pervasive Computing. In: Tamma, V., Stephen Cranefield, T.F., Willmott, S. (eds.) Ontologies for Agents: Theory and Experiences, Springer, Heidelberg (2005)
4. Fikes, R., Nilsson, N.J.: STRIPS: A New Approach to the Application of Theorem Proving to Problem Solving. In: IJCAI, pp. 608–620 (1971)

5. Levesque, H., Pirri, F., Reiter, R.: Foundations for the Situation Calculus. In: Linkoping Electronic Articles in Computer and Information Science, vol. 3 (1998)
6. Pinto, J.A.: Temporal Reasoning in the Situation Calculus. PhD thesis (1994)
7. Reiter, R.: Natural Actions, Concurrency and Continuous Time in the Situation Calculus. In: KR 1996. Principles of Knowledge Representation and Reasoning: Proceedings of the Fifth International Conference, Cambridge, Massachusetts, USA, pp. 2–13 (November 1996)
8. Pinto, J., Sernadas, A., Sernadas, C., Mateus, P.: Non-determinism and Uncertainty in the Situation Calculus. Int. J. Uncertain. Fuzziness Knowl.-Based Syst. 8(2), 127–149 (2000)
9. Scherl, R.B., Levesque, H.J.: Knowledge, Action, and the Frame Problem. Artif. Intell. 144(1-2), 1–39 (2003)
10. Papadakis, N., Plexousakis, D.: Actions with Duration and Constraints: The Ramification Problem in Temporal Databases. In: ICTAI 2002. Proceedings of the 14th IEEE International Conference on Tools with Artificial Intelligence, pp. 83–90. IEEE Computer Society, Washington, DC, USA (2002)
11. Thielscher, M.: From Situation Calculus to Fluent Calculus: State Update Axioms as a Solution to the Inferential Frame Problem. Artif. Intell. 111(1-2), 277–299 (1999)
12. Thielscher, M.: The Concurrent, Continuous Fluent Calculus. Studia Logica 67(3), 315–331 (2001)
13. Thielscher, M.: Modeling Actions with Ramifications in Nondeterministic, Concurrent, and Continuous Domains - and a Case Study. In: Proceedings of the 17th National Conference on Artificial Intelligence and 12th Conference on Innovative Applications of Artificial Intelligence, AAAI Press / The MIT Press, pp. 497–502 (2000)
14. Scherl, R.B.: Action, Belief Change and the Frame Problem: A Fluent Calculus Approach. In: Proceedings of the Sixth Workshop on Nonmonotonic Reasoning, Action, and Change at IJCAI 2005, Edinburgh, Scotland (August 2005)
15. Shanahan, M.: The Event Calculus Explained. In: Veloso, M.M., Wooldridge, M.J. (eds.) Artificial Intelligence Today. LNCS (LNAI), vol. 1600, pp. 409–431. Springer, Heidelberg (1999)
16. Miller, R., Shanahan, M.: Some Alternative Formulations of the Event Calculus. In: Computational Logic: Logic Programming and Beyond, Essays in Honour of Robert A. Kowalski, Part II, pp. 452–490. Springer, London, UK (2002)
17. Gelfond, M., Lifschitz, V.: Action Languages. Electronic Transactions on AI 3 (1998)
18. Giunchiglia, E., Lifschitz, V.: An Action Language Based on Causal Explanation: Preliminary Report. In: AAAI 1998/IAAI 1998: Proceedings of the Fifteenth National/Tenth Conference on Artificial intelligence/Innovative Applications of Artificial Intelligence, American Association for Artificial Intelligence, pp. 623–630 (1998)
19. Giunchiglia, E., Lee, J., Lifschitz, V., McCain, N., Turner, H.: Nonmonotonic Causal Theories. Artif. Intell. 153(1-2), 49–104 (2004)
20. Finzi, A., Lukasiewicz, T.: Game-Theoretic Reasoning About Actions in Nonmonotonic Causal Theories. In: Baral, C., Greco, G., Leone, N., Terracina, G. (eds.) LP-NMR 2005. LNCS (LNAI), vol. 3662, pp. 185–197. Springer, Heidelberg (2005)
21. Boutilier, C., Reiter, R., Price, B.: Symbolic Dynamic Programming for First-Order MDPs. In: IJCAI 2001. Proceedings of the Seventeenth International Joint Conference on Artificial Intelligence, Seattle, Washington, USA, pp. 690–700 (2001)

22. Großmann, A., Hölldobler, S., Skvortsova, O.: Symbolic Dynamic Programming within the Fluent Calculus. In: Ishii, N. (ed.) Proceedings of the IASTED International Conference on Artificial and Computational Intelligence, pp. 378–383. ACTA Press, Tokyo, Japan (2002)

23. Ghallab, M., Nau, D., Traverso, P.: Automated Planning: Theory and Practice. Morgan Kaufmann, San Francisco (2004)

24. Bresina, J., Dearden, R., Meuleau, N., Ramkrishnan, S., Smith, D., Washington, R.: Planning under Continuous Time and Resource Uncertainty: A Challenge for AI. In: UAI 2002. Proceedings of the 18th Annual Conference on Uncertainty in Artificial Intelligence, pp. 77–84. Morgan Kaufmann, San Francisco, CA (2002)

25. Pollack, M., Horty, J.F.: There's More to Life than Making Plans. The AI Magazine 20(4), 71–84 (1999)

26. Blythe, J.: Decision-Theoretic Planning. AI Magazine 20(2), 37–54 (1999)

27. Mueller, E.: Automating Commonsense Reasoning Using the Event Calculus. Communications of the ACM (in press, 2007)

28. des Jardins, M., Durfee, E.H., Ortiz Jr., C.L., Wolverton, M.: A Survey of Research in Distributed, Continual Planning. AI Magazine 20(4), 13–22 (1999)

29. Durfee, E.H., Lesser, V.R.: Partial Global Planning: A Coordination Framework for Distributed Hypothesis Formation. IEEE Transactions on Systems, Man, and Cybernetics 21(5), 1167–1183 (1991)

30. Lesser, V.R.: Evolution of the GPGP/TÆMS Domain-Independent Coordination Framework. In: AAMAS 2002. Proceedings of the First International Joint Conference on Autonomous Agents and Multiagent Systems, pp. 1–2. ACM Press, New York (2002)

31. Durfee, E.H.: Distributed Problem Solving and Planning. In: Luck, M., Mařík, V., Štěpánková, O., Trappl, R. (eds.) ACAI 2001 and EASSS 2001. LNCS (LNAI), vol. 2086, pp. 118–149. Springer, London, UK (2001)

32. Cohen, P.R., Levesque, H.J.: Teamwork. Technical Report 504, Menlo Park, CA (1991)

33. Wooldridge, M., Jennings, N.R.: Towards a Theory of Cooperative Problem Solving. In: Perram, J., Müller, J.P. (eds.) MAAMAW 1994. LNCS, vol. 1069, pp. 40–53. Springer, London, UK (1996)

34. Weld, D.S.: An Introduction to Least Commitment Planning. AI Magazine 15(4), 27–61 (1994)

35. Cox, J.S., Durfee, E.H.: An Efficient Algorithm for Multiagent Plan Coordination. In: AAMAS 2005. Proceedings of the Fourth International Joint Conference on Autonomous Agents and Multiagent Systems, pp. 828–835. ACM Press, New York (2005)

36. Dimopoulos, Y., Moraitis, P.: Multi-agent Coordination and Cooperation Through Classical Planning. In: IAT 2006. Proceedings of the IEEE/WIC/ACM International Conference on Intelligent Agent Technology (IAT 2006 Main Conference Proceedings) (IAT 2006), pp. 398–402. IEEE Computer Society, Washington, DC, USA (2006)

37. Cox, J.S., Durfee, E.H., Bartold, T.: A Distributed Framework for Solving the Multiagent Plan Coordination Problem. In: AAMAS 2005. Proceedings of the Fourth International Joint Conference on Autonomous Agents and Multiagent Systems, pp. 821–827. ACM Press, New York (2005)

38. Yang, Q.: Intelligent Planning: A Decomposition and Abstraction Based Approach. Springer, London (1997)

39. Valk, J.M., de Weerdt, M.M., Witteveen, C.: Algorithms for Coordination in Multi-Agent Planning. In: Vlahavas, I., Vrakas, D. (eds.) Intelligent Techniques for Planning, pp. 194–224. Idea Group Inc., London (2005)

40. Sauro, L., Gerbrandy, J., van der Hoek, W., Wooldridge, M.: Reasoning About Action and Cooperation. In: AAMAS 2006. Proceedings of the Fifth International Joint Conference on Autonomous Agents and Multiagent Systems, pp. 185–192. ACM Press, New York, USA (2006)

41. Pauly, M.: A Modal Logic for Coalitional Power in Games. Journal of Logic and Computation 12, 146–166 (2002)

42. van der Hoek, W., Wooldridge, M.: On the Logic of Cooperation and Propositional Control. Artif. Intell. 164(1-2), 81–119 (2005)

43. de Weerdt, M., ter Mors, A., Witteveen, C.: Multi-agent Planning: An Introduction to Planning and Coordination. In: Handouts of the European Agent Summer School, pp. 1–32 (2005)

44. Chen, H., Finin, T.: Beyond Distributed AI, Agent Teamwork in Ubiquitous Computing. In: AAMAS 2002. Workshop on Ubiquitous Agents on Embedded, Wearable, and Mobile Devices (July 2002)

45. Erol, K., Hendler, J., Nau, D.S.: HTN Planning: Complexity and Expressivity. In: AAAI 1994. Proceedings of the Twelfth National Conference on Artificial Intelligence, Menlo Park, CA, USA, American Association for Artificial Intelligence, vol. 2, pp. 1123–1128 (1994)

46. Amigoni, F., Gatti, N., Pinciroli, C., Roveri, M.: What Planner for Ambient Intelligence Applications? IEEE Transactions on Systems, Man, and Cybernetics, Part A 35(1), 7–21 (2005)

47. Hadad, M., Kraus, S., Gal, Y., Lin, R.: Temporal Reasoning for a Collaborative Planning Agent in a Dynamic Environment. Annals of Mathematics and Artificial Intelligence 37(4), 331–379 (2003)

48. Friedland, P., Iwasaki, Y.: The Concept and Implementation of Skeletal Plans. J. Autom. Reasoning 1(2), 161–208 (1985)

49. Miksch, S., Seyfang, A.: Continual Planning with Time-Oriented, Skeletal Plans. In: ECAI, pp. 511–515 (2000)

50. Baier, J.A., McIlraith, S.A.: On Planning with Programs That Sense. In: KR, pp. 492–502 (2006)

51. McIlraith, S., Fadel, R.: Planning with Complex Actions. In: NMR 2002. Proc. International Workshop on Non-Monotonic Reasoning, pp. 356–364 (2002)

52. Console, L., Torasso, P.: A Spectrum of Logical Definitions of Model-Based Diagnosis. Comput. Intell. 7(3), 133–141 (1991)

53. Witteveen, C., Roos, N., van der Krogt, R., de Weerdt, M.: Diagnosis of Single and Multi-agent Plans. In: AAMAS 2005. Proceedings of the Fourth International Joint Conference on Autonomous Agents and Multiagent Systems, pp. 805–812. ACM Press, New York (2005)

54. Kalech, M., Kaminka, G.A.: On the Design of Social Diagnosis Algorithms for Multi-agent Teams. In: IJCAI, pp. 370–375 (2003)

55. Coddington, A., Luck, M.: A Motivation-based Planning and Execution Framework. International Journal on Artificial Intelligence Tools 13(1), 5–25 (2004)

56. Look, G., Peters, S., Shrobe, H.: Plan-driven Ubiquitous Computing. In: Dey, A.K., Schmidt, A., McCarthy, J.F. (eds.) UbiComp 2003. LNCS, vol. 2864, pp. 66–73. Springer, Heidelberg (2003)

Active Coordination Artifacts in Collaborative Ubiquitous-Computing Environments

Marco P. Locatelli and Marco Loregian

University of Milano-Bicocca,
viale Sarca 336, 20126 Milano, Italy
{locatelli,loregian}@disco.unimib.it

Abstract. Coordination artifacts play a primary role in cooperation and, in particular, active artifacts allow for the development of flexible cooperative software systems. Their role with respect to ubiquitous-computing environments can be defined, exploited, and assessed according to different perspectives. This paper presents a notion of active artifact that relies on the seminal definition given in CSCW literature by Schmidt and Simone, and it is applied to a model for systems supporting ubiquitous-computing collaborative environments (CASMAS). A technique to configure and interact with such environments, i.e., the composition of devices' functionalities according to their high-level features, and services provided, is presented. A scenario is used as an in-depth example along the paper. The architecture of a system implementing the scenario using our reference middleware is presented.

1 Introduction

Ubiquitous-computing systems are designed to fulfill users' needs in specific settings and scenarios, where a multitude of interconnected devices have to be properly configured and orchestrated [1]. The definition and dynamic re-arrangement of such configurations (to support user cooperation) is one of the most relevant issues in this research field, and it is addressed in this paper.

An approach grounded in the notion of *active coordination artifact* [2] is presented along with the interaction mechanisms among different entities — both human and technological — with the aim of providing a complete framework for the design of flexible adaptive systems. Active artifacts autonomously support cooperation by propagating over the environment information about their internal state, that reaches other entities that can then act conveniently within the context.

Ubiquitous-computing environments are inherently characterized by the communities of persons populating them and by the activities such actors perform. The study of coordination mechanisms, meaning the ways in which actors in collaborative settings pursue their goals, led to the notion of coordination artifact as the permanent symbolic construct objectifying interaction protocols [2]. In other words, a coordination artifact can be defined as a physical or symbolic object mediating interactions, playing an enabling and/or constraining function.

B. Schiele et al. (Eds.): AmI 2007, LNCS 4794, pp. 177–194, 2007.
© Springer-Verlag Berlin Heidelberg 2007

Additionally, artifacts can be provided with a representation function, when involved in cognitive processes [3]. Such artifacts have been in use for coordination purposes in cooperative settings across centuries in forms ranging from plain time-tables, to checklists, to electronic bug reports and so on. More recently, the adoption of computational coordination artifacts opened many possibilities to support cooperative work, mainly by delegating to the artifacts the tedious routines of articulation work, enhancing systems with distributed and flexible coordination capabilities. In particular, active coordination artifacts (*active artifacts* henceforth), being computational, are able to conveniently propagate awareness and coordination information to drive the execution of activities. Although some similarities can be found between this definition of active artifacts and workflow management systems (WfMS), they are intrinsically different because an active artifact is the "object" through which persons coordinate themselves, while a WfMS acts instead as the "coordinator" of persons. In other words, while an active artifact is never *prescriptive* — meaning that it cannot induce actors to undertake actions — a WfMS always is, by definition.

The approach presented in this paper is agent-based, and the role of active artifacts is presented accordingly. To highlight the features of the mechanism, a scenario referring to education (Fig. 1) is presented in the next section, other examples have already been presented [4]. The scenario is described according to our reference model (CASMAS, Community-Aware Situated Multi-Agent Systems [5]) in Section 3, and then the architecture of a system implementing the same scenario using our reference middleware (MICA, MIddleware for CASMAS) is presented (Section 4). Finally, a discussion of related work and concluding remarks are given.

2 Scenario

In education facilities enabled by ubiquitous computing technology, classrooms are equipped with a minimal set of devices providing: people identification or localization, projection on a large surface, audio-video recording, and interaction with electronic documents. Complementarily, personal devices seamlessly integrate into an organization-wide cooperative infrastructure. In this kind of scenario, all devices are supposed to be *smart* and able to execute or participate in software applications according to the ubiquitous-computing paradigm [1]. For this reason, the term "smart" is omitted from devices' name from this point on.

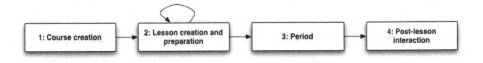

Fig. 1. Main phases of the scenario

Mrs. Jameson is a teacher of the Institute, and she is allowed to use its modern facilities. She can seamlessly work in her office or in a classroom: when she is sitting at her desk, she can use her habitual PC applications, and she is aided by the cooperative infrastructure when interacting with other devices (such as her PDA or mobile phone) and to access documents in a content management system. She can schedule lessons and prepare them by selecting the material to be used in the classroom (e.g., slides, videos), and the readings and exercises to assign. When Mrs. Jameson enters the classroom where one of her lessons is scheduled for the moment, the environment automatically sets up according to the situation: teaching materials are retrieved from the content management system and presented to the teacher on the interactive surface of her desk, the projecting equipment switchs on to display the presentation, and the audio/video equipment starts recording, possibly streaming to remote students. The system also monitors the breaks in the lesson and its ending (and stops recording) either automatically, for example if the teacher leaves the room before time, or with a manual command from the desk. After the period, both the teacher and the students can revise the lesson: the former to add or change some material, the latter to comment, ask questions, or deliver assigned homework.

The system provides a twofold support in the scenario above: technological, facilitating the orchestration of devices — and the services they provide, — and cognitive, enabling actors to interact and share knowledge within the community associated with the course. Moreover, the *lesson* can be seen as the focal point of interaction, and thus as a candidate coordination artifact.

3   The Reference Model: CASMAS

Ubiquitous-computing systems can shape up as constellations of dynamically defined and interacting *communities* of human and technological *entities*. In the model we are presenting (called CASMAS, Community-Aware Situated Multi-Agent Systems, Fig. 2), each entity is represented by two sets of agents belonging to two separate classes — grouped in two *modules*, — defined according to roles: agents can either enact *cooperation* mechanisms (within the communities to which entities belong), or supply information related to context *awareness* [6].

Communities are established in the cooperation module by aggregation points called *community fulcra*. Community fulcra are designed to contain characteristic information: entities gather around them to exploit such information and contribute to the definition of communities. Each community is represented in the model by a specific fulcrum. Entities connect to community fulcra by means of cooperation agents (**C-agents**) (Fig. 3). Entities own a distinct C-agent for each of the communities in which they participate: when created, all C-agents are provided with generic inferential capabilities and with a set of entity-specific statements and rules. By connecting to a community fulcrum, C-agents standing

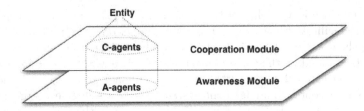

Fig. 2. Abstraction of the CASMAS reference model: each entity (person, device, or service) is modeled in two separate modules using a set of cooperation and awareness agents

for different entities can share information (*statements*) and acquire community-specific behaviors (*rules*) that are either defined at design time or injected in the fulcrum by other entities (details will be provided next). In addition, each entity owns a private *personal fulcrum* for its inner coordination: each C-agent is also connected to this fulcrum, and only C-agents belonging to an entity can access its personal fulcrum.

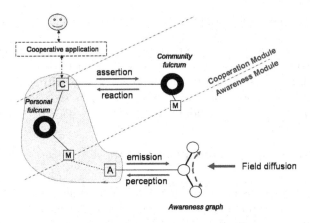

Fig. 3. Elements of the reference model

The behaviors of C-agents are influenced by the degree of participation of entities in communities, according to additional context information that is supplied by the awareness module.

The context-awareness facet of an ubiquitous-computing environment can encompass several different aspects, such as the physical position of an entity as well as its logical (sometimes social) role, such as the responsibility in an organization or a project. Aim of the **awareness module** is to manage this kind of information, and entities are therein represented by specific awareness agents (**A-agents**).

The (spatial, social, organizational) environments in which entities are situated are modeled as awareness graphs, also called *topological spaces*, and A-agents are connected to graph nodes accordingly. Each community can refer to one or more graphs (one for each aspect), therefore, each entity needs an A-agent for each graph. Similarly, the same graph could support more than one community. However, different communities may have different perceptions of the same aspect (e.g., different notions of distance with respect to the same spatial arrangement) thus requiring a more precise definition of interaction on awareness graphs.

The awareness module has been designed according to the perception-reaction paradigm [7]: the behaviors of A-agents are driven by the perception of signals, called *fields*, emitted by other agents and propagated across the awareness graph (e.g., to notify presence in a specific position). The propagation of fields is mediated in intensity according to a graph-specific and community-specific distance function evaluated in and between nodes. When a field reaches a node its intensity is computed according to the weight of the arc connecting the current node to the one from which the field is coming, and then the field (if sufficiently intense) can be propagated to adjacent nodes. If the field reaches a node where an A-agent is connected, and if it is relevant to the A-agent, the agent evaluates its local intensity according to a characteristic function: possibly, the A-agent can then emit new fields as the result of inner computation, and reach other A-agents. Additionally, A-agents can provide information for the cooperation module, to possibly trigger some reaction in the C-agents.

To this aim, special agents bridging information between the two modules are defined: manager agents (**M-agents**) are specialized C-agents that can translate information expressed in terms of fields (exported by the A-agents) into statements that C-agents can understand (by publishing them into the personal fulcrum), and, in the other direction, import fields in A-agents when requests for propagation come from C-agents (e.g., when a device localizes an entity, Section 3.2). Finally, each community fulcrum has an M-agent enforcing inter-entity coordination by causing the propagation of general community awareness information on awareness graphs (e.g., causing devices to join the community when they are needed, Section 3.2), and by applying access policies and preventing unauthorized entities to join the community.

In the following, a detailed description of active artifacts, in terms of the elements of the model, is given.

3.1   Active Artifacts in the Model

Active artifacts are first-class abstractions, to be defined at design time, and provided at run time to agents to enact the desired behaviors [8]. The process of definition of the application functionalities must be independent from the implementation of the model, and agents should dynamically enact different policies according to the desired outcome in a certain situation.

While there exist approaches adopting persistent nodes of the systems, where context information is shared, as coordination artifacts – e.g, tuple spaces in TuCSoN [3], which are conceptually similar to what we called community fulcra, — the role of active artifacts in CASMAS, according to the definition provided in the introduction of this paper, is covered by specialized *entities*.

Coordination policies are carried over the environment by specialized C-agents that can connect to the fulcra where coordination is required, providing a reference to other involved entities, and then disconnect when their presence is no longer needed, so to allow entities to coordinate differently. Awareness policies induce specific behaviors in the entities involved, but these entities can also ignore the awareness information (e.g., due to their state) without affecting the overall behavior of the community.

Active artifacts can play a functional role in helping the mediation of the articulation work among the cooperating entities involved in the community, and is characterized by the properties presented in Table 1.

Table 1. Characteristics of active artifacts

ID	The ID of the artifact, from which it is recognizable in the system.
Content	Information carried by the artifact. This field is structured, meaning that complex and manifold information can be carried, according with the definition of the specific artifact. The definition, as well as information, is domain dependent.
Access rights	What entities, individually or by role, can access the content, in terms of *read* and *update* operations.
Definition rights	What entities, individually or by role, can alter the definition of the artifact, in terms of *define* (create new properties, remove existing ones) and *adapt* (re-define existing properties) operations.
Awareness	How to elaborate and/or propagate awareness information related to changes of the internal state (upon external events); detailed specification is given in Table 2.
Coordination	How to enact and/or propagate coordination information related to changes of the internal state (upon external events); detailed specification is given in Table 3.

Activities related to awareness and coordination are triggered by contextual factors (e.g., perception of particular awareness fields, observation of coordination statements to which the artifact is sensitive) according to conditions based on artifacts' internal state, and/or to specific events. When the conditions are satisfied, the consequent effect is enacted: in response to such event receiver entities must (coordination case) or may (awareness case) react accordingly.

In Tables 2 and 3, which describe how awareness and coordination propagation work, `out-trigger` identifies the assertion of coordination information or the propagation of awareness information, `in-trigger` is the perception of either coordination or awareness information, and `function` is an operation of modification to the artifact itself. The * symbol means that the related construct can be present more than one time. A construct between square brackets (i.e., [and]) is optional. Finally, ‖ means that two activities may happen at the same time, in parallel.

Table 4 shows the definition of a lesson (as presented in the scenario, Section 2) as an example of active artifact.

Table 2. Form of awareness characteristics

`condition-on-internal-state*` → `out-trigger*` When the change in the information of the artifact happens, one (or more) awareness information are propagated.
`[condition-on-internal-state*` ∧`]` `in-trigger*` → `out-trigger*` ‖ `function*` When the artifact is aware of some kind of information (`in-trigger`), possibly guarded by the state of the information of the artifact, one (or more) awareness information can be propagated and in parallel one (or more) function can be executed. The reaction to an `in-trigger` could be inhibited by the presence of a `condition-on-internal-state`. This means that the artifact could be sensitive to awareness information depending on its state.

Table 3. Form of coordination characteristics

`condition-on-internal-state*` → `out-trigger*` ‖ `function*` When the change in the information of the artifact happens one (or more) coordination information can be asserted to the community and in parallel one (or more) function can be executed.
`in-trigger` → `function*` When the artifact senses coordination information one (or more) function are executed. Artifacts always react to perceived coordination information, in fact, a coordination `in-trigger` can not be guarded by a condition on the artifact internal state.

3.2 The Scenario in CASMAS

The creation of a new course corresponds to the creation of a new community that involves people (teacher, students) and technological entities. The following general steps are necessary:

- in the **cooperation** module: a fulcrum and its manager must be defined. For a fulcrum, it is necessary to specify statement templates, and basic behaviors (sets of rules), for the correspondent M-agent, access policies (entities able to join the community) are given;
- in the **awareness** module: the topological spaces supporting the community must be chosen — using existing ones, or adding new spaces in case they are needed. For a new space, a graph of sites (in terms of structure and possible connections to other spaces) and its corresponding field types (in terms of data and propagation function) must be specified.

With respect to the scenario (step 1 in Fig. 1), a course can be added to the environment — i.e., the set of existing entities, communities, and topological spaces — by assigning the desired properties to a new instance of a course. For example, the cooperative application of the Institute, can provide course templates to teachers. Mrs. Jameson creates a new course by using her PC: some information is inherited from the general definition of a course, mapped from the course template to an entity (e.g., default topological space, statement

Table 4. Definition of a lesson as an active artifact, default values (when significant) are underlined

ID	Assigned by the system at creation time
Content	*name* *courses* *description* *teacher* *assistants* *timeSlot* *location* *state* (Can be <u>not-ready</u>, ready, setup, running, suspended, or finished) *documents* (Each document has ID and format) *delivery* (Can be <u>co-located</u> and/or online) *comments* (Each comment has text and author)
Access rights	*teacher*: read all, update all Assistant: read all, update none Student: read all, update comments Service: read all, update none
Definition rights	*teacher*: define Content, adapt all
Awareness	AWARE OF location AND location id=*location* AND current time IN *timeSlot* → UPDATE *state*=setup ‖ PROPAGATE lesson setup for *courses* ‖ CONNECT TO *courses*
Coordination	*documents* HAS ?format AND *state*=setup → ASSERT TO _COMMUNITY_ required ?format service *state*=setup → ASSERT TO _COMMUNITY_ required record service *delivery*=online AND *state*=setup → ASSERT TO _COMMUNITY_ required streaming service IN _COMMUNITY_ ALL required ?service HAS provided ?service → UPDATE *state*=running *state*=running → ASSERT TO _COMMUNITY_ lesson running

Legend. CAPITALIZED words are elements of the (pseudo-)language; *italic* words are the elements of the Content; _COMMUNITY_ is replaced by the name of the community once the rule is loaded; Uppercase words are roles or entity types; words beginning with a ? are parametric values and identical ?words make reference to the same value. States refered are depicted in Fig. 4.

templates and behaviors), some other information can be automatically filled by the course management module of the cooperative application (e.g., the teacher as the contact person), while she has to provide other basic information such as:

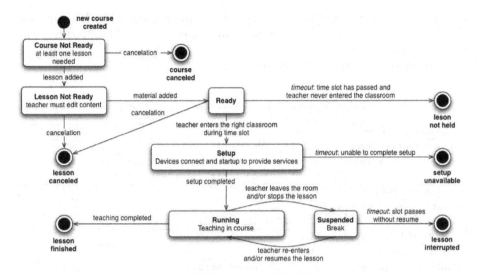

Fig. 4. Complete state diagram of the system supporting the scenario: more states than those described in the text are depicted, not influencing the meaning of the description provided

- the name of the course (e.g., "Operating Systems");
- a description (e.g., "the course is recommended to bachelor students");
- access policies (e.g., "students of the first year are not allowed to attend"), and so on.

After saving the entered data, the teacher is automatically connected to the new "Operating Systems" community: a new C-agent is created and connected to the course fulcrum, to supply interaction with the available services and devices (all those available to her in the room, as descibed later). Other authorized entities (e.g., students and teaching assistants) can join the community afterwards.

Mrs. Jameson is initially localized in her studio (by means of some localization technique or device, e.g., RFID) and working on her lessons by means of co-located devices (e.g., a PC or a digital pen to make sketches). Having already defined her course, she can prepare new lessons, specifying information such as: the topic of the lesson, with a brief description, where and at what time the lesson is going to be performed, and who is going to assist her (Table 5). Additionally, she can assign the lesson to more than one course, in case the topic is relevant for more than one group (community) of students. She can prepare slides with her favourite application, and then attach them to a specific lesson by means of the Content Management System, an entity devoted to the task of storing, selecting, and providing suitable information in a context-aware fashion. The choice of specific material defines the technological requirements for the lesson: for example, if audio clips are used, the classroom has to provide speakers. However, this has not to be considered as a direct specification of required devices, but rather as an automatic request for certain services that will cause the involvement of the entities that provide them. Mrs. Jameson can also define a lesson as being part of an e-learning program, if the lesson is going to be delivered online, the environment should provide streaming audio-video functionalities, so to reach remote students.

Table 5. Definition of the content of the lesson

Content.name	``Introduction to scheduling''
Content.courses	``Operating Systems''
Content.description	``Introduction to process scheduling: first-in first-out, round robin, shortest job first.''
Content.teacher	J. Jameson
Content.assistants	A. Brown
Content.timeSlot	(02/11/2007,10.30,12.30)
Content.location	(U7,423)
Content.state	finished
Content.documents	(cmsID.33252,presentation)
Content.delivery	online,co-located
Content.published	false
Content.comments	(``Please provide more exercises'', T. White) (``Interesting article: cmsID.7900'', R. Green)

Whenever Mrs. Jameson creates a new lesson, it can be considered to be located in the same site where she is. When she leaves her office, she moves in the institute and is localized by the system. The lessons (A-agents) follow Mrs. Jameson in the topological space (thanks to the propagation of her presence field): the presence field is perceived to be weaker, the A-agents of the lessons check the source of the field (i.e., where the teacher is), and move to the same site. The new position is exported by the M-agents of the lessons into the personal fulcrum, to be confronted with lessons' properties (Table 5). If the place where a lesson is scheduled is reached, and the time is right, then:

- the scheduled lesson connects to the communities (courses) to which it belongs (i.e., "Operating Systems") by creating the required number of C-agents (one for each course). The description of the behaviors desired for the environment is already available in the course fulcrum;
- the connection is published by propagation on the topological space. The M-agent of the lesson imports a field in the corresponding A-agent, which then propagates a field with data specifying the involved communities;
- co-located entities (e.g., devices in the same room) sense the information and the field is exported (via M-agents) to their personal fulcra; the rule in Table 6 (loaded in the devices when they were deployed in the university) is executed, and a new C-agent is created and connected to the course communities;
- the lesson (via its C-agents) asserts coordination information in the community fulcra: setup of the environment is requested;

– coordination statements induce reactions in the involved entities (i.e., due to the rule loaded in every device by design, Table 7), to which they react according to their inner behaviors.

Table 6. Example of rule loaded in the devices by configuration (domain dependent)

AWARE OF lesson setup for ?courses AND this locked=false → CONNECT TO ?courses
When a lesson propagates the information that it is setting up, if the device is not locked by someone else, the rule is executed and the device connects to the course communities of the lesson.

Table 7. Example of rule loaded in the devices by design (domain independent)

IN _COMMUNITY_ required ?service AND this provide ?service AND this locked=false → ASSERT TO _COMMUNITY_ provided ?service
When someone publishes the request for a service, if the device provides the required service (i.e., exists the statement this provide service-name) and it is not locked by someone else, the rule is executed and the availability of the required service is asserted.

Being the lesson an active artifact for the environment, its presence and the coordination information it provides trigger all devices to execute the specific behaviors of the case, according to the services they are able to provide. Such operation represents the setup of the system for the lesson that is beginning: once devices have set up, they are ready to provide the desired services, and feedback regarding the acquired status is published in the fulcrum. When all the required services are available, the lesson officially begins: its status change accordingly, a webcam starts recording and streaming the lesson, the material for the teacher is retrieved from the CMS and displayed on the desk (ready to be shown on a larger screen to the audience), and a sign can automatically light outside, above the door to warn people passing by to be quiet.

The lesson, as an active artifact, enacts coordination mechanisms during the scheduled period (as long as the teacher is in the right place): it mediates interaction among devices and human actors, and possibly handles breaks in the teaching.

Finally, the teacher moves out and the information is propagated in the awareness module, reaching the lesson that perceives a weaker presence field and stops its coordination activity with the role of current lesson but still remains connected to the community. Thanks to the persistence of the link, further interaction between the students and Mrs. Jameson is possible: the students are aware when the teacher publishes (via the CMS) new material for the lesson, and the teacher is aware of students' work and contributions. At the same time, the information is propagated to the lesson by its M-agent at awareness level. The lesson can be disconnected from the site in the topological space, as its location is no longer needed. Devices perceive the absence of a current lesson, and consequently disconnect from the communities formerly needing their services.

Flexibility and Automation in the Scenario. If the teacher enters at lesson time in a classroom that is different from the assigned one (e.g., when the room is not available for some reason), the system could try to support the new situation and assists the teacher by asking her if the current classroom should be used for the lesson. In this way, the teacher does not need use a configuration utility again to make last-minute changes. The system can have an active role in the management of unexpected situations but delegates the final decision to the teacher (or, more in general, to persons).

In practice, the lesson artifact executes the first rule in Table 8 to ask a confirmation for the new location of the lesson; the desk in the classroom is in charge of responding to such requests by executing the first rule in Table 9 and displaying a confirmation dialog. Upon confirmation, the desk executes the second rule in Table 9 and propagates the information that is then perceived by the lesson. By knowing that the lesson's classroom has changed, the lesson updates this information by executing the second rule in Table 8; thereby, the regular configuration process can begin as illustrated before.

Table 8. Rules loaded in the lesson artifact to manage a possible change in the lesson's classroom

AWARE OF location AND location id!=*location* AND location type=classroom AND current time IN *timeSlot* $\rightarrow$ PROPAGATE confirm lesson *name* at location id
If the teacher is in a classroom that is not the configured classroom for the lesson, the rule is executed and a request of confirmation to know if this is the (new) lesson's classroom is propagated.
AWARE OF location AND location id!=*location* AND AWARE OF confirmed lesson name=*name* AND current time IN *timeSlot* $\rightarrow$ UPDATE *location*=location id
If the lesson is confirmed in the classroom the rule is executed and the lesson's location is updated to the new location.

4   Deployment of the Scenario

A test middleware implementing the described model for ubiquitous-computing environments has been developed (architecture in Fig. 5): we called it MICA, MIddleware for CASMAS. In systems relying on such middleware, devices are described in terms of the services they provide, for example, the projector in the scenario is something that can show messages of some format (e.g., pictures, slides, movie clips), and its presentation mechanism has to be implemented to give and comply with such format specifications.

Table 9. Rules loaded in each classrooms' desk

`AWARE OF confirm lesson AND lesson location id=this location id AND this locked=false → ask confirm lesson name` If the desk is aware of a confirmation request for a lesson and it is not in use (it is not locked) the rule is executed and a confirmation dialog is showed on the desk.

`AWARE OF confirm lesson AND confirmed lesson name=confirm lesson name →`
`PROPAGATE confirmed lesson name`
If the lesson is confirmed in the classroom the rule is executed and the confirmation is propagated.

The middleware is based on a distributed inferential engine, called DJess [9]: a tool to deploy generic distributed inferential systems sharing a common space to exchange facts and rules. Exploiting the features of the inferential system, the middleware can realize both cooperation and awareness modules: specific types of agents (C-, M-, and A-agents) are defined as specialized inferential nodes, and an extended language is used to express environmental information and community policies, in order to drive agents' behaviors in accordance with the model.

The cooperation module is defined according to a widely adopted multi-agent architecture [10], provided with distributed inferential capability and based on a blackboard mechanism [11]. The blackboard approach makes the environment very flexible with respect to dynamic situations — e.g., entities joining and leaving communities. The blackboard mechanism of fulcra is enacted through shared working memories, where agents can assert and retract facts. Since rules can be enclosed in facts, agents can also load and unload rules. Different agents can work on the same set of facts and rules observing how they change and acting according to shared or private rules.

The awareness module is defined according to the situated multi-agent systems paradigm [12], where agents are situated on topological spaces, can propagate and perceive information on them and move from one site to an adjacent one. Topological spaces, which are represented as graphs, are defined in the shared working memory by sets of statements expressing neighborhood relations between sites. Moreover, the fields (i.e., how the propagated information is described) are represented as facts and awareness agents own rules to observe field on the site where they are situated.

In practice, the system described in the scenario can be deployed as depicted in Fig. 6. The institute provides:

- a **Department Server** where the topological spaces and the fulcra for all the communities of the institute are instantiated;
- a **CMS Server** to provide access to the documents through the CMS entities;
- the devices available in the classrooms such as the **Desk** and the **Projector**.

The teacher has her own **Teacher Server** in her office (it is a regular PC running the middleware and the client for the cooperative application) to instantiate her proxy entity and all the entities she owns such as the lessons; her other devices

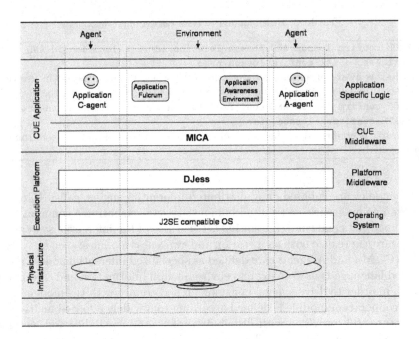

Fig. 5. General architecture of systems designed according to the model and deployed with the test middleware

(a **Mobile Phone** and a personal **Desk**) are in her office. Each student has his **Student Server** at home (owned or provided by the university).

The connections among the devices reflect the relationships between the persons and the environment. In fact, a student (through his **Student Server**) is connected only to the **CMS Server** and the **Department Server**, i.e., he has access to the university's communities and to the documents provided by the CMS but he can not use directly any resources in the institute. Instead, the teacher (through her **Teacher Server**) is connected also to her devices so she has direct access to them. The **Desk** and the **Projector** in the classroom are available only to communities (they are not intended for personal use) so they are connected only to the **Department Server**.

Middleware connections are realized over TCP/IP, and the distributed inferential engine relies on Java RMI technology: each instantiated entity refers to a RMI registry by which other entities, communities and topological spaces can be reached by name. As a consequence, when an entity perceives a field that contains the name of a community and the behavior in response to this perception is to connect to this community, the entity simply uses the name to lookup and connect to the corresponding site. For example, when the devices in the classroom perceive the "lesson setup" field, which carries the name of the course community, they can connect to the community according to the name of the course.

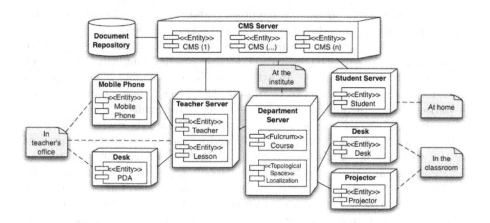

Fig. 6. Deployment of the system according to the scenario: various locations are shown, communication is provided by the test middleware

5   Discussion and Related Work

The notion of coordination artifact is grounded in research on human activities, and the embodiment as an active artifact allowed by the proposed approach represents a further step toward the design of systems that might otherwise result inadequate to support human (and human-computer) interaction. The adoption of active artifacts in ubiquitous-computing environments can provide general-purpose systems — i.e., systems that can support heterogeneous activities in the same place — with a better understanding of the current *context* [6]. Active artifacts allow to collect coordination and context-awareness policies in the same entity at design time, and also all other entities can be designed to be able to autonomously coordinate themselves by means of active artifacts. Moreover, coordinated entities do not need to look for or monitor active artifacts, because they are able to reach the communities where coordination is needed and supply the necessary information.

In some models for multi-agent systems, agents can directly communicate with one another and enact (inter-agent) coordination from a *subjective* perspective [13]. Agents exchange information about themselves and the environment by adopting an Agent Communication Language (ACL), and reason on gathered information to form a model sustaining individual beliefs, upon which each agent independently plans its own actions. In contrast, (intra-agent) *objective* coordination is achieved by separating agents' perception and coordination issues, which are delegated to artifacts that model the interaction space independently from the interacting agents [14]. Strohbach et Al. defined Cooperative Artefacts as autonomous mobile agents with embedded domain knowledge, perceptual intelligence, and rule-based inference [15]. They use the term "artefact" to refer to entities in general, whereas in this paper the term is more specific and carries different implications — moreover, we adopt a different spelling. Coordination is achieved by making artefacts communicate and compose a shared knowledge base, that dissolves after the cooperative task is performed.

The approach proposed by Omicini et Al. [16] is more similar to ours, but we adopt the notion of active (coordination) artifact in a different way. Our research guideline is that an artifact is an active coordination artifact if and only if *it is used by the different actors to coordinate themselves* in doing their activities. In particular, as introduced in Section 1, the active artifact is introduced in the environment to let entities autonomously coordinate themselves. An active artifact cannot directly induce entities to perform some task, but only provide entities with the necessary knowledge to be able to perform the right task in the right way and in the right moment. Hence, an active artifact cannot be considered to be *prescriptive* and, for example, be used to model a workflow engine or semaphores, as proposed by Omicini et Al. We agree that coordination artifacts represent an engineered approach to coordination that is useful when it is possible to design the solution to the coordination problem, and then to reify such a knowledge in suitable artifacts [16]. This seems to us much closer to the original definition by Schmidt and Simone [2], which is widely accepted in CSCW and HCI literature.

The approach proposed by Dastani et Al. is another example of a different interpretation of the concept of coordination artifact: "An *organization structure* determines the dependencies and interactions among constituting agents/multi-agent systems and is responsible for the global properties of the system. [...] we consider an *organization structure* as a coordination artifact." [17] From our point of view an organization structure can not be considered a coordination artifact because entities can not and do not use only the organization structure to coordinate their activities, rather, it is one of the sources providing context awareness, thus contributing to enact cooperation.

Our current implementation of the middleware allowed for a qualitative evaluation of the approach, whose results cannot fit with a detailed description in this paper, especially considering the aim to present a general approach and not only a specific experiment. Application designers that are not familiar with the CASMAS model could have difficulties to "think" in a distributed and service-oriented way where involved entities enact both individual and cooperative behaviors. Difficulties can also arise with thinking about entities independently from the physical devices that will host them in the environment. Fig. 6 shows that there is no fixed one-to-one mapping between devices and entities: for example, the Teacher Server executes both Teacher and Lesson entities. Hence, the best practice we have learned is to conceive the environment in terms of interactions and required functions, without constraining them according to the devices that will possibly be employed. This approach is essential to fully exploit the features of the proposed model. In our experiments so far, we did not encounter particular problems at implementation time; the prominent challenge is to identify (and keep in mind) to which fulcrum or space information are addressed or come from while defining the rules.

Briefly, the main shortcomings of the middleware at the moment are the computational requirements, which still do not allow for a deployment of entities on devices with very limited capabilities (e.g., sensors). However, successful experiments have been conducted with PCs (acting as servers as well as cooperative application clients), large screens, and mobile phones within our laboratory (some preliminary results, focusing only on technological aspects, have been recently published already). For our implementatin we do not adopt third-party middlewares for context awareness, such as the Context Toolkit [18], because they can provide "only" the *context abstraction and reasoning* part of our model. We need, and achieve support to both coordination and propagation of awareness information, in addition to the ability to enhance the behavior of any application by informing it of the context of its use [19].

6   Conclusion

Active artifacts play a primary role in cooperative software systems. In particular, their role with respect to ubiquitous-computing environment can be defined, exploited, and assessed according to different perspective. In this paper, we presented a notion of active coordination artifact that relies on the seminal definition given by Schmidt and Simone [2], and applied the very same to a model to design systems supporting collaborative environments by means of heterogeneous devices. The technique to setup and interact with such environments, i.e., the composition of devices' functionalities according to their high-level features, and services provided, is presented. The scenario can be used to have an idea of the approach, while a quantitative evaluation (e.g., performance) depends on the specific implementation of the systems. The implementation of the scenario using our reference middleware is shortly presented as a possibility of supporting current and future experiments on the model.

References

1. Weiser, M.: The computer for the 21st century. Scientific American 265(3), 94–104 (1991)
2. Schmidt, K., Simone, C.: Coordination Mechanisms: Towards a conceptual foundation for CSCW systems design. Computer Supported Cooperative Work 5, 155–200 (1996)
3. Ricci, A., Viroli, M., Omicini, A.: Agent coordination contexts in a MAS coordination infrastructure. Applied Artificial Intelligence 20, 179–202 (2006)
4. Cabitza, F., Locatelli, M.P., Simone, C.: Designing computational places for communities within organizations. In: CollaborateCom 2006, pp. 1–10. IEEE Computer Society Press, Los Alamitos (2006)
5. Cabitza, F., Locatelli, M.P., Sarini, M., Simone, C.: CASMAS: Supporting Collaboration in Pervasive Environments. In: PerCom, pp. 286–295. IEEE Computer Society Press, Los Alamitos (2006)
6. Abowd, G.D., Dey, A.K., Brown, P.J., Davies, N., Smith, M., Steggles, P.: Towards a better understanding of context and context-awareness. In: Gellersen, H.-W. (ed.) HUC 1999. LNCS, vol. 1707, pp. 304–307. Springer, Heidelberg (1999)

7. Simone, C., Bandini, S.: Integrating awareness in cooperative applications through the reaction-diffusion metaphor. Computer Supported Cooperative Work 11, 495–530 (2002)
8. Zambonelli, F., Jennings, N.R., Wooldridge, M.: Developing multiagent systems: The gaia methodology. ACM Trans. Softw. Eng. Methodol. 12, 317–370 (2003)
9. Cabitza, F., Dal Seno, B.: DJess - A Knowledge-Sharing Middleware to Deploy Distributed Inference Systems. In: WEC 2005, Enformatika, vol. 2, pp. 66–69 (2005)
10. Omicini, A., Zambonelli, F.: Coordination for internet application development. Autonomous Agents and Multi-Agent Systems 2, 251–269 (1999)
11. Gelernter, D.: Generative communication in Linda. ACM Trans. Program. Lang. Syst. 7, 80–112 (1985)
12. Weyns, D., Schumacher, M., Ricci, A., Viroli, M., Holvoet, T.: Environments for multiagent systems. Knowledge Engineering Review 20, 127–141 (2005)
13. Schumacher, M.: Objective Coordination in Multi-Agent System Engineering - Design and Implementation. In: Schumacher, M. (ed.) Objective Coordination in Multi-Agent System Engineering. LNCS (LNAI), vol. 2039, Springer, Heidelberg (2001)
14. Omicini, A., Ricci, A., Viroli, M., Rimassa, G.: Integrating objective & subjective coordination in multi-agent systems. In: SAC 2004, pp. 449–455. ACM Press, New York (2004)
15. Strohbach, M., Gellersen, H.W., Kortuem, G., Kray, C.: Cooperative artefacts: Assessing real world situations with embedded technology. In: Davies, N., Mynatt, E.D., Siio, I. (eds.) UbiComp 2004. LNCS, vol. 3205, pp. 250–267. Springer, Heidelberg (2004)
16. Ricci, A., Viroli, M., Omicini, A.: Programming MAS with artifacts. In: Bordini, R.H., Dastani, M., Dix, J., Seghrouchni, A.E.F. (eds.) Programming Multi-Agent Systems. LNCS (LNAI), vol. 3862, pp. 206–221. Springer, Heidelberg (2006)
17. Dastani, M., Arbab, F., de Boer, F.S.: Coordination and composition in multi-agent systems. In: AAMAS, pp. 439–446. ACM Press, New York (2005)
18. Salber, D., Dey, A.K., Abowd, G.D.: The context toolkit: Aiding the development of context-enabled applications. In: CHI, pp. 434–441. ACM Press, New York (1999)
19. Dey, A.K., Abowd, G.D., Salber, D.: A conceptual framework and a toolkit for supporting the rapid prototyping of context-aware applications. Human-Computer Interaction 16, 97–166 (2001)

A Communication Middleware for Smart Room Environments

Gábor Szeder and Walter F. Tichy

Institute for Program Structures and Data Organization (IPD)
University of Karlsruhe
Germany
{szeder,tichy}@ipd.uni-karlsruhe.de

Abstract. Processing sensor data to recognize and interpret human activity and human-human interaction in smart room environments is a computationally intensive task. Thus, processing components in smart rooms must be spread over multiple computers in a network. Dealing with the complexity of distributing and managing these components puts a considerable burden on these components' developers. In this paper we introduce ChilFlow, a distributed data-transfer middleware specifically designed to ease the work of smart room developers. We describe flows, the network-transparent, typed, one-to-many communication channels used for communication between processing components. We also present ChilFlow's programming interface for flows and demonstrate how it assures type-safety and network-transparency.

1 Introduction

There is a growing interest in enabling computers to provide higher-level multimodal services to facilitate collaboration between people. To provide such services computers need to continuously observe, recognize, and interpret human activity and human-human interaction using all perception modalities available. A number of sensors, such as cameras, microphones, and microphone arrays, are necessary to perceive human activity. Meeting or lecture rooms equipped with these sensors are commonly referred to as *smart rooms*.

Handling all the data collected by various sensors in a smart room raises serious issues. Having only one component for processing the data from all sensors is certainly undesirable, because this processing is such a computationally intensive task that it is virtually impossible to do on one single computer. Therefore, processing components must run on multiple computers in a distributed network.

To illustrate further issues, Figure 1 shows a sample arrangement of processing components that together realize an audio-visual speech recognition system. The sensors deployed in this scenario can be found on the left side of the picture. The sensors are a 16 channel and a 64 channel microphone array for source localization and far-field speech recognition, respectively, and a pan-tilt-zoom camera for lip reading. These sensors are connected to different computers and the data coming from the sensors are received by capture components running on these

B. Schiele et al. (Eds.): AmI 2007, LNCS 4794, pp. 195–210, 2007.

computers. Capture components and processing components are represented by squares. Communication channels are illustrated with thick lines with an arrowhead showing the direction of the data flow. As Figure 1 shows, data acquired by a sensor might be processed by more than one component at the same time. The output of a components is often further processed by other component(s). Moreover, each component might have more than one input and/or more than one output.

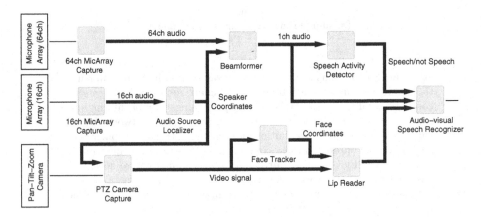

Fig. 1. Example arrangement of processing components realizing audio-visual speech recognition

During the development of a system like the one on Figure 1 the configuration of the system changes frequently. Such a system is mostly developed off-line, i.e., previously recorded data is used for testing, fine-tuning, and experiments instead of real-time captured sensor data. It is also common to simulate the output of processing components by using previously recorded data. This implies that processing components receive input from different components. Considering the system on Figure 1 for example, it could be easily turned into an off-line system by replacing the three capture components with components reading previously recorded data from hard disks. Moreover, adjacent processing components might run on the same or different computers, which in turn might vary with changing configurations.

Developers of processing components want to stay focused on enhancing processing algorithms instead of managing the connections between components and the caveats of networking. Consequently, smart rooms require a networking middleware that is inherently network-transparent and copes with the complexity of connecting and managing a large number of processing components.

In this paper we present a network-transparent, typed, one-to-many communication channel called *flow*, tuned to the communication characteristics of smart room environments. We introduce *ChilFlow*, a distributed data-transfer middleware implementing flows on top of TCP sockets. We present ChilFlow's programming interface for flows and demonstrate how it assures type-safety and network-transparency. We will show that the run-time overhead introduced by our implementation barely affects the performance of processing components under typical workloads of smart room environments.

2   Related Work

The pipes and filters (or pipeline) architectural pattern [1] divides the task of a system into several sequential processing steps. These steps are implemented as filter components and adjacent filters are connected by pipes. However, pipes are too static, because all filters in a pipe must be started at once, and no further filters can be added afterwards. Moreover, each filter component has only one single input and one single output. Although the pattern and its implementation can be varied to allow filters with more than one input and/or more than one output, the design of individual filters and the whole system could be difficult [1].

The Message Passing Interface (MPI) [2,3] provides efficient one-to-many communication primitives. However, these primitives lack the type-safety provided by flows. Moreover, to handle the possibly changing number of consumers, the developer of a data source component must take explicit actions, such as add and remove processes to or from communicators.

GStreamer [4] is a multimedia framework that allows the construction of graphs of media-handling components. These components have to be implemented as shared libraries. The libraries are loaded and the components are connected by GStreamer in a single process. This implies that an eventual fault of one component has likely fatal consequences to other components as well. GStreamer does not support networking natively, so it cannot exploit the computational power of multiple computers.

Realityflythrough [5] is a telepresence/tele-reality system that focuses on streaming video feeds from wireless networked cameras under harsh conditions to a control "room". As it primarily focuses on harsh conditions and not on the issues raised by the complex network of processing components described in previous section, it is impractical for the development of processing components in smart room environments.

A network of various processing components connected by multiple flows bears similarities with a publish-subscribe system. One could roughly consider source components as publishers, consumer components as subscribers, flows as topics, and buffers as messages or events. In some aspects, however, flows are more similar to streams in smart room environments. There are also important architectural differences. There is an event service or event broker between publishers and subscribers in traditional publish-subscribe systems [6], which is responsible for message distribution and buffering. Publishers and subscribers are unaware of each other, and communicate through the event service. In smart room environments, a central distribution component would not be practicable, as transferring sensor data requires lot of bandwidth and the central component would certainly be a significant bottleneck to the performance of the whole system. In the area of ubiquitous computing [7], the STEAM [8] publish-subscribe system resolves this issue by omitting the event broker and implementing brokering functionality at both the producer and consumer side. However, similarly to Realityflythrough, it does not address management of processing components.

The NIST Smart Data Flow System (NSDFS) [9] is a data-transfer system for smart rooms. Although it uses similar concepts, it has several shortcomings compared to ChilFlow. The NSDFS has a difficult to learn C API which offers weaker of type-safety for flows than the API of ChilFlow. Due to API limitations all flows the component wants to create or receive during its whole lifetime must be specified in advance during initialization. The API provides only blocking functions for subscribing to flows or for retrieving buffers from the buffer history. Blocking makes handling of input on multiple flows rather difficult, as developers must resort to multiple threads: one for each of the flows and one for the actual processing. Also, NSDFS consumer components are not enabled to select a subset of the data sent by the source component.

The NSDFS uses shared memory segments to store the buffer history of consumer components. This way the overhead of flow data exchange between components running on the same computer is reduced. It also reduces the network load when more consumer components running on the same computer are receiving the same flow. However, the implementation of shared memory handling suffers from severe design issues. It is not recorded, which consumer component is processing which buffer in the buffer history, hence a failed component will easily turn the buffer history into inconsistent state, mostly with fatal consequences to the whole distributed system. As components tend to fail frequently during development and testing, this is a significant drawback concerning usability.

3   Flows

Flows are the means of data exchange between processing components. They are network-transparent, typed, unidirectional, one-to-many communication channels.

- *network-transparent*: To hide the ever changing addresses (hostname, IP, port) of source and consumer processing components, flows are identified by an abstract name. Although the name of a flow bears no meaning for the underlying system, developers might choose meaningful names that reflect the data transferred through the flow (e.g. Speaker Coordinates in Figure 1). The name of a flow is specified at flow creation time by its source component. Consumer components can subscribe to a particular flow by requesting it based on its name. The system implementing flows will then in turn transparently connect the consumer to the source of the requested flow. This way developers of consumer components do not need to worry about from which source their component will receive input, where this source component runs and how to connect to it. Flow names must be unique in the system.
- *typed*: To prevent misinterpretation of data, flows are typed at two levels. First, there is a distinction between various types of flows each having specific parameters, as shown in Table 1. For example the parameters of an audio flow are

the number of channels, frequency, and number of frames in a buffer, while a video flow has horizontal and vertical resolution and color channels (e.g. RGB, monochrome). Second, the type of the data is distinguished, too. This datatype determines the bit depth of audio and the color depth of video flows.

The flow's type, parameters, and datatype must be defined together with the flow's name at the flow's creation by its source component. When a consumer component requests a particular flow by its name, it also has to specify the flow's type, parameters, and the datatype it wants to receive. If the flow with the given name has in fact a different type or parameters or datatype, then the consumer can not receive that flow.

Table 1. Flow types and their parameters in ChilFlow

Flow Type	Parameters	Datatype
Video	width, height, format	base datatypes of
Audio	channels, frequency, frames	the C++ programming
Vector	size	language
Matrix	width, height	
Data	size	user-defined

- *unidirectional*: Data is transferred only in one direction, from the source component to the consumer component(s). Bidirectional communication between two processing component is rarely needed in typical smart room scenarios. If necessary, however, the two components can be connected by two flows, one in each direction.
- *one-to-many*: It is common in smart room environments that data from a single source must be processed by more than one independent component at the same time. For example, video from a camera might be processed by a body tracker, a face tracker, a face recognizer, and a lip reader component as well. Flows support one-to-many communication transparently. The programmers of data source components do not need to take explicit actions to handle the multiple and possibly changing consumer components.

To adapt to the practice of processing component developers, data is transferred through flows in abstract units developers usually working with. Such a unit is a whole frame from a camera in case of a video flow, or the 3D coordinates with a confidence value of a speaker. These units are simply called *buffers*. Apart from the actual data, buffers also encapsulate some basic metadata (e.g. timestamp).

Consumer components have a buffer history for every received flow, where a couple of recently received buffers are stored. A newly arriving buffer is automatically stored in the history, replacing the oldest one. Buffers are then pulled from the buffer history in turn for processing. This buffer history can help compensate temporary slowdowns of the consumer component, as it prevents loosing data to a certain degree. Furthermore, the buffer history is particularly useful by such a component arrangement, like the PTZ Camera Capture, Face Tracker, and Lip

Reader triple in Figure 1. In this case the output of PTZ Camera Capture is processed by the two other components. However, to process a buffer received on this flow, the Lip Reader component also needs the Face Coordinates extracted from the same buffer by the Face Tracker component. The Face Tracker outputs these coordinates through a vector flow. Since the Face Tracker obviously needs some time to process the buffer, the resulting buffers containing the coordinates will arrive with a short delay at Lip Reader. If the Lip Reader stores some of the recently arrived video buffers in the buffer history, it will be able to find the matching video and vector buffers.

Besides the features mentioned above, flows in ChilFlow offer additional features. Most notably consumers are enabled to select only a subset of the data sent by the source component. For example in case of a multi-channel audio flow, the consumer can specify which particular audio channels it wants to receive. In case of a video flow consumers can select a sub-region of the pictures sent through the flow. In order to save bandwidth, the source component sends only the selected subset of the data through the network. However, handling of selections is still completely transparent to the source component. There are no actions needed at all to handle the different and changing selections of the different consumer components.

4   ChilFlow

This section gives an overview about the structure of ChilFlow, our distributed data-transfer middleware implementing flows. ChilFlow consists of three different kinds of components, namely daemons, controlling applications, and the processing components. This section describes the tasks of these components and how they collaborate to establish connections.

4.1   Daemons

Daemons are primarily responsible for organizing the distributed system and for coordinating connections between processing components. There is a daemon process running on each computer of the system to prevent single point of failure. Daemons are connected via TCP sockets with each other, building an overlay network. They share all information about processing components (e.g. their address) and flows (e.g. their name, parameters, source component, etc.) present in the system. When a consumer component requests a flow, daemons use this information to check the flow's parameters and to look up the address of the flow's source component. Daemons do not participate in data exchange through flows, and if a daemon fails, it will not affect already established connections between source and consumer components.

For control applications and processing components to connect to the local daemon, a TCP socket on a predefined port is inadequate, because other processes running on the same computer might interfere by binding to the same port. Hence, each daemon listens on an additional Unix domain socket for connections from local control applications and local processing components. By setting appropriate access rights on this socket it is ensured that no other processes can interfere by creating a socket under the same path. The default location of this domain socket is hard coded in all component parts, but can be overridden from a configuration file if desired. This way processing components and controlling applications can connect to the local daemon automatically without any user intervention.

Daemons are also responsible for fulfilling requests of control applications by starting or stopping daemons and processing components. These controlling requests are serialized and executed in order. This way conflicting concurrent requests are resolved, as only the first request is fulfilled; any further conflicting request will fail. For example, when multiple users want to start the same component simultaneously, the component is started on the first request; all further requests fail with a message telling the user that the component has been started in the meantime. Daemons also notify control applications about various events in the system, such as creation of a flow, exiting components, etc., and forward the standard output and error of processing components to control applications.

4.2   Controlling Applications

A controlling application serves visualization and management purposes. It offers a graphical interface for convenient starting, stopping, and monitoring daemons and processing components on different computers in the distributed system. It shows a map of the running components and the flows between them similar to Figure 1. To facilitate the arrangement of processing components on different computers, these maps of components and flows can be saved to files and later reloaded. Controlling applications also include plugins for visualizing the actual data transferred through flows (e.g. waveforms of audio flows, or the pictures transferred through a video flow). The system can be controlled by multiple controlling applications run by multiple users at the same time; a significant asset when multiple developers want to use the same sensor setup.

4.3   Processing Components

Processing components are doing the actual work in a smart room by processing data. They use ChilFlow's client library, which provides a thread-safe C++ programming interface to communicate with other component parts of the system and to send and receive data through flows.

To hide networking from the developers and avoid unfavorable interferences between processing data and networking, we opted for a multi-threaded library design. A background thread handles incoming messages, such as accepting new subscriber components, registering their selections, handling control messages from the local daemon, and receiving buffers on input flows and storing these buffers in the buffer history, while the main thread retrieves buffers from the buffer history and processes them. The background thread is hidden from the developer and does not interfere with his main thread, except the critical sections necessary for accessing shared data structures, such as the buffer history.

This approach decouples the processing in the consumer component from source component(s). Even if the main thread of the consumer is blocked or long in processing a buffer, the background thread still handles incoming messages and buffers. A failing component only affects downstream components, as their input will not be available.

The C++ programming interface of ChilFlow's client library is described in Section 5.

4.4   Connecting Processing Components Through Flows

During the initialization of a processing component, the client library creates a TCP socket for future flow data transfer. Then it connects to the local daemon through the daemon's domain socket and informs the daemon about the port of its TCP socket. The daemon will in turn inform all other daemons about the newly connected component and the address of its TCP socket, so each daemon will know where that new component can be accessed.

Once a component wants to create a flow for its output, it sends a request to the local daemon containing the flow's name, type, parameters, and datatype. If a flow with the given name already exists, the daemon rejects the components request. If it does not exists, the daemon stores all information about the flow and in turn informs all other daemons about the event. As a result each daemon will know about the new flow, its parameters, and its source component.

To subscribe to a flow, the consumer components sends a request to the local daemon containing the name, type, parameters, and datatype of the flow it wants to receive. If a flow with the given does not exists, the daemon stores the request and fulfills it when a flow with the given name is created. If such a flow exists and the requested type, parameters, and datatype do not match those of the existing flow, the request is rejected. If they match, the daemon informs the consumer about the address of the source component's TCP socket. Upon receiving the reply, the consumer connects to the source component, which registers the new consumer and starts sending its output to the consumer, too.

5   Programming Interface for Flows

ChilFlow's API for flows is based on the push-pull model for sending and receiving buffers. For illustrating the basic functions of this API, Figure 2 and 3 show the source code of a simple example[1] source component with a video flow output and a consumer component with a video flow input, respectively. These two components build a processing pipeline of two stages: the source component captures data from a videocamera or reads previously recorded data, while the consumer processes the data.

ChilFlow's classes are defined in the `chilflow.h` header file, where everything resides in the `ChilFlow` namespace (lines 1 and 2). The initialization of the client

---

[1] To keep the included source code short and simple, we omitted exception handling from these examples.

```
1#include <chilflow.h>
2using namespace ChilFlow;
3extern void process_buffer(
4     VideoInputFlow<unsigned char>::Buffer & buffer);
5int main(int argc, char * argv[])
6{
7     unsigned int width = 640, height = 480, history_size = 25;
8     Main * cf = Main::create(argc, argv, "sample consumer component");
9     VideoInputFlow<unsigned char> * flow
10         = cf->subscribe_video_flow<unsigned char>("sample video flow",
11             VIDEO_RGB, width, height, history_size);
12     while (cf->is_running()) {
13         VideoInputFlow<unsigned char>::Buffer * buffer
14             = flow->get_newest_buffer();
15         process_buffer(*buffer);
16         buffer->release();
17     }
18     flow->close();
19     cf->finalize();
20     return 0;
21}
```

Fig. 2. An example source component with a video flow output

library is done in line 8 by calling `Main::create()`. This single call encapsulates the initialization of the networking back-end, creation of the TCP socket for future flow data transfer and establishing connection with the local daemon through its socket. The last string argument of this method is the name of the processing component. This string will appear in the map of controlling applications. The returned `Main` object is a handle for the connection to the daemon and the entry point for creating and subscribing to flows.

The video flow for the output of this component is created by the template method `Main::create_video_flow<T>()` in line 10. The method name indicates the type of the flow explicitly. The first string argument specifies the name of the flow, while the remaining arguments specify the parameters of the flow (color channels and resolution). The template parameter `unsigned char` defines the primitive datatype representing the actual data. The datatype is determined inside the client library by using run-time type information. In this case the `unsigned char` datatype means that each color channel in a pixel is represented by 8 bits. The returned `VideoOutputFlow<T>` object stands for the source-side endpoint of the flow. There are other methods and classes to work with other types of flows, for example `Main::create_vector_flow()` or `AudioOutputFlow<T>`.

The real work is done in the `while` loop in lines 12–17. The `Main::is_running()` helper method returns true as long as this component is not stopped by the user through a controlling application. Lines 13–14 retrieve an output buffer from the buffer history. This buffer will be filled with data in the `fill_buffer()` function.

Providing this function is the developers responsibility. Line 16 sends the buffer to all consumers subscribed to this flow. If any of the customers has selected only a sub-region of the frames, then this `Buffer::send()` method will send only that selected sub-region to reduce network load. If the buffer was not provided with a timestamp in the `fill_buffer()` function, the current time will be automatically assigned.

Once the component is stopped, it should exit gracefully. The flow is closed by calling `VideoOutputFlow<T>::close()` in line 18. This method will also send a message to all consumer components and the local daemon to notify them about the close event. Finally, the `Main::finalize()` method in line 19 disconnects the component from the local daemon and frees all resources used by the library.

Note, that there is no indication of handling consumer components in any way. They are handled completely transparently in a background thread, as described in Section 4.3. Also note that both the type and datatype of the flow are reflected throughout the code from the creation of the flow to the method signature of the `fill_buffer()` function (lines 3–4).

The structure of the consumer component shown in Figure 3 is quite similar to the structure of the source component, hence only the differences will be described.

The component subscribes to a flow for input by calling the template method `Main::subscribe_video_flow<T>()` in line 10. The method name indicates the type of the flow explicitly. The first string argument specifies the name of the flow the components wants to receive. The `history_size` argument specifies

```
 1 #include <chilflow.h>
 2 using namespace ChilFlow;
 3 extern void process_buffer(
 4     VideoInputFlow<unsigned char>::Buffer & buffer);
 5 int main(int argc, char * argv[])
 6 {
 7     unsigned int width = 640, height = 480, history_size = 25;
 8     Main * cf = Main::create(argc, argv, "sample consumer component");
 9     VideoInputFlow<unsigned char> * flow
10         = cf->subscribe_video_flow<unsigned char>("sample video flow",
11             VIDEO_RGB, width, height, history_size);
12     while (cf->is_running()) {
13         VideoInputFlow<unsigned char>::Buffer * buffer
14             = flow->get_newest_buffer();
15         process_buffer(*buffer);
16         buffer->release();
17     }
18     flow->close();
19     cf->finalize();
20     return 0;
21 }
```

Fig. 3. An example consumer component with a video flow input

the number of buffers that should be kept in the buffer history. The three remaining arguments specify what parameters the requested flow should have. Any of these parameters could be null, meaning that those parameters will equal the parameters specified by the source component. The template parameter **unsigned char** requests the primitive datatype the data should be represented with. This single method call encapsulates all communication between the consumer component and the local daemon and the source component, respectively, that is required to establish the connection between the source and consumer components. If a flow with the given name does not exists, this method will block until one is created. If such a flow exists, but either its type or parameters or datatype differ from what is requested, the component is not allowed to subscribe to the flow, and an exception is thrown. If everything matches, a **VideoInputFlow<T>** object is returned that stands for the consumer-side endpoint of the flow and provides methods for retrieving buffers from the buffer history easily.

Lines 13–14 retrieve the most recent buffer from the buffer history. If that buffer was already processed, this method will block until a new buffer arrives. The returned **Buffer** object contains not only the actual data sent by the source component, but it also encapsulates brief information about the buffer itself, such as its timestamp or the dimensions of the selection in effect. Other methods are also available for retrieving buffers from the buffer history based on the buffer's timestamp or its position in the buffer history. The data in the retrieved buffer is processed by the **process_buffer()** function (lines 3–4). Providing this function is the developer's responsibility. After the processing finished, the buffer must be released (line 16).

Note, that there is no indication of any network address or alike where the component should connect to. Just like the source component, both the type and datatype of the flow are reflected throughout the source code from the subscription to the flow to the method signature of the **process_buffer()** function. This way the accidental misinterpretation of received data is effectively prevented. Also note that merely two function calls were needed in each program to reach the point where the two components are connected.

When handling input on multiple flows simultaneously the previously described **subscribe_*_flow()** and **get_*_buffer()** methods might well be inappropriate because of their blocking behavior. Therefore, ChilFlow's API also offers non-blocking methods and helper classes to facilitate handling multiple input flows. Each blocking **subscribe_*_flow()** and **get_*_buffer()** methods have non-blocking counterparts. These methods return immediately when the requested flow does not exists or the requested buffer has not arrived yet, respectively. One of the helper classes deals with synchronization of input on multiple flows. The consumer component can register which flows should be synchronized in a **Synchronizer** object. This object's **wait()** method will return when there are unprocessed buffers in the flows' buffer histories with the same timestamp. As the clocks of different computers are not perfectly synchronized, the exact match of timestamps is barely feasible. Hence, an optional threshold value can be specified that determines how large timestamp difference is allowed to treat buffers synchronized.

A detailed description of ChilFlow's API can be found in [10].

6   Evaluation

In our prototype implementation of ChilFlow flows are realized on top of regular TCP sockets. In this section we measure the run-time overhead of our approach using CPU usage and throughput as metrics. We also examine the programming overhead of ChilFlow's API.

6.1   Performance

For the measurements we created two data source and two data consumer benchmark programs: one using TCP sockets directly and one using ChilFlow's flow implementation for data transfer. Both the TCP and ChilFlow programs took the same actions. During initialization the source and consumer programs established a TCP socket or flow connection, respectively, then they were synchronized in a barrier. After the barrier the source program sent given number of buffers with given size to the consumer. The buffer sizes covered values typically used in smart room environments: from a few bytes for a flow of 3D coordinates to 1MB for an RGB video flow with a resolution of 640x480 pixels. The number of buffers in each measurement was choosen large enough so that each measurement ran at least ten minutes. In case of the ChilFlow benchmark 128 buffers were kept in the buffer history. Once the last buffer was sent from the source and received at the consumer, the two programs synchronized again in a barrier. Time was measured from leaving the first barrier to leaving the second barrier. Neither the initialization nor the clean-up phase was included in the results. All measurements were repeated five times and the results' average was taken.

All benchmarks were run on identical computers equipped with two 1300Mhz Intel Itanium2 processors and 1GB of memory interconnected by 1Gbit Ethernet. The computers run Red Hat Enterprise Linux AS Release 4 operating system.

Figure 4 shows the ratio of CPU usage of the benchmark program using ChilFlow and that of the benchmark program using TCP sockets directly for both the source and the consumer. The benchmark using ChilFlow has certainly higher CPU overhead than the TCP benchmark, caused by the infrastructure needed to transparently handle the buffer history, multiple input flows from multiple source components, multiple consumers, and their selections. For large buffer sizes the number of buffers transferred in a second is orders of magnitude smaller than for small buffer sizes (around 100 for buffers of 1MB size and around 100000 for buffers of 16B). Hence, for large buffers the actual socket functions dominate the CPU usage and ChilFlow's overhead is relatively small. Towards smaller buffer sizes the implementation of flows on top of TCP sockets starts to dominate, especially on the consumer side, where the synchronization of threads and handling of the buffer history results significant overhead.

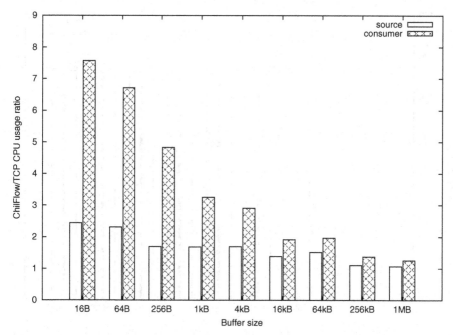

Fig. 4. The ratio of CPU usage of benchmarks using ChilFlow and TCP sockets in case of different buffer sizes

Figure 5 shows the throughput of TCP sockets and flows implemented in ChilFlow on top of TCP sockets in case of one source and one consumer using different buffer sizes. The benchmark program using ChilFlow was able to match the maximum available bandwidth of the 1Gbit Ethernet connection for buffer sizes larger than 4kB and at 4kB just slightly lower. For smaller buffers the throughput degrades significantly. The TCP benchmark program performs better; performance degrades only for buffers smaller than 1kB.

We have found that the performance degradation is merely caused by the CPU being a bottleneck. Even for the benchmark using TCP sockets directly we observed 100% CPU usage at the consumer for buffer sizes smaller than 1kB. As shown above, ChilFlow's CPU overhead is higher, hence the performance degradation extends to somewhat larger buffer sizes.

Although in real-world smart room scenarios buffer sizes usually vary from a few bytes to around 1-1.5MB, the number of buffers sent in one second shows significantly less variation. The buffer rate of video flows and flows carrying information extracted from video flows usually matches the frame rate of the videocamera, which is around 15-30 frames per second. The buffer rate of audio flows and flows carrying information extracted from audio flows is usually a bit higher, but still only around 100 buffers per second. These buffer rates are more than two orders of magnitude smaller than the buffer rate at the point

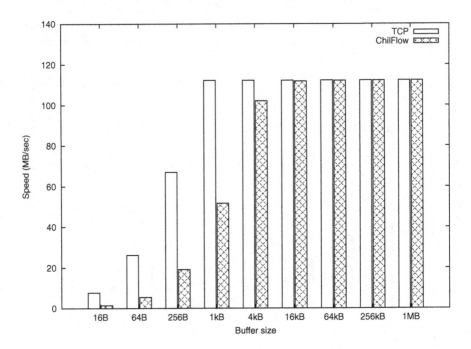

Fig. 5. Comparing throughput of ChilFlow and TCP sockets using different buffer sizes

where the throughput starts to degrade. As a consequence, the performance of typical processing components is barely influenced by ChilFlow's overhead.

6.2 Programming Overhead

As shown in Section 5, merely two function calls are needed to reach the point, where the source and consumer components are connected through a flow and can exchange data. Also, each subsequent subscription to a flow or creation of a flow requires only one additional function call, and is accomplished without explicitly specifying any network addresses or taking care about accepting connections. This is only a fraction of the code required to establish a connection using TCP sockets directly. Exchanging data is also greatly simplified, as handling multiple consumers, their selections, and the buffer history is treated transparently to the programmer.

ChilFlow's programming interface also offers advantages over the API of the NIST Smart Data Flow System (NSDFS) [9]. Handling input on multiple flows with the NSDFS is cumbersome, as its API offers only blocking functions to retrieve buffers from the buffer history, and the programmers must resort to using multiple threads: one for each of the flows and one for processing. The non-blocking methods and the helper classes for synchronizing input on multiple flows in ChilFlow simplify this issue. In contrary to ChilFlow, the NSDFS does not offer type safety, as data in buffers is accessible through void pointers and the actual datatype is specified using enumerations. Neither enables the NSDFS to consumers to select a subset of the data (e.g. sub-region of video frames) sent by the source component.

7   Conclusion and Future Work

We have presented ChilFlow, a distributed data-transfer middleware specifically targeted for smart room environments. We introduced flows, the network-transparent, typed, one-to-many communication channels used in ChilFlow for communication between processing components. We demonstrated how Chil-Flow's programming interface for flows assures type-safety and network transparency.

As future work we will optimize the client library to reduce the CPU overhead. We plan to evaluate the impact of using shared memory to reduce network load when multiple components running on the same computer are receiving the same flow. We are looking for techniques where a failing component will not influence other components using the same shared memory segments. We also investigate deploying reliable multicast to further reduce network load.

Acknowledgments

The authors would like to thank Joachim Neumann, Keni Bernardin, and Uwe Meyer for their suggestions about the design of ChilFlow, and Frank Padberg for comments on an early draft of this paper.

The work presented here was funded by the European Union (EU) under the integrated project CHIL – Computers in the Human Interaction Loop (Grant number IST-506909).

References

1. Buschmann, F., Meunier, R., Rohnert, H., Sommerlad, P., Stal, M.: A System of Patterns. John Wiley & Sons, Chichester (1996)
2. The MPI Forum: MPI: A Message Passing Interface. In: Proceedings of the 1993 ACM/IEEE conference on Supercomputing, pp. 878–883 (1993)
3. Gropp, W., Lusk, E., Thakur, R.: Using MPI-2 – Advanced Features of the Message Passing Interface. MIT Press, Cambridge (1999)
4. GStreamer: an open source multimedia framework.
   http://gstreamer.freedesktop.org
5. McCurdy, N.J., Griswold, W.G.: A systems architecture for ubiquitous video. In: MobiSys 2005. Proceedings of the 3rd international conference on Mobile systems, applications, and services, pp. 1–14. ACM Press, New York (2005)
6. Object Management Group: CORBA services: Common object services specification. Technical report (1998)
7. Weiser, M.: Ubiquitous computing. Computer 26(10), 71–72 (1993)

8. Meier, R., Cahill, V.: Steam: Event-based middleware for wireless ad hoc network. In: ICDCSW 2002. Proceedings of the 22nd International Conference on Distributed Computing Systems, pp. 639–644. IEEE Computer Society Press, Washington, DC, USA (2002)

9. NIST Smart Data Flow System.
   http://www.nist.gov/smartspace/nsfs.html

10. Szeder, G.: The ChilFlow API. http://www.ipd.uni-karlsruhe.de/CHIL/ChilFlow/Documentation/libchilflow/html/

Evaluating Confidence in Context for Context-Aware Security*

Marc Lacoste, Gilles Privat, and Fano Ramparany

France Telecom R&D/Orange Labs
{marc.lacoste,gilles.privat,fano.ramparany}@orange-ftgroup.com

Abstract. We propose a software framework that augments context data with a range of assorted confidence/reputation metadata for dimensions such as security, privacy, safety, reliability, or precision, defined according to a generic context confidence ontology. These metadata are processed through the network of federated distributed software services that support the acquisition, aggregation/fusion and interpretation of context, up to its exploitation by context-aware applications. This solution for qualifying and gauging context data makes possible its use in more critical applications of context awareness, such as adaptation of security mechanisms. We show how to implement with our framework a quality-critical application like contextual adaptation of security services, where security is tailored to the protection requirements of the current situation as captured by relevant context data.

1 Introduction

Qualifying Confidence in Context. Ambient intelligence has enlarged context-awareness beyond its classical uses with application-centric, system-centric or static user context, and re-centered it towards physical context. Physical context is acquired through distributed sensors in various modalities and may undergo several stages of processing, aggregation, fusion and abstraction, until it is exploited by context-aware applications.

The heterogeneous and unreliable nature of context data and the potentially error-prone interpretation to which low-level data are subjected are a major hindrance to the generalization of context-awareness. Most actual uses of context-awareness are still mainly limited to simple low-level context (such as location). Applications of higher-level context remain restricted to innocuous adaptations that do not substitute for the user's decision (such as recommendation systems). Using context for automatic adaptations in more critical applications requires a more watertight model of context acquisition and management, and a thorough confidence assessment of the context data transmitted to applications.

Confidence in context data has several dimensions that are mostly independent and incommensurable, and cannot be aggregated in a single scalar confidence parameter.

---

* This work was performed in project E2R II which has received research funding from the EU's Sixth Framework programme. This paper reflects only the authors' views and the EU is not liable for any use that may be made of the information contained therein. The contributions of colleagues from the E2R II consortium are hereby acknowledged.

B. Schiele et al. (Eds.): AmI 2007, LNCS 4794, pp. 211–229, 2007.

Precision and reliability are classical parameters for physical measurements. Their representation depends on the corresponding modality of physical data. They may also vary according to other environment parameters.

Security of context data may be treated in a way similar to security of content data and also includes several dimensions (e.g., authenticity, secrecy, integrity, etc.).

Safety of context is as well a dimension of confidence, yet of a different nature. It is most of the time associated with the *use* of context rather than with its sources: context used for triggering alarms in a remote monitoring application is more safety-critical than information about user presence transmitted to a remote user in a context-aware instant messaging application. This is related to privacy, a complementary, non-technical aspect of confidence that must also be considered.

Adapting Security to Context. Under the implicit assumption that stronger security is always preferable, a major trend in security to use highest common denominator, one-size-fits-all solutions for all applications that require some form of protection. Yet, overkill security places an unwarranted burden on the user, and is completely in contradiction with the overall objective of ambient intelligence: replacing, as much as possible, explicit interaction with implicit interaction, and relieving the user of the cognitive load of undue or redundant interactions.

Flexible security architectures make it possible to adapt security, not only to the requirements of the application, but also to those of the current situation, captured as context. Such security adaptations clearly fall under the most critical applications of context, where confidence in the context information triggering actions of reconfiguration has to be guaranteed. An obvious security loophole would be created if security could be relaxed on account of context data that could be spoofed by an attacker. Context-aware security is thus an ideal use case for the secure management of context described in this paper.

Managing Quality of Context for Context-Aware Security. We propose to integrate the management of quality-of-context metadata tightly with that of context data proper, using separate planes of the same distributed architecture. The different dimensions of quality of context are accounted for. Each of them is processed along a different data path, either from context acquisition up to its interpretation and exploitation, or down from applications when handling requests for particular types of context data with specific security requirements. We also show how security services like access control can be adapted to the current security context with this architecture.

The remainder of this paper is organized as follows. We give in section 2 a few sample applications which require confidence assessments of context data to trigger adaptations of security. Section 3 gives an overview of an architecture that integrates secure context management with a set of security mechanisms that are reconfigurable on the basis of context data. Section 4 describes the design of the context management infrastructure and the ontology of confidence to define the context metadata. Finally, section 5 presents the component-based security subsystem upon which we apply contextual adaptation, and the actual implementation that validates these solutions.

2   Example Applications

Location-Based Access Control and Secure Information Services. This scenario considers a relaxed security model that does not require strong identification or authentication from users, unlike traditional techniques relying on biometric or physical tokens such as smart cards. The basis of security is implicit, reduced to the user's location, and is defined by being inside some security perimeter. Traditional physical security mechanisms are assumed to be available for access control, so that only the users who are legitimately present within the target perimeters (corresponding in Figure 1 to the home and a home office) will be authorized to access the resources corresponding to these environments.

The idea is to avoid imposing an additional authentication step to grant these users access to services that may be specific to these locations and do not require strong per-person identification and authentication.

Assuming the physical location itself is secure, it should not be possible for an attacker to spoof this location by feeding applications with false location data, masquerading as issued by a legitimate location-detection source. The authenticated location data that the application would require to replace a password could be seen as a *secure location certificate* by reference to known authentication solutions.

The physical properties of the underlying location-determination technologies and its modelled representation do also come into play [15]. To specify that a target is within a given perimeter, the underlying model of space is set-based rather than cartesian.

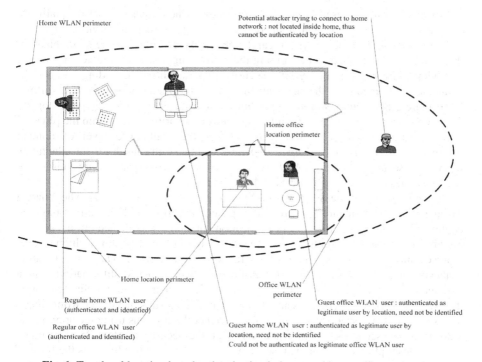

Fig. 1. Two-level location-based authentication in home and home office perimeters

Proximity-Based Interfaces. In this example, typical of smart spaces and ambient intelligence, a user interacts with services on the basis of his position relative to various interface devices or anchors within a room. This piece of context could be used in the same way as the position of a mouse on a desktop, or for more indirect adaptations like changing the focal length of communication (from wide-angle to telephoto) depending on how close the user is to a display. The *safety* requirements of this application are much less stringent than in the previous example. On the other hand, the *precision* requirements are much stronger, demanding location-detection with a (Cartesian) precision of about a few tens of centimeters.

Various contextual parameters could alter the confidence in the position detection technique used in this application. In the case of a vision-based technology, the possibility to mix targets when several persons are present in the room could downgrade reliability. For a radio technology such as WiFi-based fingerprinting, a surge of electromagnetic interference could also alter precision and reliability. The application could respond to these changes by selecting other position detection technologies, or aggregating several technologies for better results. We have implemented such an application with multi-technology location detection and are currently in the process of integrating location precision and reliability metadata in the data fusion mechanism.

3   Overall Architecture

Overview. We now present a generic architecture where management of quality of context serves as basis for contextual adaptation of several security services.

A context-aware security system can be abstractly described as the assemblage of three high-level components performing the monitoring, decision, and action steps of the adaptation process of system security functionalities according to context parameters extracted from the environment. This description can be refined as follows (see Figure 2). A *Context Management Infrastructure* collects and aggregates context data. A *Security Context Provider* infers the current security context from the physical context. An *Authentication Manager* qualifies the confidence level of context information. A *Decision-Making Component* evaluates the need for an adaptation from the security context. A *Flexible Security Sub-System* is the target of reconfigurations in terms of policies and mechanisms.

Reconfiguration of the Security Sub-System is performed as follows. The Context Management Infrastructure first provides a generic description of the current physical context. Low-level data (e.g., raw location inputs) is collected from sensors distributed in the environment, aggregated, and abstracted into a higher-level representation (e.g., a description of a situation or an activity). The Authentication Manager then performs a confidence evaluation of this context information, which will serve to reconfigure the security functionalities. For instance, unreliable context data will be ignored for critical adaptations. Evaluation results may range from simple levels (e.g., of trust, security, or reliability) to richer descriptions using the appropriate ontologies (see section 4). After this assessment, the Security Context Provider infers from it a description of the ambient security context, which typically takes the form of a set of security attributes, such as security levels in the simplest case. More complex representations are also possible using dedicated security ontologies. The authenticated security context then serves as input to the Decision-Making Component to trigger or not a reconfiguration of the Security Sub-System, for instance to relax the strength of authentication, to change cryptographic key lengths, or to select the type of authorization model adapted to the current network. The decision is finally transmitted to the Security Sub-System to be adapted. The reconfiguration operation is performed by changing the needed component. Security Sub-Systems should be flexible enough to be reconfigured, by tuning security configuration parameters, or by replacing them with other components offering similar security services. Specific support mechanisms are needed to guarantee the safety and security of the reconfiguration process. The new security configuration then constitutes the basis for future adaptations.

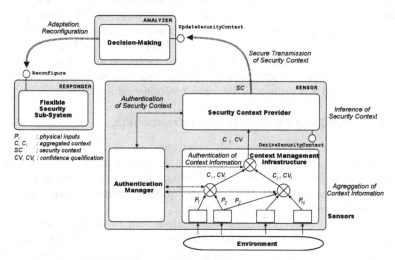

Fig. 2. Components of a context-aware security system

Main Interfaces. For each step of the reconfiguration activity, the relationships between these components can be abstracted with a small number of interfaces:

Monitoring: `DeriveSecurityContext` interface. Based on information retrieved from sensors, the Context Management Infrastructure notifies the Security Context Provider of changes in the physical context. This will trigger a computation of the new security context, by reasoning on the aggregated sensor data.

Analyzing: `UpdateSecurityContext` interface. When a new security context is computed from the environment, one has to check whether a reconfiguration of the Security Sub-Systems is needed..

Responding: `Reconfigure` interface exported by each Security Sub-System. If a decision to reconfigure a Security Sub-System is taken, the reconfiguration process needs to be performed safely and securely. This interface is also in charge of translating a high-level decision to perform a reconfiguration to low-level adaptation actions specific to each Security Sub-System. A flexible Security Sub-System for authentication, authorization, and cryptography would typically include specializations of the `Reconfigure` interface such as `ChangeASP` to select a new authentication mechanism or *Authentication Service Provider (ASP)*, `ChangeAuthorizationPolicy` to enforce a new authorization policy, and `ChangeCryptoAttributes` to change cryptographic configuration parameters.

4   An Enhanced Context Management Infrastructure

We now focus on the components of the architecture dealing with context acquisition and processing. This architecture has been fully implemented as a comprehensive context management system in the AMIGO project [35]. Context management amounts to acquire data from various sources such as physical sensors, user activities, or running applications, and to combine or abstract away these pieces of heterogeneous data into consistent *context information* that is provided to context-aware applications. The *Context Management Infrastructure (CMI)* is the software that supports the plugging of context sources and the transport of context information from context sources to context-aware applications. We now introduce the main features of the CMI and the associated context information model.

4.1   A Distributed Context Management Infrastructure

The main functional entities in the CMI architecture are represented in Figure 3a. Our design principle has been to provide a well-defined interface (named `ContextSource`) to context-aware applications (also called *context consumers*). This interface enables applications to query context information or to subscribe/unsubscribe to context change events.

The CMI architecture prescribes the encapsulation of physical sensors or any devices that could provide context information within a software layer that implements the `ContextSource` interface. Pure data processing systems such as a context history management system or a dedicated context reasoning system that abstracts away or aggregates context information could also implement this interface.

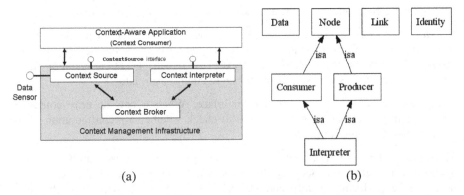

(a)   (b)

Fig. 3. The Context Management Infrastructure: (a) architecture; and (b) structural ontology

The corresponding entities are called *context sources* (or *context producers*) since they constitute the primary source of context information. The CMI uses a high level language for exchanging context information between context sources and consumers, irrespective of the type of context (user, environmental, or device contexts). A *context interpreter* is a special context source which takes as input a set of possibly heterogeneous context data (generally physical measurements) and processes them to produce further context data (usually an abstract context such as a user activity).

Context sources, consumers, and interpreters are organized into a graph, where nodes are processing elements that handle and transform context data, and edges represent information flow between nodes. These nodes can discover one another dynamically using a *context broker*. The concepts used to describe the structure of the CMI are summarized in the structural ontology shown in Figure 3b.

After a comprehensive analysis of ambient intelligence applications, a context ontology was defined to identify the types of context information relevant to context-aware applications and the relationships among these types [34].

Context information is described using the Resource Description Framework (RDF). In our modelling approach, a piece of context information is a RDF fragment which relates entities that are instances of concepts of the context ontology to other entities, or to literate values (strings, numerical values, or URIs). A textual serialized format based on XML is used to transmit this information between context sources and context-aware applications. Based on this information, the context broker is able to connect context consumers to context sources. Context sources register to the context broker by providing a description of their capabilities as soon as they are deployed or come into the environment.

Context sources are designed as web services, providing a standard interface to context consumers. Our infrastructure draws inspiration from many similar context management systems proposed in the literature [12][20][26][36] from which SOCAM [20] is a prototypical example. More precisely, the job of SOCAM context management service is to collect sensor information and forward this information in a single place so that information could be easily aggregated. The drawback of such system is that they centralize the management of context information in a single place, which is contradictory to the concept of context. For instance, SOCAM would provide information about a person activity environment (a special case of context information), whereas this information might not be contextual if it were independent from the current person task. Moreover, with such a system, the scope of context management would be only efficient in a limited geographical area. Among the work mentioned previously, the Context Toolkit [36] had a pioneering influence. These architectures either applied object-orientation, component-based design, or SOA software paradigms. The latter approach fits the dynamic nature of ambient intelligence and pervasive computing environments, where devices and humans appear and disappear, and interact in a loose and ad hoc fashion.

The CMI relies on standard technologies for: (i) *binding applications to context sources:* applications interact with context sources using the SOAP protocol [39], a well-established standard for communication between web services; and (ii) *querying context information:* context consumers use SPARQL [40] for querying context sources on specific context information.

4.2 An Ontology of Confidence: Metadata Attached to Context

To each context information handled by the CMI is attached metadata that convey the security and quality of that piece of information. Metadata may also be associated with a context source, thus qualifying the confidence we may have in the processing of context information by that context source. These metadata contribute to the making of a *reputation* related to the context information itself, or to the process that yields that information.

A reputation has several dimensions, each one representing one way of qualifying the confidence we might have in a context information or in its processing. The relationships between those dimensions are described with an *ontology of confidence* (see Figure 4), which can be extended to refine the description of the reputation.

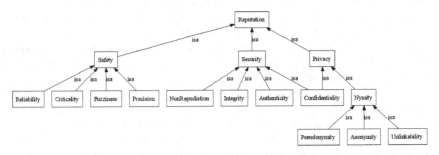

Fig. 4. The ontology of confidence

The root concept of this hierarchy is the *reputation*, which measures how much we may trust a piece of context data or information. This qualification comprises the following sub-concepts, pertaining to the fields of *safety*, *security*, and *privacy:* *reliability* that ensures a specific level of quality of service; *criticality* that measures the effects and consequences of an undesired event; *fuzziness* that characterizes a data in the fuzzy logic representation framework (crisp vs. fuzzy); *precision* that quantifies the similarity of multiple values measured under the same circumstances; *confidentiality* that prevents unauthorized divulgation of information; *integrity* that avoids inappropriate modification of information; *authenticity* that ensures that the completeness and accuracy of information has not been altered; *non-repudiation* that guarantees that the author of some information is unable to deny his/her authorship; *nymity* that measures the degree of anonymity of a context information [17]; *anonymity* that qualifies the fact of not being identifiable within a set of subjects; *unlinkability* where one may perform multiple accesses to a resource or a service without letting other entities know the relationships between these operations; and *pseudonymity* which refers to the use of a pseudonym as an identifier [32].

4.3 Mapping the Quality of Context to the CMI Architecture

The architectural concepts of the CMI described in section 4.1 are endowed with specific context qualities depending on their nature, thus giving rise to relationships

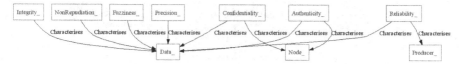

Fig. 5. Sample relationships between structural and confidence ontologies

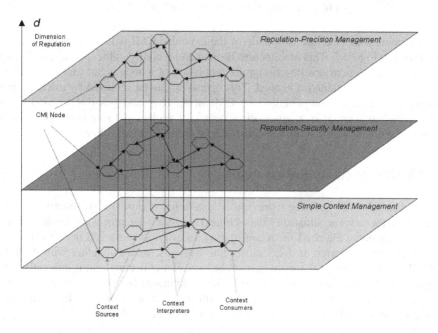

Fig. 6. Architecture for managing several planes of context metadata

between structural and confidence ontologies (see Figure 5). Criticality will rather characterize context consumers, producers, and intermediary nodes of the CMI. Precision, fuzziness, reliability, confidentiality, authenticity, integrity, and non-repudiation are qualities that apply to context information itself – although reliability, authenticity, and confidentiality might also characterize CMI nodes.

As introduced earlier in the paper, the standard CMI forms a network of nodes that are context sources, consumers, or interpreters. We extend the CMI to consider confidence qualification of context information by managing reputation. As shown in Figure 6, the overall architecture of this enhanced CMI can conceptually be viewed as overlays of the CMI that add to the components of the standard CMI dedicated *Reputation Managers* for each dimension d or concept defined in the confidence ontology (d = precision, security, reliability, etc.). The role of these new components is to process the reputation metadata specific to each dimension d. For instance, there will be Managers for Reputation-Precision, Reputation-Security, Reputation-Reliability etc.

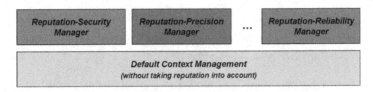

Fig. 7. Architecture of a node of the extended CMI

The internal architecture of a node of the extended CMI will thus be organized as presented in Figure 7. This architecture is open and reconfigurable. More specifically, the number of dimensions describing the reputation of a node is not limited, and new dimensions may be added if needed. This operation can be achieved by inserting new Reputation Manager components in a CMI node. It is also possible to modify the processing associated to a given dimension, by replacing the current Reputation Manager with another that implements the new processing algorithm.

5   Flexible Security Sub-systems

The enhanced CMI described previously can infer a trustworthy security context related to the current situation. This context can then be processed by a decision engine to evaluate the need for reconfiguring security, as presented in section 3. We now focus on the design of the Security Sub-Systems, which, together with the CMI described previously, is the main part of the overall architecture that is currently fully implemented. We apply the benefits of component-based design to achieve adaptability in such sub-systems. We illustrate this approach by presenting implementation and evaluation results for an authorization sub-system.

5.1   A Component-Oriented Approach to Flexibility

Component-based design is a simple but powerful manner to achieve flexibility of configuration in a system: in this paradigm, functionalities can be simply adapted or inserted by adding or replacing components. This approach is thus well suited to the dynamic needs of ambient intelligence environments.

We specify the architecture of the Security Sub-Systems using Fractal [7]. This generic component model is based on a minimal number of concepts (see Figure 8): a *component* is a run-time entity built from a *controller*, which supervises the execution of a *content* possibly including other components (*sub-components*). A *composite component* reveals the organization of its content. A *primitive component* is a black-box to encapsulate legacy code. A component only interacts with its environment through well-defined *interfaces*, which may be provided or required. Components interact by establishing *bindings* between their interfaces. Fractal manages reconfiguration independently from component functionality by separating *control interfaces* from *functional interfaces*. The main control interfaces of Fractal cover: (i) containment relationships and bindings between components (BindingController interface); (ii) configuration of component properties (AttributeController interface); (iii) dynamic reconfiguration, by adding or removing sub-components

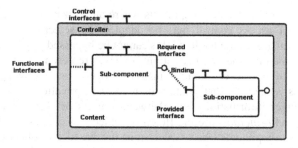

Fig. 8. Main concepts of the Fractal component model

(ContentController interface); and (iv) life-cycle management, for instance, suspending or resuming component execution (LifeCycleController interface).

5.2 Flexible Access Control

Architecture. These concepts can be applied to enforce several classes of authorization policies with a single mechanism, and select the policy best matching the security context. We introduced support for policy-neutral access control at the OS-level with a security framework called CRACKER *(Component-based Reconfigurable Access Control for Kernels)* [24], specified with Fractal, and implemented on the Think [14] component-based OS framework for limited devices. CRACKER clearly separates policy enforcement from decision-making. The framework is independent from a security model, with the exception of a single component computing permissions according to a specific model. This component can be replaced at run-time to support other security models. Flexible authorization is achieved with minimal intrusiveness, since the OS is already built from components.

CRACKER represents each kernel resource by a software component. Access control on resources is enforced by associating security controllers to the corresponding components. Controllers are specified in the description of the kernel architecture. This automatically attaches a *Reference Monitor (RM)* to intercept invocations on the component interfaces. Policy decision-making is encapsulated in a separate *Policy Manager (PM)* component (see Figure 9).

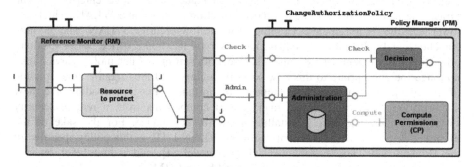

Fig. 9. The CRACKER security architecture

RMs can be shared between components where authorizations are enforced. Thus, the granularity of access control may be adapted, by selective insertion of RMs. Hardware mechanisms guarantee that RMs cannot be bypassed.

The PM contains the authorization policy, represented by an efficient implementation of the access control matrix. We use the following terminology: *objects* are passive entities that contain or receive information; *subjects* are active entities that trigger information flows between objects or change the system state (e.g., threads); and *principals* are indifferently subjects or objects. CRACKER views all principals as components. Access decisions are based on collections of security attributes found in common authorization models, such as security levels, domains, types, or roles. Customized attributes can also be defined for specific models. Subject and object attribute collections are stored in specific tables called *SID-tables*, indexed by *security identifiers (SIDs)* assigned to principals. Each newly created principal is assigned a new attribute collection depending on the current authorization model. Then, permissions are computed, assigned according to the authorization policy, and inserted into the access matrix representation.

The PM exports interfaces for checking permissions (Check) and for policy management (Admin). It contains the following sub-components. The *Administration component* stores the SID-tables and the access matrix. The SID-table entry of each principal contains a reference to the corresponding component, and the associated collection of security attributes. The access matrix is an optimized table of permissions, indexed by pairs of subject and object SIDs. Authorization is made at the method level. The *Decision component* decides whether the current subject is allowed to access the requested object. Given subject and object SIDs, this component asks the Administration component for the permission corresponding to the requested operation (using the Admin interface). Access is then granted or denied. The *Compute Permissions (CP) component* defines the authorization policy. It computes permissions as specified in the authorization model and policy, and fills the access matrix accordingly (Compute interface).

Adaptation Capabilities: An Example. Since the Administration and Decision components are completely independent from a security policy or model, reconfiguring the authorization policy only amounts to changing the CP component To illustrate this reconfiguration process, we consider the two-level location-based security scenario illustrated in Figure 1. When guest user Alice enters the home office, she had first been authenticated by location on the home WLAN, which has lower security requirements. Coming from a low-security WLAN, she is now authenticated by location as a legitimate user of the home office WLAN, where protection requirements are stronger. The security settings of her mobile device may no longer be appropriate to this new security context, and thus require an adaptation of the device security functionalities: for instance, by downloading the new authorization policy and related management components from a remote security service provider, and safely installing them on the device. For the sake of the example, we consider a low-security network WLAN-DTE, with a policy specified in the Domain and Type Enforcement (DTE) model [4]; and a high-level security network WLAN-MLS enforcing a Multi-Level Security (MLS) policy [5].

The considered subjects are two threads T1 and T2 running simple counters on Alice's PDA. The system resource to protect is the screen of the PDA. Access control is performed on a single write operation: only authorized threads are allowed to write on the screen. We also define a non-secure zone of the PDA screen where threads may write freely.

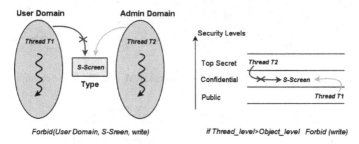

Fig. 10. Security policies: DTE and MLS cases

WLAN-DTE contains two security domains, Admin and User. The security policy is the following: threads in the User domain (e.g., T1) may only write on the non-secure zone, while threads in the Admin domain (e.g., T2) may write both on the secure and non-secure zones. In WLAN-MLS, three security levels are considered: Top secret, Confidential, and Public, the levels of the screen, T1, and T2 having the values shown in Figure 10. The policy is a simple confidentiality policy (no write down). Thus, T1 may write on the screen, while T2 cannot. The security policies were specified using ASL policy specification language [23]. This example was implemented on Think for several devices (iPAQ PDA, Nokia 770 Internet Tablet), with the outputs shown in Figure 11 for each WLAN. Figure 12 shows the relationships between the different Think components running on Alice's PDA, and where RMs have been inserted to perform access control checks.

The reconfiguration of the PM is performed as follows. A change of access control policy is triggered by a call to the PM ChangeAuthorizationPolicy control interface. A new CP component containing the MLS authorization policy is introduced in the PM, using its ContentController control interface. The Think

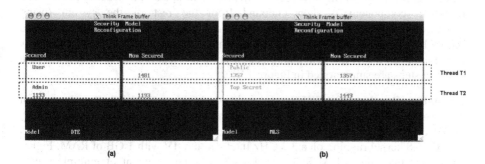

Fig. 11. Output on Alice's device: (a) for WLAN-DTE; (b) for WLAN-MLS

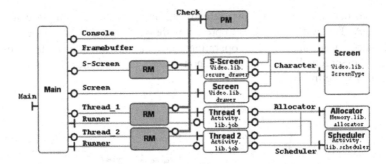

Fig. 12. Think implementation components, RM, and PM in the example

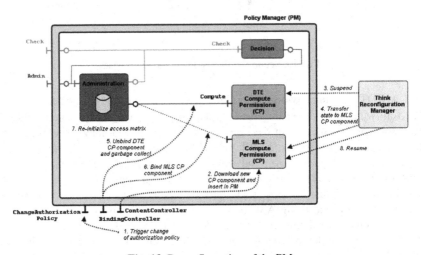

Fig. 13. Reconfiguration of the PM

reconfiguration framework is then invoked [33]. Using a set of interceptors, this framework ensures that the components to be replaced are in a stable state, when about to be reconfigured. The DTE CP component is thus suspended. The DTE CP component state is then transferred to the MLS CP component, either to translate existing permissions in the new security model, or to update the security policy. The DTE CP component is then unbound from the rest of the system (using the BindingController control interface) and garbage collected. At this point, the MLS CP component is bound to the other components of the PM. The access matrix is re-initialized with the new authorization policy. Execution then resumes. These different steps are summarized in Figure 13.

Evaluation Results. CRACKER was evaluated both quantitatively (access control overhead in terms of performance and system size) and qualitatively (adaptability compared to other authorization frameworks). We ran a simulation of Think on a Linux 2.6.8 kernel running on a 3.2 GHz Intel Pentium IV with 1 GB of RAM. Figure 14 demonstrates that CRACKER enables effective enforcement of multiple access

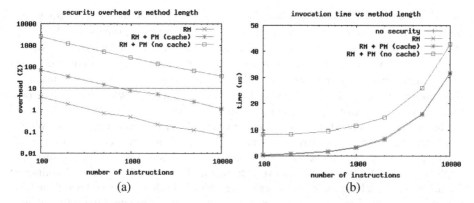

Fig. 14. (a) Relative overhead of access control checks for different method lengths in number of instructions; (b) Absolute times in the same conditions in microseconds. The overhead is calculated by comparison with the execution time without any security checks. Overheads are given for pure policy enforcement (RM interception alone), policy enforcement and decision when permissions have already been computed, and when they must be recalculated (first access control check, or reconfiguration of security policy). The protected method performs basic integer arithmetic processor instructions.

control policies with reasonable performance overhead, while keeping reconfiguration cost within reasonable bounds. Indeed, when permissions have already been computed, the overhead is lower than 10% for component sizes of 1 KB or higher – assuming components only contain the method code, and that 1 byte processor instructions are executed. The component size overhead is also satisfactory and makes the architecture applicable to embedded settings. The architecture seems to scale well, both in terms of number of components, or complexity of the system authorization policy. More complete evaluation results are available in [24].

6 Related Work

A number of distributed architectures deal with network-based confidence in a general sense [19][25], neither attaching it specifically to context, nor addressing its different possible dimensions systematically as we proposed here. Most of this work corresponds to generic reputation management systems, architected in a decentralized or peer to peer fashion [6][11][41], or specifically applied to sensor networks [44]. These systems cannot handle separately the different and potentially incommensurable dimensions of reputation as we propose here.

A significant body of work has also been dedicated to either one type of confidence data (e.g., authentication), or one type of context data (e.g., time or location [18][37][46]) Location has also been extensively addressed from the viewpoint of data protection and privacy [31]. The closest work on quality of context (QoC) management comes from [27], but does not consider the multidimensional aspect we have proposed here. It is also worth mentioning the work done by Judd et al. [26], that has addressed the incorporating of meta-information such as confidence, accuracy and update time information into context data. In this work, meta-information and context information itself have been formatted as p-tuples and stored in a dedicated relational database. As pointed out by later work on context modelling [12], modelling context using languages lacking semantics ground hamper interoperability and scalability. For this reason, we have adopted the web ontology language OWL which has more facilities than p-tuples for expressing semantics, see [29].

Related to this context modelling issue, the search for a common context ontology has been one source of disagreement for years. Indeed, as any piece of information could potentially be considered as context information for a specific task or application, building a comprehensive context ontology would amount to building a language for modelling the entire world. Attempts along this line have been launched some 20 years ago [28], that have proved that the resources required to do the job are enormous and incommensurate with the result yield. For this reason we prefer to bank on the openness of ontology description languages, such as OWL, which makes possible the extension of context description and on ontology alignment and matching which helps dealing with independently developed ontologies [13].

The quest for the right balance between security and flexibility has also spawned a whole line of research in the fields of reconfigurable security architectures and adaptive security mechanisms, security of smart spaces, and security of autonomic computing systems.

Adaptive security mechanisms are found in flexible protocol stacks for wireless networks [21], context-aware access control systems [1] and context-aware security architectures [3][9][43], or architectures supporting disconnected modes [2][45]. Such schemes suffer from limited flexibility, being restricted: either to a specific application setting, such as optimising the performance of security protocols for wireless networks [21]; or to a particular security mechanism such as authorization [43][45]. Our solution remains independent from the network architecture, and can support several types of adaptive security mechanisms.

Many software systems have also been developed to support smart spaces such as intelligent homes, where users are immersed in massively sensed and actuated space, integrated in an extended information system able to respond to changes in the physical context through actuators. Most of these systems remain limited to closed environments, and generally adopt centralized security architectures. They also rely on extended versions of RBAC (Role-Based Access Control) [10][42] for authorization. Our framework addresses open environments, allowing for instance to insert new security mechanisms, can operate in a decentralized manner, and is not tied to a particular access control model.

Finally, self-protection is a key property of autonomic systems [16]: the overhead of security management is reduced by enforcing policies with minimal human intervention. Emphasis was mostly put on security of system configuration, detection and prevention of unusual events (intrusions), and appropriate recovery (self-healing), rather on contextual adaptation of security functionalities. The architecture proposed in [8] is quite similar to our framework, but does not seem to have been fully implemented, many studies remaining concentrated on theoretical foundations.

7 Conclusion

We have presented a concept and corresponding architecture that build upon and generalize the classical view of distributed context management, to allow for more secure exploitation of context by attaching various types of context metadata to context data. We have shown how it can be applied to contextual security using a flexible security framework that lends itself to full reconfiguration on the basis of contextual criteria. This work was motivated by a desire to overcome the limitations of present-day context management: its brittleness, lack of scalability, poor reliability, the difficulty to delineate the perimeter of relevant context data, and the ad hoc nature of the rules or numeric mechanisms that implement context fusion, aggregation or interpretation. It is but a first step towards a more robust and scalable use of context.

Future work should lead towards the use of context in a way that fits within the general framework of autonomic systems [38], making it possible, not only to adapt system parameters, but also to reconfigure the system on the basis of context as we have shown here, and, one step further, to reconfigure the use of context itself when the environment changes. This may mean reconfiguring the use of some types of context data (e.g., excluding some from the relevance perimeter or including others) on the basis of other types of context. This choice can be achieved by including a contextual relevance parameter in the context metadata. Only when they can self-configure and self-optimize in this way will context-aware systems achieve their full potential and be really applicable in practice.

References

[1] Almenárez, F., Marín, A., Campo, C., García, C.: TrustAC: Trust-Based Access Control for Pervasive Devices. In: Hutter, D., Ullmann, M. (eds.) SPC 2005. LNCS, vol. 3450, Springer, Heidelberg (2005)

[2] Almenárez, F., Marín, A., Díaz, D., Sánchez, J.: Developing a Model for Trust Management in Pervasive Devices. In: IEEE Workshop on Pervasive Computing and Communication Security, IEEE Computer Society Press, Los Alamitos (2006)

[3] Al-Muhtadi, J., Ranganathan, A., Campbell, R., Mickunas, M.: Cerberus: A Context-Aware Security Scheme for Smart Spaces. In: International Conference on Pervasive Computing and Communications (PerCom) (2003)

[4] Badger, L., Sterne, D., Sherman, D., Walker, K., Haghinghat, S.: Practical Domain and Type Enforcement for UNIX. In: IEEE Symposium on Security and Privacy, IEEE Computer Society Press, Los Alamitos (1995)

[5] Bell, D., La Padula, L.: Secure Computer System: Unified Exposition and Multics Interpretation. Technical Report no MTR-2997, MITRE Corporation (1975)

[6] Blaze, M., Feigenbaum, J., Lacy, J.: Decentralized Trust Management. In: IEEE Symposium on Security and Privacy, Oakland, California, USA (1996)

[7] Bruneton, E., Coupaye, T., Leclerc, M., Quéma, V., Stéfani, J.-B.: The Fractal Component Model and its Support in Java. Software - Practice and Experience (SP&E) special issue on Experiences with Auto-adaptive and Reconfigurable Systems 36(11-12), 1257–1284 (2006)

[8] Chess, D., Palmer, C., White, S.: Security in an Autonomic Computing Environment. IBM Systems Journal 42(1), 107–118 (2003)

[9] Covington, M., Fogla, P., Zhan, Z., Ahamad, M.: A Context-Aware Security Architecture for Emerging Applications. In: Annual Computer Security Applications Conference (ACSAC) (2002)

[10] Covington, M., Moyer, M., Ahamad, M.: Generalized Role-Based Access control for Securing Future Applications. In: National Information Systems Security Conference (NISSC) (2000)

[11] Damiani, E., De Capitani, S., Paraboschi, S., Samarati, P., Violante, F.: A Reputation-Based Approach for Choosing Reliable Resources in Peer-to-Peer Networks. In: ACM Conference on Computer and Communications Security (CCS), Washington DC, USA (2002)

[12] Ebling, M., Hunt, G., Lei, H.: Issues for Context Services for Pervasive Computing. In: Guerraoui, R. (ed.) Middleware 2001. LNCS, vol. 2218, Springer, Heidelberg (2001)

[13] Euzenat, J., Pierson, J., Ramparany, F.: A Context Information Manager Component for Dynamic Environments. In: International Conference on Pervasive Computing (2006)

[14] Fassino, J.P., Stefani, J.B., Lawall, J., Muller, G.: Think: A Software Framework for Component-Based Operating System Kernels. In: USENIX Annual Technical Conference (2002)

[15] Flury, T., Privat, G.: An Infrastructure Template for Scalable Location-Based Services. In: Smart Objects Conference (SoC), Grenoble (May 2003)

[16] Ganek, A., Corbi, T.: The Dawning of the Autonomic Computing Era. IBM Systems Journal 42(1), 5–18 (2003)

[17] Goldberg, I.: A Pseudonymous Communications Infrastructure for the Internet. PhD thesis, University of California at Berkeley (2000)

[18] Gonzáles, A., Salas, L., Ramos, B., Rigaborda, A.: Providing Personalization and Automation to Spatial-Temporal Stamping Services. In: International Workshop on Secure Ubiquitous Networks (SUN) (2005)

[19] Grandison, T., Sloman, M.: A Survey of Trust in Internet Applications. IEEE Communications Surveys 4(4), 2–16 (2000)

[20] Gu, T., Pung, H.K., Zhang, D.Q.: A Middleware for Building Context-Aware Mobile Services. In: Vehicular Technology Conference (VTC) (2004)

[21] Hager, C.: Context Aware and Adaptive Security for Wireless Networks. PhD thesis, Virginia Polytechnic Institute and State University (2004)

[22] Housley, R., Polk, W., Ford, W., Solo, D.: Internet X.509 Public Key Infrastructure Certificate and Certificate Revocation List (CRL) Profile. RFC 3280 (April 2002), http://www.ietf.org/rfc/rfc3280.txt

[23] Jajodia, S., Samarati, P., Subrahmanian, V.: A Logical Language for Expressing Authorizations. In: IEEE Symposium on Security and Privacy, IEEE Computer Society Press, Los Alamitos (1997)

[24] Jarboui, T., Lacoste, M., Wadier, P.: A Component-Based Policy-Neutral Authorization Architecture. In: French Conference on Operating Systems (CFSE) (2006)

[25] Jøsang, A., Ismail, R., Boyd, C.: A Survey of Trust and Reputation Systems for Online Service Provision. Decision Support Systems (2005)

[26] Judd, G., Steenkiste, P.: Providing Contextual Information to Pervasive Computing Applications. In: PerCom 2003 (2003)

[27] Hübscher, M.C., McCann, J.: Adaptive Middleware for Context-Aware Applications in Smart Homes. In: Workshop on Middleware for Pervasive and Ad Hoc Computing, Toronto (2004)

[28] Lenat, D., Guha, R.V.: Building Large Knowledge-Based Systems: Representation and Inference in the Cyc Project. Addison-Wesley, Reading (1990)

[29] McGuinness, D., van Harmelen, F.: OWL Web Ontology Language Overview. W3C Recommendation (2003), http://www.w3.org/TR/owl-features/
[30] Myers, M., Ankney, R., Malpani, A., Galperin, S., Adams, C.: Internet X.509 Public Key Infrastructure: Online Certificate Status Protocol – OCSP. RFC 2560 (June 1999), http://www.ietf.org/rfc/rfc2560.txt
[31] Myles, G., Friday, A., Davies, N.: Preserving Privacy in Environments with Location-Based Applications. IEEE Pervasive Computing 2(1), 56–64 (2003)
[32] Pftizmann, A., Hansen, M.: Anonymity, Unlinkability, Unobservability, Pseudonymity, and Identity Management - A Consolidated Proposal for Terminology. Technical University of Dresden (2005)
[33] Polakovic, J., Ozcan, A.E., Stefani, J.-B.: Building Reconfigurable Component-Based OS with Think. In: EUROMICRO 2006 (2006)
[34] Ramparany, F., Euzenat, J., Broens, T., Pierson, J., Bottaro, A., Poortinga, R.: Context Management and Semantic Modelling for Ambient Intelligence. In: International Workshop on Future Research Challenges for Software and Services (FRCSS) (2006)
[35] Ramparany, F., Poortinga, R., Stikic, M., Schmalenströer, J., Prante, T.: An Open Context Information Management Infrastructure. In: IE 2007. 3rd IET International Conference on Intelligent Environments, Ulm, Germany (September 2007)
[36] Salber, D., Dey, A.K., Abowd, G.: The Context Toolkit: Aiding the Development of Context-Enabled Applications. In: Conference on Human Factors in Computing Systems (CHI) (1999)
[37] Sastry, N., Shankar, U., Wagner, D.: Secure Verification of Location Claims. In: ACM Workshop on Wireless Security, pp. 1–10. ACM Press, New York (2003)
[38] Saxena, A., Lacoste, M., Jarboui, T., Lücking, U., Steinke, B.: A Software Framework for Autonomic Security in Pervasive Environments. In: International Conference on Information Systems Security (ICISS) (to appear, 2007)
[39] SOAP Specifications. http://www.w3.org/TR/soap/
[40] SPARQL Specifications. http://www.w3.org/TR/rdf-sparql-query/
[41] Suryanarayana, G., Erenkrantz, J., Taylor, R.: An Architectural Approach for Decentralized Trust Management. IEEE Internet Computing 9(6), 16–23 (2005)
[42] Undercoffer, J., Perich, F., Cedilnik, A., Kagal, L., Joshi, A.: A Secure Infrastructure for Service Discovery and Access in Pervasive Computing. ACM Mobile Networks and Applications (MONET): Special Issue on Security in Mobile Computing Environments 8(2), 113–125 (2003)
[43] Wullems, C., Looi, M., Clark, A.: Towards Context-aware Security: An Authorization Architecture for Intranet Environments. In: International Conference on Pervasive Computing and Communications Workshops (PerCom) (2004)
[44] Yao, Z., Kim, D., Lee, I., Kim, K., Jang, J.: A Security Framework with Trust Management for Sensor Networks. In: IEEE Workshop on Security and QoS in Communication Networks (SecQoS), Athens, Greece (2005)
[45] Zhang, K., Kindberg, T.: An Authorization Infrastructure for Nomadic Computing. In: Symposium on Access Control Models and Technologies (SACMAT) (2002)
[46] Zugenmaier, A., Kreutzer, M., Kabatnik, M.: Enhancing Applications with Approved Location Stamps. In: IEEE Intelligent Network Workshop (IN), Boston, MA, USA (2001)

A Compiler for the Smart Space

Urs Bischoff and Gerd Kortuem

Lancaster University, Lancaster LA1 4YW, UK

Abstract. Developing applications for smart spaces is a challenging task. Most programming systems narrowly focus on the embedded computer infrastructure and neglect the spatial aspect of this fusion between a physical and a virtual environment. Hence, application logic is not implemented for the smart space but for the embedded network, which is only one aspect of the system. Our programming system supports an abstract model of a smart space. A high-level language is used to implement the application logic for this model. In this paper we show how a compiler translates code written for this abstract model into a distributed application that can be executed by a computer infrastructure. The compiler allows for a clear separation between the application code and its execution in a concrete network. This simplifies the development and maintenance of an application because the application programmer can focus on the actual application logic for the smart space instead of issues related to a concrete network.

1 Introduction

High-level programming languages provided the basis for the development of complex computing systems. Compared to assembly programming early programming languages (e.g. COBOL or FORTRAN) simplified the programming task considerably. Even though these languages were developed in the 50's, millions of lines of code written in these languages are still in use today. The secret behind this success is that they were designed for an abstract computer model instead of a concrete hardware platform. A compiler is responsible for the translation between the code written for the abstract computer model and code that can be executed by the computer hardware. This separation allowed the independent development of hardware and software over the years.

Today, we are working on the ubiquitous computing vision of smart spaces consisting of large numbers of sensors and actuators. And we are faced with the challenging task of programming this new type of computer infrastructure. Similar to how assembly programming did not scale to complex applications, system design focused on individual network nodes does not scale to networks consisting of large numbers of sensor and actuator nodes. We must consider how to model these smart spaces and design suitable programming abstractions.

A smart space embeds interconnected technologies that are, more or less, responsive to the state of the environment. A problem pointed out in [1] is that our experience in building smart spaces is limited by the set of concepts we know at

B. Schiele et al. (Eds.): AmI 2007, LNCS 4794, pp. 230–247, 2007.

the time of development; we are constantly faced with better technology becoming available. Unlike a mobile phone it is not possible to replace the infrastructure of a smart space every few months. As emphasised by Rodden and Benford [2], living and work environments are also subject to continuous transformation; they are modified by the people who inhabit them in a variety of ways, for a variety of purposes and with different frequencies. This observation also has an effect on the requirements of a computing infrastructure of a smart space and its applications. As such, they are subject to similar changes as the rest of our living and work environments. As users we want to change or extend the application logic from time to time. With better technology becoming available, the network or parts of it should be exchanged without greatly affecting the running applications. Or by adding nodes and replicating tasks we want to make the application more reliable. Upgrading and modifying embedded software is difficult because of the generally tight coupling between hardware and software. Having to deal with distributed applications makes changes to the application even harder.

In this paper we present a novel programming paradigm and compiler for smart spaces. In our programming paradigm a smart space is not just the end product of a fusion between a physical and virtual environment but it is a fundamental abstraction that is used during the whole life cycle from the design to the deployment of such a space. The application developer does not implement the application logic for a network that happens to be embedded in a physical environment, but for an abstraction of the actual space that should exhibit smart behaviour. A high-level language is used to define the application logic for this space abstraction. A compiler translates the high-level application code into a representation that can be executed by the embedded network. It splits the application code into a set of tasks and operators, and assigns them to individual network nodes. This top-down approach allows the application programmer to move away from system problems of the individual nodes to the actual programming problem of the smart space as a whole. Hence, the global application does not have to be expressed in terms of a set of distributed tasks for individual nodes. Furthermore, because the logic is implemented for the smart space itself (and not for the embedded network), the network infrastructure can evolve independently of the application logic.

This paper is organised as follows. Section 2 presents the abstract concept of a programmable smart space. In Sec. 3 we describe our programming system that integrates this smart space model. Section 4 introduces an application scenario that is used in this paper to illustrate the technical detail of the compiler addressed in Sec. 5. In Sec. 6 we focus on the mapper, which is a core component of the compiler. We evaluate it in terms of a case study. Section 7 gives a brief overview of related work. Finally, Sec. 8 concludes this paper.

2   Programming a Smart Space

An application programmer wants to write an application for a space to make it "smart". For example, a room should turn off its lights if nobody is inside.

This point of view is in contrast to the prevalent programming paradigm focused on the embedded network infrastructure. Implementing this example, the application programmer would have to address the motion sensors to find out whether there is motion in the room. And if no motion is detected, a command can be sent to the light switch to turn the lights off. The ubiquitous computing vision of technologies that *weave themselves into the fabric of everyday life until they are indistinguishable from it* [3] cannot support such an explicit technology focus on programming. Our novel programming paradigm supports the definition of the application logic for the smart space. The actual technology disappears in the background; it is irrelevant for the logic and is interchangeable.

Figure 1 illustrates this programming paradigm. It shows a floor of an office building. Each room should be made "smart" by embedding some logic into it. For example, each room should turn off its light when nobody is inside. Additionally, the office occupants might want to individualise their office and update it with additional logic. The kitchen is a different type of space which requires different logic; it should detect when the stove is turned on and nobody is monitoring it. Finally, there is a fire alarm that concerns the whole floor. What is important to notice is that we want to embed logic into the actual room. The embedded sensor and actuator network is not relevant at this point. Our programming paradigm supports this point of view. By focusing on the space instead of the embedded computer infrastructure, we can separate the implementation of the application logic from the underlying hardware. The application developer can deal with the space abstraction instead of the details of the underlying network such as types and number of nodes. A compiler is responsible for mapping the application logic onto the computer infrastructure of a smart space.

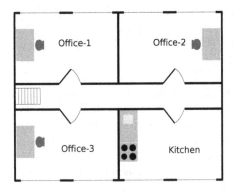

Fig. 1. A floor in an office building as a smart space

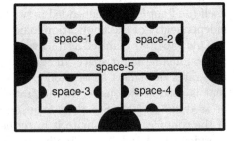

Fig. 2. Example of the abstract model of five smart spaces. Each one has interfaces for communication with other spaces and the physical environment.

2.1   Abstract Smart Space Model

In order to support this programming paradigm, an abstract model of a smart space is necessary. Figure 1 shows that there can be several separate smart spaces (e.g. offices and kitchen), which are all contained within another smart space (office floor). And each space exhibits its own logic. Communication between these spaces might be necessary (e.g. the kitchen might want to send an alarm to an occupied office if the stove is turned on).

Figure 2 illustrates an example of the abstract model of smart spaces. There are several smart spaces. Some are contained within another one. Each smart space has four distinct interfaces. One interface is used to observe the environment and another one to affect the environment. The two remaining interfaces provide the communication channels to send/receive state information to/from other smart spaces. A space uses its sensor observations to update its internal state. It can then use this state information to affect the state of the physical environment.

2.2   Infrastructure Assumption

The computer model of a standard high-level programming language is based upon several requirements for the the underlying computer (e.g. computer has memory and can do comparisons). Similarly, the abstract smart space model makes some assumptions about the structure and capabilities of the underlying network:

- Nodes in the network can communicate with each other.
- A node belongs to a symbolic location that it is assigned to or it can assign itself to (e.g. node 23 is in room 213). This information is necessary to find a mapping between the smart space model and the actual network infrastructure.
- Properties of network nodes are known (e.g. node 23 has a temperature sensor). The nodes could either describe themselves or the properties are well-known facts.

3   System Overview

The programming paradigm introduced in Sec. 2 is directly supported by our system called RuleCaster. It provides a high-level language and implementation for the smart space model. In the following we outline this system with a focus on the two main problems mentioned earlier: (1) defining the global application in terms of separate local actions, and (2) accommodating changes.

By dealing with smart space not only as a physical entity but also as an abstract computer model we realised the concept of a programmable space. The advantage of this approach is that the application developer can implement applications for the smart space as one logical entity; *the smart space is the computer.* The application developer is provided with a high-level language for application development.

As mentioned earlier, dealing with evolutionary changes to the application requirements and the infrastructure is a complex job for application developers, which touches upon several life-cycle phases. We can identify three major classes of changes that a smart space application undergoes throughout its life-cycle. These are changes to the

- logical structure,
- physical structure and
- computing infrastructure.

The logical structure describes how functional elements and application states are connected for describing the application logic. Changes to the logical structure refer to changes in the observable behaviour of an application. For example, while an application might initially be defined to open the window when the room is too hot, a new application logic might turn on the air conditioning instead.

The physical structure describes where computational elements are executed and where application states are stored in the network infrastructure. Changes to the physical structure of an application refer to changes in the distribution of computing tasks to individual nodes. For example, a task initially performed by a central node is distributed over several nodes in order to improve reliability and decrease energy consumption.

The infrastructure is the actual network that stores and computes the application states. It is the distributed runtime environment. Changes to the infrastructure refer to changes in the underlying hardware and runtime system (e.g. network system). For example, the infrastructure might need to be updated when a new generation of hardware devices becomes available with different processor, memory or radio. Another example is modifying the infrastructure by adding or removing nodes.

Our programming system supports these classes of changes by separating them into three separate models: logical structure, physical structure and infrastructure. Changes to any of these three models can be directly propagated to the running application by recompilation and re-deployment.

Figure 3 illustrates the architecture of our system. The logical structure of an application is defined in the RuleCaster Application Language (RCAL) — a high-level language designed for the smart space model. The physical structure is implicitly described by the compiler that translates the logical structure into an executable representation.

The infrastructure consists of the actual sensor-actuator node hardware running a middleware that executes the application. This middleware is based around a service-based architecture. Services give access to the interface between the network and the physical world (i.e. sensors and actuators).

In this paper we exclusively focus on the description of the compiler and the generation of the physical structure of an application.

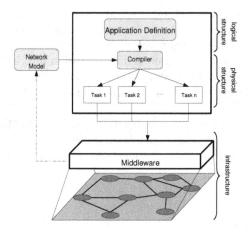

Fig. 3. The system architecture

4 Application Scenario

In order to simplify the discussion in the remainder of this paper we introduce a simple application scenario. As an example we use a smart office building.

4.1 Scenario

Bob is the environmental officer at Green University. He wants to reduce the electrical energy consumption. One of the first ideas is to turn off the lights in an office if there is enough day light coming through the windows or if nobody is in the office. And instead of using the HVAC system to control the temperature, he wants the windows to be opened automatically if the outside temperature can be used to reduce the office temperature.

4.2 Scenario Implementation in RCAL

The scenario application is implemented in RCAL — a state-based programming language for a smart space (i.e. office). Based on sensor observations the smart space determines the current state of the space. Rules are used to define the state transitions. And states can trigger the activation of an actuator. More information about this language can be found in [4]. Figure 4 shows a simplified version of the application code. For space reasons we only show a small part of the whole application, which we are going to use in the rest of this paper. Communication with other spaces is not shown. Lines 2-8 declare the interface of the office space. For example, line 3 declares a sensor `indoorTemperature` that delivers one value at a time (i.e. the indoor temperature).

Lines 10-14 define the first state transition rule. This rule is applied if the space is in a state `lightOn` (the rule that defines this state is not shown). If the rule in line 11 or the one in line 13 is satisfied, the state `lightOn` changes into a state `lightShouldBeOff`, which means that the lights should be turned off. The rule in line 11 is satisfied if both conditions `light.average(X)` and `bright(X)` are satisfied. The condition `light.average(X)` delivers the average light sensor reading of this space in the variable `X`. The condition `bright(X)` is defined in a rule in line 12. It accepts the light value `X` as input. It is satisfied if this value is more than 20. Similarly the rule in line 13 is satisfied if the observed motion is less than 2.

Lines 16-18 define the transition from the state `lightShouldBeOff` to the state `lightOff`. This transition depends on the rule in line 17 that is satisfied if the condition `lightSwitch(0)` is satisfied. As a side-effect this condition turns the light off.

```
1     SPACE(office) {
2     INTERFACE:
3         SENSOR(indoorTemperature/1),
4         SENSOR(outdoorTemperature/1),
5         SENSOR(motion/1),
6         SENSOR(light/1),
7         ACTUATOR(window/1),
8         ACTUATOR(lightSwitch/1).
9
10    PRE_STATE(lightOn) [
11        STATE :- light.average(X), bright(X).
12        bright(X) :- X>20.
13        STATE :- motion(X), X<2.
14    ] POST_STATES(lightShouldBeOff).
15
16    PRE_STATE(lightShouldBeOff) [
17        STATE :- lightSwitch(0).
18    ] POST_STATES(lightOff).
19
20    ...
21    ...
22
23    }
```

Fig. 4. The implementation of the application scenario

4.3   The Smart Space Model and Infrastructure

In order to execute the application logic a smart space requires certain services from the underlying infrastructure. Figure 5 depicts the smart space model of an office space on the left hand side and the infrastructure of an office on the right hand side. The logic implemented for the smart space model requires a number of services for observing and affecting the physical environment: for example, the service `indoorTemperature/1` is required to get the indoor temperature. The infrastructure can provide these services with its sensors and actuators. The compiler is responsible for mapping the smart space model onto a concrete infrastructure. In general there is not a one-to-one mapping; as shown in this example, the indoor temperature is measured by three different sensor nodes.

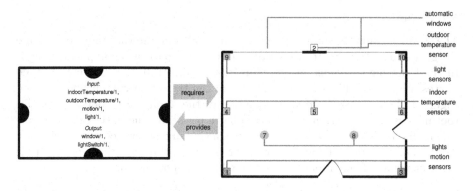

Fig. 5. The smart space model and a possible infrastructure

5   Compiler

Applications are written for an abstract computer model of a smart space. A
compiler has to find a mapping between this abstract model and the concrete
smart space infrastructure. In other words it has to translate the high-level application code into executable code for the network. The compiler consists of
several subcomponents that implement the different phases of the whole compilation process. Figure 6 depicts these components. In the following we address
each component individually.

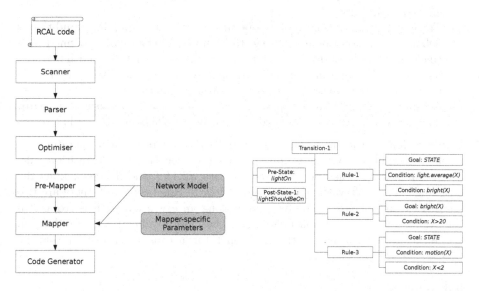

Fig. 6. The architecture of the compiler   **Fig. 7.** The syntax tree of a state transition rule

5.1 Scanner

The scanner reads the application code and builds an internal representation of the syntax as a tree. State transitions are the core part of the application code. In the following we focus on one transition to illustrate the different compiler phases. Figure 7 depicts the syntax tree of the transition rule in lines 10-14 of Figure 4. This tree is a direct translation of the application code syntax. The root node is the transition node, which has a pre-state, one post-state and three rule nodes as children. Each rule node has a goal and several condition children. Additionally there is a number of other nodes in this tree that represent the other elements of the application code, which are not shown.

5.2 Parser

The input to the parser component is the syntax tree. The parser translates this syntax representation into a semantic representation. A semantic representation contains information about the actual execution of the application. The core part of the semantic representation are the task graphs. Each transition rule tree is transformed into a task graph consisting of several operators connected with communication channels. The parser proceeds in several steps:

1. Initialise a *START*, *OR* and *END* operator and connect them with a channel.
2. Extract the top-level state rules. These are the rules whose satisfaction cause a state change. Their rule goal is STATE. Initialise a representative operator for each condition and connect them with a channel. Rename the variables because the scope of a variable is changed from the individual rule to the whole task graph. Attach these operators to task graph between the *START* and *OR* operators.
3. Traverse task graph and replace operators whose corresponding condition is defined by an additional rule (e.g. the condition bright(X) is defined by a rule). The rule is transformed into an operator-channel list and integrated into the task graph at the replaced operator's position. The variables are renamed to conform with the existing variable names.
4. Assign types to operators. Operators that correspond to a sensor or actuator interface declaration are labelled with either *SENSOR* or *ACTUATOR*.

Figure 8 depicts the task graph generated by the parser. Each operator represents a condition. A task graph specifies the execution of a transition rule. Execution starts at the operator labelled with *START* and proceeds along the outgoing channels towards the operator *END*. In this task graph there are two parallel execution paths. The execution along an execution path is stopped if the evaluation of a condition fails (e.g. if the motion value *V2* is less than 2). If one execution path reaches the *END* operator, it causes a transition from the pre-state to the post-states.

5.3 Optimiser

The optimiser is an optional component. It accepts a task graph as input and produces a task graph as output. The goal of the optimiser is to minimise the

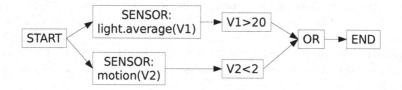

Fig. 8. The task graph of a rule

flow of information between the operators by rearranging them without altering the observable behaviour of the application. Actuators need special attention because they provide the interface for output to the environment, which is directly observable.

The optimiser of our system tries to "push" an operator that uses data as close as possible to the operator that produces the relevant data. The following operation is applied to rearrange operators:

> Two operators that are directly connected with a channel can swap position if both have exactly one input and one output channel, none of them is an *ACTUATOR*, *START* or *END* operator and the successor operator does not depend on data of the predecessor operator.

The optimiser cannot rearrange any operator in our example because neighbouring operators depend on each other; e.g. the operator with condition *V2<2* depends on the output of *motion(V2)*. Figure 9 shows a different example where two operators could be swapped. The advantage of the new task graph is that the execution could already be stopped at the second operator if the comparison condition cannot be satisfied.

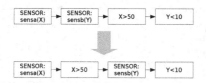

Fig. 9. The optimiser rearranges the operators of the task graph

5.4   Pre-mapper

The pre-mapper component prepares the task graph for the actual mapping process. As shown in Figure 6 it requires the network model as input. The network model contains an abstract representation of every network node. This representation consists of three parts:

Services. Each node offers a number of services. For example, a node that has a light sensor, offers a sensor service that can deliver a light value. Or another node provides a service that compares two numbers.

Attributes. Each node has some static features called attributes. The attributes that are used by the pre-mapper are the symbolic locations. Each node can belong to several locations (e.g. node-3 belongs to *office* and *building-CS*).

Properties. Properties are dynamic features of nodes. The battery level or connectivity information are properties. The pre-mapper does not need any node property information.

The pre-mapper is responsible for the following steps:

1. It identifies each sensor operator in the given task graph. If the operator explicitly specifies an aggregator (e.g. average), it splits the operator into an aggregator operator and a sensor operator. Otherwise it attaches a generic OR aggregator to the sensor operator.
2. For each sensor/actuator operator in the task graph it counts all nodes in the respective space that provide the corresponding sensor/actuator service. Then, it splits the corresponding sensor/actuator operator into several instances and assigns one to each of the corresponding sensor/actuator service nodes (i.e. it labels the operator with the id of the node).

The output of the pre-mapper component is depicted in Figure 10. After the pre-mapper phase every sensor and actuator operator is assigned to a network node.

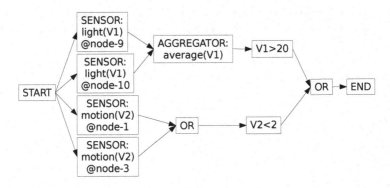

Fig. 10. The pre-mapper splits the sensor/actuator operators into several instances and assigns each one to a separate node that can provide the required service

5.5   Mapper

The mapper is the core component of the compiler. It assigns the operators (that have not been assigned yet by the pre-mapper) given by the task graph to nodes in the smart space network. Those nodes will be responsible for the execution of the assigned operators. Similarly to the pre-mapper it requires network information given by the network model.

The observable behaviour of an application is defined in the logical structure of the application. The observable behaviour must not be changed by the mapper. However, the mapper can influence the quality of an application.

For example, a centralised solution and fully distributed solution have different characteristics in terms of reliability and energy consumption [5]. Depending on the requirements the compiler can use a different mapper. And different mapper components require different mapper-specific parameters.

In general terms, the mapping problem can be reduced to finding a matrix P such that $P(k, i) = 1$ if operator k is assigned to node i under the constraint C. We assume that an operator k can only be assigned to one node i, thus $P(k, j) = 0$ for all $j \neq i$. Although redundant placement of operators can be useful, we do not consider this in the paper. Let C denote a constraint matrix such that $C(k, i) = 0$ if operator k has to be assigned to node i, $0 < C(k, i) < \delta$ if operator k can be assigned to node i, and $C(k, i) = \delta$ if operator k cannot be assigned to node i given a constant δ. The elements of the constraint matrix could be seen as preferences to where operators should be placed. Or they could be interpreted as the cost for executing a certain operator k on a node i. We will give more details about two specific mapper components in Sec. 6.

The output of the mapper component is a task graph whose operators are assigned to network nodes. Figure 11 depicts the assignment of a mapper.

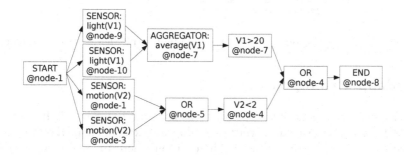

Fig. 11. The mapper assigns every operator of the task graph to a network node

5.6   Code Generator

The code generator transforms the task graph into byte code that can be executed by the stack machine interpreter in our system-specific middleware. The execution of an application is based on the idea of a token that is passed from operator to operator along the execution paths. Tokens transport relevant sensor data from one operator to the next one. Each node has a handler that accepts tokens and forwards them to the required operator. An operator extracts the relevant data from the token and evaluates the given rule condition. If the condition cannot be satisfied, the token is killed. Aggregators combine several input tokens into one output token. For each output channel the operator generates a token containing the data required by its successor operators and sends it to the node executing the first successor operator.

Figure 12 illustrates the byte code of an operator that is executed by *node-7*, which is responsible for the evaluation of the condition *V1>20*. Operators send and receive data through channels that connect them with other operators. In line 1 data field 0 of the token in incoming channel 0 is loaded and pushed onto the stack. The value 20 is pushed onto the stack in line 2. The command eval calls a node service; in this example it is the service lessThan, which pops the two top numbers from the stack and compares them. If the comparison succeeds, it pushes the value 1 onto the stack. If it fails, the value 0 is pushed onto the stack. In line 4 the top stack value is removed and compared to 0. If it is equal to 0, execution jumps over the next line. If the top stack value is 1, execution continues at line 5, where the send command tells the outgoing channel 0 to send a token through the channel to the next operator. These channels are set up at the beginning when the operators are deployed. In this example, the token does not have to carry any application data (e.g. sensor data) because successor operators do not require any specific data. The end command in line 6 finishes execution.

```
1    iload 0 0 //push data field 0 from channel 0 onto stack
2    ipush 20 //push the value 20 onto the stack
3    eval lessThan //call the service lessThan
4    ifeq 2 //jump over next line if service evaluation has returned 0
5    send 0 //send data in channel 0
6    end //operator execution finished
```

Fig. 12. Operator code that is interpreted by the middleware of our system

6   Mapper Component

The mapper component of the compiler was introduced in Sec. 5.5. It is the core part of the compiler. Deciding where operators are executed and states are stored in the network are its main tasks. The decision where the states are stored is equivalent to the decision where the START and END operators of a task graph are placed.

In this section we describe two exemplary mappers that can be selected as compiler plugins at compile-time. Both mappers assign task operators to nodes that are contained in the smart space that is described by the smart space model; i.e. if the smart space is an office, all operators are executed by nodes that are actually in the office. In general this is not a necessary requirement, because *free* operators, which are operators that are not of type *SENSOR* or *ACTUATOR*, could be executed anywhere; e.g. sensor data could be analysed anywhere.

Both mappers initialise the following parameters for mapping the task t (cf. Sec. 5.5):

- S is the set of nodes contained in the space of t.
- $C(k, i) = 0$ if operator k has already been assigned to node i by the pre-mapper.
- $C(k, i) = 1$ if node $i \in S$ and node i can execute operator k.
- $C(k, i) = 2$ if node $i \notin S$ or node i cannot execute operator k.
- $P(k, i) = 0$ for every k and i.

6.1   Centralised Operator Mapping

The first mapper chooses one random node in the space that corresponds to the task that has to be mapped onto the infrastructure. It then assigns every free operator to this node. If it cannot find such a node that is able to execute the required operators, the compilation fails and the mapper returns a description of the additional requirements for the infrastructure. Pseudocode of the mapper is shown in Figure 13.

```
1     for each k do
2         if there is i such that C(k,i)=0 then
3             P(k,i) = 1; mark k;
4
5     find random i such that
6         for each unmarked k C(k,i)==1
7     if found i then
8         for every unmarked k
9             P(k,i) = 1;
10    if not found i then
11        ERROR;
```

Fig. 13. Algorithm of centralised operator mapping

Figure 15 illustrates the output of this mapper when applied to our example task. The sensor operator on nodes 1, 3, 9 and 10 send their data to node 7, which executes the remaining operators and stores the state information.

6.2   Decentralised Operator Mapping

In contrast to the first mapper, the decentralised operator mapper chooses a different random node for each free operator. Similar to the first mapper this mapper can also fail to find a node for every operator. In such a case it can provide an exact description of the additional requirements for the infrastructure. Figure 14 illustrates algorithm of the mapper component.

```
1     for each k do
2         if there is i such that C(k,i)=0 then
3             P(k,i) = 1; mark k;
4
5     for each unmarked k do
6         find random i such that
7             C(k,i)==1
8         if found i then
9             P(k,i)=1; mark k;
10        if not found i then
11            ERROR;
```

Fig. 14. Algorithm of decentralised operator mapping

Figure 16 depicts the output of this mapper. The sensor operators on nodes 9 and 10 send their tokens to an operator on node 7 that computes the average. This average is compared with 20 by another operator on node 7. Then, the

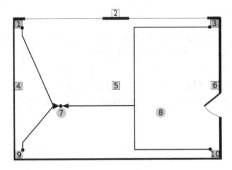 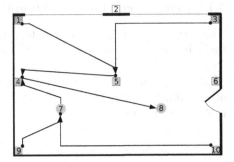

Fig. 15. The first mapper assigns operators in their corresponding space centrally

Fig. 16. The second mapper assigns operators to random nodes in their corresponding space

token is forwarded to node 4. Sensor nodes 1 and 2 send their tokens to an aggregator on node 5. The resulting token is forwarded to node 4. Node 4 sends the token to the *END* operator on node 8.

6.3   Discussion

The observable behaviour of the application is not directly affected by the chosen mapper. However, the mapper can influence the qualitative (or non-functional) aspects such as energy consumption, privacy or reliability of the running application. The main focus of this paper is on the technical aspects of the compiler; and we want to leave a qualitative discussion open for future work.

7   Related Work

The development of small low-powered computers, sensors and wireless radios has made impressive progress in recent years. This is only partly the consequence of Moore's law and better materials being developed in research labs. The potential economic impact of this technology (not just for the smart space, but in general) shows great potential beyond research labs (e.g. [6]). Several companies produce ready to use hardware platforms (e.g. Crossbow, Ember, Freescale or Texas Instruments) and industry-driven communication standards have been published (e.g. Zigbee [7]).

This technological development and the trend of moving away from a single computer per user has cleared the way to the development of smart spaces. Several research groups have developed first-generation prototypes of the smart home as an example of a smart space to study the computing needs in our everyday lives ([8,9,10]).

Currently, the main technological focus is on integrating suitable hardware into the environment, and on developing services that analyse sensory data in order to identify high-level contexts. One existing problem is that these systems are generally purpose-built. This makes the development or maintenance of applications a challenging task because expert knowledge is required.

RuleCaster is related to *macroprogramming* approaches, which have emerged as a potential solution for simplifying the development of applications for these embedded distributed computers. Common to all these approaches is that they address the whole network as one programmable unit instead of the individual nodes.

The Kairos macroprogramming system [11] extends traditional programming languages with three specific abstractions: node, one-hope neighbours of a node and remote data access. Its runtime system supports the execution of applications using these abstractions. In contrast to Kairos RuleCaster providesnode-independent abstractions. A RuleCaster application is expressed in a network-independent way. Kairos provides node-dependent abstractions and therefore forces the programmer to express global application behaviour in terms of nodes and node state. Accordingly, every node executes the same code. The RuleCaster compiler has more freedom and generates specific code for each individual node depending on the properties and capabilities of the respective node, which is more suitable for a heterogeneous network environment.

Similar to RuleCaster Regiment [12] is also based on a declarative language. Functional programming constructs are used to build applications. As a fundamental programming abstraction it uses the concept of a region, which is a collection of data signals originating from a set of nodes. Regiment applications describe the manipulation of regions. This is related to the abstract smart space model used in RuleCaster. However, Regiment addresses a different class of applications. While RuleCaster focuses on state-based sensor-actuator applications, Regiment is designed for extracting time-varying sensor data streams from a sensor network.

COSMOS [13] is comprised of a programming language and an operating system. Similar to Regiment it addresses processing and aggregation of time-varying sensor data streams. The basic building blocks of a COSMOS application are functional components (FCs) that transform input streams into output streams. These FCs are interconnected via asynchronous data channels to implement a sensor network application. Compared to RuleCaster, COSMOS is on a much lower abstraction level which makes application development hard and error-prone. The assignment of functional components to nodes (or classes of nodes) is specified by the application programmer. This simplifies the mapping process but makes the development of complex applications difficult.

At the core of an ATaG [14] macroprogram are abstract tasks. An abstract task encapsulates the processing of data. The flow of information between abstract tasks is defined in terms of input/output relations. To achieve this, abstract channels are used to connect tasks. ATaG is a suitable approach for implementing high-level sensor network applications. However, the separation between the logical structure and the physical structure is not as strict as in RuleCaster. On the one hand this simplifies the task of the compiler. On the other hand, it makes it more difficult to change the physical structure of an application.

8 Conclusion

Our compiler-based approach provides support for programming and maintaining a smart space through a number of measures:

- Our approach does not force the application programmer to express the application logic of a smart space in terms of distributed actions for the underlying infrastructure. This method would be cumbersome because the programmer has to deal with many issues related to distributed programming which make application development difficult, time-consuming and error-prone. Instead the application programmer can program the smart space as one logical entity. And the compiler is responsible for the distribution.
- Our smart space model addresses the evolutionary changes of a smart space by separating the infrastructure from the application logic. They can evolve independently. The compiler accommodates changes by finding a new mapping of the application logic onto the infrastructure.

Smart spaces promise a visionary concept about how computers and the physical environment can create an integrated system. If we want to realise this vision outside research labs, we have to address issues related to programming and maintenance of the related computer infrastructure. We believe that providing a unified abstraction of the environment and the embedded infrastructure in terms of a smart space model is a step into the right direction.

References

1. Helal, S.: Programming pervasive spaces. IEEE Pervasive Computing 4(1), 84–87 (2005)
2. Rodden, T., Benford, S.: The evolution of buildings and implications for the design of ubiquitous domestic environments. In: Proceedings of the SIGCHI conference on Human factors in computing systems, pp. 9–16. ACM Press, New York (2003)
3. Weiser, M.: The computer for the 21st century. Scientific American (1991)
4. Bischoff, U., Sundramoorthy, V., Kortuem, G.: Programming the smart home. In: Proceedings of the 3rd IET International Conference on Intelligent Environments (2007)
5. Ahn, S., Kim, D.: Proactive context-aware sensor networks. In: Römer, K., Karl, H., Mattern, F. (eds.) EWSN 2006. LNCS, vol. 3868, Springer, Heidelberg (2006)
6. Hatler, M., Chi, C.: Wireless sensor networks: Growing markets, accelerating demand. OnWorld (2005)
7. Alliance, Z.: Zigbee specification (2006), http://www.zigbee.org
8. Kidd, C.D., Orr, R., Abowd, G.D., Atkeson, C.G., Essa, I.A., MacIntyre, B., Mynatt, E., Starner, T.E., Newstetter, W.: The aware home: A living laboratory for ubiquitous computing research. In: Streitz, N.A., Hartkopf, V. (eds.) CoBuild 1999. LNCS, vol. 1670, pp. 191–198. Springer, Heidelberg (1999)

9. Intille, S.S.: Designing a home of the future. IEEE Pervasive Computing 1(2), 76–82 (2002)
10. Helal, S., Mann, W., El-Zabadani, H., King, J., Kaddoura, Y., Jansen, E.: The gator tech smart house: A programmable pervasive space. Computer 38(3), 50–60 (2005)
11. Gummadi, R., Gnawali, O., Govindan, R.: Macro-programming wireless sensor networks using Kairos. In: Prasanna, V.K., Iyengar, S., Spirakis, P.G., Welsh, M. (eds.) DCOSS 2005. LNCS, vol. 3560, Springer, Heidelberg (2005)
12. Newton, R., Morrisett, G., Welsh, M.: The Regiment macroprogramming system. In: IPSN 2007. Proceedings of the 6th international conference on Information processing in sensor networks, pp. 489–498. ACM Press, New York (2007)
13. Awan, A., Jagannathan, S., Grama, A.: Macroprogramming heterogeneous sensor networks using COSMOS. SIGOPS Oper. Syst. Rev. 41(3), 159–172 (2007)
14. Pathak, A., Mottola, L., Bakshi, A., Prasanna, V.K., Picco, G.P.: Expressing sensor network interaction patterns using data-driven macroprogramming. In: Proceedings of the Fifth IEEE International Conference on Pervasive Computing and Communications Workshops, IEEE Computer Society Press, Los Alamitos (2007)

Situated Public News and Reminder Displays

Jörg Müller, Oliver Paczkowski, and Antonio Krüger

University of Münster, Münster, Germany

Abstract. In this paper we present concepts for and experiences with a Situated Public Display system deployed in a university setting. We identify the rate with which information is updated as an important property to distinguish different kinds of information. With a first slideshow based prototype it was very difficult for users to predict whether information was updated since they last looked. To solve this problem, we took a broader view and conducted a contextual inquiry to investigate how people deal with paper based posters. We deduced an information flow diagram that identifies roles of people and categories of posters and noticeboards. We identified actionables, that is, posters that offer people to take a specific action, as a special type of information to support. We identified two strategies, planning and opportunism, to deal with actionable information. We present a system using two kinds of displays, News Displays and Reminder Displays, to support both strategies. We show how auctions can be used for Reminder Displays to select those information chunks that are most important in a particular context. Finally, we present an evaluation and lessons from the deployment.

1 Introduction

Due to falling costs of electronic displays and their potential value, we predict electronic displays soon to cover much of public space. Digital displays offer a whole new way of presenting information in public spaces, essentially because the cost of changing information is so low. Public Displays prove especially useful in scenarios where other communication forms like email, mail or the web are infeasible. This is usually the case when the identities of information providers and interested people are unknown to each other or computers are not used by everyone. On most public displays that are installed nowadays, however, information is presented as slideshows or scrolling text. We argue that both presentations are unsuitable for users that pass the displays often, because it is difficult for them to tell whether information was updated. We propose using two different kinds of displays, News Displays and Reminder Displays, instead. Imagine the following scenario. A student passes the digital display installed at the entrance of his department (a News Display) every day. One day, as he has a quick glimpse on it to see whether there is something new, he notices that there is an interesting talk next week, and notes it in his calendar. One week later, just before the start of the talk, a guest researcher who has just arrived passes the lecture hall. He sees the talk announcement on a different display (a Reminder Display) in front of the lecture hall and decides to attend spontaneously.

B. Schiele et al. (Eds.): AmI 2007, LNCS 4794, pp. 248–265, 2007.
© Springer-Verlag Berlin Heidelberg 2007

News Displays show new information chunks as soon as they are created. These displays support the process of planning well ahead, for example for regular visitors to a place who see the displays often. Reminder Displays show chunks which are considered important at the current time and location by the system. They support the process of acting opportunistically, for example for one-time visitors to a place. Note that the same information chunks are shown on News Displays when they are new and again on Reminder Displays when they are considered important. Thus many people will see chunks first on News Displays and then be reminded by Reminder Displays just in time.

Main contributions of this paper are:

- The identification of the update rate of information as an important criterion informing the design of public displays.
- A consolidated information flow model, that categorizes information chunks, noticeboards and roles of users as found in a university scenario.
- The identification of actionables as a major kind of information chunks to support, together with planning and opportunism as strategies to deal with them.
- A workflow of how people deal with actionables that shows tasks and resources that need to be supported.
- A restructured information flow model that drives system design.
- An information system consisting of News and Reminder Displays, which integrates the findings and was successfully deployed and evaluated in a university setting.

2   Related Work

Work on Situated Public Displays has been done in three broad areas. They were used for *continuous support of small groups* (e.g. members of a workgroup), to provide *shared workspaces for small groups*, and for *support of large groups* (e.g. the inhabitants of a building). For continuous support of small groups, systems like CWall [6], Plasma Poster Network [4], Notification Collage [7], MessyBoard [5], Hermes Door Displays [3], and Semi-Public Displays [10] provide public displays where members of a workgroup can post content, mostly via a web form or email. In these systems, all workgroup members can post content, because peer control works well in small groups. Some of these systems also generate content automatically, like Semi-Public Displays, that show who is currently in the lab from keyboard activity. Most of these systems are interactive and evaluated by expert users in the respective research groups. For these users, many of these systems proved valuable over a long time period from a few months up to several years. The BlueBoard [16] and MERBoard [19] systems provided shared workspaces for small, co-located groups, and a log-on was required to use them. For many tasks, however, people preferred to gather around laptops, and the systems were most successful for specialized tasks, like the SOLtree application of MERBoard. For support of large groups, however, less work has been done. The GroupCast [12] and BlueScreen [14] systems were evaluated only by smaller

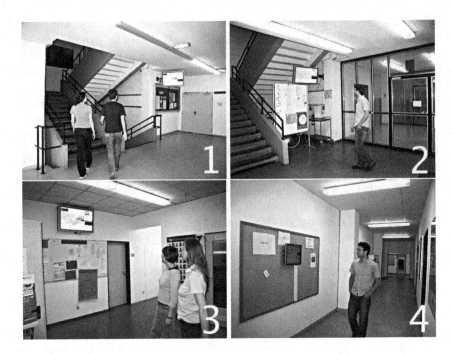

Fig. 1. Some News Displays (1,2) and Reminder Displays (3,4) installed at the department building

groups, although their design can well be applied to very large groups. In Group-Cast sensors were used to determine which people are nearby, and information regarded to be of mutual interest was displayed to spark informal conversations. BlueScreen also sensed nearby people, and used auctions to show ads to people who have not yet seen them. ECampus [18] is an effort to deploy displays throughout a whole university campus. It supports a large user population. Currently, eCampus does not focus on the utility of information shown, but more on soft values. For example, in an underpass bus station, content created by artists is shown on large displays. In most systems for a large user population, content creation is limited to authorized users, because peer control is too weak to suppress inappropriate content. [11] provides a good survey for systems that support small groups together with the advice to carefully integrate systems into users' workflow.

3   Requirements Analysis

From the systems reviewed in related work, only the eCampus system focuses on support of large groups, but less on the utility for the users. The goal of our system was to provide useful information for large user groups. To understand the values of our users towards a Situated Public Display system, we conducted a laddering analysis [15] interviewing 24 students. The study revealed that the most important values students want to support are *success, fun* and *social interaction*. We decided to focus on the value of *success* first, and build a system that would provide useful information for students on a daily basis. The system should complement, but not replace the paper based noticeboards that are in use in our building. In order to gain first experiences, we deployed a first prototype early. Since the prototype seemed not to work as we expected with the user population, we decided to conduct a Contextual Inquiry to understand more thoroughly the needs of our users.

Fig. 2. The layout of the first prototype

3.1 First Prototype

Design. Since it was too difficult to dynamically update information with PowerPoint and we had flexibility problems with HTML, we decided to deploy the system as a Java application running full screen. The bigger part of the displays showed information chunks similar to paper based posters. Information chunks from different institutes were shown in slides, where display duration depended on the number of letters on the slide and was about 20 seconds on average. Each institute was assigned a number of slides, and two information chunks announcing information like news or seminars could be displayed on each slide. On average 5 slides were shown, resulting in a cycling time of approximately 100 seconds until all items were shown. Peak utilization was 12 slides, resulting in a cycling time of approximately 4 minutes. In addition to the information chunks, different information modules with information that was updated more often were shown on the right. We implemented modules like a clock, rain radar, bus departures, cafeteria menu, flight departures, video streams, and building facility opening times, which could easily be replaced to fit the context of the display.

In contrast to the poster like information chunks, this information is not edited manually but extracted automatically from diverse sensors in the building (e.g. information on how many public computers are available), and sources derived from the web. We tried to design the presentation of modules so that users can tell very fast whether something was updated, and then extract the information as fast as possible. For bus departure times for example, we used a presentation very similar to that used at real bus stations.

Results. The system was running for 8 months. After an initial hype, the system began to suffer from disusage. An observation of our users suggested that the problem might be that most users do not stay in front of the display but only have a short glimpse instead. We observed 20 random users who happened to pass by the display installed in the secondary entrance within half an hour. Only one user watched the display for about one minute. 10 others glimpsed at the display for about two seconds, and 9 users did not look at all.

Discussion. The most important benefit of digital displays over paper based displays is that information can be updated at any time. Obviously, not for all information it is useful to always update it. The weather data for example usually doesn't change significantly within 15 minutes, the cafeteria menu changes once a day, and for information chunks it is not predictable when new chunks arrive. We call the rate with which significant changes are expected the *update rate* of information. Note that update rate doesn't refer to the technical refresh rate, but rather to the rate by which users can expect significant changes. Users looking at the displays are usually interested in new information. Thus they should be enabled to either predict whether anything has changed or to decide this very quickly by looking at the display. We concluded that the main problem with our first prototype is that slideshows don't support this behaviour. In order to tell whether anything has changed, users have to wait for a whole cycle to see all the slides. This is especially annoying for people who pass the displays regularly. Our hypothesis was that people try to estimate the cost of waiting against the expected benefit of information gained. This is difficult if no cue is available whether anything is new. Thus, because people can't estimate the benefit of waiting, they mostly don't wait but walk away instead.

3.2 Contextual Inquiry

Inspired by the problems from the first prototype, we decided to do a Contextual Inquiry [2] to determine the real needs of our users. The goal of the study was to understand how people in our department use posters and noticeboards to spread and gather information.

Method. For the interviews we tried to cover all relevant stakeholder groups for the system. We interviewed 21 users from four different institutes, which were three undergraduates, six graduate students, seven secretaries and five faculty members. The interviews took place after the first prototype was deployed. The interviews took place within a period of three weeks and interview duration was between 30 and 90 minutes. We started with a short conventional interview of 10 to 15 minutes to determine the responsibilities and typical tasks of users regarding posters. We then went with the user to the place where they would normally carry out these tasks and had them explain to us how they do this. Thus, for users who created posters, we went to their workplaces, and for users who put up or read posters, we went to the noticeboards they normally use. This process can be described as apprenticeship compressed in time, where we acted as apprentices, analyzing and understanding the typical tasks of the users. This approach is important because users usually have no explicit understanding of their own work, so it is important to observe them in context. In addition to the interviews, we collected examples of posters and took photos of all noticeboards used in our department in order to find categories of posters and boards. After the interviews we created information flow models, work sequence models and artifact models. We consolidated the data over all interviewees into an affinity diagram and a consolidated information flow model.

Results. In the consolidated information flow model (figure 3) we focused on how information chunks are created, distributed and consumed. Users are categorized into sources, filter/forwarders and sinks of information. *Sources* in our case are mostly faculty and secretaries, for whom it is important that their information reaches all interested sinks. Therefore, they distribute posters over multiple noticeboards, highlight important facts and use a corporate identity to increase the probability that interested sinks read the poster. Then they send the information to filter/forwarders (who can be themselves). *Filter/forwarders* are mostly secretaries and decide whether a poster is worth posting and where to post it. Sometimes it is important that people can rely on information they filtered, so they put stamps on filtered posters or post them on locked noticeboards. They put down old and non-approved posters and maintain an archive of those. Everyone could act as an information *sink*, consuming information that was created by sources. Since there are many students, they form the most important subgroup. Sinks like to quickly evaluate the expected benefit of looking at posters against the opportunity costs of used time. Therefore they often only have a quick look and a longer one only if they have enough time or are really interested. They like to quickly identify the source and key points of a poster, and like to have pictures on it to quickly identify if they have already read it. Most sinks like to have important information centralized in certain places, so they know where to find it. Many look for new information in the morning, are interested in cafeteria menu around noon and in weather data when they leave the building. Students had different information needs at the beginning than at the end of the semester, and needs differed between first and higher semesters. Some sinks keep a well maintained calendar and note all actions they want to take in calendars and to-do lists. We refer to this strategy as *planning*. Other sinks prefer to attend events for which they see posters spontaneously. We refer

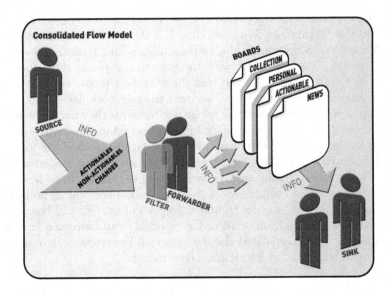

Fig. 3. The consolidated information flow model. Actionable, change, and non-actionable information chunks are created by sources and put onto noticeboards by filter/forwarders. Sinks read these chunks on news boards, dedicated actionable boards, personal boards and collection boards.

to this behaviour as *opportunism*. For important events, these sinks rely on being reminded by friends. Most sinks however use both strategies depending on the context.

We studied more than 60 posters and categorized them into actionables, changes and non-actionable information chunks. *Actionables* offer people to take a clearly defined action within a certain window of space and time. These are for example deadlines for exam registrations or talk announcements. Actionables have deadlines, so it is important to see them on time, while the time until the deadline can vary from one day to several months. *Changes* to actionables were mostly cancellations or changes of the date. They often came as colorful posters, but sometimes the original poster was just changed with a thick pen or post-it. *Non-actionables* are all chunks that are neither actionable nor changes to actionables, for example new project or publication announcements or snippets from newspapers, which serve mainly representation purposes. Other examples are lists of exam grades or operating instructions for machines. We extracted the parts that were shared by most information chunks, which were a title, a clearly visible notion of the source of the chunk, for example the institute logo and contact address, the date of creation, a text and a picture, and for actionables the time and location of the action opportunity. All posters were only hung at locations where sources believed the sinks would see them. Posters for students of Geoinformatics for example were placed in the respective area of the department.

We studied more than 30 noticeboards and observed four different categories, which we called news boards, dedicated actionable boards, personal boards and collections. *News Boards* are installed at the entrances and are intended for highly urgent chunks. Sometimes even the doors of the building were used as news boards. News boards are glanced at by most people while passing them. As it is very hard to keep the boards up to date, most of them degenerate to collections. *Dedicated actionable boards* hold only actionables of a specific kind, and are guaranteed to be complete and reliable. In our department, a dedicated board that holds all available excursions is locked behind glass and has a single board maintainer. These boards can be placed anywhere, as long as everyone knows where they are. People go there specifically to have a look at this board. *Personal Boards* belong to a person or group and hold all kind of chunks that are related to these. In our department, most professors and workgroups have one that is located next to their workplace, and sometimes the office door is used as a personal board. They often hold representative chunks, and people go there explicitly if they look for something related to this person, but also have a glimpse as they pass by. *Collections* are mostly large boards where anything is put that does not fit anywhere else. Each institute of our department has one, and most of the posters there are diverse actionables.

Discussion. From the contextual inquiry we gained models and categories for posters, noticeboards, stakeholders and the respective information flow. For the redesign of the displays we decided to focus on the distinction between action-able and non-actionable information chunks. Whether a specific chunk is really actionable for someone depends of course on the context, like the time, location or role of that person. A seminar announcement for example can be actionable for a student, but not for faculty. Of course, actionable information can also be useful to people who do not want to take the action. Seeing the talks given in a certain institute gives a feeling of what is going on in that institute even if one does not attend the talks. For dealing with actionables, we identified the strategies of planning and opportunism. The choice of strategy also depends on the context: A one-time visitor to a place would need to rely on opportunism, while for someone who visits a location every day it would be entirely possible to plan ahead. We also saw that information need of interviewees depends heavily on context, specifically time, location, interests and intent.

4   Design

In consequence of the insights we gained in the requirements analysis we re-designed the information system for information chunks.

Because the major part of the posters we studied were actionables and changes, we decided to focus our redesign to support these, while also supporting non-actionables as a side effect. To enable users to decide whether something is important to them we color code chunks in the colors of the institute that created it. We also show an image, the creation date, the name of the institute, the author, a prominent title and a textual description. For actionables, we also show the time and location of the action opportunity.

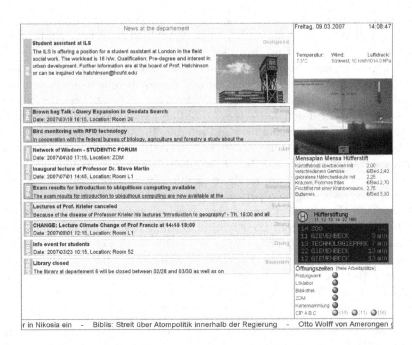

Fig. 4. The layout of the News Display. A list with new information chunks is at the left, while other information modules are shown at the right (e.g. time, weather, cafeteria menu, bus departures, building facility opening times and a news feed). For chunks, details are shown in turn (chunks translated from German).

For actionables, the main question is whether to act or not. We adapted the workflow of how to deal with actionables presented in [1] for the case of public displays (figure 5). We propose to use two kinds of displays, News Displays and Reminder Displays, to support the whole spectrum of strategies between pure planning and pure opportunism.

News Displays (see figure 4) are intended to support planning. They don't adapt to the context and simply show all actionables in the order they were created by sources. They enable users to answer the question "What is here and now new?". We adapted the metaphor of an email inbox, so new chunks are shown on top of a list, and gradually move downwards as new chunks are added. Users can glance at the first chunk and see whether they know it, and if they don't, read chunks from the list until they get to the first one they already know. With this strategy, users are guaranteed never to miss a chunk as long as they pass News Displays regularly, like once or twice a day. On the other hand, it doesn't help much if users pass News Displays more often. Thus, News Displays should be installed in spaces where the number of different people who see them is maximized. Good places for News Displays would be at the entrances, where all users in the building are guaranteed to see them twice a day.

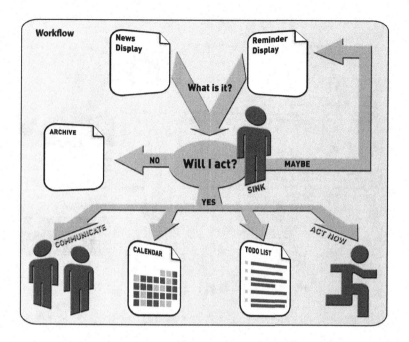

Fig. 5. The workflow of how to deal with actionables. People see actionables on News or Reminder Displays. They have to determine what the actionables are about and then decide whether they want to act. If they decide not to act, the actionables are available for later reference in the archive. If they cannot decide yet whether to act, for example because of missing information, they will be reminded later that the decision is still due. If they decide to act, they can act immediately, communicate or delegate the actionable to someone else, or copy the actionable to their calendar or to-do list.

Reminder Displays (see figure 6) are intended to support opportunism. They show actionables next to the time and location where they take place. Users are enabled to answer the question "What is here and now *important?*". We adapted the layout of newspapers, so readers can start reading the headlines of the biggest and most important chunks and then also read the small ones if they have time. Because many users will already have seen the chunks on News Displays, we use images to facilitate recognition and remind people of the actionables. Reminder Displays adapt to time and location, trying to always show those chunks with maximum utility for the user in a specific context. For Reminder Displays, the more often users see them, the better, because the probability is higher that they are reminded of an important event. Thus, Reminder Displays should be placed in locations where the total viewing time for all users is maximized. That would be for example in places where many users hang out, or main hallways where many users pass often.

All information chunks are also accessible through an archive online. We try to have all important actionables on the displays, so that there is no need for people to regularly search the paper based noticeboards anymore. Because paper

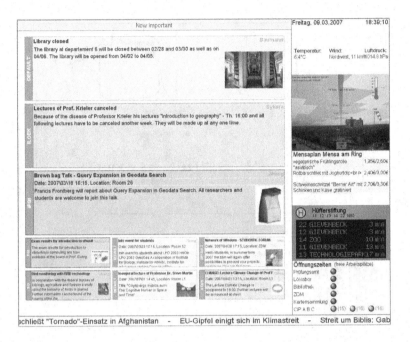

Fig. 6. The layout of the Reminder Display. The most important information chunks, depending on the current time and location, are shown on the left (chunks translated from German).

based noticeboards are much cheaper, provide higher resolution and more space, we still support them for reference information. Users do not need to search them for important actionables, but details to actionables that were presented on the displays can be looked up there. Because such reference information needs a low update rate anyway, paper is ideally suited for this task.

Note how the process of planning a user's time is now distributed over the displays and the user himself. Instead of copying all actionables that are assumed to be of interest to the user's calendar, he is only provided suggestions. From the set of all actionables available, the newest are shown on News Displays and those the system believes the user could be interested in are shown on Reminder Displays. A lot of screen space is useful to present the user many possibilities. From this subset the user finally decides which really to attend, going there directly, or copying them to his calendar or to-do list.

The submission tool should fit into the sources workflow. We restructured the information flow as depicted in figure 7. We decided to provide one interface to submit information chunks for sources, filters and forwarders alike. We argue that communication between those can take place via telephone, direct communication, email or paper as usual and need not to be changed. For the submission tool to fit into the users workflow we considered it crucial that the tool is fast and easy to use as well as reliable. We started by providing each user

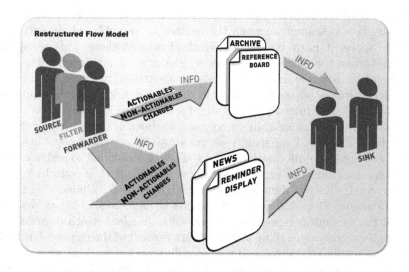

Fig. 7. The redesigned information flow model. Sources, filters and forwarders are supported with the same interface for chunk submission. Communication between these roles takes place in oral form, by email, paper or telephone. The sources create chunks in the categories actionable, change, and non-actionable, and submit these chunks simultaneously to News and Reminder Displays and paper-based reference boards. Sinks can be planners who pass News Displays regularly and read all new chunks to decide whether to copy them to their calendar or to-do list. Sinks can also act opportunistically, see chunks on Reminder Displays and decide to act immediately. In case sinks want to see details for chunks they saw on the News & Reminder Displays, they can see extended versions of chunks on paper-based reference boards or online archives.

a local Java client, but changed to a web application by March 2007 for easier access, higher reliability and easier administration. A chunk can be created in two simple steps, filling out the necessary fields and approving the generated previews. We decided to support the most important features paper has, so users can use all important fields we identified for posters, highlight important facts and use their institute's corporate identity. Sources can also change chunks by crossing words out or adding yellow post-its to them. They can see, edit and remove all chunks that were created by colleagues from the same institute, and reliability is guaranteed because only people with the password can submit chunks with a certain institute's corporate identity. We consciously decided not to make the submission tool available for anyone. Because inappropriate content could lead to a negative appearance of the university to users, we decided only to give access to the submission tool to sources that can be held responsible for the content they posted. To provide additional benefit for sources, new chunks are available on the institute's web page, as an RSS feed, and a paper version resembling the posters we studied can be generated with a single click.

Reminder Displays adapt to context using auctions. Obviously screen space on public displays is limited, so when the number of available chunks exceeds the available space, it must be decided which chunks to show. This is especially important when the number of sources scales up, for example when the system is deployed for a whole university or as an advertising platform for a city. On Reminder Displays we want to provide the chunks with highest utility for a certain context. [14] introduced the use of auctions for allocating scarce screen space to information chunks. In our system, auctions are used to allocate space on Reminder Displays. Each month sources are given a certain budget in a virtual currency to assign to information chunks. They are assumed to assign a budget to information chunks in proportion to how important they consider a certain chunk to be. By default a fixed budget is assigned to each chunk.

On Reminder Displays, every 10 seconds all slots available are sold in an auction. Each chunk is represented by an software agent which makes a bid in the virtual currency depending on the current context of the display. The highest bidders are displayed on top, and the lower bidders below. Non-actionables bid a high amount when they are created and a smaller amount when they become old. The bid of actionables depends on the context, which currently is only the location and time until deadline, and is highest just before the event. A detailed bidding strategy for actionables is presented in [13].

5 Experiences

We evaluated the deployment by analyzing the submitted chunks and by conducting paper based as well as web-based questionnaires. The system has been deployed in a university department building with more than 2000 students and 70 faculty members. We installed two 42" News Displays at the entrances and five Reminder Displays of various sizes from 19" to 42" throughout the building. The displays were wall-mounted and attached to hidden PCs for flexibility. The first slideshow based prototype (section 3) was running for 8 months from 10-2005 until 4-2006 before being replaced by the News & Reminder system in 5-2006. To this date, the News & Reminder system is running for 12 months, making for a total of 20 months. The new web-based submission tool was introduced in 03-2007. Maintenance effort to keep the system running is about 4 hours a week for 7 displays.

Usage statistics. In 17 months, 23 sources created 236 actionables, like talk announcements, 21 changes, like the cancellation of a lecture, and only 15 non-actionables, like the announcement of a new project. Unfortunately, the data for the first 3 months was not recorded. The overall number of 272 created chunks is not very high, but submission is stable over a long period of time (see figure 8). 9 groups submitted 132, 36, 32, 19, 16, 16, 14, 5 and 5 chunks, respectively. The most active sources submitted 78, 32, 26, 24 and 22 chunks, respectively, the least active four sources only created one chunk. 154 of the 272 chunks created contained an image.

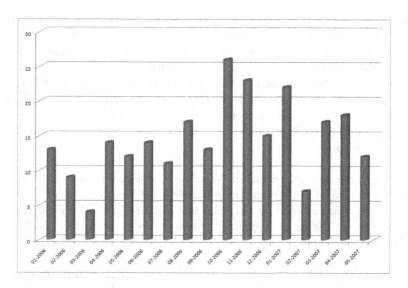

Fig. 8. The number of chunks submitted to our system. In total 272 chunks were submitted. The first prototype was used from 10-2005 until 4-2006. The News & Reminder system was used from 05-2006 on. The data for 2005 was lost. Usage was approximately one post per work day and periodically dropped in term breaks (e.g. 02-2007).

Sources Questionnaire. To further investigate the utility of the system, we interviewed 7 sources regarding their usage of the system. We used a questionnaire to establish how often and for what users they believed to use the system.

Sources reported that they posted between 0.5 and 2 digital chunks ($\mu = 1.6$) and between 1 and 10 paper posters ($\mu = 4.3$) a month. 5 said to post mostly events to the displays, again 5 said to post mostly job offers as posters. For both chunks and posters, only one ever received feedback that anyone has read the item. Most sources said they would prefer getting more feedback. 6 out of 7 sources said they feel they should post more chunks to the display. Four said they submit less because it costs too much time to make a submission, one forgot the password and for another the submission tool didn't work. Asked for additional features, only one wanted to be able to update existing chunks and highlight this.

Sinks Questionnaire. During one day, we interviewed 28 randomly selected students who were sitting in the computer pools regarding their usage of the system. All sinks we interviewed said they know and use the displays. Three sinks reported not to glance shortly at the displays when in the building, the remaining 25 stated to glance between twice a week and 30 times per day ($\mu = 3.9$). A short glance was estimated to be between 1 and 60 seconds ($\mu = 10.2$). In addition, 21 sinks reported to sometimes stop in front of the displays. They reported to do so between twice a week and 5 times a day, for a duration between 20 and 300 seconds ($\mu = 86$). 14 of 28 sinks even reported to look to the display for a mean of less than 5 seconds. 23 of 28 sinks reported to regularly use the information chunks, 14 to use cafeteria menu, 10 to use rain radar, and 3 to use bus, time, and news ticker information, respectively. All sinks liked the locations where the displays are installed. 21 sinks used the News Display in the secondary entrance, and 18 used the News Display in the first entrance. 11 users reported to use a Reminder Display in a main hallway. Only one sink reported to use the other Reminder Displays. On a scale from 1 (very good) to 6 (very bad), users graded the system between 1.3 and 3.3 ($\mu = 2.2$). 23 out of 28 said they would object to have the displays removed.

Utility/Attractivity Questionnaire. We asked 15 students from a course in geoinformatics to rate our system in terms of utility and beauty [9]. According to the answers, both factors are well balanced but can be improved. People described our system with the terms 'technical', 'presentable', 'innovative', 'good', 'easy', 'useful' and 'enjoyable'.

Discussion. The submission seems to have plateaued at approximately one chunk per work day. Although the computer science institute had by far most submissions (132) all groups regularly use the system. One student was often called by various groups to submit items on their behalf and submitted 78 chunks, but having 23 sources from 9 groups and with various levels of computer expertise suggests that the system is attractive for different people. The change to the web based submission tool didn't change the amount of submissions significantly, and number of submissions varies widely between sources. We believe that the main problem is that chunk submission is not yet fully integrated in many users' workflows. For many older sources, the workflows have evolved over many years, and despite our efforts it seems quite difficult to change them. Also, many sources hesitate to submit many chunks because they don't want to congest the system. The time requirement to submit chunks was considered crucial by sources, and we took effort to minimize this. Only 50% of the chunks contained images, probably because it takes more time to find an adequate image.

We found it very promising that all of the 28 randomly selected sinks knew the displays and reported to use them at least twice a week. This is probably because to enter the building, users have to pass the displays. Because the digital displays are eye-catching, we experience it natural to at least have a quick glimpse on them. It is striking that the News Displays are used much more than the context adaptive Reminder Displays. The main reason is probably that News Displays are installed in places where much more people pass by. It is also possible that in a university environment more people rely on planning instead of opportunism. Additionally, some information modules like cafeteria menu are used much more than others, like building facility opening times. It is possible that some kind of information is simply more interesting, or that some modules are easier to understand than others. Concluding, it is interesting to see that a large population has integrated the technology into their everyday life.

6 Conclusions and Future Work

Known issues that proved important for Situated Public Displays From the experience of 1.5 years of deployment, we found many well-known lessons approved in the context of Situated Public Displays:

Deploy or Die. We agree with the 'Deploy or Die' argument of Sharp [17], that ubicomp is at the point where it must make its way out of the lab to really weave itself into everyday life of ordinary users. Many of our experiences, like that people won't wait in front of slideshows, would have been much more difficult to observe in a closed lab.

Do Requirements Analysis. We want to emphasize that it is important to make a thorough *Requirements Analysis* to really understand how technology can fit into users' workflows [2]. If one does not do this, one risks making false assumptions, for example that most users will stay in front of displays for a longer time.

Provide immediate benefit for all stakeholders. We also want to underline that it is very important to provide *immediate benefit for all stakeholders* [8]. If only one group has a benefit (for example students) while another group must do more work (for example secretaries) the system will suffer from disusage. Thus we aimed at improving the cost/benefit ratio for sources by making the systems easy to use and fit into the workflow, and also by providing side effects, like automatic poster generation.

Provide 24/7 reliability by using standard hard and software. To gain the trust of ordinary users, it is urgently important to provide 24/7 reliability [18,3]. From the beginning we tried to minimize risk. Some displays with WiFi network connection (although standard) proved too unreliable, so we had to put network cables to all display locations. For production deployments, centralized systems where servers control multiple displays are suitable, while for research purposes where you may want to install a Bluetooth stick at each display one PC per display is useful. To avoid the perception of a broken system, we implemented various levels of caching and fall-back modes that show locally stored content and images.

New lessons learned. In addition to these well known lessons, we learned some new lessons more specific to Situated Public Displays that we hope will help other ubicomp researches and practitioners.

The update rate of information is especially important. Different kinds of information have different update rates. People should be enabled to make a quick cost/benefit estimation of the effort of system usage and the payoff. The first question users have when they approach a display is whether there is something new. The design should enable users either to predict or to determine this very quickly. With slideshows, for example, people do not know whether there is something new until they waited for a whole cycle.

Identify sources, filters and forwarders and win their support. Because content is king, it is important to have sources constantly deliver new chunks. Sinks will only rely on the system if the majority of all actionables is posted on the displays. We identified content creators and won their support early during the contextual interviews, which also significantly increased the sources trust in our system.

Identify actionables, changes and non-actionable information chunks.
From the posters we studied, the vast majority was actionables, with a smaller number of changes and only some non-actionables. The same structure was reflected in the chunks that were created for our system. In a company, presumably much more non-actionable information would be posted. In a city center however, many advertisements would be actionable, pointing directly to the shop. The specific mixture however depends on the environment of the deployment.

Support planning with News and opportunism with Reminder Displays. Some environments are closed and have only regular visitors, like certain companies where employee information would be shown on the displays. Most of the users there will plan well ahead and thus News Displays are very suitable. Other environments are open and have many one-time visitors, like city centers and shopping malls where advertisements would be shown on the displays. In these setting more users will act opportunistically and thus Reminder Displays are more suitable. Most environments, like our university, are however somewhere on a continuum between these extremes, such that a mixture of News and Reminder Displays is best.

Place Displays in entrances and waiting areas. We provide News Displays at the entrances to the building, so users are guaranteed to see them twice a day. Reminder Displays on the other hand are installed in working and waiting areas, such that the total viewing time is maximized.

We proposed the notion of update rate as well as the distinction between actionable and non-actionable information to categorize different kinds of information. We developed the concepts of News and Reminder Displays as ways to present actionable information to planners and opportunists alike. In the future, we want to generalize these concepts to other areas beyond universities, where Situated Public Displays can be deployed. In particular, actionable advertisements can offer users diverse action opportunities like discounts, shows or special events. Thus, News and Reminder Displays could be deployed in shopping malls, city centers, airports or amusement parks to enable people to participate in more action opportunities and make better use of their time.

References

1. Allen, D.: Getting Things Done: The Art of Stress-Free Productivity. Penguin (Non-Classics) (December 2002)
2. Beyer, H., Holtzblatt, K.: Contextual Design: A Customer-Centered Approach to Systems Designs. Morgan Kaufmann, San Francisco (1997)
3. Cheverst, K., Fitton, D., Dix, A.: Exploring the evolution of office door displays. In: O'Hara, K., et al. (eds.) Public and Situated Displays, pp. 141–169. Kluwer International, Dordrecht (2003)

4. Churchill, E., Nelson, L., Denoue, L., Girgensohn, A.: The plasma poster network: Posting multimedia content in public places. In: INTERACT 2003, IOS Press, Amsterdam (2003)
5. Fass, A., Forlizzi, J., Pausch, R.: Messydesk and messyboard: Two designs inspired by the goal of improving human memory. In: Proc. Conf. Designing Interactive Systems (DIS), pp. 303–311. ACM Press, New York (2002)
6. Grasso, A., Mühlenbrock, M., Roulland, F., Snowdon, D.: Supporting communities of practice with large screen displays. In: O'Hara, K., et al. (eds.) Public and Situated Displays, Kluwer International, Dordrecht (2003)
7. Greenberg, S., Rounding, M.: The notification collage: Posting information to public and personal displays. In: Proc. Human Factors in Computing Systems (CHI), pp. 515–521. ACM Press, New York (2001)
8. Grudin, J.: Why cscw applications fail: problems in the design and evaluation of organization of organizational interfaces. In: CSCW 1988, pp. 85–93. ACM Press, New York (1988)
9. Hassenzahl, M., Beu, A., Burmester, M.: Engineering joy. IEEE Softw. 18(1), 70–76 (2001)
10. Huang, E.M., Mynatt, E.D.: Semi-public displays for small, co-located groups. In: Proc. conference on Human factors in computing systems (CHI), pp. 49–56. ACM Press, New York (2003)
11. Huang, E.M., Mynatt, E.D., Russell, D.M., Sue, A.E.: Secrets to success and fatal flaws: The design of large-display groupware. IEEE Computer Graphics and Applications 26(1), 37–45 (2006)
12. McCarthy, J.F., Costa, T.J., Liongosari, E.S.: Unicast, outcast & groupcast: Three steps toward ubiquitous, peripheral displays. In: Abowd, G.D., Brumitt, B., Shafer, S. (eds.) Ubicomp 2001. LNCS, vol. 2201, pp. 332–345. Springer, Heidelberg (2001)
13. Müller, J., Krüger, A.: How much to bid in digital signage advertising auctions. In: Adjunct proceedings of Pervasive (2007)
14. Payne, T.R., David, E., Jennings, N.R., Sharifi, M.: Auction mechanisms for efficient advertisement selection on public displays. In: Brewka, G., et al. (eds.) ECAI, pp. 285–289. IOS Press, Amsterdam (2006)
15. Reynolds, T.J., Gutman, J.: Laddering theory, method, analysis and interpretation. Journal of Advertising Research 28(1), 11–31 (1988)
16. Russel, D.M., Sue, A.: Large interactive public displays: Use patterns, support patterns, community patterns. In: O'Hara, K., et al. (eds.) Public and Situated Displays, pp. 3–17. Kluwer, Dordrecht (2003)
17. Sharp, R.: Deploy or die: A choice for application-led ubiquitous computing research. In: Workshop on What makes for good application-led research in ubiquitous computing?, in Conjunction with Pervasive 2005 (2005)
18. Storz, O., Friday, A., Davies, N., Finney, J., Sas, C., Sheridan, J.: Public ubiquitous computing systems: Lessons from the e-campus display deployment. Personal and Ubiquitous Computing 5(3), 40–47 (2006)
19. Trimble, J., Wales, R., Gossweiler, R.: Nasa's merboard: An interactive collaborative workplace platform. In: O'Hara, K., et al. (eds.) Public and Situated Displays, pp. 18–44. Kluwer International, Dordrecht (2003)

A Web 2.0 Platform to Enable Context-Aware Mobile Mash-Ups

Diego López-de-Ipiña, Juan Ignacio Vazquez, and Joseba Abaitua

University of Deusto, Avda. Universidades 24, Bilbao, Spain
{dipina,ivazquez}@eside.deusto.es, abaitua@fil.deusto.es

Abstract. Context-aware systems allow users to access services and multimedia data according to their current context (location, identity, preferences). Web 2.0 fosters user contribution and presents the web as an application programming platform where third parties can create new applications (mash-ups) mixing the functionality offered by others. We deem that applying Web 2.0 principles to the development of middleware support for context-aware systems could result into a wider adoption of AmI. This work provides a platform which combines social context-aware annotation of objects and spatial regions with sentient mobile devices enabling multi-modal human to environment interaction in order to enable advanced context-aware data and service discovery, filtering and consumption within both indoor and outdoor environments.

Keywords: Context-awareness, Web 2.0, mobility, location, middleware, NFC, Internet of Things.

1 Introduction

Ambient Intelligence (AmI) environments are usually instrumented with a plethora of sensors and actuators in order to proactively provide users with smart services that enhance their daily activities. Unfortunately, this heavy infrastructure requirement (costly and difficult to install and maintain) has been the reason why AmI adoption, even in the indoors case, is still far from being the norm.

Nowadays, a user is usually accompanied anywhere at anytime by a constantly more capable mobile device that can act as his proxy/intermediary by sensing (GPS, RFID, NFC, barcode reading) and communicating (Wi-Fi, Bluetooth, GPRS/UMTS) with the surrounding environment, and so enabling rich interactions with it. Conventionally, either the user explicitly controls through the device services discovered in the environment (explicit interaction) or the environment triggers autonomously services based on users' context, profile and preferences published by the device (implicit interaction). In all these situations, context acts as an important source to filter down and select the most suitable services for the user at his current contextual situation.

However, it would be desirable that users accompanied by smart mobile devices could profit from surrounding smart services without having to be within an

B. Schiele et al. (Eds.): AmI 2007, LNCS 4794, pp. 266–286, 2007.

intelligent highly instrumented environment. In fact, a key aspect for the successful massive adoption of AmI will be to foster the use of off-the-shelf globally accessible infrastructure, without imposing costly investments and cutting edge infrastructure deployment and installation hassles.

In the last two years the Web 2.0 approach has revolutionised the way we use the web. On one hand, it enables the active participation of users with new content such as wiki pages, blogs or online multimedia tagged repositories such as Flickr or YouTube. On the other hand, Web 2.0 transforms the Web into an application enabling platform. Currently, many different organisations such as Yahoo!, Google or Microsoft, publicise diverse types of functionality (such as maps, advertisement, weather info or photo repositories) accessible through REST or SOAP APIs. Thus, a popular trend is being to define new web applications by mixing and integrating the functionality offered by others. These new applications are being termed in Web 2.0 jargon as mash-ups.

Sentient Graffiti (SG) is our proposition for providing a simple, Web 2.0-inspired, globally accessible AmI infrastructure enabling natural interaction (touching, pointing or being close to nearby augmented objects) that simplifies context-aware application creation and deployment. It is a platform which merges the Ubiquitous Web (UW) or Internet of Things (IoT) concepts, where all physical objects are web resources accessible by URIs, providing information and services that enrich users' experiences in their physical context, with Web 2.0, where users accompanied by mobile devices or web browsers can browse, discover, search, annotate and filter surrounding smart objects in the form of web resources.

The main aim of the SG platform is to make possible the Internet of Things vision by lowering the barrier of developing and deploying ecosystems of smart everyday objects providing services within any indoor or outdoor environment. The focus in this work lies on maximizing the developer audience rather than concentrating on providing highly advanced features. It is based on the spontaneous annotation by a community of users of objects, places or even other people with web accessible multimedia content and services which can then be discovered and consumed by mobile users, whose contextual attributes match those of the annotations.

In other words, Sentient Graffiti is the result of combining the capabilities of last generation sentient mobile devices, the Web 2.0 as an application enabling platform, rather than just as a collection of hyperlinked documents, the UW/IoT concept where physical object services are published, discovered and accessed; and social annotation of the physical environment. The following facts justify that such a combination may constitute a promising user-driven Web 2.0-based middleware for AmI:

- Current mobile devices multimedia (e.g. camera and media playback), sensing (e.g. GPS, Bluetooth, RFID, NFC and barcode readers) and communicating (e.g. GPRS, UMTS, Bluetooth, Wi-Fi) capabilities make them ideal sentient intermediaries between us and our environment. Good examples of such devices are Nokia N95 (includes built-in GPS, high resolution camera, Wi-Fi, Bluetooth, GPRS/UMTS) or Nokia NFC 6131 (includes built-in RFID reader, high-resolution camera, Bluetooth and GPRS).

- Mobile Web 2.0 mash-ups, where users contribute with content and create integrated mobile applications mixing information from diverse distributed sources will increasable become commonplace and be presented as smart services in an environment.

- The web of everyday physical resources proposed by UW/IoT suits perfectly to AmI, making their development interlinked to a more extensive adoption of AmI in previously unconsidered settings such as cities or cars.
- Folksonomies, i.e. automatic taxonomies generated from social annotations, linked with context information (identity, location, profiles) provide efficient discovery, filtering, and consumption mechanisms for the massive web of resources (smart services provided by physical objects) which constitute UW/IoT.

The structure of the rest of this paper is as follows. First, related work on mobile Web 2.0, UW/IoT and middleware support for AmI is reviewed. In section 3, the Sentient Graffiti concept and related terminology are presented. Section 4 explains the internal details of Sentient Graffiti. Section 5 reviews the multi-modal human to environment interaction mechanisms offered by Sentient Graffiti and the benefits brought forward to interaction by adopting NFC technology. Section 6 overviews some example applications developed with this middleware. Finally, section 7 proposes some future work and concludes the article.

2   Related Work

The two most remarkable features of Web 2.0 [15] versus the traditional web are: a) *Read/Write Web*, the user stops being a passive subject, a consumer of data published by others, but he contributes continuously with new information (e.g. blogs, wikis) and b) *Web as a platform*, the web can be seen not only as a huge collection of interlinked documents but as a set of web applications offering open APIs (REST or Web Services) that can be composed to create sophisticated applications combining data from diverse sources, namely *mash-up web applications*.

Lately, significant research and industry effort [9] is underway in order to translate the Web 2.0 paradigm to mobile computing. Some interesting examples of this effort are Moblogs, i.e. blogs whose content is updated from a mobile device in order to answer what a user is doing at every moment such as Jaiku (http://jaiku.com), or mobile versions of Web 2.0 sites such as Flickr (http://m.flickr.com). In this work we propose to go a step further progressing from Mobile Web 2.0 into Mobile Context-Aware Web 2.0, which should ease the discovery and consumption of smart services from mobile devices.

The concept of Ubiquitous Web (UW) was first considered on the W3C Workshop on the Ubiquitous celebrated on March 2006 [22]. However, before this workshop initiative, other researchers had already considered the convergence of web-related technologies and ubiquitous computing. A fine example of this was the CoolTown project [10]. Its main goal was to support "web presence" for people, places and things. They used URIs for addressing, physical URI beaconing and sensing of URIs for discovery, and localized web servers for directories in order to create a location-aware ubiquitous system to support nomadic users. This vision resembles very much the definition of Ubiquitous Web as a net of knowledge where every physical object is web-accessible and interlinked. Other researches [1][13] have coined the term

Internet of Things (IoT) to refer to the same idea, being this term currently more popular than the UW one.

Sentient Graffiti is a Web 2.0-based platform also following the UW/IoT approach, but emphasizing the need to minimize the deployment requirements (making use of off-the-shelf hardware and sensing technology) on the environments, stressing the importance of user collaboration and providing different human to environment natural interaction modes (touching, pointing, proximity, location). Furthermore, earlier projects such as CoolTown did not consider the communicatory, social and navigational implication of the mass usage of a context-aware information system, as it is the case of SG and other related research such as GeoNotes [5] or InfoRadar [17].

Several research projects have also attempted to lower the barrier of deploying simple context-aware applications anywhere, both within controlled indoor and uncontrolled outdoor environments. Some good examples are stick-e notes [2], GeoNotes, Active Campus [5], CoolTown, InfoRadar, Place-Its [20], Mobile Bristol [8] or Semapedia [18]. A common feature of these projects addressed to non- or lightly- instrumented environments has been the adoption of a "virtual Post-It metaphor". This metaphor was first proposed by the stick-e notes project, which defined an infrastructure enabling the edition, discovery and navigation of virtual context-aware post-it notes. Everything (a location, an object or even a person) can be augmented with an XML document (stick-e note) which can later be discovered and matched, taking into consideration the contextual attributes associated to a tag. A key aspect on mobile mass annotation systems as these is to address the trade-off between creating an open and social information space while still enabling people to navigate and find relevant information and services in that space. The more contextual information used in the content matching process the better filtering results that are obtained.

Sentient Graffiti is in our opinion the only of the above mentioned systems which successfully combines several context attributes (identity, precise and proximity location) and keyword-based user preference filtering, inherited from famous Web 2.0 sites such as del.icio.us or Flickr. SG stresses the importance of user participation; users create graffitis, tag them with keywords and then comment or add further tags to other users' annotations. Moreover, it can associate graffitis to objects tagged by a diverse range of technologies, TRIP [12] ringcodes (enabling interaction by pointing) or RFID tags (enabling interaction by touching), precise location (GPS) and to Bluetooth coverage areas (proximity attribute). Similarly to InfoRadar, it usefully deviates from the Post-It metaphor in that notes can be posted and retrieved remotely and to remote places through a Web 2.0 site. Finally, previous ubiquitous context-aware messaging systems do not provide an open API which enables third party applications to use SG's capabilities to mash-up context-aware applications. This feature gives SG a Web 2.0 platform, i.e. application enabling nature.

A few industrial systems such as Navizon (http://www.navizon.com), Socialight (http://socialight.com), Context Watcher (http://portals.telin.nl/contextwatcher) or Tagzania (http://www.tagzania.com) have also combined the "Post-It metaphor" and Web 2.0 approaches. However, the context-based filtering they propose is limited, it only encompasses location and keyword filtering. They disregard other interesting context attributes as object identity, proximity, advanced privacy control (who is allowed to receive what notes) or complex temporal restrictions (lifespan, validity timetable and garbage collection), which are all addressed in Sentient Graffiti. Besides, their mobile clients compared to the SG are very limited: a) they are not able of presenting web services, only simple multimedia content, b) only offer list-based views and not more intuitive map views, c) only work outdoors (GPS) or through coarse-grained Wi-Fi based indoor location [19], and d) allow for very limited user participation.

For a few years now, other researchers have also noticed the importance of providing middleware support for aiding on context-aware application development and deployment. Some good examples of this are the Context Toolkit [4] and Context Tailor [3] systems. The Context Toolkit consists of context widgets and a distributed infrastructure that hosts the widgets. Context widgets are software components that provide applications with access to context information while hiding the details of context sensing. The Context Tailor system decouples triggering (when) from effecting (how) in order to simplify context-aware application programming. Moreover, it applies machine learning techniques to enrich the triggering phase. Compared to these two systems, Sentient Graffiti is more generic and simple, it does not require any special purpose development and deployment of widgets or context-sensing and inferring infrastructure. Sentient Graffiti already provides the context repository and inference infrastructure. End users only need either to construct novel applications which profit from such infrastructure or simply limit to their user-friendly multi-modal mobile and web clients.

Few research works have attempted wide-scale ubiquitous computing deployment. To date, most 'ubiquitous' computing experiments have been far from ubiquitous, generally restricted to specific laboratories or research groups. Pioneering work on this area was carried out by the Active Campus [5] and Mobile Bristol [8] projects, which chose a university campus and a city respectively as ideal settings for wide-scale deployment. With Sentient Graffiti we also attempt to encompass global uncontrolled deployment settings such as a city (outdoors) or a faculty building (indoors).

An interesting technology which has emerged lately and which seems as an ideal candidate to help on providing a more natural way of interaction between the user and the environment is Near-Field-Communication (NFC) [6][13][14]. This technology is a combination of contact-less identification and interconnection technologies that enables wireless short-range communication between mobile devices, consumer electronics, PCs and smart objects. NFC offers a simple, touch-based solution that allows consumers to exchange information and to access content and services in an intuitive way. The emergence of NFC should simplify human to environment interaction, giving place to the Touch Computing paradigm [21], where users have only to wave their representing mobile devices in front of everyday objects augmented with RFID tags and visual markers or other NFC-aware devices in order to trigger the smart services offered by them. In fact, the combination of RFID and visual tagging of everyday physical objects and NFC-enabled devices will foster the UW/IoT vision where every resource that surrounds us and its associated services are available through some kind of networking (Bluetooh, Wi-Fi, GPRS/UMTS) and programming infrastructure (web service, semantic web service, RSS feed and so forth), easily discovered and consumed through our mobile devices. Sentient Graffiti, as an UW/IoT-enabling platform, also leverages on the promising NFC technology as it will be later reviewed.

3 Sentient Graffiti: Definition, Concepts and Functionality

Sentient Graffiti enables mobile and web users to profit from the benefits of Ubiquitous Computing in uncontrolled environments, only requiring in exchange, the participation in a community of users interested on publishing and consuming context-aware empowered annotations and services. Users annotate objects and spatial regions with multimedia data or web services which are only made available to other users when those match the context attributes (location range, period of time, and so forth) previously assigned to the resources.

3.1 Sentient Graffiti Terminology

A *virtual graffiti* within SG is defined as a virtual post-it note in the form of an XML document which combines some content (multimedia presentation or web service front-end) with some keywords summarising the content, and some contextual attributes (profile of creator, location, time interval and so on) which restrict who, when and where can those annotations be seen.

Virtual graffitis are edited through a PC web browser or, on the move, through a mobile client and then published on a back-end server. We currently support two types of graffiti content: multimedia presentations in SMIL format (including video, audio and images) and URLs pointing to web service front-ends.

Before a graffiti is edited it has to be associated to a spatial region, using accurate (GPS) or proximity (Bluetooth) location, or to an object using its identity given by a barcode or a RFID tag (see TRIP [11] ringcode and RFID tag examples in Fig. 4).

Users bookmark graffitis with keywords. Although a user may always create new keywords, the system suggests previously chosen keywords to encourage keyword sharing.

In order to prevent users from being overloaded with all the graffitis associated to a location or object, only those with contextual attributes that match users' current context are provided. Contextual attributes input into the system are: filtering keywords or *graffiti domains* (explicitly indicated by the user), graffiti presentation distance range selected, location and identity of user (implicitly input by his accompanying mobile device running the SG Mobile Client). Moreover, graffitis are returned ordered by usage, i.e. most visited and recently created graffitis come first. Thus, Sentient Graffiti tracks community usage of graffiti to enable such ordering behaviour. On the other hand, an important issue to tackle in mass annotation systems is that of spam. Users should reject inappropriate graffitis so that the system stops providing them. In conclusion, Sentient Graffiti aims to undertake both context and usage-based filtering.

Another important issue is garbage collection of non-active graffitis. Sometimes it will be interesting to consume a graffiti only once whereas other times a fixed number of times or indefinitely. Besides, a graffiti may be valid forever or only for a certain period of time. Sentient Graffiti takes into account all these criteria in order to clean up expired or consumed graffitis. Those grafittis removed are archived in order to keep a historical of graffitis and allow past graffiti context retrieval.

An interesting extrapolation of Web 2.0 principles to Sentient Graffiti is what we have called *WikiGraffiti*, i.e. graffiti consumer participation on a graffiti by adding

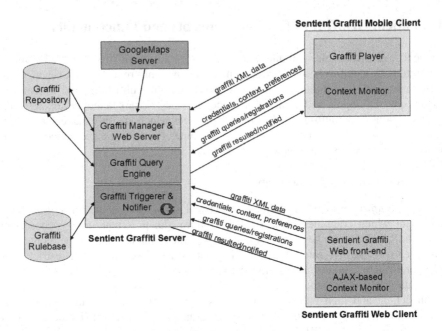

Fig. 1. Sentient Graffiti System Architecture

personal comments, additional multimedia content or keywords. This idea may be useful to encourage user participation and the creation of communities of graffiti-ers.

A *graffiti domain* is a group of user-set related keywords qualifying a graffiti category. Graffiti domains are interesting for graffiti filtering. For instance the graffiti domain Deusto_University may be associated to the graffiti qualifying keywords   university,   engineering,   deusto,   student, computer_science and so on. A user registering his interest on viewing only Deusto_University domain's graffitis will automatically view only graffitis qualified by at least one of its set of associated keywords.

3.2 Sentient Graffiti Functionality

Sentient Graffiti presents a client/server architecture, as shown in Fig. 1, where users run a SG client in either their mobile device or a computer's web browser, whilst a server-side component, namely Sentient Graffiti Server, stores, indexes and matches user annotations against user's current context published by SG clients. It is important to note that Sentient Graffiti clients can be either the provided generic ones (in web and mobile form) or any special-purpose custom-developed ones using the HTTP API offered by the SG platform.

From a user's perspective, the modus operandi of Sentient Graffiti can be described as a two-fold process:

- *Graffiti annotation.* Users of SG clients (mobile- or web browser-based) add annotations to objects or spatial regions consisting of:
  a. Descriptions (e.g. multimedia content or web service front-end URL)

b. Keywords, describing annotated resources and enabling their classification and
c. Contextual attributes which define the conditions to be met by consumers of
    those annotations. Some of those attributes will be set automatically by the SG
    client (who created the annotation, where and when) whilst others will be
    explicitly set by the user (location range where the tag should be viewed, who
    can see it, when and for how long).

A sample of GraffitiXML, an XML derivative used to describe the information
associated to graffitis and exchanged among SG clients and back-ends is shown in
Fig. 2.

- *Graffiti discovery and consumption.* Users equipped with a mobile device or
  remotely through a web browser running the SG client, move (physically or
  virtually) through an annotated (virtually graffiti-ed) environment, browse and
  consume the available annotations matching the user's current context, profile and
  preferences. This interaction may take place in an explicit, i.e. the user interacts with
  the application requesting available annotations either by user input, pointing to a
  surrounding marker or touching a nearby RFID tag, or implicit manner, i.e. the
  system alerts the user when new annotations are available corresponding to his
  current contextual attributes. User explicit interaction through a mobile or web client
  is supported in the back-end by the Graffiti Query Engine module whilst implicit
  interaction by the Graffiti Trigger and Notifier module (see left-hand-side of Fig. 2).

From a system's point of view, SG can be seen as both a Context-Aware Folksonomy
and a Context-Aware Mobile Mash-up. As a Context-Aware Folksonomy,
SG establishes a spontaneous classification of the objects and spatial regions
annotated and their relationships. Thus, it is possible to link annotations of

```
<graffiti>
  <head>
    <general>
      <id><!-- unique ID --></id>
      <title><!-- graffiti title --></title>
      <description><!-- description --></description>
    </general>
    <keywords><!-- qualifying keywords --></keywords>
    <context-attributes>
      <implicit>
        <who></who>
        <when><when>
        <where type="gps|TRIP|RFID|BT_MAC"><!--coord or IDs--></where>
      </implicit>
      <explicit>
        <who><!-- who can see the graffitis --></who>
        <within><!-- viewing location range --></within>
        <when><!-- hour range --></when>
        <during><!-- period of availability --></during>
        <times><!-- how many times --></times>
      </explicit>
    </context-attributes>
  </head>
  <body type="SMIL | WebService">
    <!-- SMIL file content or web service url -->
  </body>
</graffiti>
```

Fig. 2. GraffitiXML Sample Denoting the Information Associated to a Graffiti

resources sharing all or a subset of keywords. As a Context-Aware Mash-up, the mobile and web-based SG clients combine geographical information in the form of maps (e.g. obtained from maps.google.com) and the SG back-end supplied descriptions.

3.3 Sentient Graffiti Deployment

Fig. 3 shows how the Sentient Graffiti infrastructure may be deployed. A cluster of central servers stores graffitis together will all their metadata so that appropriate filtering, discovery and triggering of them can be carried out.

A user equipped with a PC browser may comfortably access the SG back-end from his office or home, as shown on the right hand side of Fig. 3. By means of an advanced Web 2.0 front-end, the user may create, discover and consume graffitis, commenting or adding new content to them.

A user equipped with a last generation mobile device including a camera and Bluetooth, and optionally with a Bluetooth-enabled (see Fig. 4) or built-in the phone RFID reader, will in an indoor environment (see centre of Fig. 3) access either through a global access network such as GPRS/UMTS or a locally available network (Bluetooth or Wi-Fi) to the SG back-end. The sentient capabilities of a mobile device (camera enabling image processing of barcodes or RFID reader), enable the user to

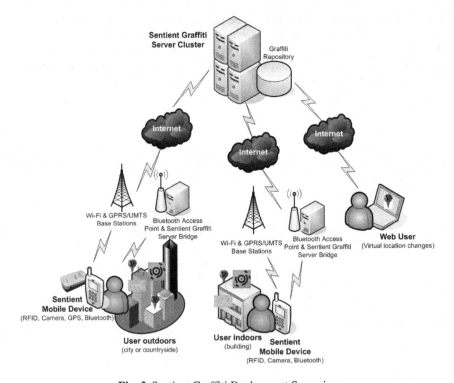

Fig. 3. Sentient Graffiti Deployment Scenarios

Fig. 4. Advanced mobile device including Wi-Fi, Bluetooth, GPRS/UMTS and camera (center), TRIP tag and Bluetooth GPS device (left) and RFID tag and Bluetooth RFID reader (right)

associate graffitis to tagged objects or review the graffitis attached to those objects. Noticeably, an organisation may deploy within its premises a network of Bluetooth accessible SG Server Bridges. These bridges enable users to create, discover and consume graffitis only active within the bridges' Bluetooth access point coverage. The bridge itself caches the last accessed graffitis associated to its domain. Thus, even users not equipped with sophisticated camera phones or RFID readers, can still profit from the Sentient Graffiti infrastructure without incurring in network communication costs (GPRS or UMTS).

Likewise, a user in an outdoor environment may use its advanced mobile device to annotate objects and spatial regions, discover and consume graffitis in his surroundings. In these outdoor environments, the user may also use the sentient capabilities (accurate location) provided by a built-in or Bluetooth-enabled GPS device attached to his mobile device (see Fig. 4), or the previously commented sensing capabilities (TRIP, RFID and Bluetooth proximity) to annotate, discover and consume graffitis.

4   The Sentient Graffiti Platform

In this section, we explain why Sentient Graffiti should be regarded as a context-aware application-enabling platform rather than as a plain context-aware application. Besides, some relevant implementation details are offered.

4.1   Graffiti Notification and Query

Two components within SG help on the graffiti filtering process: Graffiti Triggerer and Graffiti Querier (review left-hand-side of Fig. 1). The mission of the *Graffiti*

Triggerer is to infer suitable graffitis for a user and filter out all the ones unlikely to be of interest. The *Graffiti Querier* allows for the on-demand context-aware interrogation of the Graffiti Repository.

In the Graffiti Triggerer, an ECA rule based [19] inference engine at the back-end populates its knowledge base with contextual attribute changes received from users' SG clients, and infers sets of active annotations which have to be notified to those users' SG clients, where they are depicted. The graffiti inference is supported by a set of generic rules stored in a rule base which embodies the intelligence of SG. Those rules (see Fig. 5) do not only determine what new annotations need to be transmitted to a SG client but they are also in charge of garbage collecting expired annotations. This component enables a SG client to operate on a PUSH manner, without user intervention. On the other hand, the Graffiti Querier enables a SG client to operate on a PULL manner, communicating with the back-end under user's explicit command.

```
{
  graffiti (?graffiti_id, ?graffiti_title, ?graffiti_desc, "GPS",
?graffiti_creation_date, ?graffiti_content) and

  graffiti_location(?graffiti_id, ?graffiti_location,
?graffiti_viewing_range) and

  graffiti_tags(?graffiti_id, ?graffiti_tagSet) and

  graffiti_visibility_restriction(?graffiti_id,
?graffiti_viewing_restrictions) and

  user (?user_id) and

  test (validUserFilter(?user_id, ?graffiti_viewing_restrictions))
and

  ( user_location_restriction(?user_id, ?user_location, 0) or

     (user_location_restriction(?user_id, ?user_location,
?user_viewing_distance) and

       test(validDistanceFilter(?user_location, ?graffiti_location,
?user_viewing_distance))

     )

  ) and

  user_tag_restrictions(?user_id, ?user_tagSet) and

  test(validTagFilter(?user_tagSet, ?graffiti_tagSet))

}

=>

{

  notifyEvent(SG$ShowGraffitiForUser(?user_id, ?graffiti_id));

}
```

Fig. 5. Simplified pseudo-coded ECA rule which would trigger whenever a user equipped with a GPS device and having specified his location and tag restrictions enters in the vicinity of an active graffiti

4.2 The Sentient Graffiti HTTP API

Sentient Graffiti is not only thought as a practical mobile context-aware application. More importantly, SG aims to provide a platform useful to construct real-life context-aware mash-up applications. The functional requirements addressed by this platform on behalf of applications are:

- Model every physical object (identified by TRIP or RFID tag) or spatial region (GPS or Bluetooth proximity) whose information or services may be consumed.
- Make available to users only the annotations associated to surrounding resources available under their current contextual conditions or desired filtering requirements.
- Facilitate explicit user-controlled interaction with the smart object and spatial regions encountered by a mobile user or a web user, both in a PUSH and PULL manner.

As a proper Web 2.0-based system, Sentient Graffiti offers an HTTP-based API which enables third-party programmers to develop applications that profit from its functionality. The HTTP API provided requires third-party clients to issue HTTP

Fig. 6. Sentient Graffiti Web Interface: a) setting time and tag restrictions to a graffiti (top left), b) adding content to a graffiti (top right), c) setting location range and user constraints (bottom left) and d) viewing a graffiti (bottom right)

POSTs with a `Content-Type` header set to `application/octet-stream`, where the body content is a binary data chunk including any of the following methods and their associated parameters: `LOGIN_USER`, `GET_GRAFFITIS`, `GET_GRAFFITIS_BY_TRIP`, `GET_GRAFFITI_DETAILS`, `GET_MAP_TILES`, `SET_USER_LOCATION`, `SET_USER_FILTERS`, `SAVE_GRAFFITI`, `CANCEL_GRAFFITI`, `LOGOFF` or `ACTIVATE_PUSH_MODEL`.

The `ACTIVATE_PUSH_MODEL` method activates Sentient Graffiti PUSH operation mode. This method requires passing as parameter, apart from the current user location and filtering constraints (viewing location range, keywords or graffiti domains if they have been specified), either the `IP_address` (assigned by the network operator in the case of GPRS/UMTS or the network router in Wi-Fi) or the `Bluetooth_MAC` address of the mobile device. The knowledge of this network address allows the Graffiti Triggerer module (review again left-hand-side of Fig. 1) in the Sentient Graffiti back-end to contact a daemon in the SG mobile client which is listening out for new active graffiti notifications received through server-side issued `NOTIFY_GRAFFITIS` invocations. Once the PUSH mode has been activated, the Context Monitor (see right-hand-side of Fig. 1) in the SG Mobile Client issues `SET_USER_LOCATION` invocations to the back-end whenever significant location changes take place (by default 10 meter-movements or more from an earlier reported location).

4.3 Sentient Graffiti Implementation

A Java implementation of the SG server-side has been completed which runs on a Tomcat application server and uses the Java EE frameworks Tapestry and Hibernate,

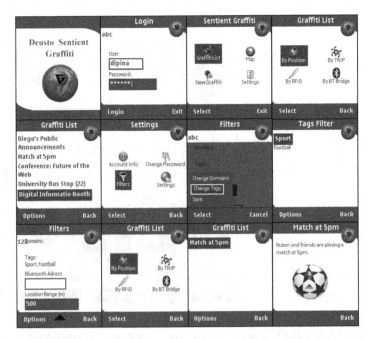

Fig. 7. A logged in user searches for graffitis by location, views all the graffitis available in its location, and repeats the graffiti search after establishing a keyword and location filter

Java expert system shell (Jess), Google Maps API and MySQL. A Web 2.0 front-end client for SG, using the Dojo AJAX framework, has also been completed. Fig. 6 shows some snapshots of such front-end, illustrating how to create graffitis, assign constraints and view them.

A Java ME Sentient Graffiti client, using J2ME Polish (http://www.j2mepolish. org/), is also available which enables the creation, search, discovery and play-back of graffitis from mobile phones (currently available for Nokia 6330, N90, N91, N95 and NFC 6131 devices). Fig. 7 depicts a scenario where a user with a mobile device and a GPS first discovers graffitis in its surroundings by position, secondly obtains a list view of the graffitis around him, and finally repeats the search by position after having established tag and location filters.

5 Multi-modal Interaction and NFC in Sentient Graffiti

Sentient Graffiti aims to simplify the mobile phone-mediated interaction of users with data and software services offered by augmented everyday objects (posters, doors, locations, sculptures and so on). Users equipped with a Sentient Graffiti-enabled mobile phone simply have to lie within a specific geodesic location range, nearby a Sentient Graffiti-powered Bluetooth server or point their devices to visual or RFID tags stuck to Sentient Graffiti-aware objects in order to discover and consume their services. The generic SG Mobile Client provided enhances user to environment interaction by enabling the following four interaction mechanisms:

- *Pointing* – the user can point his camera phone to a bi-dimensional visual marker and obtain as result all the graffitis associated to such marker which are relevant and can be seen by him. Fig. 9 shows such scenario.
- *Touching* – the user can use a mobile RFID reader bound to a mobile through Bluetooth to touch an RFID tag and obtain all the relevant graffitis associated to that tag. Fig. 4 shows the ID Blue (http://www.cathexis.com/) pen-like Bluetooth-enabled RFID reader that we used to enable this interaction mode.
- *Location-aware* – mobiles equipped with a GPS in outdoor environments can obtain all the relevant nearby graffitis in a certain location range which are relevant to the user. Fig. 4 shows the Bluetooth-enabled GPS device used to test the location-aware graffiti retrieval capacities of Sentient Graffiti.
- *Proximity-aware* – the SG Mobile Client can retrieve all the graffitis published in nearby accessible Bluetooth servers when the device is in Bluetooth range from the server. Fig. 10 shows such interaction mechanism, where a user by means of proximity interaction scans for nearby Sentient Graffiti Bluetooth servers, finds one installed in a near digital information booth and browses through the private and public notes available for him in that context.

In order to further improve the support for human-to-environment interaction offered by Sentient Graffiti we have adopted NFC technology. The adoption of this technology on the mobile client has brought out improvements on the way users retrieve public and private virtual graffitis associated to surrounding resources. Our initial implementation of the Sentient Graffiti Mobile Client supported only non NFC-aware mobiles. The adoption of NFC technology and the implementation of a

Touch2Launch service as part of the Sentient Graffiti MIDlet for the Nokia NFC 6131 device (using the Nokia NFC SDK [6]), has provided the following improvements for the touching and proximity aware interaction modes:

- *Touching interaction through NFC.* So far, enabling touching interaction required the complicated scenario of pairing a Bluetooth RFID reader such as the ID Blue with a mobile device, and then force the user to carry both the mobile and the RFID reader, to be able of touching the RFID tags identifying intelligent service enhanced surrounding objects and so obtain the graffitis associated to them. This cumbersome scenario is now simplified for users with a Nokia NFC 6131, since the device itself is able of reading smart object identifying RFID tags. The combination of the Push Registry MIDP 2.0 [16] and NFC technology prevents a user from even having to have the Sentient Graffiti application started in their mobile before undertaking an interaction with an augmented object. As soon as the user approaches his device to an RFID tag attached to an object, the Sentient Graffiti Mobile Client is started thanks to the MIDP 2.0 Push Registry functionality and configured to retrieve all the virtual graffitis associated to the read RFID tag. Fig. 8 shows a user initiating a session of Sentient Graffiti Mobile Client on his Nokia NFC 6131 by touching an RFID tag.

Fig. 8. Touch interaction through NFC

- *Proximity-aware interaction through NFC.* An important drawback of the scenario shown in Fig. 10 is that the user had to wait until the Bluetooth discovery process concluded (about 10 seconds) to figure out whether that information point contained a Bluetooth SG server providing virtual graffitis of his interest. The use of NFC-technology has simplified this scenario considerably. Now, the binding between an NFC-enabled device (Nokia NFC 6131) and the Bluetooth server is carried out by simply touching with the mobile an RFID tag attached to the information point. Such tags offer Bluetooth connection details such as the Bluetooth MAC address of the server and the port where a service is waiting for mobile client requests. Moreover, thanks again to the combination of the Push Registry capacity of MIDP 2.0 and NFC, it is not even necessary that the user has the Sentient Graffiti Mobile Client started. By pointing his device to the information point tag, the application is automatically initiated, and most importantly, correctly configured so that it automatically retrieves virtual graffitis for the user from that Bluetooth Sentient Graffiti Server.

In conclusion, incorporating the Touch2Lounch service into the Sentient Graffiti MIDlet for the Nokia NFC 6131 has simplified both touch and Bluetooth proximity-aware interaction with nearby smart objects. Thus, NFC makes Sentient Graffiti even more suitable as a platform to enable the discovery and consumption of services within UW/IoT by further simplifying two of its natural (pointing, touching) interaction supported modes.

6   Sentient Graffiti Examples

Several proofs of concept applications have been developed with SG to evaluate its potential.

6.1   Marker-Associated Graffitis: Virtual Notice Board

In a university building, professors and researchers are usually scattered through several offices and labs in different floors. Students, researchers and academic staff often go for tutorials or comments to other staff offices. A common pattern followed is to leave a Post-It note outside an office to warn people with whom there was an appointment about the temporal absence from the office, when someone will be back and where that person is at that moment. Unfortunately, those notes are not very aesthetic and even more annoyingly are often seen by people that should not be aware of them.

The Sentient Graffiti platform can serve to improve this scenario. A person only needs to place a distinctive marker (TRIP or RFID tag) on the door of his office. From then on, he can associate graffitis to that marker, creating immediately a context-aware virtual notice board. Graffitis associated to that marker can act as announcements addressed to office visitors. The main advantages of using SG over the traditional use of Post-Its, are:

- Each announcement can only be viewed by the people marked as possible viewers. On graffiti creation we can identify whether the graffiti is public, only viewable by a group of specified users or our contacts.
- The graffiti has an expiration time or a number of maximum views associated that ensures it does not lie on the virtual board forever.
- A user can remotely create or view a graffiti. If a user is off sick, he can remotely from home, with the help of the web SG client, create a graffiti associated to his office TRIP marker. Besides, people aware of this user's virtual notice board may remotely check his notes.
- Graffitis enable user participation, since users can add comments, new content or even associate new keywords to a graffiti. So, a user visiting the office of an absent colleague could leave a comment addressed to his missing colleague to be read when he is back.

Fig. 9 shows how a user obtains through a camera phone running the SG Mobile Client a list of two graffitis. One of them is public and viewable by everybody, whilst the second one is addressed directly to him. Placing a marker on an object, indoors or outdoors, turns such item into a smart object offering a myriad of services in the form of graffitis linked to such marker. For instance:

- A lecturer could leave a graffiti which as content included a pointer to a web service front-end through which students visiting that office could book an appointment.
- A daemon using the SG HTTP API could annotate the TRIP marker with a graffiti indicating whether the user is currently in his office or not. The user presence in the office could be determined by different mechanisms, e.g. Ubisense, RFID or a pressure sensor on his chair.

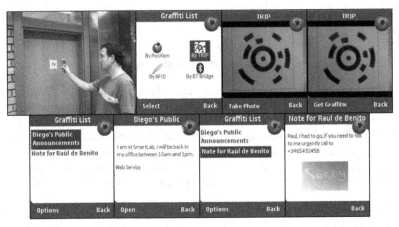

Fig. 9. A user arrives to an office, discovers a TRIP marker and through the SG Mobile Client finds out the graffitis associated to that marker and reviews them

Obviously graffitis can be assigned to a marker with very different purposes. An easy way of distinguishing them is by graffiti keyword or domain filtering. For instance, graffitis used as notes in a board could be tagged with the keyword NOTICE_BOARD, whereas graffitis used for location purposes could be assigned the keyword USER_LOCATION. Thus, it would be possible to create a location service which inspected all the graffitis in a setting of type USER_LOCATION, and produced a view of them over a building map. This scenario would prove the mash-up enabling functionality provided by SG since in this case we would use a brand-new client with a specific (location-awareness) behaviour, rather than using the generic mobile client provided.

6.2 Bluetooth-Range Graffitis: University Services Booth

The Faculty of Engineering of the University of Deusto is equipped with several digital information booths (see top left frame in Fig. 10), each hosted in an embedded computer with a tactile screen, from where students and visitors get university information and access academic services, e.g. course registration, marks look-up and so on.

These digital booths have been enhanced by attaching to them a Bluetooth access point and installing the SG Server Bridge software. The faculty webmaster regularly publishes graffitis bound to the Bluetooth MAC addresses of these booths, only visible in their Bluetooth coverage:

- Public graffitis are used to provide nearby users announcements of general interest, e.g. a conference notice, university news and so forth.
- Graffitis addressed to specific groups, e.g. students registered for a course who are alerted about a lecture cancellation.
- Graffitis for a specific person, e.g. exam mark notification.
- Graffitis associated to a tag, e.g. OPEN_DAY, so that potential students visiting our university get an overview about interesting facts in the university in the form of graffitis. In this case, the lifespan of those graffitis is set to one day, so that immediately after the open day those graffitis are removed.

On the other hand, the SG-aware booths also enable students and staff to create their own graffitis. For example, users may create new graffitis tagged with the keyword ACOMMODATION so that students looking for housing can view them.

Something important about the SG booths is that they only enable the creation, discovery and browsing of graffitis attached to their Bluetooth MAC address. Their main advantage is that it is absolutely free for the student, given that all the communication is carried out through Bluetooth. Fig. 10 shows a user with a Bluetooth-enabled mobile device discovering both a public web service graffiti and a private multimedia graffiti.

As mentioned before, the interactions between NFC-aware mobile devices and Sentient Graffiti booths are further improved by allowing, through NFC technology, automatic Bluetooth pairing between devices and Sentient Graffiti Bluetooth Servers.

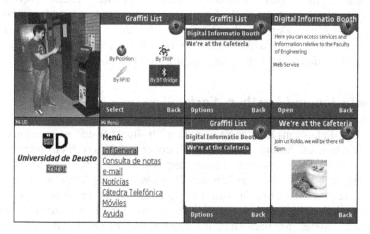

Fig. 10. A user nearby a Digital Booth obtains: a) generic university information offered as a web service graffiti, b) information specifically addressed to him through a multimedia graffiti

6.3 Outdoor Graffitis

Sentient Graffiti can also be applied to outdoor scenarios where the precise location information of the user is known either by GPS or using marker technology (TRIP or RFID).

A Bus Position Alerter service has been prototyped which informs to users present nearby a bus stop about the arrival time of forthcoming buses. A specially designed server-side application communicates with the SG platform through its HTTP API in order to periodically publish a graffiti announcing the waiting periods for next buses arriving to bus stops. Those graffitis are constantly updated with new bus location information. The information shown is retrieved from the Web 2.0 site http://www.bilbobus.info which offers real time data about the location of buses in the city of Bilbao.

This prototype could further be extended to offer users in a bus stop alternative transport options, such as nearby available taxis or underground stations. All those graffitis would be tagged with the same keyword in order to foster filtering, e.g. BILBAO_TRANSPORT. Other interesting applications scenarios enabled through Sentient Graffiti for outdoor environments could be context-aware city tours or publicity campaigns.

Note that Sentient Grafftiti encourages third parties to create mash-ups which access to its infrastructure by means of the SG HTTP API and mix the data obtained from its back-end with info from other Web 2.0 applications. The Bus Position Alerter prototype illustrates how the data provided by Sentient Graffiti through its HTTP API is combined with data provided by another organisation (bilbobus in this example) in order to create a new integrated mash-up application. In this particular case, the Bus Position Alerter back-end uses the method SAVE_GRAFFITI to publish new bus arriving notifications in the form of graffitis and CANCEL_GRAFFITI to cancel them once the buses are gone from a bus stop. On the other hand, the Bus Position Alerter mobile client invokes the ACTIVATE_PUSH_MODEL method transferring the user's current context details such as location, identity, graffiti viewing range (20m) and tag filters (BILBAO_TRANSPORT) as parameters. A rule like the one shown in Fig. 5 takes care of client notification when an alerting situation is found.

7 Conclusion and Further Work

Web 2.0-based platforms such as Sentient Graffiti should foster the creation of mobile social communities, where users may discover based on their current context everyday physical objects and regions augmented with multimedia and service annotations, with which they can interact. Moreover, those platforms should promote a more extensive adoption of Ambient Intelligence in previously unconsidered locations (cities, cars, hospitals, homes) without imposing important deployment and maintenance hassles. Sentient Graffiti's combination of an HTTP API and built-in inference engine provides both simplicity and reasoning power for AmI application development. Furthermore, the multi-modal interaction mechanisms offered by the Sentient Graffiti Mobile Client (touching, pointing, Bluetooth proximity- and location-awareness) clearly simplify the way that a user can discover and request services from the environment. Finally, the adoption of NFC technology has made Sentient Graffiti even more suitable as a candidate platform to enable the discovery and consumption of services provided within the Internet of Things by automating the activation and configuration of its mobile client when simply pointing or touching augmented objects.

Binding graffitis, authors and consumers to an ontology would enable associations among different author graffitis, the author themselves and graffiti consumers. A current research line is to automate, as an off-line process, the association of tag and user entries to Dublin Core and FOAF ontology entries, respectively. For that purpose, a Folk2Onto tool is being developed which converts the Sentient Graffiti folksonomy, i.e. the user-created spontaneous taxonomy of graffitis based on the keywords assigned to them, into an Ontology combining the vocabularies of Dublin Core (for graffitis) and FOAF (for users).

Further work is required to ease the provision of graffitis to consumers. Currently all the available graffitis according to a user's current context are offered sorted by date and consumption rate. However, it would be desirable to offer those graffitis sorted by their specific importance for users. Such improved sorting of graffitis could be possible if graffiti consumption patterns were identified. In essence, we aim to adopt some of the mechanisms used by search engines to offer the most relevant pages as first results to the graffiti domain.

Finally, we plan to pass from the proof of concept scenarios explained to a real deployment of the Sentient Graffiti within our university campus. So far, the only real user experience with Sentient Graffiti took place in two open day sessions in May where student candidates (two groups of ten people) visited the university premises accompanied by mobile phones running Sentient Graffiti which allowed them to obtain further information about locations tagged with TRIP markers. Although the experience was positive, only accurate information on the practicality of the platform can be obtained through a much more detailed user study. Therefore, currently we are focusing on analysing the role this system may play on constituting a mobile context-aware social network of our students, a group of twenty during a term, sharing their knowledge as an ecosystem of annotations. This real deployment should help us evaluating the practical usability and real performance (especially in the PUSH mode) of the Sentient Graffiti platform.

Acknowledgements

Thanks to the Cátedra Movistar of the University of Deusto (http://www.ctme. deusto.es) for funding this research. We are very grateful to Raúl de Benito and Rubén Abuín for their excellent implementation work on Sentient Graffiti.

References

1. Broll, G., Siorpaes, S., Rukzio, E., Paolucci, M., Hamard, J., Wagner, M., Schmidt, A.: Supporting Mobile Service Usage through Physical Mobile Interaction. In: 5th Annual IEEE International Conference on Pervasive Computing and Communications, White Plains, NY, USA (2007)

2. Brown, P.J.: Triggering information by context. Personal Technologies 2(1), 1–9 (1998)
3. Davis, J., Sow, D., Blount, M., Ebling, M.: Context Tailor: Towards a Programming Model for Context-Aware Computing. In: International Middleware Conference, Workshop Proceedings, Rio de Janeiro, Brazil, pp. 68–75 (2003)
4. Dey, A.K.: Providing Architectural Support for Building Context-Aware Applications. PhD thesis, Georgia Institute of Technology (2000)
5. Espinoza, F., Persson, P., Sandin, A., Nyström, H., Cacciatore, E., Bylund, M.: GeoNotes: Social and Navigational Aspects of Location-Based Information Systems. In: Abowd, G.D., Brumitt, B., Shafer, S. (eds.) Ubicomp 2001. LNCS, vol. 2201, pp. 2–17. Springer, Heidelberg (2001)
6. Forum Nokia: Nokia 6131 NFC SDK: User's Guide v1.1. Forum Nokia (2007), http://sw.nokia.com/id/77d9e449-6368-4fde-8453-189ab771928a/Nokia_6131_NFC_SDK_Users_Guide_v1_1_en.pdf
7. Griswold, W.G., Shanahan, P., Brown, S.W., Boyer, R., Ratto, M., Shapiro, R.B., Truong, T.M.: ActiveCampus: Experiments in Community-Oriented Ubiquitous Computing. IEEE Computer 37(10), 73–81 (2004)
8. Hull, R., Clayton, B., Melamed, T.: Rapid Authoring of Mediascapes. In: Davies, N., Mynatt, E.D., Siio, I. (eds.) UbiComp 2004. LNCS, vol. 3205, Springer, Heidelberg (2004)
9. Jookar, A., Fish, T.: Mobile Web 2.0, FutureText (2006) ISBN: 0954432762
10. Kindberg, T., Barton, J., Morgan, J., et al.: People, Places, Things: Web Presence for the Real World. In: WMCSA 2000. MONET, vol. 7(5) (2002)
11. López-de-Ipiña, D., et al.: An ECA Rule-Matching Service for Simpler Development of Reactive Applications. IEEE Distributed Systems Online 2(7) (2001)
12. López-de-Ipiña, D., Mendonça, P., Hopper, A.: TRIP: a Low-cost Vision-based Location System for Ubiquitous Computing. Personal and Ubiquitous Computing 6(3), 206–219 (2002)
13. Michahelles, F., Thiesse, F., Schmidt, A., Williams, J.R.: Pervasive RFID and Near Field Communication Technology. IEEE Pervasive Computing 6(3), 94–96 (2007)
14. NFC Forum: About page (2007), http://www.nfc-forum.org/aboutnfc/
15. O'Reilly, T.: What Is Web 2.0 – Design Patterns and Business Models for the Next Generation of Software (2005), http://www.oreillynet.com/pub/a/oreilly/tim/news/2005/09/30/what-is-web-20.html
16. Ortiz, E.: The MIDP 2.0 Push Registry, Sun Developer Network (2003), http://developers.sun.com/mobility/midp/articles/pushreg/
17. Rantanen, M., Oulasvirta, A., Blom, J., Tiitta, S., Mäntylä, M.: InfoRadar: group and public messaging in the mobile context. In: NordiCHI 2004. Proc. 3rd Nordic Conference on Human-Computer interaction, vol. 82, pp. 131–140. ACM Press, New York (2003)
18. Semapedia. org: Hyperlink your world (2007), http://www.semapedia.org/
19. Sohn, T., Griswold, W.S., et al.: Experiences with place lab: an open source toolkit for location-aware computing. In: ICSE 2006. Proc. 28th international Conference on Software Engineering, pp. 462–471. ACM Press, New York (2006)
20. Sohn, T., Li, K., Lee, G., Smith, I., Scott, J., Griswold, W.G.: Place-Its: A Study of Location-Based Reminders on Mobile Phones. In: Beigl, M., Intille, S.S., Rekimoto, J., Tokuda, H. (eds.) UbiComp 2005. LNCS, vol. 3660, pp. 232–250. Springer, Heidelberg (2005)
21. The Touch Computing Project (2007), http://www.nearfield.org/about/
22. W3C, Workshop on the Ubiquitous Web (2006), http://www.w3.org/2005/10/ubiweb-workshop-cfp.html

A Matter of Taste

Alois Ferscha

Institut für Pervasive Computing
Johannes Kepler Universität Linz
Altenberger Strasse 69, 4040 Linz, Austria
ferscha@soft.uni-linz.ac.at

Abstract. Ambient information systems, often referred to as ambient displays, peripheral displays or informative art systems (IAS), aim at providing users with information considered relevant at arbitrary points of work or living engagement, in easy and quickly to convey, aesthetic and artful style. Adhering principles of visual perception, visualization and design, information coming from various different (hardware and software) sensors is aggregated through abstraction and selective omission, and displayed at the periphery of a user's attention. A broad range of visual metaphors ranging from the fine arts, abstract art, naive art, comic drawings up to photographic images or technical drawings have been proposed, but all grounded on the "I-throw-it-out-there-and-watch" design paradigm[1], totally excluding the user, his background knowledge and his aesthetic appreciation from the design process. This paper advocates for a user-oriented, participatory design process for IASs. Addressing canvas style IASs, i.e. displays that decorate apartments, offices, foyers and the like in the first (but not the only) place, in our approach the choice of the IAS canvas *theme* is left to the user. To steer the (design) process of identifying *symbols* within a chosen theme we have developed categories of metaphors like *color*, *space*, *shape*, *abstraction*, *scale* and *dimension*, and discuss their potential with respect to preattentive and interpretative cognition. From experiments with users we find, that the choice of themes and the identification of metaphoric symbols are considered as a means of personal emotional expression (or in other words, as "*a matter of taste*"). Aesthetic attractiveness turns out to be a dominant factor of IAS appreciation. A general purpose software framework for IASs is presented, implementing sensor data acquisition, context recognition, aggregation and filtering, as well as 2D/3D graphics engine, dynamically controlling the visual appearance of themes and symbols.

Keywords: pervasive computing, ambient information systems, peripheral displays, informative art, ambient intelligence, intelligent user interfaces.

1 Informative Art

In an age in which computers are everywhere and nowhere, where tiny computing devices are continuing to pervade into everyday objects, users presumably do, and

---

[1] The term was created and used by Gregory D. Abowd in his PERVASIVE 2007 Tutorial "Evaluation of Real Deployments in Ubicomp", in J. Krumm, . Pfeifer (Eds.): Pervasive Computing Tutorials 2007, Fifth International Conference, Pervasive 2007, Toronto, Canada, multicon verlag 2007.

B. Schiele et al. (Eds.): AmI 2007, LNCS 4794, pp. 287–304, 2007.
© Springer-Verlag Berlin Heidelberg 2007

increasingly will not notice them anymore as separate entities. Appliances, tools, clothing, accessories, furniture, rooms, machinery, cars, buildings, roads, cities, even whole agricultural landscapes increasingly embody miniaturized and wireless, thus invisible information and communication systems. Information technology rich systems and spaces are being created, radically changing the style of how we perceive, create, think, interact, behave and socialize as human beings, but also how we learn, work, cultivate, live, cure, age as individuals or in societal settings. A major issue in such technology rich settings is how we perceive information, how we interact with digital media, how we manage to sustain attentive to information of interest, how we stay aware of the dynamics and changes of information, or how we manage perceptual complexity and information overload.

With all the technological options that fertilize and accelerate the pervasive and ubiquitous computing field of research, we are taught to maintain a certain skeptical view on things and scenarios that are "technologically possible" [30] (see also footnote 1) – and are challenged to remain grounded in the real world, encouraged to propose systems that augment the real world, that facilitate human interactions – that are "socially acceptable". Designing and building pervasive computing systems and applications has become more an "artistic challenge", rather than an "engineering task", as addressed in [4], relating the aim of the "Gesamtkunstwerk" of the "Vienna Moderne" (1895-1930) (*The aim for the "Gesamtkunstwerk" (the "total artwork") lead to the unification of art and the re-evaluation of the role of craftsman and designers. The understanding of an artist dedicated to the Gesamtkunstwerk was "to impress beauty upon every aspect of our lives, that the artist should no longer simply paint pictures, but rather create whole rooms, or even whole dwellings, with wallpapers and furniture as well as paintings".*) to the aim of a hypothetic "Gesamtcomputer", reinterpreting Weiser's Vision as follows: "*The understanding of a computer scientist dedicated to the "Gesamtcomputer" is to impress computing upon every aspect of our lives, that the computer scientist should no longer simply build personal computers, but rather create whole rooms, or even whole dwellings, with wallpapers and furniture as well as personal computers.*"

In an attempt of relating the understanding of science and the understanding of art, [31] postulates scientists to see only the "*observed in the material world*", while the artist sees the "*spiritual*": "*While the scientist describes and predicts, the artist distills and presents. Interpreting science [...] means balancing the desire of scientists to spew data with the artistic urge to create a transcendent experience.*" In quintessence, "Informative Art" is art with electronics, with content and presentation being primary, while technology, form and function is fused and secondary. Following Buckminster Fuller's belief, that as technology advances, art begins to resemble science [30], this paper addresses the process of "creating an experience" from "data spews" by means of artful display installations, often referred to as informative art or ambient displays.

This work is organized as follows. We first (Section 2) identify the focus of this paper as being concerned with ambient information systems of visual type only (visual displays). We give an indication in which areas of application such systems have been developed so far, and discuss how this was done. We assess the design process for IAS system based on user studies (Section 3), and identify shortcomings and misconceptions. For systems dealing with visual art as information displays (informative art systems, IASs) we propose a user centered, participatory design process, in which the choice of the visual "theme" of an IAS is left to the user. To steer the (design) process of identifying symbols within a chosen theme we present categories of metaphors, and discuss their potential with respect to pre-attentive and interpretative cognition. We have developed a versatile IAS architecture and have implemented a corresponding software framework in order to display 2D/3D IAS theme dynamics in arbitrary canvas like settings. Finally, findings are discussed (Section 4).

2   Visual Informative Art

2.1   Ambient Displays: Creating Experience from Data

A variety of definitions for ambient information systems have been proposed in the literature, using slightly different characterizations [28]. Their common core is the aim to deliver information through visuals that are quickly and easily perceived while doing other tasks [19]. As an example, ambient displays are understood as "*aesthetically pleasing displays of information which sit on the periphery of a user's attention. They generally support monitoring of non-critical information*" [16]. Ambient displays have been proposed to provide users with information considered relevant at arbitrary points of work or living engagement, originating from many different – mostly geographically dislocated– sources, and presented at the periphery of human (visual) perception [14]. Monitoring the display should cause minimal distraction from the user's focus of attention [10] [15]. The display and its delivered experience move to the focus of attention only if desired or appropriate in a certain situation, hence justifying the synonym "peripheral display". Everyday life examples of peripheral displays are thermometers and barometers in the kitchen window weather station, wall clocks, windsocks at bridges on the highway, etc. The purpose, type, physical appearance, modality of interaction and notification level of ambient information systems is manifold [29]. While physical, touchable, auditory and even olfactory display types have been proposed, justifying the more general term "ambient information systems" [29], we here restrict to displays of visual type and artistic nature.

As of today, we observe a whole landscape of colorful expressions of art connotating information, motivated with different aims, designed according to different principles and exhibiting a variety of different characteristics. Common to all of them is the fact that information dynamics are subtly encoded by modifying the shape, color and appearance details of some elements of the graphical or pictorial artwork, or of its overall impression. The application domains are ample: ambient information systems have been designed to support for group awareness in work groups in virtual [6] [7] [9] or in physical [23] [26] [27] [28] space settings, for knowledge dissemination in enterprises [19], for users of instant messaging systems [2][3], for deaf users [11], to keep in touch with family members [22], or to display a cities health information in public places [1] – to name a few. Metaphorically, abstract art has been proposed to serve as the visualization paradigm for contextual information [24], design principles and guidelines have been developed [13] [16], upon which software frameworks and development toolkits [17] [18] have been built. Evaluation guidelines have been developed [13][16], and assessment studies have been conducted, e.g. relating comprehension of peripheral displays (i.e. how well a user understands and uses such artifacts) to the time span of their use [12].

For a technical discussion of IASs consider the two expressions of physical and visual ambient displays in Fig. 1. While an USB-memory stick growing and shrinking according to the degree of "loadedness" is designed as an information displaying physical artifact (Fig. 1, *left*), the figural informative art installation (Fig. 1, *right*) is designed to rely on a (computer) screen for output. While the former is a design that augments a real world physical object, the latter one abstracts from a physical representation and assumes a 2D graphical representation.

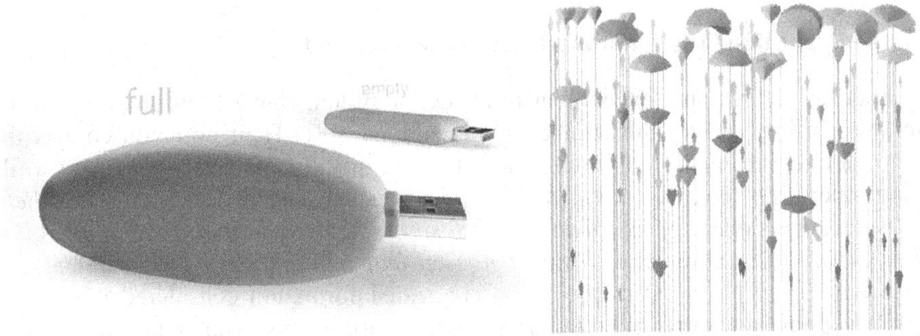

Fig. 1. A physical object (memory stick) designed for the purpose of being an ambient display – it intuitively displays the amount of used storage by the shrinking and growing size of the object (Flashbag: http://www.plusminus.ru/flashbag.html, left). The People Garden [33] figural Informative Art design shows user activities in terms of message densities from posting onto a message board (*right*).

Representation, i.e. the distinction of having a physical (or tangible) object or a 2D visualization is just one design dimension, among the many discussed in the literature [15] [29]. Further design dimensions are the number of *information sources, level of abstraction, transition, notification level, intrusiveness, modality* of use, degree of *interactivity, location*, and *aesthetics* – which we briefly discuss along the PeopleGarden IAS: PeopleGarden proposes a flower and garden metaphor to visualize participation of members of a web community on a message board [33] (*information source*). Community members posting to the message board are abstracted as flowers, with the height of the stem indicating the time span of their contribution history. Petals abstract the number of posts, with blue petals indicating posts, and red petals indicating replies (*low level of abstraction*, i.e. the source data is displayed with little modification). A single message board is abstracted by a whole garden of flowers, with an inherent legibility of the meadow metaphor delivering an "at-a-glance" impression of the board activity: active boards appear as a flower rich, luscious bloom flower garden, while a fading group with just a few participants occasionally checking the board appears "as a neglected garden, with a scattering of tall, scraggly plants that are mostly stem and little flower" [15] (*high level of abstraction*, i.e. the source data is displayed in a collective aggregate of the individual participant activities). On both levels of abstraction (contributor and board), the "at-a-glance" impression delivers an intuitive understanding of the underlying situation, resembling the evocative character of the flower metaphors. The visual encoding of posting patterns to flower growth and shape is based on a direct mapping of the data as it evolves, thus conveying a *slow transition* in the visual appearance within the display. Fast *transition* as a design option would allow to express fast switches in the level of attentiveness of the user. The *notification level* of an IAS is the indication of the degree at which a system alerts the user, and maybe enforces actions to be taken in the indicated situation. *Notification level* metrics like *ignore, change blind, make aware, interrupt* and *demand attention* have been proposed in the literature [16] [17] [18]. The *modality* of PeopleGarden is one of pure visual perception. IASs however are not limited to visual designs, but could as well involve *auditory, haptic, olfactory* or *degustation* elements. The degree if *interactivity* is reduced to a one way communication in PeopleGarden, and the *location* where one would typically deploy and operate a display like this is the *private* desktop. IASs have been designed for *public* installations as well.

2.2 Design Dimension Aesthetics

The design dimension of *aesthetics* is one that is claimed important by almost all contributions to informative art designs [29], but is presumably the least understood [6] [8]. Again, to explain it with an example, the aesthetics of PeopleGarden are borrowed from naïve art (*primitivism*), which is a style characterized by simplicity and the lack of formal qualities of painting (like unrefined color, perspective, etc.), resulting in charmingly awkward artwork. The design finds the good balance between simplicity of the visual elements and their descriptive power (stem and bloom of flowers), and copes well with the problem of semantic overloading of the symbolic representation (it uses just one visualization concept and thus avoids ambiguities in interpretation : "*If a visualization evokes meaning beyond the direct mapping of the data, there needs to be information in that data that guides the choice and shape of the visualization. If there is no such guiding information, then the evocative quality of the visualization is likely to be misleading and inappropriate*" [15]). Beyond some appropriateness of the visualization concepts, the design dimension of aesthetics is not addressed.

In almost all the systems proposed in the literature (see Fig. 2) we find that aesthetics follow the "I-throw-it-out-there-and-watch" design paradigm, totally excluding the user and his personal appreciation of beauty from the design process. This is even true for the Kandinsky systems [8], the first contribution postulating that an ambient display has to be aesthetically interesting in the first place, and convey information in the second place (here an artist specifies the aesthetic template of a collage, which then is used to present photographic images). So far, we have to conclude, are there no general rules steering the process of finding themes and display elements for IASs, and hypothesize, that they are highly dependent to the individual aesthetical appreciation of a user. Observing that the theme of wallpaper, a poster or a painting decorating the living environment of a person is an expression of personal taste, we advocate for a user-oriented, participatory design process, and propose to leave the choice of visual metaphors and the overall visual appearance of the display with the user.

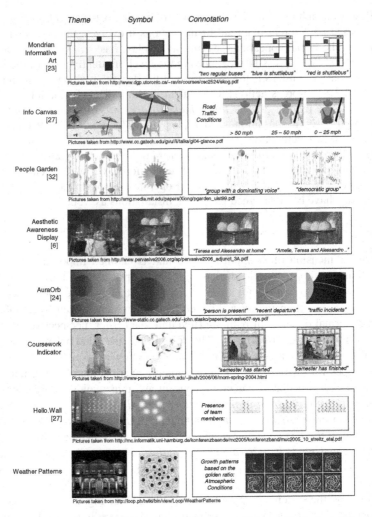

Fig. 2. Aesthetics in previous work structured according to *Themes*, *Symbols* and *Connotations*

2.3 Appreciation of Informative Art Aesthetics

To investigate whether and to which extent IAS themes underly an individual appreciation of visual design we conducted an empirical study aiming at the isolation of personal preferences with respect to (i) *visual appearance*, (like e.g. color, form, shape, etc.), (ii) *concreteness* and (iii) *harmonic embedding* into everyday environments (see Fig. 3). Taking the goal of designing a canvas like IAS for a home (Fig. 3, *left*) or office (Fig. 3, *right*) setting, it is important to not only investigate on the aesthetics of what the display shows (visual appearance, indicated by the orange canvas in Fig. 3), but also its physical shape (frame like, rectangular, oval, sculpture like; concreteness), and how it fits into aesthetics of other artifacts in such environments.

Fig. 3. Questioning on the desired visual appearance, concreteness and harmonic embedding of IAS into everyday environments. Living room setting (left). Office setting (right).

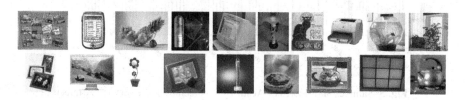

Fig. 4. Questioning on the desired visual appearance, concreteness and harmonic embedding of IAS into everyday environments. Living room setting (left). Office setting (right).

A set of artifacts typically available in home or office scenarios were selected, representing computing technology (Phone/PDA, Monitor, Printer), media technology (Bigscreen, Touchpad), gadgets (Lightcolumn, ColorBricks, FlowerLamp, Laserpod), appliances (Humidifier, Scent), decorations (Painting, Photos, Poster, Pinboard), "natural" things (Fruits, Plants, Aquarium) and dishware (TeaPot). The choice of artifacts aimed at identifying personal preferences according the three criteria in Fig 3.

To this end, a group of n=20, all students of art, design, computer science and mechatronics at an age from 21 to 29, was asked to respond on the aesthetic appreciation of decorative artifacts at the levels (1) "I would never want to have such a thing in my environment", (2) "I don't like it, but I could try to live with", (3) "I would appreciate to have such thing" and (4) "Wow, this thing is fascinating!". The group was informed on the principle purpose of the poll, namely to develop a metric for the aesthetic appreciation of IASs – physical or visual – but was not concerned with any particular purpose or connotation of an artifact at display.

The survey (scores in Fig. 5) indicates evidence for the appreciation of artifacts that are not related to (media or computer) technology, like computers, printers or monitors. On the other hand, everyday items exhibiting a certain decorative character like pin boards, fruit bowls, the aquarium or the tea pot found fascination. The variation in the sample was smallest with "living" artifacts like fruits, plants and animals(fish), indicating that people strictly prefer "natural" settings over "technical" ones. In that preference, they cannot even be "fooled" by a "techno-natural" artifact like the FlowerLamp, which is consistently declined. The Bigscreen artifact which

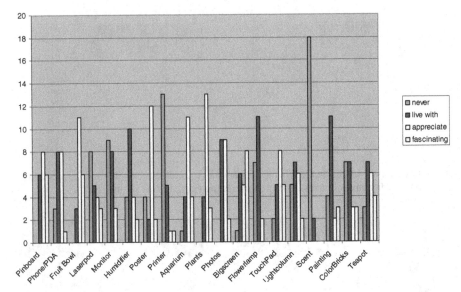

Fig. 5. Samples and Scores of Aesthetic Appreciation of Everyday Artefacts

seems to contradict the central message from the survey was appreciated for what it displays (a natural landscape expressing the beauty of nature in the mountains), rather than what it is (a media technology artifact).

The findings of this survey lets us hypothesize, that users, based on their cultural background, cognitive skills, situative environment, contextual settings, but most of all their aesthetic appreciation, have dedicated, individual and personal attitudes towards the preferred overall appearance of an IAS. Empirical evidence explicates critical importance to the design dimension of aesthetics, and suggests to respect the individual aesthetic sense of users at highest priority throughout the whole IAS development process – in particular at the very beginning, since eminently already the choice of an IAS theme is a (very personal) *"matter of taste"*.

3 Informative Art to Your Taste

We have attempted the design dimension of aesthetics already with previous work [6], relating the choice of the visual elements of an ambient display to factors that seem to be highly impacting aesthetic appreciation: the *cultural context* (geolocation, cultural background of society, etc.) within which information is being displayed, the *application context* (e.g. team awareness, event notification, time series monitoring, etc.) within which the IAS is used, the *environmental setting* (like home, transport, office, public places) where the IAS is installed, the extent to which individuals have the freedom of choice for a personal emotional expression (*personal aesthetic appeal*), and the *disruption free transition* in the visual appearance of color, light, smoothness, shininess, brightness, etc. The way how a certain IAS theme is chosen follows a user-centered design approach: While the theme is allowed to be chosen by the user, the symbols are derived as the result of a metaphor driven structured design process.

3.1 Categories of Metaphor

The main IAS design concern is the choice of a *theme* which (i) meets the aesthetic appreciation of the user, and (ii) at the same time provides sufficient degree of metaphoric freedom within the contained *symbols*, to be able to encode the information to be delivered with the display. Previous work [24][27][32] has followed a creative artistic approach to design *themes* and *symbols*, and present the result "as is" to the user (see Table 1).

In an approach based on information visualization principles, an analysis of (i) which information is to be displayed, (ii) how it is displayed, depicted and conveyed, and (iii) how *external representations* (information conveyed using an artifact of some kind) are related to *internal representations* (information maintained in the human mind) precedes the design activities. From theories of visual perception it is well known, that the process of perceiving information visually performs in two phases:

(i)   in the first phase, the *preattentive phase*, low level features are extracted from the raw images projected to the retina in highly parallel, neural processing schemes. This phase detects features like size, shape, orientation, proximity, curvature, color, shading or texture very fast, way before we are attentive to them or aware of them. These basic features can carry meaning, and are then called *sensory symbols*. A box embracing a set of dots, or a line connecting two areas to indicate connectivity would be simple examples. Sensory symbols, require no learning, are stable across cultures, time and individuals.

(ii)   in the second phase, the *interpretative phase,* objects and relations are identified and related to previously stored information in working memory, one by one. This comparatively slow second phase is goal-driven, i.e. we attend to the information that is most relevant for our goals. This phase detects features of arbitrary kind, so called *arbitrary symbols*. They only carry meaning by convention, they must be learned, are easy to forget, are embedded in culture and applications, and can evolve (e.g. "emoticons" within email cultures). Arbitrary symbols can be overlearned, even to the extent that they seem like sensory symbols (e.g. the number digits 0 – 9 to everybody has been learned so well, that they are perceived just like sensory symbols. For most of us it would be impossible to relearn their meaning).

Most visualizations, or visual impressions fall along the continuum between sensory and arbitrary symbols, and (visual) metaphors build on the preattentive and interpretative recognition of symbols. Metaphors used in human computer interfaces for example, like "folders" or "trash" for document management, ground on arbitrary symbols that have been learned in the office domain, and are exploited in the computer domain. Generally, (interface) metaphors combine visuals, actions and procedures in order to exploit specific knowledge that users already have of other domains. In some sense the "borrow" ideas from the familiar in order to understand the unfamiliar. Consequently, the perception of a metaphor is closely coupled to an individuals knowledge and experience. Metaphors are specific to the individual.

This is one more reason to involve the user of an IAS already at the time of *theme* choice. Selecting a theme according to the users appreciation, not influenced or affected by any constraints rooted in design, implementation or technology, preserves the chance of a systematic exploitation of knowledge the user already has wrt. the visual context of the theme. Sometimes it is even necessary to change or reconfigure the theme at runtime, due to e.g. learning based changes, cultural changes, or even changes in the target audience.

The second step is then to identify *symbols* contained in that chosen theme, so as to be able to exploit the mechanism of preattentive and interpretative recognition. Having the user participate in the symbol identification process helps to reflect his knowledge, and thus his perceptual aptitude for metaphors (We are guided by the assumption that symbols favored by the user will implicitly reflect a better metaphoric perception of the connotated information, but do not have empirical evidence for this yet.). Symbol identification hence is a process at the confluence of respecting user preference and adhering to visualization principles. In order to steer this process, we have developed guidelines for identifying concepts in themes and symbols along (i) *color*, (ii) *space*, (iii) *shape*, (iv) *abstraction*, (v) *dimension* and (vi) *orientation*. We discuss them based on artwork which might be considered to serve as themes (see Fig. 6 – 10).

Color. An intuitive category of metaphor is *color*. Mapping data values to color attributes (*color coding*) is a well understood from scientific visualization. For IADs, the metaphoric expressiveness of color is of interest. As for example wrt. *sense*, blue is perceived as hard, red as rough, yellow as soft and pink as very soft; wrt. *temperature*, blue is perceived as neutreal, red as spicy or crisp, green as bitter, yellow as sweet, pink as sweetish; wrt. *taste* blue is perceived as hard, red as rough, yellow as soft and pink as very soft; and wrt. *hazard* green is perceived as safe, blue as uncritical, yellow as slightly critical, pink as critical, red as dangerous.

An example of a *theme* illustrating in an impressive way combinations of ranges of color is given in Fig. 6. The theme could serve as an awareness display for a workteam (one square per team member). Variations of the color appearance of one team member (Fig. 6, *right top*) could encode "mood" (neutral, happy, bitter), or the

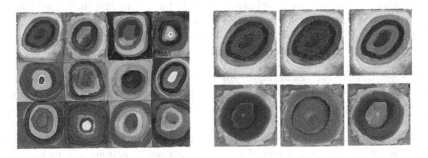

Fig. 6. Wassily Kandinsky (1886-1944), Squares with Concentric Circle, 26.3x29.3 in, http://www.www.artexpression.com (*left*), and a set of symbol variations (*right*)

agenda of a work day (Fig.6, *right bottom*) (research=red, teaching=green, administration=blue). Color is an effective, yet problematic category of metaphor. It can be percieved very differently in different situations by different people. It is less feasible for representing quantitative data, but more for categorization or the expression of emotions.

Space. When forming images, our mind separates *figure* and *background*. Figure is often described as the "*useful field of view*" (UFOV), i.e. the area from which useful visual information can be extracted in a single glance. It is roughly oval shaped, and varies in size depending on information density and cognitive load. It is the part of an image which we attend to, while background gives context. The more variation the background has, the more difficult it is to perceive and interpret figure (visual clutter).

 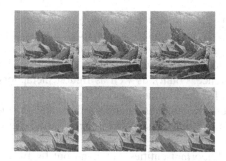

Fig. 7. Caspar David Friedrich (1774-1840), Das Eismeer (The Arctic Sea) – "Die gescheiterte Hoffnung", (1823/24), oil on canvas, 96,7x126,9 cm, Hamburger Kunsthalle, http://www.hamburger-kunsthalle.de (*left*), and figure / background variation (*right*)

An example of a theme encouraging to alter the perception of *space* by varying the amount of detail in the figure (*right top*), or in the background (*right bottom*) is given in Fig.7. Aside figure/background variation, the scene in the painting encourages to alter the perception of *space* by subtle modifications of depth cues like shading, lighting and shadowing, occlusion, attenuation, changes in perspective of parts of the scene, stereopsis, accommodation and texturing. Candidates for IAD symbols are the floe peak for expressing e.g. dynamic information (at the viewers focus) by varying the shading and lighting, the distant peak for less prominent information items by varying e.g. the attenuation from visible to totally invisible, the chunks of ice to express information by modifying their texture and relative position, and maybe the nuggets to indicate discrete value information by e.g. adding and removing individual nuggets of different size, shape and color to the scene.

Shape and Abstraction. Promising strategies driving the selection of IAD *symbols* are identification of *shapes* and form in a theme that offer certain degrees of freedom for harmonious variation, and the identification of abstract or figural elements that can support variations of the degree of *abstraction* used for information visualisation. A well interpreted piece of artwork expressing these categories of metaphor is given in Fig. 8. While the female character in the painting is coated in a texture with strictly

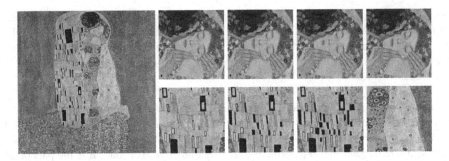

Fig. 8. Gustav Klimt (1862-1918), Der Kuß, (1907/08), oil on canvas, 180x180cm, Österreich-ische Galerie, Wien, http://www.belvedere.at (*left*), and IAD symbol variations (*right*)

curly, circle like and roundly ornament *shapes*, the male character is coated in a strictly rectangular, geometric and squarish ornament shaped texture. Both abstract ornament (color, size, proximity, inclusion, alignment, direction, horizontal, vertical, inside, outside, cyclic, spin, connection, hole, crack, fissure, boundary, presence, absence, count), as well as figural metaphors can be attempted based on this theme. As for the abstract concepts, spatial areas of the two coats in the theme allow to express the amount (number of rectangles (Fig.8, *right bottom*, *left* to *right:* ranging from "few", to "some", to "many"), number of curls) or the proportion of information entities.

Important entities can stand out by further size and color coding, selective omission can simplify visualisations, and spatial arrangement of ornaments can help to better organize information. As for the more figural concepts, connotating information into the facial expression of characters appears as a very rich, yet intuitively perceivable symbolic instrument. Much like *Chernoff Faces*, which are motivated to visualize multivariate data in the shape of a human face (eyes, eyebrows, nose, mouth etc. represent values of variables by their shape, size, placement and orientation), the figural face in the theme could encode multivariate information entities. With the realism of this painting, the idea behind using faces for data visualisation because humans can easily recognize faces and notice small changes therein without difficulty, is even enforced (Fig.8, *right top*, *left* to *right* shows indicative lip and eyebrow variation).

Scale and Dimension. The metaphor categories identified so far are less suitable for the encoding of information entities that represent quantitative data, given e.g. in scalar, vector or tensor format. For visualisations that need to reflect information on a metric scales (discrete or continuous), the relative "distance" of information entities (translation, rotation, scaling), their relative importance as perceived facts, or the size of the information domain as such, the identification of symbols supporting the metaphor categories of *scale* and *dimension* are important. By *metaphor of scale* we refer to learned symbols on standards of measurement or estimation (like a ruler), or an entity of reference by which to gauge or rate. A *metaphor of dimension* is based upon properties of space, or an extension in a given direction. A *theme*, which due to its strictly geometric composition (straight lines, segments, string cords, rulers, tickers)

Fig. 9. Rudolf Hausner (1914-1995), Adam maßstäblich, (1972), 54,0x55,5cm, signed, http://www.artnet.com (*left*), and symbol variations (*right*).

bears a rich variety of IAD symbol candidates is given in Fig. 9. The variation of the number, spatial position (in the front, in the back) and relative height of the pillar meters in Fig. 9 (*right*) intuitively encode quantitative data like economy indexes or stock analysts ratios.

Activity. IADs used for the purpose of delivering awareness in families, work teams, interest groups or discussion forums demand for "at-a-glance" perceivable symbols of the activities of individuals. Fig. 10 identifies symbol candidates from an activity awareness IAD. The level of attentiveness to a shared electronic document is encoded in the raising and lowering of the head (Fig. 10, *right upper*), the availability for interaction is encoded into body postures (think, turned away, ready for discussion) (Fig. 10, *right lower*). As a drawing study with detailed figure only for some parts of the human body, the theme in an outstanding way supports UFOV, highlighting indicative body postures as attentional spotlights.

Fig. 10. Leonardo da Vinci (1452-1519), Study of nude men, pen and ink on paper, http://www.www.kunstkopie.de (*left*), and a set of symbol candidates (*right*, (a), (b), (c), (d))

3.2 Aesthetic Appreciation

Having proposed a participatory design process, and having developed a series of design metaphors, all implemented in our *IAS software framework,* we have again tested the aesthetic appreciation of our metaphors against the ones proposed and used in previous work.

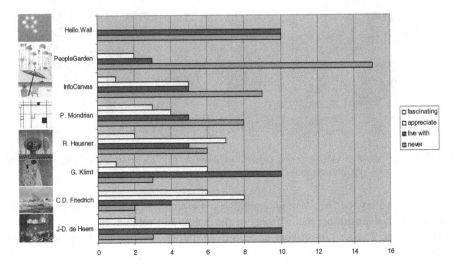

Fig. 11. Aesthetic appreciation of Informative Art themes: then and now

Involving the same group as with the survey in 2.3, we now asked to respond on the metaphors and overall appreciation of ambient displays levels (1) "I would never want to have such a display", (2) "I don't like it, but I could try to live with", (3) "I would appreciate to have such display" and (4) "Wow, this is fascinating!". The results of the survey are summarized in Fig. 11. Surprisingly enough, the traditional styles of ambient displays like the Hello.Wall, PeopleGarden and InfoCanvas do not find much of aesthetic appreciation, PeopleGarden not at all. Well known artwork, like G. Klimt, The Kiss, is considered mouldy due to its worldwide popularity, but people would accommodate to it, given it is installed. To some extent the same is true for de Heem's Stilleven, and Redström's Mondrian metaphor. The most fascinating impressions are delivered by monumental artwork that does not have broad popularity, and somehow reflects a very personal expression of taste (C.D. Friedrich's Arctic Sea). The style of "Phantastic Realism" ("Wiener Schule des Phantastischen Realismus") by R. Hausner – which was intentionally chosen as a compromise combining stylistic elements from fine arts and photo realism with pictorial elements from engineering (meters, scales, strings, etc.) – turned out to polarize appreciation: about the same amount of respondents strictly declined and appreciated the artwork as an ambient display – a minority was fascinated.

3.3   IAS Software Framework

We have developed a versatile IAS software framework, which implements sensor data acquisition, context recognition, data aggregation and dissemination, privacy preserving data filtering, as well as a 2D/3D graphics engine to dynamically control the visual appearance the IAS display (Fig. 12).

The *Theme Control Engine* as container dynamically manages the life cycle of a symbols, which are implemented as individual software components (*Symbol Control*

Engines, SCEs), packaged in OSGi bundles. An SCE is responsible to visualize an information entity associated with a spatial (2D or 3D) subregion of the whole theme, by transforming changes in the data in real time into visual effects concerning this subregion.

The framework is implemented on top of an OSGi runtime environment (OSCAR), involves physical sensors like noise, temperature, light and humidity sensors, accelerometers and gyroscopes, WLAN and GPS positioning systems, RFID based identification sensors, card readers, HR frequency and even ECG sensors. Soft sensors are processes collecting data from the Internet via http, from computational processes (exe, dll) or from special purpose monitoring systems. A complex context analysis subsystem handles multi sensor data fusion, context extraction and context prediction. High end graphics components (OGRE 3D, Flash) implement the dynamics of themes and symbols. An XML based configuration management tool allows to "hot-plug" sensors, or to "hot-swap" themes and symbols at runtime. The IAS software framework is fully functional and has been used in an activity awareness application "connecting" dislocated workteams from four different continents.

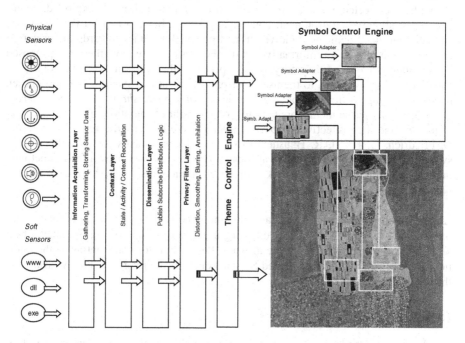

Fig. 12. The IAS SF collects information of interest via hardware or software sensors (Acquisition Layer), identifies the context (Context Layer), distributes context information according to a publish subscribe principle (Dissemination Layer), and restrains it with respect to privacy policies (Privacy Filtering Layer). The *theme* control engines generates the visual appearance from the chosen *theme*, the *symbol* control engine encodes information into symbol visuals (not necessarily rectangular), which are overlayed into the *theme*.

4 Conclusion

"Informative Art" in one of its earliest appearances was considered as computer augmented pieces of art or computer generated artwork, turning an aesthetical object into an information display [24]. The aim of such displays to deliver information through visuals that are quickly and easily perceived while doing other tasks [19], i.e. provide users with information considered relevant at arbitrary points of work or living engagement, but at the periphery of human (visual) perception [14] is better coined by the more recent term "ambient information system" [29]. In any way, monitoring such a display should cause minimal distraction from the user's focus of attention.

Several contributions have appeared in the literature, addressing the issue of encoding information of interest in an *aesthetical pleasing* style, using the one or the other design driven approach. In most of these cases, the design work conducts information visualisation concepts, display strategies, as well as decorative, aesthetic and artistic composing, but not involving the user beforehand. Typically, the user is consulted once the informative art display system is ready at hand, and concerned for usability engineering studies ("I-throw-it-out-there-and-watch" design paradigm).

We have collected evidence, that users, based on their cultural background, cognitive skills, situative environment, contextual settings, but most of all their aestehtic appreciation, have dedicated, individual and personal attitudes towards the preferred overall appearance of an informative art display system. We have therefore proposed a *metaphor* driven, participatory design process, that guarantees sovereignity of choice of a display *theme* to the user. Our process identifies *symbols* out of a chosen *theme* according to the metaphor categories *color, space, shape, abstraction, scale* and *dimension*. These metaphors help to find the right connotation of the information of interest and the respective *symbols* of a *theme*. We have used original artwork (C. D. Friedrich, G. Klimt, R. Hausner) to support our arguments for metaphor driven symbol selection. Our informative art design process is support by a fully functional informative art software framework, within which many display systems have already been built.

Acknowledgements. I wish to thank the anonymous reviewer for rigorously commenting on this work (and by that throwing a whole new light on it), Bernadette Emsenhuber for preparing some of the artwork, Petra Thon for contributing to the questionnair, and my SS2007 Embedded Systems class for helping as a survey group and the lively interactions.

References

1. Ames, M., Bettadapur, C., Dey, A.K., Mankoff, J.: Healthy Cities Ambient Displays. Extended Abstracts of UbiComp (2003),
   http://guir.berkeley.edu/pubs/ubicomp2003/healthycities.pdf
2. De Guzman, E.S.: M.S. Thesis: Presence Displays: Tangible Peripheral Displays for Promoting Awareness and Connectedness, University of California, Berkeley (December 2004)
3. De Guzman, E.S., Yau, M., Gagliano, A., Park, A., Dey, A.K.: Exploring the design and use of peripheral displays of awareness information. In: CHI 2004. Extended Abstracts on Human Factors in Computing Systems, pp. 1247–1250. ACM Press, New York (2004)

4. Ferscha, A.: PERVASIVE 2004 opening address.
   http://www.pervasive2004.org/opening_ferscha.pdf
5. Ferscha, A.: Workspace Awareness in Mobile Virtual Teams. In: WETICE 2000. Proceedings of the 9th International Workshops on Enabling Technologies: Infrastructures for Collaborative Enterprises, pp. 272–277. IEEE Computer Society Press, Los Alamitos (2000)
6. Ferscha, A., Emsenhuber, B., Schmitzberger, H., Thon, P.: Aesthetic Awareness Displays. Advances in Pervasive Computing 2006. In: Adjunct Proceedings of the 4th International Conference on Pervasive Computing. books@ocg.at vol. 207, Austrian Computer Society (OCG), Vienna (2006)
7. Ferscha, A., Johnson, J.: Distributed Interaction in Virtual Spaces. In: Proc. of the 3rd International WS on Distributed Interactive Simulation and Real Time Applications, IEEE Computer Society Press, Los Alamitos (1999)
8. Fogarty, J., Forlizzi, J., Hudson, S.E.: Aesthetic Information Collages: Generating Decorative Displays that Contain Information. In: UIST 2001. Proceedings of the 2001 ACM Symposium on User Interface Software and Technology, pp. 141–150. ACM Press, New York (2001)
9. Gutwin, C., Greensberg, S.: A Framework of Awareness for Small Groups in Shared-Workspace Groupware. Technical report 99-1, Department of Computer Science, University of Saskatchewan, Canada, http://www.cpsc.ucalgary.ca/grouplab/papers/
10. Heiner, J., Hudson, S., Tanaka, K.: The Information Percolator: Ambient Information Display in a Decorative Object. In: ACM Symp. on User Interface Software and Techn., pp. 141–148. ACM Press, New York (1999)
11. Ho-Ching, F.-W., Mankoff, J., Landay, J.A.: Can you see what I hear? The Design and Evaluation of a Peripheral Sound Display for the Deaf. Group for User Interface Research, Computer Science Division, University of Berkeley,
    http://guir.berkeley.edu/projects/ic2hear/Masters-final.pdf
12. Holmquist, L.E.: Evaluating the comprehension of ambient displays. In: CHI 2004. Extended Abstracts on Human Factors in Computing Systems, Vienna, Austria, ACM Press, New York (2004)
13. Hsieh, G., Mankoff, J.: Peripheral Displays Evaluation,
    http://www.cs.berkeley.edu/projects/io/peripheral_evaluation/
14. Ishii, H., Ullmer, B.: Tangible Bits: Towards Seamless Interfaces between People, Bits and Atoms. In: Proceedings of the Conference on Human Factors in Computing systems, pp. 234–241. ACM Press, New York (1997)
15. Mankoff, J., Dey, A.K.: From conception to design: a practical guide to designing ambient displays. In: Ohara, K., Churchill, E. (eds.) Public and Situated Displays, Kluwer, Dordrecht (2003),
    http://www.intel-research.net/Publications/Berkeley/072920031038_155.pdf
16. Mankoff, J., Dey, A.K., Hsieh, G., Kientz, J., Lederer, S., Ames, M.: Heuristic Evaluation of Ambient Displays. EECS Department, University of Berkeley, CA, USA, http://www.cs.berkeley.edu/projects/io/publications/660-mankoff.pdf Also: Proceedings of the SIGCHI Conference on Human Factors in Computing Systems, pp. 169–176. ACM Press, New York (2003)
17. Matthews, T., Dey, A.K., Mankoff, J., Carter, S., Rattenbury, T.: A toolkit for managing user attention in peripheral displays. In: UIST 2004. Proceedings of the 17th Annual ACM Symposium on User interface Software and Technology, Santa Fe, NM, USA, October 24-27, 2004, pp. 247–256. ACM Press, New York (2004)

18. Matthews, T., Rattenbury, T., Carter, S., Dey, A.K., Mankoff, J.: A Peripheral Display Toolkit. EECS Department, University of California, Berkeley Technotes, UCB//CSD-03-1258 (2003), http://www.eecs.berkeley.edu/Pubs/TechRpts/2003/CSD-03-1258.pdf

19. McCarthy, J.F., Costa, T.J., Huang, E.M., Tullio, J.: Defragmenting the organization: Disseminating community knowledge through peripheral displays. In: ECSCW. Workshop on Community Knowledge at the 7th European Conference on Computer Supported Cooperative Work, pp. 117–126 (2001)

20. Matthews, T.: Designing and Evaluating Glanceable Peripheral Displays, Technical Report UCB/EECS-2007-56, EECS Department, University of California, Berkeley (May 2007), http://www.eecs.berkeley.edu/Pubs/TechRpts/2007/EECS-2007-56.html

21. Miller, T., Stasko, J.: The InfoCanvas: information conveyance through personalized, expressive art. In: CHI 2001. Extended Abstracts on Human Factors in Computing Systems, pp. 305–306. ACM Press, New York (2001)

22. Mynatt, E., Rowan, J., Jacobs, A., Craighill, S.: Digital Family Portraits: Supporting Peace of Mind for Extended Family Members. In: Proceedings of the SIGCHI conference on Human factors in computing systems, pp. 333–340. ACM Press, New York (2001)

23. Prante, T., Stenzel, R., Röcker, C., Streitz, N., Magerkurth, C.: Ambient agoras: InfoRiver, SIAM, Hello. Wall. In: CHI 2004. Extended Abstracts on Human Factors in Computing Systems, Vienna, Austria, April 24-29, 2004, pp. 763–764. ACM Press, New York (2004)

24. Redström, J., Skog, T., Hallnäs, L.: Informative art: using amplified artworks as information displays. In: Proceedings of DARE 2000 on Designing Augmented Reality Environments, pp. 103–114. ACM Press, New York (2000)

25. Stasko, J., Doo, M., Dorn, B., Plaue, C.: Explorations and Experiences with Ambient Information Systems. In: Workshop at Pervasive 2007: Designing and Evaluating Ambient Information Systems. 5th International Conference on Pervasive Computing, Toronto, Canada, pp. 36–41 (2007)

26. Streitz, N., Magerkurth, C., Prante, T., Röcker, C.: From information design to experience design: smart artefacts and the disappearing computer. Interactions 12(4), 21–25 (2005)

27. Streitz, N.A., Nixon, P.: The Disappearing Computer. Guest Editors' Introduction to Special Issue. Communications of the ACM 48, 33–35 (2005)

28. Streitz, N.A., Rocker, C., Prante, T., Alphen, D.V., Stenzel, R., Magerkurth, C.: Designing Smart Artifacts for Smart Environments. Computer 38(3), 41–49 (2005)

29. Tomitsch, M., Kappel, K., Lehner, A., Grechenig, T.: Towards a Taxonomy for Ambient Information Systems. In: Workshop at Pervasive 2007: Designing and Evaluating Ambient Information Systems. 5th International Conference on Pervasive Computing, Toronto, Canada, pp. 42–47 (2007)

30. Vesna, V.: Bucky Beat: Buckminster Fuller, the Anticipatory Design Scientist, Foreshadows the Complex Persona of a Contemporary Media Artist. ArtByte, 1(3) (August/September 1998)

31. Walker, K.: Interactive and Informative Art. IEEE MultiMedia 10(1), 4–10 (2003)

32. Wisneski, C., et al.: Ambient Displays: Turning Architectural Space into an Interface between People and Digital Information. In: Streitz, N.A., Konomi, S., Burkhardt, H.-J. (eds.) CoBuild 1998. LNCS, vol. 1370, pp. 22–32. Springer, Heidelberg (1998)

33. Xiong, R., Donath, J.: PeopleGarden: creating data portraits for users. In: UIST 1999. Proceedings of the 12th annual ACM symposium on User interface software and technology, pp. 37–44. ACM Press, New York (1999)

User Centered Research in ExperienceLab

Boris de Ruyter, Evert van Loenen, and Vic Teeven

Philips Research Europe, HTC 34,
5656 AE Eindhoven, The Netherlands
{Boris.de.Ruyter,Evert.van.Loenen,Vic Teeven}@Philips.com

Abstract. With the introduction of the Ambient Intelligence vision, a shift from usability towards end user experience research has been proposed. Such experience research requires new methods and instruments beyond the traditional usability research labs. This paper describes the ExperienceLab infrastructure, its way of working and the lessons learned from using this infrastructure.

Keywords: User Centered Research, Ambient Intelligence, Experience research.

1 Introduction

The design of Ambient Intelligence (AmI) environments differs markedly from the design of classical single device systems. AmI environments introduce new options for services and applications, by focusing on the desired functionality, rather than on the devices traditionally needed for each individual function. The fact that the technology will be integrated in these environments introduces the need for novel interaction concepts that allow the user to communicate with their electronic environment in a natural way.

When aiming at user experiences, requirements engineering for AmI environments has to take a step beyond the development of scenarios and the translation of use cases into system requirements. System functionalities that generate true user experiences can be determined in a reliable way by exposing users to feasible prototypes that provide proofs of concept. These are called experience prototypes, and they can be developed by means of a user-centered design approach that applies both feasibility and usability studies in order to develop a mature interaction concept. More specifically, this means that laboratories are needed which contain infrastructures that support fast prototyping of novel interaction concepts and resemble natural environments of use. Moreover, these experience prototyping centers should also be equipped with an observation infrastructure that can capture and analyze the behavior of people who interact with the experience prototypes. Philips' ExperienceLab is an example of such an experience and application research facility. It combines feasibility and usability research into user-centric innovation, leading to a better understanding of (latent) user needs and the technologies that really matter from a user perspective [1].

B. Schiele et al. (Eds.): AmI 2007, LNCS 4794, pp. 305–313, 2007.

1.1 From Usability to User Experiences

Nowadays, the technological possibilities to enhance life are vast; to quote the prototypical engineer, "tell us what you want and we can make it". But, what do people really want? Once we better understand the needs and desires of people, the output of a structured idea generation process is expected to yield product or system concepts that show an increased potential to truly enhance our lives. In a first research and design phase, (latent) user needs are explored using various methods, such as focus groups, context mapping, ideation and scenario evaluations. Of course, such claims should be validated by evaluating the anticipated user benefits before a selection is made to bring certain concepts into a next research and design phase. In a next iteration cycle, more detailed user requirements need to be uncovered and fed into the generation and implementation of concrete design solutions. Next, the utility and usability of the proposed solutions can be checked by conducting carefully planned user tests. This iterative process which is carried out by multi-disciplinary teams and in which user involvement plays a crucial role is called User – Centered Research [2].

Throughout the User Centered Research cycle there is a strong involvement from end – users based on studies in *context* (e.g. context mapping studies), in the *laboratory* (e.g. the ExperienceLab) and in the *field* (e.g. longitudinal field trials). While the context studies are focused on the initial requirements for AmI environments, the laboratory studies will focus on the end –user's acceptance and the usability of the proposed AmI prototypes. Through field studies the longer term effects of the AmI prototypes will be investigated.

ExperienceLab, as an instrument for User – Centered Research, is designed to become the place where researchers and designers can team up with end-users to realize a shared and tangible vision of the future of electronic systems. Given the application domain of AmI environments there is a need to extend the traditional utility measures (such as effectiveness and efficiency) towards user experiences. The real user benefit of AmI environments will be found in their impact in terms of user experiences they generate. For this, the ExperienceLab offers a complete environment for the conceptualization, implementation and evaluation of Ambient Intelligence systems that bring true user experiences.

2 ExperienceLab

ExperienceLab offers a unique environment, both physically and intellectually, for researchers and their partners inside and outside Philips to give concrete form to the Ambient Intelligence vision. By developing and integrating advanced technologies in the area of Ambient Intelligence, ExperienceLab, currently consisting of a HomeLab, ShopLab and CareLab, is an innovation center for the development of novel consumer products and services, and it therefore makes a substantial contribution to the implementation of the Philips strategy in the domain of Lifestyle and Wellbeing.

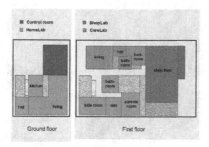

Fig. 1. The ExperienceLab floorplan (note: service areas surrounding the ExperienceLab are not labeled)

2.1 HomeLab

The HomeLab is build as a two-stock house with a living, a kitchen, two bedrooms, a bathroom and a study. At a first glance, the home does not show anything special, but a closer look reveals the black domes at the ceilings that are hiding cameras and microphones. Equipped with 34 cameras throughout the home, HomeLab provides behavioral researchers a perfect instrument for studying human behavior inside HomeLab. Adjacent to the Home there is an observation room.

When HomeLab started in 2001, one way mirrors were placed between the living and observation room. The idea was to have a direct view into the living. But time learned that observers preferred the camera images. The different viewing angels and possibility to zoom into details were reasons to abandon the mirrors. The observation room is equipped with four observation stations. Each station has a large high resolution flat screen showing a collection of six different images from the cameras in the house. The observer is free to choose which cameras he wants to use and what the pan, tilt and zoom position of every individual camera has to be. And he can route two of the roughly 30 available microphones to the left and right channel of his headphones. Each observer has an application running to feed the behavioral data to the storage system, synchronized to the video data. In the early days of HomeLab this setup was used in the real time situation. Four observers had a hard time to follow the progress of the experiment. Nowadays it is more common to first have the video data stored on the capture stations and do the behavioral data collection afterwards. Also events and sensor data are time-stamped and appended to the video data. This way of working is much more efficient and a single observer can collect all the relevant data.

Broadband Internet facilities enable various ways to connect parts of the HomeLab infrastructure to the Philips High Tech Campus network or even to the outside world. A wireless Local-Area Network (LAN) offers the possibility to connect people in HomeLab without running cables. However, if cables are required, double floors and double ceilings provide nice hiding places. Corridors, adjacent to the rooms in HomeLab, accommodate the equipment that researchers and developers need to realize and control their systems and to process and render audio and video signals for the large flat screens in HomeLab. Light control systems (LON and amBX) can be accessed by the researchers and offer their prototypes the possibility to affect the light settings in the rooms.

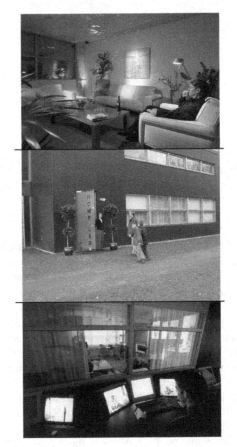

Fig. 2. HomeLab: user centered design environment for advanced studies in multimedia concepts for the home

2.2 ShopLab

The ShopLab research program builds on the insight, that shopping itself has become an important leisure activity for many people, and that flexible atmospheres are needed to enhance shopping experiences. On the other hand many retail chains want to maintain a clear house style for branding reasons.

This introduces the challenge of combining these two major aspects. One approach to this, studied in ShopLab, is that one atmosphere design will be sent to all stores and slightly adapted there to meet local conditions. With the introduction of solid state (LED) lighting, a wide range of new options to create such atmospheres using color and dynamic effects is becoming available. However, tuning these atmospheres requires controlling several hundred lamp settings, introducing a complex overall control challenge. Another approach studied to enhance the shopping experience is the introduction of interactivity, in the form of interactive shop windows, interactive signage and reactive spots. Adaptation of these shop atmospheres also requires input

Fig. 3. ShopLab: augmented environment with advanced vision and lighting concepts for retail studies

from smart environments that detect people's presence and product interests while they are in or near a shop.

The ShopLab is used extensively to perform user studies, both with retailers and with end-users (shoppers). By involving these users in all phases of the design process, including the evaluation of the experience prototypes, important insights in the actual experiences of users are obtained early on in the development process.

2.3 CareLab

This CareLab resembles a one-bedroom apartment for seniors and is equipped with a rich sensor network to study the contextual settings in which people will use the health and wellness applications.

Fig. 4. CareLab: realistic aware environment with advanced sensing and reasoning capabilities to study consumer health and wellness propositions in a home context

The sensor information is processed and combined to extract higher-order behavioral patterns that can be related to activities and states, such as the presence of people, the state of the home infrastructure, etc. With the CareLab it is possible to explore at an early stage the user's acceptance for these solutions and to assess the interactive and functional qualities of these solutions before deploying these into field settings. Results will be used to improve applications of innovative technologies, to eliminate imperfections and to explore new applications.

2.4 Infrastructure

The possibility to study user experiences of test participants during their stay in ExperienceLab is one of its primary functions. A tailor-made control system has been developed in-house to collect and analyze observational data. The system controls the cameras and the routing of the video and audio signals. Human activities, postures, facial expressions, social interactions and user-system interactions can be recorded and digitally stored to study patterns, trends and relationships.

3 Studying User – System Interaction

When setting up an experiment in ExperienceLab, the researcher designs a coding scheme for the observation session. A coding scheme lists all prototypical behaviors that are expected to be observable during the session. These behaviors should be structured as an orthogonal classification system: during the classification of behavior it should not be possible to classify one behavior in more than one category. The observers mark the occurrence of these behaviors during the ExperienceLab session by means of pressing keys on a keyboard. Additional, more and more behavioral events are registered automatically through the use of sensors.

Once the coding scheme is developed it is saved into the scoring system. Very similar to questionnaires, the coding schemes are standardized and reused. For example, coding schemes for problem solving behavior or user-system interaction in voice controlled environments have been developed and reused over several experimental sessions.

If applicable, a detailed user profile for test participants is established in collaboration with a consumer marketing intelligence department. The user profile is then provided to a recruitment agency for test participant recruitment. As a rule these participants are externally recruited to not have any affiliation with Philips as such affiliation could influence test results. Depending on the focus of the research question a test methodology is designed. If longitudinal data collection is needed we setup field trials during which the experimental systems are installed into the homes of end-users.

Data analysis can consist of a simple frequency analysis up to a sophisticated data mining analysis for finding hidden patterns in the data set [4]. For this ExperienceLab is equipped with a software tool capable of detecting repeated patterns that are hidden to observers and very hard or impossible to detect with other available methods (Fig. 5). It is particularly suitable for analyzing behavioral data.

This tool is able to detect patterns that are obscured by other events, and finds patterns that no form of frequency count, lag sequential or time series analysis can identify. As such, it is an effective way to detect patterns in user-system interaction [3] and to identify the precursors or consequences of specific behavioral events. This

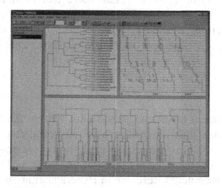

Fig. 5. Pattern analysis of behavioral data

tool has been used extensively in studies of human communication, spoken dialogues, gestures, protocol analysis, etc.

4 Lessons Learned

Since the opening of ExperienceLab in 2001, there are several lessons learned with respect to the use of the ExperienceLab.

1. *Real-time observation is less important, off-line scoring is preferred.* When equipping the ExperienceLab with observation tools, it was assumed that researchers would code observations in real-time. However, over the years we have learned that off-line scoring after the experiments is preferred. This has a consequence for the way data is collected and made available for scoring since now researchers need portable solutions and export the observational data from the ExperienceLab system.

2. *Developing good coding schemes is as much effort as developing a questionnaire.* Coding schemes provide an extensive classification of potential observable behavior. This coding scheme is used to code the recorded behavior. Developing good coding schemes takes time and reuse of these coding schemes (like for questionnaires) is desired.

3. *New methods and instruments to measure the subjective user experience in an objective way are needed.* Although the user experience is by nature subjective, there is a need to capture and analyze user experiences by means of objective methods.

4. *ExperienceLab is a catalyst for improving technology transfer into the business.* Traditionally, research results are communicated through scientific publications and presentations. Over the years ExperienceLab has proven to be a very effective communication tool within a large corporate environment. Although the original goal of the ExperienceLab was to support usability and feasibility research, there is a need to reserve capacity for demonstration and dissemination events.

5. *Having a support team is essential when operating an ExperienceLab.* Since the opening of the ExperienceLab there has been a permanent software engineering team available for technology integration and maintenance of the infrastructure. Similarly, there is a need for a team of behavioral scientists to guide the empirical research in ExperienceLab.

5 Conclusions

The design and assessment of interactive systems, that are targeted to be introduced into the market within a timeframe of five to ten years, remains a methodological challenge. Instruments such as the ExperienceLab provide research a powerful tool for testing early user acceptance and usability of futuristic AmI propositions.

Challenges for User Centered Research in ExperienceLab involve the development of innovative methodologies and tools for data collection and data analysis. As more automated data collection techniques (e.g. sensors) are becoming available there will be a need for more suitable data analysis techniques to make sense out of the rich datasets that will be collected in AmI environments. The use of the T-patterns techniques has given some very promising results into the analysis of complex behavioral patterns as collected in AmI environments.

Although lots of data can be collected through observational techniques, the challenge of collecting data on subjective user experiences remains. Today we are using standardized questionnaires to assess the user experience that is subjective by nature. The future challenge will be to deploy psychophysiological techniques to complement or even automate the assessment of subjective user experiences.

References

1. Aarts, E., Eggen, B.: Ambient Intelligence Research in HomeLab. Neroc Publishers, Eindhoven, The Netherlands (2002)
2. de Ruyter, B.: User Centred Design. In: Aarts, E., Marzano, S. (eds.) The New Everyday: Vision on Ambient Intelligence, 010 Publishers, Rotterdam, The Netherlands (2003)
3. http://www.noldus.com/site/content/files/case_studies/pu_usab_ruyter.pdf
4. Magnusson, M.S.: Hidden real-time patterns in intra- and inter-individual behavior: description and detection. European Journal of Psychological Assessment 12, 112–123 (1996)

Enhancing the Shopping Experience
with Ambient Displays:
A Field Study in a Retail Store

Wolfgang Reitberger[1], Christoph Obermair[1], Bernd Ploderer[2],
Alexander Meschtscherjakov[1], and Manfred Tscheligi[1]

[1] ICT&S Center, University of Salzburg
Sigmund-Haffner-Gasse 18, 5020 Salzburg, Austria
{wolfgang.reitberger,christoph.obermair,alexander.meschtscherjakov,
manfred.tscheligi}@sbg.ac.at
[2] Department of Information Systems, The University of Melbourne
111 Barry Street, Carlton, Victoria 3010, Australia
berndp@pgrad.unimelb.edu.au

Abstract. This paper discusses the prototypical implementation of an ambient display and the results of an empirical study in a retail store. It presents the context of shopping as an application area for Ambient Intelligence (AmI) technologies. The prototype consists of an ambient store map that enhances the awareness of customer activity. The results of our study indicate potentials and challenges for an improvement of the shopping experience with AmI technologies. Based on our findings we discuss challenges and future developments for applying AmI technologies to shopping environments.

Keywords: ambient displays, field study, awareness, shopping experience, shopping environments, retail store.

1   Introduction

We are investigating and enhancing the shopping experience in real life. For this purpose we chose to equip a retail store with ambient intelligence (AmI) technologies – especially ambient displays – in order to create a new shopping experience. Usually researchers try to improve the online shopping experience to compensate for what is missing compared to shopping experiences in "real shops". Our approach is to enhance the shopping experience by merging the advantages provided by online shops with the benefits of shops in the real world. Our application is an ambient store map, which integrates the awareness of the activity of other customers, a feature that was previously limited to online shopping, with other qualities of retail shops such as sensual perception or social interaction. In order to research our application we deployed a prototype in a retail store where we conducted a three-day field study. We report our findings from the field and discuss their implications for the design of AmI applications for shopping environments.

B. Schiele et al. (Eds.): AmI 2007, LNCS 4794, pp. 314–331, 2007.

The paper starts with a background on ambient displays and then leads to a discussion of the context of shopping, including shopping experience and environments. We then present an overview of our study including the method and the prototype. The last chapters discuss our findings and conclusions.

2   Background

The aim of our research is to investigate the potentials of ambient displays to enhance the shopping experience in real life. Our focus is on interactive aspects that convey potentials for an enhancement of the shopping experience through interactive technology. There has been considerable research in the usability of websites [1] and online shopping systems [2,3], but only a few field studies – with "real shoppers" in "real shops" – have been conducted.

2.1   Ambient Displays

Mark Weiser's vision of ubiquitous computing [4] and its follow-up concept ambient intelligence (AmI) [5] describe the pervasion of the everyday world with digital technology. This enables computing systems to anticipate the user's needs and to support the user in fulfilling these needs. AmI is embedded into the environment of the users and adapts to their requirements and reacts to their presence. It took several years for interaction designers to cope with the major challenges that unfolded with the dawn of ambient intelligence. Finally interaction concepts like ambient displays or implicit interaction were born.

The term *ambient display* was coined by Wisneski et al. [6]. Their work was inspired by preceding research from the mid-nineties. It's two main influences are calm computing [7] and tangible user interfaces [8]. Ambient displays integrate digital information into the physical environment, manifesting themselves as ambient media, i.e. "subtle changes in form, movement, sound, color, smell, temperature, or light" [6].

The main purpose of ambient displays is to present information in the periphery of the users' attention, in order to keep them aware of certain aspects which are of relevance for them. Changes of such relevant aspects will affect the ambient display, and consequently attract the center of the users' attention. Following this idea, many different types of ambient displays (for many different purposes) have been proposed since then, e.g. [9,10,11].

There is also a second meaning for *ambient display*. As display screen technologies rapidly evolved in terms of size and cost in the past few years, it became feasible to deploy them not only on desktops but anywhere in a user's surrounding, e.g. [12,13]. This second kind of ambient displays don't necessarily operate peripherally, but are rather intended as information and communication technologies, i.e. as substitutes for todays desktop computers.

Nevertheless, the focus of our work lies on ambient screen technologies, which provide information implicitly and peripherally.

Designing Ambient Media. Due to the peripheral nature of ambient displays, the way users interact with them is quite different from traditional interfaces: "Ambient display users are passive in obtaining information from a display. Users do not *use* the displays as they would use computers; they *perceive* the displays" [14]. This is why Mankoff et al. adapted Nielsen's heuristics [15] for the domain of ambient displays, providing not only hints for evaluating ambient displays but also for designing them. Their ambient heuristics cover criteria such as *information design, aesthetics,* or *unobtrusiveness,* which are of high importance for the success of an ambient display.

Moreover, Dey & De Guzman [16] recently described a user-centered design process for building ambient displays. They successfully designed two presence awareness displays by conducting contextual inquiries, cultural probing, focus groups, and a field study.

Implicit Interaction. According to Schmidt [17] implicit inputs are "actions and behaviors of humans, which are done to achieve a goal and are not primarily regarded as interaction with a computer, but captured, recognized and interpreted by a computer system as input". Implicit output is "output of a computer that is not directly related to an explicit input and which is seamlessly integrated with the environment and the task of the user". This means that an AmI environment reacts to input which is not explicitly entered by the user, but is given by the users' context.

This is important in terms of unobtrusive technology which is able to support people in their tasks and needs. As we want to enhance the "real life" shopping experience on the one hand side, we mustn't oblige shop customers to adapt to something completely new in an already familiar environment. Therefore, such an enhancement has to be deployed unobtrusively without affecting people's habits.

Awareness. Dourish & Bellotti define awareness as "understanding of the activities of others, which provides a context for your own activity" [18]. They further argue that "awareness information is always required to coordinate group activities". A rather similar notion of awareness was given by Wisneski et al. [6]: "Awareness is the state of knowing about the environment in which you exist; about your surroundings, and the presence and activities of others. Awareness is essential in collaboration to coordinate the activities in a shared workspace."

AmI technologies such as Telemurals have been used to foster interaction between users and serve as a social catalysts [19]. The Telemurals connect users in remote spaces by giving them mutual awareness through a video representation on an ambient screen.

McCarthy et al. [20] discuss three applications of ambient displays. *UniCast* is geared at individual users in their offices and can peripherally display information that is of interest to the user but not urgent. *OutCast* extends this concept and is directed towards co-workers in the vicinity of the users office. *GroupCast* follows a different approach and aims to foster social interaction between users in the workplace. It can identify people nearby and display content according to their personal interest. The goal is that people with similar interests might start a conversation about a shared topic.

Brignull et al. [21] see the issues of social embarrassment as one of the main obstacles preventing people from interacting with public ambient displays. They suggest to overcome this issue by designing the application in a way that encourages users to easily change between different states of awareness. The users should cross the threshold to focal awareness and further to participation and back again easily, without becoming self-conscious.

Awareness is a concept, which can also be found in many online shops. One example is to recommend products which might be of interest for you due the fact that many other customers also bought a similar combination of products. Another example is the concept of co-shopping: a certain product gets cheaper and cheaper, when there are more people who are willing to buy this product.

Cues in the Environment. Considering organization and coordination in natural systems (e.g. insect colonies) the common principle of *cues in the environment* has been derived as a design guideline for AmI [22,23]. In natural systems these cues are environmental context factors, which are collectively generated by a group of individuals (e.g. pheromone trails of ants, waiting lines at bee hives). These individuals are not creating these cues explicitly through a conscious action but rather implicitly through their behavior. Due to the evolutionary pressure, these cues are simple but yet efficient. They coordinate the group behavior and lead to the emergence of a new quality: collective intelligence [24].

These cues are – like ambient displays – perceived peripherally. Thus, ambient displays are a promising way to provide such cues for groups of humans, in order to raise the collective intelligence of the group. The idea is to raise the users' awareness of their group and their environment in order to persuade them to behave in a more collectively intelligent manner. This can be achieved by manifesting information about relevant aspects peripherally in the users' surroundings, which would otherwise remain hidden from them.

In our research, we found the principle of *cues in the environment* to be promising way for enhancing the "real life" shopping experience. Our strategy for that purpose is to provide shop consumers with ambient information about the shop activities in order to achieve awareness about other consumers' activities. This information is of an implicit nature, since it can be derived automatically by the AmI system. There is no need for the shop customers to perform any special actions when in the store.

The perCues framework [22,23], which emerged from the *cues in the environment* principle is of particular interest. This framework lays the foundation for applications that foster awareness in order to increase a groups' collective problem solving capability and coordinate collectively intelligent behavior. The process that underlies this framework consists of four steps that form a feedback loop: (1) acquire the current group state, (2) determining a way how to foster awareness for the current group state, (3) displaying an appropriate representation of the group state which motivates the group members to improve the

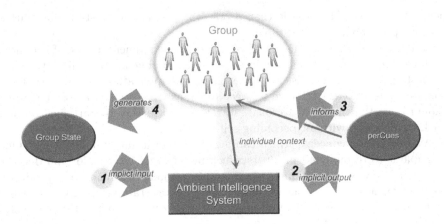

Fig. 1. The perCues framework: The underlying process consists of four steps, which utilize an ambient intelligent system to form a feedback loop in order to provide a collective benefit. The framework can also take into account a person's individual context by providing services, which lead to an individual benefit.

group state, and (4) the resulting group behavior which raises an updated group state (see Fig. 1).

The perCues framework considers not only the collective state of a group, but also takes a user's individual context into account. This way, a perCues application can primarily offer a high individual benefit, which is an incentive for using the application. The actions that lead to this individual benefit, have to be in line with the overall strategy of improving the group state. Thus, this actions also help to establish the goal of raising a more convinient group state.

2.2 Shopping Experience

As indicated above, the context of the user and the environment in which an ambient display is situated plays an important role for the design and the purpose of the ambient display. Especially the context of shopping in real life is a big challenge for designing an ambient display. In shopping malls advertisement messages are omnipresent. Therefore designers have to find a middle course between the ambient nature of ambient displays and the necessity not to be ignored within the flashy shopping world.

Online Shopping vs. Retail Shops. Online shopping has some advantages, which cannot be provided by shopping malls, like almost limitless choice or the convenience to buy something from wherever you are – presumed there is an internet access available – at any time you want. There is no waiting in checkout lines and you could get all the information you need instantly and you can get information about products not only from the retailers but also from other consumers. When you buy for instance a book at Amazon you are provided with information in which further products other consumers, who bought the same book, were interested in. The key question is, how can user generated information be distributed among consumers within the retail shopping context?

Underhill [25] claims that there are three important benefits which can only be offered in "real shops": (1) *sensory perception* like grasping, trying on and trying out, smelling and other sensual stimuli, (2) *immediate gratification*, and (3) *social interaction*. Therefore the shopping experience in retail stores is completely different to the experience shoppers get when buying in online stores. The question is, how we can use the advantages of online shopping in the real live shopping environments.

Industry Studies. There are currently investigations on the future of shopping by some major companies to enhance the consumers' experience throughout the purchasing process.

Cap Gemini Ernst & Young, Intel, Cisco Systems, and Microsoft have conducted a study in consumer buying behavior by surveying 2.500 consumers in five European countries [26]. Their findings show that only a positive shopping experience will determine the degree of customer satisfaction and loyalty. Consumers want retailers to help them to save time, make shopping easier and treat them with respect, honesty and fairness. The authors also state that technology like self-service applications or mobile devices for accessing information have a great potential to improve the shopping experience.

Philips Design Research presented a study on the Future of Shopping in 2003 [27]. It presents findings what changes technologies could bring to enhance the consumers' shopping experience. They predict that there will be a transfer of power and control from retailers to consumers. The technology opportunities like ubiquitous, ambient and pervasive computing will create a more intuitive, personalized, and empowered retail experience.

The advantages of AmI within the shopping environment can be experienced at the METRO Group Future Store in Rheinberg, Germany [28]. Commerce and industry can test technological solutions to make shopping more convenient for the customer. Utilized techniques are the Personal Shopping Assistant (PSA), a mini-computer mounted on the shopping trolley, information displays and Everywhere Displays as a guidance to the selected item, Smart Scales which automatically identify products the costumer is weighing, the RFID based Smart Shelf, and advanced Self Check-outs.

2.3   Related Work

Research in AmI has investigated how mobile shopping applications like personal digital assistants (PDAs) or shopping trolleys with mounted displays can improve the shopping experience in retail stores.

Newcomb et al. [29] have carefully examined people's grocery shopping habits by performing usability tests within the shopping environment and presented a handheld application to support shoppers. They noticed that it was key to perform observations and evaluations within the retail environment and they mentioned that situated interactions in the store, where the user utilizes the interface while shopping, became the greatest challenge for designing the interface.

Bohnenberger et al. [30] developed a decision-theoretic location-aware shopping guide and tested their prototype in a real shopping mall. They noted that shoppers using these intelligent shopping guides tend to focus on getting the products on their shopping list as quickly as possible which seems to discourage the kind of recreational and exploratory shopping that is often desired by shoppers and retailers.

Another interesting approach is to combine the benefits of the physical and digital worlds in a mixed-reality setting by targeting an in-store scene, augmented by a PDA and a shopping trolley with mounted display [31]. Whereas The PDA works as a communication channel between the shopper and the products. The focus lies on direct interaction and the concept of anthropomorphization (i.e. assigning inanimate objects human-like characteristics). The input modalities available to the users include speech, handwriting and gestures. As Newcomb [29] mention that the intrusive shopping environment could be crucial when interacting with devices in these ways.

Pinhanez and Podlaseck [32] apply their studies on frameless displays to shopping environment. They have designed and implemented projections within the retail environment to attract shoppers or inform them about special products. A similar approach is done in [33] where text and imagery projection into physical environments as well as vision systems and sensors for user interaction are used to design a retail store. In [34] the concept of Product Associated Display (PADs) is presented. The PADs provide visual feedback to users interacting with physical objects in a shopping scenario. Therefore the PADs are projected public displays which give information about the associated shopping items.

3   The Ambient Store Map Prototype

Some of the related approaches demonstrate how advantages of AmI can be applied to real live shopping environments. However, none of them exploits the wealth of information generated by other customers in a shop as it is done in online shopping systems. Our aim is not to present another ambient method to draw shoppers attention to products, but to make use of an ambient display to provide customers with information about the activity of other customers.

To assess the enhancement of the shopping experience in the fusion of "real life" and online shopping, we implemented an AmI application and deployed it in a retail store.

3.1   Design Process

During the iterative design process in which we explored the design space for our application, we decided to use a map metaphor to visualize the activity data. One reason for this decision was that a first visit to the mall where the application would be deployed showed that static maps were already used to give customers an overview of the mall and its shops. Additionally, by using a map we could build on the previous knowledge of the users and their existing experience with maps. The use of darker and lighter colors to indicate different levels of activity also follows the standard map conventions in other contexts, where e.g. darker colors indicate higher altitudes or higher temperatures. We then refined our design iteratively by informally testing it with users. The resulting design had a more organic feel than the first version and also blended in well with the rest of the store.

For the design of our AmI application we also considered the Ambient Display heuristics of Mankoff et al. [14]. These heuristics served as a meaningful reference during the design iterations. The most valuable heuristics were: *sufficient information design* (i.e. displaying "just enough" information, not too much and not too little); *consistent and intuitive mapping* (i.e. keeping cognitive load at a minimun); *aesthetic and pleasing design* (i.e. integrating the display into its intended setting seamlessly); *useful and relevant information* (i.e. providing helpful information for the users in the intended setting); and *"peripherality" of display* (i.e. designing the display for unobtrusiveness).

Nevertheless, not all of the heuristics were applicable to our application, e.g. *user control and freedom*, or *flexibility and efficiency of use*. The heuristics which correspond to our application are highlighted in Sec. 5.

3.2   Technical Prototype

Our AmI prototype measured and displayed the customer activity in the retail store where it was deployed. The store we chose, already had a wall-mounted 84-inch plasma screen which usually shows commercial spots. For the three days of our field study we utilized this display to provide the shop customers with awareness information which otherwise would have remained hidden for them.

The prototype was an (implicitly) interactive map view of the store. This map displayed the customer activity within the store (see Fig. 2). Its implicit nature draws from the fact that the customers didn't have to do anything special to provide the map with data. The customer activity was measured automatically by the AmI system.

The prototype was based on the perCues framework [22,23], which has been described in Sec. 2.1. By applying insights gained from the field of Collective Intelligence to the design of AmI environments, this framework lays the foundation for applications that increase a group's collective problem solving capability and coordinate collectively intelligent behavior. This is achieved by fostering awareness for the current situation as well as among the group members.

We adopted the perCues framework (see Fig. 1) for our study requirements and built the AmI prototype according to this framework (see Fig. 3). In the following paragraphs we will describe how the prototype works.

Customer Behavior. The customers in the retail store exhibit a certain behavior. They walk through the store and stay at certain shelves. We used a video camera with a wide angle lens which was mounted on the ceiling. This provided us with a video image which contained a good overview of most areas in the store. This video stream was the only "user-generated" input for our application.

Fig. 2. The AmI prototype deployed in a retail store. A large ambient screen shows a map view of the store which indicates areas of high customer activity within the store.

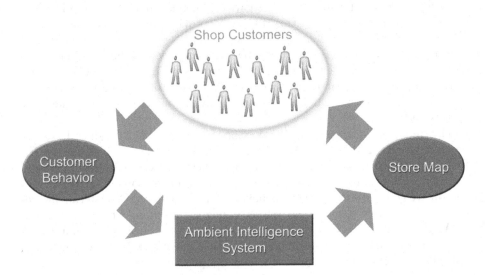

Fig. 3. The perCues framework applied to our AmI prototype. The customer behavior server serves as (implicit) input for an ambient intelligence. The information about customer behavior is visualized on a store map, which is displayed on the large ambient screen in the store. Customers being aware of the behavior of the other customers have the possibility to adapt their own behavior.

Ambient Intelligence System. Next, we derived the customer activity for distinct regions in the shop. For that purpose we defined a set of static regions in the store (e.g. in front of the shelves, between the shelves or in front the ambient screen) on the video camera image. When the system is active, a motion detection is applied to the video stream in real-time. This provides us with motion information for each single region, which is in fact an indicator for the activity in the corresponding region.

Store Map. The activity information derived in the previous step, is then visualized on the ambient screen in the retail store. The visualization is a map view of the store.

On the map we show the customer activity for each defined region. Thus, we had to map the previously defined regions on the camera image to the image of the store map. Fig. 4 shows a screenshot of the map view as it was displayed in the store. The intense red areas indicate regions of high activity. We also implemented the possibility to adjust the time-interval for displaying the activity: All the calculated activity information were stored in a database. Thus, we could either choose to display long-term customer activities (e.g. the activity within the past 60 minutes), or to use only a rather short time-interval (e.g. only the past 3 seconds). This leads to a decay effect – when there's no more activity in a certain area, the intensity of the red color fades to gray. While a long interval would result in a rather static visualization, a shorter interval allows for displaying real-time customer activities in the store.

Adapted Customer Behavior. Customers who recognize the store map have now the possibility to adapt their behavior in the store according to the behavior of other customers in the store. This adaption could happen in different ways and depends on individual preferences as well as the configuration of the time interval for displaying activity. For example, if the store map is configured to provide real-time information on the customer activities in the store, a customer might exploit the activity information in order to avoid heavy traffic between the shelves by first visiting other areas of the store with less activity. This obviously could be done by just looking at these areas, but within large retail stores it may be hard or even impossible to overlook the whole store.

To give another example, the store map could also be configured for displaying long-term activity, let's say the past 30 minutes or even the whole day. This way the store map indicates regions, which are likely more popular than other regions. A customer could check what kind of products are popular or whether there are any special offers at the corresponding shelves. In this case the benefit for the users could be compared to popularity rankings employed by websites such as Amazon.

As we mentioned before, we strive to combine the advantages of online shopping systems with those of "real" shops. Online systems recommendations are often based on fine grain demographic data like age, sex or long time shopping habits. Since we do not have these informations of customers in a shopping mall

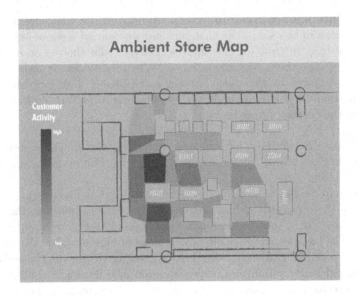

Fig. 4. A screenshot of the store map as displayed on the ambient screen in the retail store. Shop customers can see where in the store there has been much activity in the very recent past (e.g. 15 minutes). A higher intensity of the red areas indicates a higher activity in that particular area.

we only can take advantages on the customers' short time shopping habits – their activity through a specific time period.

4 Study

We deployed the AmI prototype in a retail store in a shopping mall for a duration of three days. The study was conducted during the regular opening hours of the mall. Therefore we were able to recruit a considerable number of participants. Additionally the study was carried out in the participant's actual context: shopping. The customers who visited this retail store were our test participants.

4.1 Prototype Settings

The first challenge was to specify the prototype parameters. As indicated in Sec. 3.2 a balance must be found between visualizing short-term or long-term customer activities. Since the group activity was at the center of our interest, we aimed for displaying rather long-term cumulated customer activities. Based on our observation during the first hours of deployment, we found that a time-interval of 30 minutes for the displayed customer activities was most suitable. This setting allowed us to display rich long-term information without having a too static visualization.

4.2   Methods

We applied several methods to collect qualitative data about the consumer experiences in the retail store, thereby focusing especially on the technical prototype. The aim of all methods was to investigate the shopping experience as unobtrusive as possible.

First we directly observed about 400 customers in the shop. In this way we investigated social interactions with companions or shop personnel, products and areas of special interest, and the usage of technology such as mobile phones, MP3 players and similar personal devices. The special interest of our observations was targeted towards the perception of the ambient display, the duration of fixation as well as the actions followed by that (e.g. does the customer show the display to his or her companion, explore the functionality, or mark any comments).

The second method was to conduct short in situ interviews with 50 customers, who had just investigated the ambient display. In this way we aimed to find out if the customers understood the information delivered through the ambient display. Furthermore we asked them for suggestions of how to improve the technical prototype and which kinds of information they would want.

Finally we used video material recorded through a Spectacles Camera. The Spectacles Camera is a pair of ordinary sports glasses with a built-in video camera (see Fig. 5). During the three days of the study we asked 37 consumers

Fig. 5. A customer with the Spectacles Camera. This rather unobtrusive glasses have a small camera built in, which allows us to record a video of the participants visual field.

in front of the shop if they wanted to enter the shop using the Spectacles Camera. Up to a certain distance the video could be seen as a live-stream on a display in front of the shop. For a detailed analysis the video was recorded on a mobile HD recorder connected to the Spectacles Camera. The purpose of the Spectacles Camera was twofold: first it served as demo for the university's exhibition and second it served as a research tool that enabled us to see what the customer was seeing. In the latter regard it is similar to the Microsoft SenseCam [35], a research device worn around the neck that produces fisheye photos triggered through sensor input. However the Spectacles Camera produces, albeit only for a short time, a live video including audio. The combination of immediate consumer perspectives through the Spectacles Camera, interview statements and direct observations over four days enabled us to gain valuable insights into general shopping behavior in this context as well as into the perception of the ambient display.

5   Results and Discussion

In this chapter we present the results of the three-day study of our ambient store map. The prototypical application was deployed in a retail store in a major shopping mall during regular store hours. Based on our findings we discuss impacts on the design of AmI applications for shopping environments. In brackets we also indicate when a finding matches or violates one of the Ambient Display heuristics by Mankoff et al. [14].

5.1   Situated Visualization

Our findings indicate that the data presented on the screen was easy to interpret and to understand for most users. 46 of the 50 customers who were asked in short in situ interviews understood the information delivered through the ambient display (*sufficient information design* [14]). Yet we discovered several issues regarding the usefulness of the data presented and the design of the visualization.

The ambient store map was rotated by 90 degrees in relation to the store. This made the mapping of the representation of the store to the physical store difficult for some of the users (*consistent and intuitive mapping* [14]). Users also suggested that the map should include additional information, such as the contents of a particular shelf and cues that would make the orientation easier, e.g. the position of the entrance door (*useful and relevant information* [14]).

In order to resolve the mapping problem, future developments will integrate displays, which are situated on the shelf into our solution. These displays could present location specific information such as the past activity or the popularity of this shelf.

An additional possibility would be to integrate PDAs as a personal display for each customer into the system. Such a device could be used to give personalized activity information to the user. The user could define points of interest and also set the time interval for displaying customer activities. This would be in line with the perCues framework, which also considers an individual benefit for the users (see Fig. 1).

To further improve the system, a direct visualization on the floor of the store could be utilized. This visualization could include the paths that previous customers took through the store and also the activity levels in particular areas.

5.2   Usefulness of the Information on the Map

Another finding of our study is that while most users were able to grasp the information presented on the screen the usefulness of this information was considered unclear by some of the users. Users understood that the display presented a map of the store but it was not clear to what purpose (*useful and relevant information* [14]). Especially when there was an occasional lack of customer frequency, e.g. in the early morning or at lunchtime, there were not always enough users to generate rich activity patterns on the map. A critical mass of users is necessary in order to generate meaningful data and to provide a useful service to the users of the map (*error prevention* [14]).

To overcome the problem of poor visualizations during periods of lower customer frequency, a larger time interval for displaying the customer activities (see Sec. 3.2) would be the solution. For example choosing a time interval of 45 minutes instead of 30 minutes would result in a slower decay of the displayed customer activities and thus compensating the lower activity.

5.3   Calm vs. Engaging Interface

In Weiser's vision, ubiquitous computing is a calm technology, which is unobtrusively embedded into the environment of the user. The shopping environment in which our application was deployed is the exact opposite of a calm environment. It is loud, obtrusive and glaring, with an overwhelming number of sensations bombarding the customer. We observed that even though our map was large and placed prominently in the store, some customers failed to take notice of it. They just passed by it, their attention grabbed by the many other points of interest in the store, like the display of a new shoe, shelves with items on sale or screens with promotional video clips (*"peripherality" of display* [14]).

In conclusion, the design of a ambient display in a retail store must take into account the distinct properties of a shopping environment. When designing the interactive store map, we aimed to make it an example of calm computing, with implicit input and peripheral and unobtrusive output. Based on our findings we agree with Rogers [36] that making AmI engaging for the users is an important goal. Regarding the design of AmI applications in shopping environments there is a delicate balance between creating an application that is calm enough not to get on the users nerves, but yet visible and engaging so that the user's take notice of it.

5.4   Individual vs. Collective Awareness

As stated in Sec. 4.1 it was one of the design challenges to find the right balance between a short and long time interval as basis for the displayed customer activity.

The actual setup of our application displays the collective behavior of the shoppers over a period of 30 minutes. The result was a map which only changed gradually over time based on the collective customer activity.

During our field study we discovered that the users liked to see their own impact on the map as well. This was the case when we set the time interval to one minute or less so that the individual activity could change the map easily. The users immediately became more interested in the map, since the map reacted instantly to their behavior (*visibility of system status, useful and relevant information design* [14]). This finding indicates that the display of the individual position is a key affordance also of an ambient store map, just like the "you are here" signs on traditional public maps.

One challenge for future development of the ambient store map concept will be the integration of the individual impact with the collective impact. The user should be able to grasp the collective activity and yet see the impact of his own behavior as well.

5.5   Disproportional Influence of the Activity of the Sales Staff on the Visualization

When we designed the application we assumed that the activity of the sales staff would be negligible in comparison to the much larger customer activity. This assumption was confirmed during the three days of deployment.

Nevertheless, the customer frequency was rather low during certain periods (see Sec. 5.2). At these particular times the activities of the store employees and our own movements were accounting for a large part of the visualized activity and the displayed activity was not purely the customer activity (*error prevention, useful and relevant information* [14]).

To alleviate this problem we suggest to differentiate between staff and customer activity. As suggested by a user the application could be further improved by showing the current location of staff members on the screen, thus making them easier to find for the customers.

5.6   Privacy vs. Information Disclosure

The potential application scenarios for our interactive store are twofold: On the one hand, the map can serve as a tool for the customers, raising their awareness of the activity in the shop and potentially improving the overall shopping experience. On the other hand the map can be used by the shop owner or the marketing department in the company who owns the shop in order to change the shop design based on empirical data about the actual customer behavior.

One of Rogers' objectives for persuasive AmI technologies is that the information collected by such systems should benefit the users whose information is collected themselves and not others [36]. In line with this objective, our application is geared towards the first scenario. The monitoring and tracking of the users directly benefits themselves and other customers in the same position, for example by helping them to find areas of interest in the shop (*useful and relevant information* [14]). Our application is not set up for the second scenario, which would be precisely a form of monitoring which is critiqued by Rogers [36].

6 Conclusion and Future Work

We have presented an overview of the possibilities for AmI technologies in shopping environments. As an example for such technologies we developed an ambient store map which displays customer activity and deployed it in an actual retail store. We researched this application during a three days field study.

Our findings offer implications for the design of AmI applications in shopping environments. Our study showed the importance of striking a balance between individual and collective awareness in terms of the visualization. We also discovered that in such environments the AmI application is facing a tough competition for the attention of the user, making user engagement a key design challenge. Additionally, the user feedback indicated that the information richness of the visualization adds to its perceived usefulness and that adding more situated displays would be beneficial to the users.

A next step to conduct more research regarding designs that strike the balance between being engaging and being unobtrusive with a particular focus on improving the shopping experience. We also want to investigate further enhancing our application by adding situated displays which are located throughout the store and present activity and popularity information regarding particular locations, e.g. shelves.

As ambient displays are used to provide information peripherally, it is uncertain whether a person realizes the information. But an ambient display should not distract persons from their main tasks. Consequently, a major design challenge for future work is the shift of information from the periphery of the user's attention to the center of the user's attention. This transition from the background to the foreground has to be performed in a cognitively adequate way, in order to make an ambient display helpful and efficient instead of distracting and annoying.

Acknowledgements

This research is partially funded by the Austrian Federal Ministry for Transport, Innovation, and Technology under the FIT-IT contract FFG 809532/9295.

References

1. Nielsen, J., Tahir, M.: Homepage usability: 50 websites deconstructed. New Riders Publishing (2002)
2. Sjölinder, M., Höök, K., Nilsson, L.G.: Age difference in the use of an on-line grocery shop: implications for design. In: Proc. CHI 2000, pp. 135–136. ACM Press, New York (2000)

3. Limayem, M., Khalifa, M., Frini, A.: What makes consumers buy from internet? a longitudinal study ofonline shopping. IEEE Transactions on Systems, Man and Cybernetics, Part A 30(4), 421–432 (2000)
4. Weiser, M.: The computer for the 21st century. Scientific American, 94–104 (1991)
5. Aarts, E., Marzano, S.: The New Everyday: Views on Ambient Intelligence. 010 Publishers, Rotterdam (2003)
6. Wisneski, C., Ishii, H., Dahley, A., Gorbet, M.G., Brave, S., Ullmer, B., Yarin, P.: Ambient displays: Turning architectural space into an interface between people and digital information. In: Streitz, N.A., Konomi, S., Burkhardt, H.-J. (eds.) CoBuild 1998. LNCS, vol. 1370, pp. 22–32. Springer, Heidelberg (1998)
7. Weiser, M., Seely Brown, J.: The coming age of calm technology. Technical report, Xerox PARC (1996)
8. Ishii, H., Ullmer, B.: Tangible bits: towards seamless interfaces between people, bits and atoms. In: CHI 1997, pp. 234–241. ACM Press, New York (1997)
9. Holstius, D., Kembel, J., Hurst, A., Wan, P.-H., Forlizzi, J.: Infotropism: living and robotic plants as interactive displays. In: Proc. DIS 2004, pp. 215–221. ACM Press, New York (2004)
10. Jafarinaimi, N., Forlizzi, J., Hurst, A., Zimmerman, J.: Breakaway: an ambient display designed to change human behavior. In: CHI 2005, pp. 1945–1948. ACM Press, New York (2005)
11. Gustafsson, A., Gyllenswärd, M.: The power-aware cord: energy awareness through ambient information display. In: Ext. Abstracts CHI 2005, pp. 1423–1426. ACM Press, New York (2005)
12. Pinhanez, C.: The everywhere displays projector: A device to create ubiquitous graphical interfaces. In: Abowd, G.D., Brumitt, B., Shafer, S. (eds.) Ubicomp 2001. LNCS, vol. 2201, Springer, Heidelberg (2001)
13. Streitz, N., Magerkurth, C., Prante, T., Röcker, C.: From information design to experience design: smart artefacts and the disappearing computer. Interactions 12, 21–25 (2005)
14. Mankoff, J., Dey, A.K., Hsieh, G., Kientz, J., Lederer, S., Ames, M.: Heuristic evaluation of ambient displays. In: CHI 2003, pp. 169–176. ACM Press, New York (2003)
15. Nielsen, J.: Heuristic evaluation. In: Nielsen, J., Mack, R.L. (eds.) Usability Inspection Methods, pp. 25–62. John Wiley & Sons, Inc., New York (1994)
16. Dey, A.K., de Guzman, E.: From awareness to connectedness: the design and deployment of presence displays. In: CHI 2006, pp. 899–908. ACM Press, New York (2006)
17. Schmidt, A.: Interactive context-aware systems interacting with ambient intelligence. In: Riva, G., Vatalaro, F., Davide, F., Alcañiz, M. (eds.) Ambient intelligence, IOS Press, Amsterdam (2005)
18. Dourish, P., Bellotti, V.: Awareness and coordination in shared workspaces. In: CSCW 1992, pp. 107–114. ACM Press, New York (1992)
19. Karahalios, K., Donath, J.: Telemurals: linking remote spaces with social catalysts. In: CHI 2004, pp. 615–622. ACM Press, New York (2004)
20. McCarthy, J.F., Costa, T.J., Liongosari, E.S.: Unicast, outcast & groupcast: Three steps toward ubiquitous, peripheral displays. In: Abowd, G.D., Brumitt, B., Shafer, S. (eds.) Ubicomp 2001. LNCS, vol. 2201, pp. 332–345. Springer, Heidelberg (2001)
21. Brignull, H., Rogers, Y.: Enticing people to interact with large public displays in public spaces. In: INTERACT 2003, IOS Press, Amsterdam (2003)

22. Tscheligi, M., Reitberger, W., Obermair, C., Ploderer, B.: percues: Trails of persuasion for ambient intelligence. In: IJsselsteijn, W., de Kort, Y., Midden, C., Eggen, B., van den Hoven, E. (eds.) PERSUASIVE 2006. LNCS, vol. 3962, pp. 203–206. Springer, Heidelberg (2006)
23. Obermair, C., Ploderer, B., Reitberger, W., Tscheligi, M.: Cues in the environment: a design principle for ambient intelligence. In: Ext. Abstracts CHI 2006, pp. 1157–1162. ACM Press, New York (2006)
24. Lévy, P.: Collective Intelligence: Mankind's Emerging World in Cyberspace. Plenum Publishing Corp., Cambridge, MA (1997)
25. Underhill, P.: Why we buy. The Science of Shopping. Simon & Schuster, New York (1999)
26. Cap Gemini Ernst & Young, Intel Corporation, Cisco Systems, Inc. and Microsoft Corporation: Transforming the shopping experience through technology: A study in eurpoean consumer buying behaviour. Executive Summary (2003)
27. Roux, C., Regienczuk, B.: The future of shopping. Philips Design Research (2003)
28. Metro, A.G.: Welcome to the future store: A journey into the future of retail. Brochure (2006)
29. Newcomb, E., Pashley, T., Stasko, J.: Mobile computing in the retail arena. In: CHI 2003, pp. 337–344. ACM Press, New York (2003)
30. Bohnenberger, T., Jacobs, O., Jameson, A., Aslan, I.: Decission-theoretic planning meets user requirements: Enhancements and studies of an intelligent shopping guide. In: Gellersen, H.-W., Want, R., Schmidt, A. (eds.) PERVASIVE 2005. LNCS, vol. 3468, pp. 279–296. Springer, Heidelberg (2005)
31. Wasinger, R., Wahlster, W.: The anthropomorphized product shelf: Symmetric multimodal human-environment interaction. In: Aarts, E., Encarnação, J. (eds.) True Visions: The Emergence of Ambient Intelligence, pp. 291–306. Springer, Heidelberg (2006)
32. Pinhanez, C., Podlaseck, M.: To frame or not to frame: The role and design of frameless displays in ubiquitous applications. In: Beigl, M., Intille, S.S., Rekimoto, J., Tokuda, H. (eds.) UbiComp 2005. LNCS, vol. 3660, pp. 340–357. Springer, Heidelberg (2005)
33. Sukaviriya, N., Podlaseck, M., Kjeldsen, R., Levas, A., Pingali, G., Pinhanez, C.: Augmenting a retail environment using steerable interactive displays. In: CHI 2003, pp. 978–979. ACM Press, New York (2003)
34. Spassova, L., Wasinger, R., Baus, J., Kruger, A.: Product associated displays in a shopping scenario. In: ISMAR 2005, pp. 210–211. IEEE Computer Society Press, Washington, DC, USA (2005)
35. Hodges, S., Williams, L., Berry, E., Izadi, S., Srinivasan, J., Butler, A., Smyth, G., Kapur, N., Wood, K.: Sensecam: a retrospective memory aid. In: Dourish, P., Friday, A. (eds.) UbiComp 2006. LNCS, vol. 4206, pp. 177–193. Springer, Heidelberg (2006)
36. Rogers, Y.: Moving on from weiser's vision of calm computing: Engaging ubicomp experiences. In: Dourish, P., Friday, A. (eds.) UbiComp 2006. LNCS, vol. 4206, pp. 404–421. Springer, Heidelberg (2006)

Expected Information Needs of Parents for Pervasive Awareness Systems

Vassilis-Javed Khan[1], Panos Markopoulos[1], Boris de Ruyter[2], and Wijnand IJsselsteijn[1]

[1] Eindhoven University of Technology, Den Dolech 2, 5600MB, Eindhoven,
The Netherlands
{v.j.khan,p.markopoulos,w.a.ijsselsteijn}@tue.nl
[2] Philips Research, Media Interaction, Prof. Holstlaan 4, 5656AA, Eindhoven,
The Netherlands
boris.de.ruyter@philips.com

Abstract. This paper examines the communication needs of busy parents that can be served by awareness systems: systems supporting a continuous and semi-automated flow of information about the activities of communicating individuals. We report an online survey involving 69 participants. This survey focused on whether the types of information offered by awareness systems as these are introduced in current research literature are appreciated by busy parents. The results show a) that information items that allow personalization and expressing intentionality are more desired than those than low granularity and automatically sensed information that is easy to collect automatically b) the attitudes regarding the information that people wish to share about themselves is almost identical to what they wish to know of their partners and c) survey methods focusing on information do not need to differentiate between the direction of information flow or whether this is symmetric, since people report almost identical preferences.

Keywords: Awareness systems, Communication needs, Pervasive computing.

1 Introduction

Among the pervasive computing community there is a growing interest for using pervasive computing to support informal, social communication. The target group of such efforts is usually family members, close intimates, friends. For example, contact lists currently available on mobile phones can be augmented with presence information or other contextual information that provides a context and a trigger for communication or coordination of the activities of individuals, e.g., [11]. Our research focuses especially on the communication needs of busy parents; our earlier work on intra-family communication needs focused originally on cross generational communication and on supporting elderly. However, during the field trials of our prototype for intra-family awareness [10] we found out that busy parents were a very promising user group who had pronounced needs for frequent communication over and above mobile phones and text messaging.

B. Schiele et al. (Eds.): AmI 2007, LNCS 4794, pp. 332–339, 2007.

The communication between couples has attracted the interest of researchers in this field, who have focused mostly on poetic and playful forms of communicating affect through physical artifacts connected over distance. Examples include Strong and Gaver's conveyance of presence by a feather in a plastic cone that floats when the distant partner picks up a picture frame of the couple [13]; Tollmar and Joakim's light 'orb' that glows when a remote family member walks into their apartment [15]; Brave and Dahley's two sets of cylinders that roll and rotate in unison as they are manipulated by separated partners [1]; Vetere's virtual hug realized through an inflatable vest that can be triggered to inflate from a remote partner. These works have inspired a lot of the developments in research on awareness systems for intra-family communication, but there has been little empirical research to understand the needs regarding what communication is needed between couples (and especially busy parents). Some fundamental questions that arise are:

A.   Is a sustained flow or trickle of information between parents wanted at all?
B.   Are there any other communication needs to be exchanged except intimacy?
C.   Should the information exchange be symmetric?

In an earlier interview study [8] we examined questions A and B. The results of that study indicated that parents do not really want to communicate during the day. For example, we found out that parents, while separated during the day, refrain from initiating communications with each other for fear of interrupting their work, unless for an emergency or a change of plans. Contrary to our initial expectations, parents did not report as much a need for directly communicating affective communication, e.g., to indicate that they think of each other, or to display affection over the phone. Moreover, in most cases parents use a practical reason to communicate as a pretext for a richer, more affective communication, something also found before in the case of cross-generational communication, see [10] for example. With the present study we set out to validate this result, by triangulating the interview study with a different research method focusing on exactly this issue. The survey was designed to uncover what types of information sharing busy parents wish to achieve, considering the range of information sharing that is typically addressed by awareness systems.

Question C above, has been examined at a theoretical level. For example, the concept of social translucence [3] has been put forward as a way to describe the symmetric needs for transparency and accountability between users of communication systems. The concept of minimum information asymmetry has been also proposed by Landay and Hong [4], as a way to ensure privacy protection between connected individuals. Apart from these theoretical analyses, many systems that are presented for intra-family awareness are essentially asymmetric, as for example the well known Family Portrait [12], which supports one way information flow from a lonely elderly to their close family. Such assertions have a strong logical and theoretical basis but as yet, there is little or no support from empirical research. The survey described aims to address this point.

2 Method

We reviewed related literature on Awareness systems. We included in this review papers published in conferences such as Mobile HCI, CHI, CSCW and Ubicomp. We included only papers describing systems rather than theoretical and empirical works in this domain. In each case, we examined the essence of the information that the awareness system helped communicate abstracting away from context capture mechanisms and the presentation medium. For example, Cadiz, et. al. describe in their paper [2] Sideshow, an awareness system that displays among other information traffic conditions at a particular location in the city. This is displayed on a PC based application. For our survey we retained only the fact that traffic conditions are communicated. Thus the statement we formed is presented in Table 1.

The review included 16 papers. Our overall impression is that the information exchange through the described systems varies in detail, but overall it seems to cluster around the repeating themes of location, availability, presence and activity descriptions.

In addition to the literature review, we added statements regarding information needs of busy parents that we obtained from the transcriptions of the interview study we had conducted earlier with 20 Dutch working parents [8]. In total we had 41 seed statements describing awareness information that can be exchanged between busy parents by using an awareness system. This list is of course not exhaustive, as one might be able to dream up an infinite range of information types, at different levels of details and referring to different aspects of people's lives. Rather, this list was meant to capture the range of concerns of researchers in awareness systems and to put this set of concerns to the test but also to base our own designs of awareness systems on stated communication needs and preferences of parents.

An essential tenet of awareness systems is that people will not explicitly engage in direct communication of some information, (as one would with a notification or a messaging system), but that information about one's context or activities is made continuously available and others can choose to inspect it or not. Put in another way, this suggests that there is a difference between actively wanting to share information to not minding if others view it. To implement this distinction in our survey, we asked participants to rate each statement using the following scales: I want, I don't want but I don't mind, I don't want. For our analyses, we rate these answers as 1, 0 and -1. The I don't want but I don't mind scale might initially sound bizarre. However there might be cases that someone would not mind sharing information and at the same time someone would want to receive this information, or the other way round.

Exchanging information implies both sharing and receiving. For our purposes we wanted to find out what information couples find useful to share and what to receive. Therefore for each of the types of information identified as above, we asked a question regarding the willingness to share and a question regarding the willingness to receive this information. For example, for information regarding traffic at the location of the partner the two questions were those shown in Table 1.

Table 1. Example of the two statements we formed

share	receive
My spouse is informed about the traffic conditions near the location I am	I am informed about the traffic conditions nearby the location my spouse is

At this point a methodological issue arose. Since we wanted to ask two questions we could think two ways of asking; disjoint or conjoint. For example, when asked about the traffic conditions in the location a person is, we could first ask the question: "How willing are you to share this information?" (about the statement: "My spouse is informed about the traffic conditions near the location I am") and then "How willing are you to receive this information?" (about the statement: "I am informed about the traffic conditions nearby the location my spouse is"). Or we could ask the question at the same time: "How willing are you to share/receive this information?" (about the statement: "I am informed about the traffic conditions near the location my spouse is and my spouse is informed about the traffic conditions near the location I am").

This methodological issue reflects upon the nature of an awareness system as well. Asking disjointed questions suggests a system that is asymmetric whereas the conjoined question on sharing and receiving suggests a system that is symmetric. To examine whether attitudes of partners are influenced by an assumed symmetry or not, we split participants asking half of them two questions (separately about sharing/receiving: disjoint) and the other half one question (conjoint).

We created an online application which assigned in counter balance the participants to the two ways of asking them the questions. The application presented the statements to the participants in randomized order and recorded their ratings.

2.1 Participants

69 people were recruited through advertisements placed at an online forum for parents as well as by sending email adverts to secondary schools. 34 of them saw the statements in two steps (for receiving and for sharing) as explained previously. 35 of them saw the statements in one step as explained previously. The order, in this case, both within a statement and overall was randomized.

2.2 Hypotheses and Analysis

The study had two hypotheses.

H1: When couples are asked in a way representing an asymmetrical exchange of information they would be willing to exchange more information than when asked in a way representing a symmetrical one.

H2: Spouses are willing to receive more information than they are willing to send.

For testing H1 we had to compare the two ways participants rated the statements. In one case participants answered two questions (about sharing and then about receiving) and in the other case they answered one question (about sharing and receiving). To compare the two we had to merge the two ratings participants gave when answering two questions. By merging, we had one rate to compare it against the rate participants gave when answering a single question. We merged the rates as following. We first converted the 1 and 0 scale items to logical True and the -1 scale item to logical False. We then took the logical conjunction of the rating of each participant who answered the two questions. For example, if a participant rated the question: My spouse is informed about the traffic conditions near the location I am with I don't want (-1, thus logical False) and for the question: I am informed about the traffic conditions nearby the location my spouse is (1, thus logical True) then the result of the logical conjunction would be False (since True AND False = False).

We calculated the proportion of participants choosing a statement. For that we added up the I want, I don't want but I don't mind scales and divided by the number of the participants answering that particular method (34 and 35 respectively).

We wanted to find out whether the difference between the two ways of asking was significant. For that reason we calculated the significance interval at 95% for each and every statement as well as for the overall mean of percentages of the first way of asking. We then checked whether the proportion of the second way was inside the interval. If so this meant that it the difference of proportions is not significant [7]. To illustrate an example we will examine one statement. The statement about being "a few minutes idle behind my computer" after the re-rating had 10 participants (out of the 34, i.e. 29%) who wanted to either share or receive it. To calculate the confidence interval we need to calculate the margin of error. The margin of error is then calculated by the following formula:

$$1.96\sqrt{\frac{\hat{p}\times(1-\hat{p})}{N}}$$

Where $= 0.29$ and N=34, error $= 0.15$ and therefore the confidence interval is {0.14 to 0.44} or {14% to 44%}.

The same statement had 13 participants (out of the 35, i.e. 37%) who wanted to either share or receive it when asked in the second way. The 37% is included in the confidence interval {14% to 44%}. We can therefore conclude that the difference between the two ways of asking is not significant for this particular statement.

For testing the second hypothesis we plotted a table with the frequency ratings for the I want, I don't want but I don't mind scales and divided by the number of the participants answering that particular method (34). We then again calculated the significance at 95% for each and every statement as well as for the overall mean of percentages.

3   Results

For the first hypothesis we repeated the analysis described for one statement in the previous section for each of the 41 statements. For all 41 statements there was no significant difference. Hence we can conclude that generally there is no significant difference between the two ways of surveying preferences by users.

The same holds for the second hypothesis for each and every statement except the statement: My spouse is informed that I am away from my office, I am informed that my spouse is away from his/her office where it a significant difference appears between the two. It seems that couples would like to receive this information than send it to their spouses.

3.1   Content of Information Exchange

We were interested in the statements that emerge to be most and least wanted to be shared and received.

Least wanted statements to be shared are presented in Table 2. They appear in both ways of asking. All of these statements represent very detailed information. It seems that parents are not interested in that. If we also view the statements that do not want to be shared but parents do not mind to share them anyway (Table 3) they also seem to be detailed and two of them are related to computer activity. On the other hand (and this is what we would expect) parents seem to be interested in sharing broader information like how they are feeling and if they do not want to be disturbed (Table 4).

Table 2. Least wanted statements to be shared

My spouse is informed about the general noise level of the room I am in
My spouse is informed that I am a few minutes idle behind my computer
My spouse is informed about what the title of my next meeting is

Table 3. Statements that do not want to be shared but parents do not mind to share them anyway

My spouse is informed that I am logged out from my computer
My spouse is informed that I am having a break
My spouse is informed about my Instant Messenger status

Table 4. Most wanted statements to be shared

My spouse is informed that I am wishing him/her a good day
My spouse is informed about how I am feeling today
My spouse is informed that I do not want to be disturbed now

Least wanted statements to be received are presented in Table 5. One of them is also found in Table 2(does not want to be shared as well). As was the case with sharing information that parents do not want to also receive very detailed information. The same idea is also reflected with the statements that do not want to be received but parents do not mind to receive them anyway (Table 6). They all represent information which is very detailed. It is naturally not surprising that the statements that are most wanted to be received are exactly the same with the ones that want to be shared with the exact same order (Table 7). This again reflects the wish of having symmetric exchange of information.

Table 5. Least wanted statements to be received

I am informed that my spouse is a few minutes idle behind his/her computer
I am informed about how many times my spouse spoke with other people today
I am being informed about what is going on in the room my spouse currently is

Table 6. Statements that do not want to be received but parents do not mind to receive them anyway

I am informed that my spouse is engaged in an Instant Messaging conversation with another user
I am informed about when my spouse is close to the supermarket
I am informed about the medication my spouse has taken during the day

Table 7. Most wanted statements to be received

I am informed that my spouse is wishing me a good day
I am informed about how my spouse is feeling today
I am informed that my spouse does not want to be disturbed now

In conclusion, it is clear from the data that very detailed information is not really wanted by parents and it is high-level information that would make more sense for them to be exchanged.

4   Conclusions and Discussion

We presented an online survey of 69 busy parents regarding their communication needs. According to the data we got we can draw the conclusion that parents are willing to exchange information between them. Design implications for our results are that more expressive means of conveying emotions and intentions are needed; emotional communication is valued more than communicating trivia enabled by technology.

Furthermore, since no significant difference was found between the two ways of asking participants, we can draw the conclusion that there is no difference in the way researchers of awareness systems would ask their participants. For simplicity and efficiency, in future surveys we recommend only surveying the need to 'share information'.

The found balance on willingness to share or receive information supports the "Principle of Minimum Asymmetry in Information Flow" proposed by Jiang, et. al. for designing ubiquitous information systems [5] and the concept "Social translucence" by Erickson and Kellogg [3].

There are limitations to the method of online surveys, such as not having control of the participants who are answering (self-selection bias) and the often discrepant expressions of attitudes to the actual behavior of people as users. However, our results have interesting implications for both design and research methodology aspects of awareness systems. To address these limitations an experience sampling study [9] is currently under way to examine the preferences and attitudes of people as they move in different contexts and engage in their daily activities.

Acknowledgments. This research would not be possible without IOP-MMI.

References

1. Brave, S., Dahley, A.: inTouch: A Medium for Haptic Interpersonal Communication. In: CHI 1997, pp. 363–364 (1997)
2. Cadiz, J.J., Venolia, G., Jancke, G., Gupta, A.: Designing and deploying an information awareness interface. In: CSCW (2002)
3. Erickson, T., Kellogg, W.A.: Social translucence: an approach to designing systems that support social processes. ACM TOCHI 7(1), 59–83 (2000)
4. Hong, J.I., Landay, J.A.: An Architecture for Privacy- Sensitive Ubiquitous Computing. In: Mobisys 2004, Boston, MA, pp. 177–189 (2004)
5. Jiang, X., Hong, J., Landay, J.: Approximate Information Flows: Socially-Based Modeling of Privacy in Ubiquitous computing. In: Borriello, G., Holmquist, L.E. (eds.) UbiComp 2002. LNCS, vol. 2498, pp. 176–193. Springer, Heidelberg (2002)
6. Jones, D.M., Bench-Capon, T.J.M., Visser, P.R.S.: Methodologies for ontology development. In: Proc. ITi and KNOWS Conference of the 15th IFIP World Computer Congress, pp. 62–75. Chapman- Hall, Sydney, Australia (1998)
7. Kapadia, R., Andersson, G.: Statistics explained. In: Making Inferences. ch. 11, p. 200. Ellis Horwood Limited (1987)
8. Khan, V.J., Markopoulos, P., Mota, S., IJsselsteijn, W., de Ruyter, B.: Intra-family communication needs; how can Awareness Systems provide support? In: Proc. Intelligent Environments (2006)
9. Kubey, R., Larson, R., Csikszentmihalyi, M.: Experience sampling method. Applications to communication research questions. Journal of Communication 46(2), 99–120 (1996)
10. Markopoulos, P., Romero, N., van Baren, J., IJsselsteijn, W., de Ruyter, B., Farshchian, B.: Keeping in Touch with the Family: Home and Away with the ASTRA Awareness System. In: CHI 2004 (2004)
11. Oulasvirta, A., Raento, M., Tiitta, S.: ContextContacts: re-designing SmartPhone's contact book to support mobile awareness and collaboration. In: MobileHCI 2005, vol. 111, pp. 167–174. ACM Press, New York (2005)
12. Rowan, J., Mynatt, E.D.: Digital family portrait field trial: Support for aging in place. In: CHI 2005, pp. 521–530 (2005)
13. Strong, R., Gaver, B.: Feather, Scent and Shaker: Supporting Simple Intimacy. In: CSCW 1996, ACM Press, New York (1996)
14. Sugumaran, V., Storey, V.C.: Ontologies for conceptual modeling: their creation, use, and management. Data & Knowledge Engineering 42(3), 251–271 (2002)
15. Tollmar, K., Joakim, P.: Understanding Remote Presence. In: Proc. NordiCHI (2002)
16. Vetere, F., Gibbs, M., Kjeldskov, J., Howard, S., Floyd Mueller, F., Pedell, S., Mecoles, K., Bunyan, M.: Mediating intimacy: designing technologies to support strong-tie relationships. In: CHI 2005 (2005)

Assemblies of Heterogeneous Technologies at the Neonatal Intensive Care Unit

Erik Grönvall[1], Luca Piccini[2], Alessandro Pollini[1],
Alessia Rullo[1], and Giuseppe Andreoni[2]

[1] University of Siena, Communication Science Department, Via Roma 56,
53100 Siena, Italy
{gronvall,pollini,rullo}@media.unisi.it
[2] Politecnico di Milano, Bioengineering Department, Via Golgi 39,
20133 Milan, Italy
{luca.piccini,giuseppe.andreoni}@polimi.it

Abstract. Ambient Intelligence, pervasive and unobtrusive computing research is introducing new perspectives in a wide range of applications. The Neonatal Intensive Care Unit represents a complex and multi-output context aimed at monitoring and controlling biological signals and parameters in premature newborn. This paper details some methodological and design options for developing technologies that allow end-user composition and control. These options enhance consistent user experiences in environments where different devices, services and processes co-exist. In particular we describe the notion of assemblies of monitoring devices, interpreted as the combination of sensors, tools and services in a distributed and unobtrusive computational and monitoring environment. We report on the importance of flexibility and user-control in the use of such technological assemblies in a neonatal intensive care unit, describing an early prototype of such monitoring system.

Keywords: premature newborn, design, open architecture, palpable computing, biosensors, assemblies and user control.

1 Introduction

The introduction of digital technologies into health care scenarios requires specific considerations related to the characteristics of the domain, the activities executed in the environment and the different skills of the actors involved.

The notion of ambient computing has been consolidating with a focus on the design of distributed, pervasive and reactive systems that are able to communicate with the users and to continuously adapt to their needs and expectations. Traditionally, the main goal of ambient or ubiquitous computing applications was to make the technology transparent or invisible to the users. Transparency or invisibility of these systems can enable users to receive help, and get information by the utilization of background cues that sustain their everyday tasks. However, when these applications are more deeply considered, one can recognize that this sort of

B. Schiele et al. (Eds.): AmI 2007, LNCS 4794, pp. 340–357, 2007.

technological disappearance is not always possible or even desirable [1]. When for example an error occurs within these systems, the user would benefit from the visibility of the current system state, which would permit the inspection of the error and allow the user, if possible, to take the necessary correctional measures. Therefore to effectively use these applications the users must always remain in control [2]. This is especially true in emergency or breakdown situations in critical safety domains, such as for example a Neonatal Intensive Care Unit [3]. Thus, what are the requirements for the ambient devices in such setting? How do they address these potential errors?

A premature birth dramatically alters the stabile situation of a normal pregnancy and the child development in the uterus by destroying the safe configuration of 'filters' between the child and the external world. The premature child can not stand yet the environmental stimuli which he is suddenly exposed to. The newborn shifts from a condition of protection, characterized by postural stabilization and natural stimuli, to a condition within the environment of the incubator that is characterized by excessive and painful stimulations. This in turn can cause a high level of stress that is then reflected into the clinical conditions of the baby.

The Neonatal Intensive Care Unit (NICU) represents an example of a socio-technical fragility that challenges the design of ambient computing technologies intended as a support to the premature babies' necessities and to the collaboration among the individuals acting in the ward. It has been investigated how novel bio-sensors can be introduced in a Neonatal Intensive Care Unit and what are the requirements for introducing such technologies in this kind of environment.

In order to address these research issues we adopted palpable computing as an emerging conceptual framework developed within the EU funded project PalCom (PalCom, http://www.ist-palcom.org). Palpable computing grounds on the notion of ambient computing which is focused on the design of distributed, pervasive and reactive systems able to communicate with the users and to continuously adapt to their needs and expectations. The palpable computing paradigm purposely addresses the way in which humans meaningfully interact with and make sense of distributed computational systems available in the environment.

2 The Case Study: The Neonatal Intensive Care Unit

At the NICU, the space built around the incubators represents the main setting of interactions that enable the relationships between different individuals. In fact, it not only embodies the work practice of the medical staff that aims to take care of the baby, it also represents the major setting in which relationships between the child and the external world is constructed. The incubator system is configured according to the baby conditions and it is dynamically re-configured as the newborn status changes and, indeed, the neonatal ward represents a rather changing environment.

Current incubators can not be intended as autonomous units. Each incubator works in conjunction with a number of machineries which support the different functions of the newborn. Moreover each device has its own alarm system that is adjusted according to each baby's status.

The continuous control and monitoring of newborns parameters is obtained through medical personnel collaboration and the cooperation of individuals with specific skills, heterogeneous backgrounds and different organizational values [4]. Medical emergencies require the continuous re-definition of action-plans and re-arrangement of work flows, creating ad hoc solutions for each specific situation. Such a complexity can generate latent situations of conflict that affect the safety of the patients and the security of the work environment [3].

Participatory design sessions [5-8] were organized to understand both the problems and the best practices or successful experiences of the medical staff, which are in turn used as leverage for design processes. This situation engenders different phenomena of interference and a sort of 'side effect' behaviour. In order to deal with the number and typologies of the sources of information, all the devices are set in a way to distinguish each signal from the others. During meeting and interviews with the medical personnel they mentioned that the diverse alarm configurations (both visual and acoustic) sometimes get them confused, creating potentially dangerous situations and contradictory behaviours due to the misunderstandings of the machineries values. The Pulse Oximeter, the ventilator and the humidifier are exemplar stand-alone machineries with their own alarm systems. The Pulse Oximeter mainly allows the monitoring of the baby's SpO_2 and heart rate. In medicine, oxygen saturation (SpO_2) measures the percentage of haemoglobin binding sites in the bloodstream that are occupied by oxygen. The Pulse Oximeter is equipped with an alarm configuration that provides both a visual and an acoustic feedback in order to readily alert the medical staff of any problem that may arise. Beside the Pulse Oximeter the ventilators is used in combination with the humidifier in order to regulate the temperature of the air flow. The ventilator is equipped with its own acoustic alarms and a visual configuration of alarms that display the different parameters, i.e. the ventilator peak, exhalation pressure, air flow, inhalation time and oxygen percentage. The humidifier is also provided with its own acoustic alarm to detect any increase or decrease in the water temperature.

These two machineries, the ventilator and the Pulse Oximeter, are strictly connected and any malfunction in one device would affect the other's function by changing the baby's condition. Nowadays, the neonatologist performs the coupling between the two, by an interpretation of the situation and by combining the information from the different machineries that work in conjunction with the incubator. The different components of the incubator have a strong, logical connection since they share a mutual influence on each other through the baby. Despite this strong correlation, the incubator does not create a system with the other external components: they are not functionally connected and each one works independently from each other. This aspect is fundamental for understanding the distributed nature of this setting.

Furthermore, the only way in which these different parts are interconnected is through the child, i.e. through the reflection of their functions into the child status (by influencing the baby's parameters).

2.1 Making Sense of Machines

From a direct observation of the activity in the ward, a number of scenarios have been collected to understand the current work practice adopted by the medical personnel and what are the interconnections among the machineries in use. In the following we illustrate a real scenario occurred at the NICU, generated by a variation in the SpO_2 value of the baby [9].

Indeed when a variation in the SpO_2 value occurs, the medical staff first decides to control the newborn and then to check if the SpO_2 sensor is correctly positioned on the baby. This is to decide whether to change the sensors' position or substitute it with a new one. If the mismatch is still present after this first assessment, they control the respirator. Since the baby is intubated; the nurse and the neonatologist arrange the hypothesis that the value from the Pulse Oximeter is correlated with the function of the respirator. There's not any direct coupling between the two machineries, but of course any anomalies in breathing would directly affect the amount of oxygen in the blood. The nurse tries to restart the respirator while the neonatologist performs manual ventilation. After the re-start, the respirator now works properly. The newborn is currently under the neonatologist direct care while the nurse checks the new values provided by the Pulse Oximeter shifting her attention from machinery to another. The neonatologist and the nurse assume that the Pulse Oximeter was correctly working while the fault was in the respirator. The way in which this trial and error strategy is applied depends on the previous experiences of the nurse and the neonatologist. The medical staff generates different hypotheses about the system status, continuously checking the conditions of the baby and trying to understand which is the source of the mismatch. In the current practice it is not possible to figure out the functional relations among the different equipments necessary for the child survival; although a malfunction on one device (e.g. the respirator) directly effects the functioning on another device (e.g. the Pulse Oximeter) which in turn directly influences the baby status (e.g. change in the SpO_2 value).

3 Our Approach: Making Technology Palpable

The study herein discussed is part of the EU funded PalCom project, which aims at building an innovative research framework within the field of Ambient Computing, denominated Palpable Computing. Balancing heterogeneity and automation with awareness and control is one the goals of Palpable Computing. The paradigm purposely addresses the way in which humans meaningfully interact with the distributed computational systems that are available in the environment [10]. Palpable computing aims at supporting user control by composing and de-composing assemblies of devices and services that communicate and exchange data [11]. The word palpable, in effect, embodies these aspects. "Palpable" has a double folded meaning: in one sense it means 'tangible' and 'perceivable through the senses'; it can also be interpreted as 'plainly observable', 'noticeable', 'manifest', 'obvious' 'clear'. In the Palcom approach, this notion of palpability is integrated by the concept of assembly [2, 10-11]. The assembly is intended as an enabler of palpability by the way in which it permits the logical, functional and physical combination of different services and devices and the dynamic management of these multitude of elements [3]. In fact, the assemblies can be created by the users and modified according to their evolving necessities. The assembly can also be inspected through the use of the network enabled among the assembly components. In this way, the functional connections and the component status can be inspected using the discovery protocols among the assembly parts.

The assemblies are physical and logical entities, at the NICU consisting for instance of a web cam and an EEG sensor that the neonatologist can set up to study any correlation between the baby's movements and the development of the central nervous system and convulsions [3]. The creation of assemblies implies that each part of the assembly is easy to understand on the logical level (what can be done with this, with what can be combined and for what purpose), the functional level (how to use it) and on the physical level (it must be possible to see what fits together and to actually build/rebuild the structure).

These characteristics define the notion of assemblies as dynamic collections of devices, services and communication in which palpability emerges as a property-in-use of the systems, such that it responds to the user's need for flexible and adaptable tools. At this light, the palpability framework explores the manipulation of hardware and soft components in combination with the possibilities to make the computational opportunities noticeable and understandable for the users.

The palpable nature of technologies can be further analyzed by three critical issues that challenge the design of ambient/ubiquitous/pervasive systems: *visibility*, *construction/deconstruction* and *automation and user control*. These concepts are part of the 'palpability framework' consolidated within the project.

Visibility. The changing needs of mutable contexts of interaction, as well as the emerging necessities that arise when for example a system breakdown occurs, require an update of the notion of computation invisibility. This notion should be complemented with the possibility to notice and understand what is going on at the chosen level. Indeed visibility and invisibility represents the two extremes along an axis and the system should be able to dynamically move from one extreme to the other depending on the situation and on the activity.

Construction/Deconstruction. The possibility of putting together different devices and services and of creating networks that share the available resources and support new or distributed functions, demands that the parts are both easy to understand on a logical level (what can be done with this, what can go together with and for what purpose), a functional level (how is it used) and on a physical level (it must be possible to see what fits together and to be able to actually build/rebuild).

Automation and user control. In ambient computing systems, system automation is one of the main strategies used to manage complex settings and predictable variables. When introduced in our environments, the technological solutions have to find a balance between automatic system processes and the possibility that the user has to make sense of them and of remaining in control. This balance should take place between what the system offers and what are the specific needs of the users.

These aspects are profoundly linked with a set of requirements emerging in the current practice at the Neonatal Intensive Care Unit. In this perspective, palpable computing has been adopted as an emerging conceptual framework developed in order to inform the design of technologies at the Neonatal Intensive Care Unit. As described before, a palpable system relies upon features that are coupled with both the hardware and software architecture on the system where it is implemented. The introduction of dynamic construction and deconstruction of assemblies in a clinical context implies that the participating devices could face to the several constraints proper of such scenario. Despite of generic solutions suitable for common clinical applications, "palpable" biosignals monitoring devices should be capable to create a distributed but homogeneous system. Its core should be able to adapt its configuration and its behaviour continuously in order to follow the modifications and the inspection directives received from other palpable devices and information gathered by the unit itself. This dynamic process can lead to the desired goal of the whole architecture, according to the identified conditions and reducing the possibility of fault.

4 PalCom Architecture

The palpable prototype system we have designed at the Neonatal Intensive Care Unit relies upon features that are coupled with both the hardware and software architecture on the system where it is implemented. Concepts, theories and applications presented in this paragraph depend upon the reference implementation of a palpable software architecture, as implemented by the PalCom project.

The state of the art regarding Palpable Computing software systems is that they are built up by small self-contained units or subsystems that solve user tasks through intercommunication. This approach of treating services and systems can be referred to as a Service-Oriented Architecture (SOA) [12]. The foundation of the Service-Oriented Architecture is that a number of services exists and can communicate among each other. The SOA is a way of designing a software system to provide services to both end-user applications and to other services through published and discoverable interfaces [12]. In 2000, Brown describes SOA in his book as follows: "Applications must be developed as independent sets of interacting services offering well-defined interfaces to their potential users. Similarly, supporting technology must be available to allow application developers to browse collections of services, select those of interest, and assemble them to create the desired functionality" [13].

The services are autonomous and can work in distributed settings, they exists without constrains given by the context or other services. SOA enables the services to run and be located on different platforms in a distributed network. The nature of these distributed services and the SOA provides the mean for connecting these services and allow them to communicate and exchange data. The way in which this is implemented is through the use of Assemblies.

4.1 Palpable Assemblies and Service compositions

An assembly from an implementation or software perspective can be described as a description of how a set of services should be 'loosely' grouped together, or how they should interact among them. In the same way, an assembly from the perspective of a user can be described as "some combination of devices or services that is meaningfully considered a cohesive whole by the user." - M. Ingstrup, K. M. Hansen

[11]. This possibility for a user to construct, reconstruct and deconstruct collections of services in a distributed setting (i.e. assemblies) throughout an activity, or over time (i.e. from a software perspective, in runtime), is an important feature to enable user control and visibility.

The assembly concept, from a software perspective is related to software components and their connectors [11]. The different runtime components or services are assembled through the use of a descriptor called an Assembly Script. These scripts can be loaded at runtime, or be applied or altered later by the user.

4.2 Discovery

The dynamic construction and deconstruction of assemblies implies that the available services are distributed and able to discover and interact with each other. The discovery process can in principle reside on any of the participating devices. PalCom objects thus recognize each other and their own heterogeneity among the assembled devices. Therefore, the software objects in the Palpable Open Architecture can be run on a variety of different devices, from microprocessors to biosensors monitors. Within the project many examples of application prototypes are provided to clearly show these software properties [2, 14]. By mean of the PalVM, the virtual machine developed within the PalCom project, palpable software objects can potentially be instantiated in everyday technologies as well as in personal objects.

Each resource can function as an isolated component of the original system in which they were embodied (e.g. a single peripheral of the laptop) and can be purposely collected in newly created assemblies for explicit activities and uses. As assemblies become increasingly dynamic there's an urgent need for handling resources and debugging processes in detailed and useful ways. Managing resources and inspecting processes proves to be dramatically critical in the use of dynamic assemblies. Indeed the quality of the service mainly relies on the different levels of accuracy of the created assemblies [14].

4.3 Resilience

Applications, systems and users might insert faults and prohibited behaviour into modern, distributed computer systems. Technical breakdowns and malfunction might occur as well within a system. Resilience within the palpable architecture aims at suppress or compensate these non-normalized situations by applying the, at the time and situation, most appropriate counter-measures. This can be shifting preferred input and/or output device (e.g. network interfaces and information displays), re-allocating memory or even allocating memory on other devices to compensate heavy system load. These decisions are (if not made by a user, at least) made visible to the user, to empower the user to understand the error situation and drive the activity to overcome the failure [15]. To support this activity and others, three middleware managers exists to control and maintain the lifecycle of the Palcom services and components. These are:

- the Assembly Manager, responsible for the creation and lifecycle management of PalCom Assemblies. [16]

- the Resource Manager, maintains an up-to-date directory of all active (and if required, inactive) 2nd Order Resources. [16]
- the Contingency Manager, maintains resource and assembly resilience by monitoring failure and problem conditions and applying both reactive and proactive compensation policies and mechanisms. [16]

5   The BioAssembly Designed for NICU

Nowadays many efforts are devoted to design smart monitoring and telemonitoring devices, capable to detect human signals while the subject is at work, during sport activities or simply at home without interfering with his/her spontaneous behavior. This kind of monitoring is based on the concept of using sensors and transducers embedded in the surrounding environment, clothes and other wearable objects. This is generally known as unobtrusive measure of biosignals [17-19], where new sensors and transducers represent the implementation of the physical layer in basic interface between subjects and acquisition systems.

Unobtrusive monitoring devices can become a part of a complete system able to optimize the health-care processes reducing also the failures. It is important to discriminate the problem of realizing wearable and embedded sensors and the problem of the design of systems capable to collect data [18, 21]. PalCom architecture is well suited for a critical monitoring scenario, where the characteristics of the babies are more demanding in respect of adult or elderly people (for whom wearable monitoring devices were primarily developed). Designing biomedical devices for PalCom implies to face problems related to the design of sensors and monitoring devices, the quality of the acquired data, the cost of the systems and the comfort of the user during the usage. In particular unobtrusive monitoring offers new perspectives for the creation of a PalCom architecture in an incubator system, where it is necessary to gather as much information as possible, without interfering with the premature children and interacting with other standard clinical devices.

Novel research within the domain provides interesting solutions for sensors and transducers, but, besides the interesting prototypes realized, they still do not reach a really flexible, smart and embedded solution suitable for the application described in this paper. Furthermore it is difficult to find a complete solution for the many different signals monitored in an incubator. In our work we proposed and demonstrated the possibility to realize an unobtrusive disappearing biosignals monitoring systems fully integrated in a PalCom assembly, which can acquire signals through wearable and environmental sensors and transducers.

The BioAssembly described in details in the following paragraph consists of the BioBelt prototype developed within the project, the use of the current existing Pulse Oximeter, the use of a software Ventilator simulator, the PalCom (communication) Nodes and the Assembly Browser, used to manage the devices and the communication. The above-described Open Architecture is introduced in an incubator setting and integrated, through the BioAssembly, with other standard medical devices in order to provide an adaptable and reliable monitoring station for newborns able to monitor SpO2, electrocardiogram (ECG), Heart rate (HR), breathing rate (BR), movement and skin temperature (SKT).

ECG. The standard measurement of electric biosignals (e.g. ECG) requires a low resistance and stable electrical contact between the skin surface and the electrodes. This requirement is typically met by applying the Ag-AgCl electrodes on the subjects' skin, with a film of conductive gel in order to reduce the artefacts generated at the interface. This traditional solution is suitable for a clinical assessment at the physicians laboratory but, obviously, cannot be used in the frame of an unobtrusive acquisition of the signals. In this latter case the electrodes cannot be directly applied on the subjects body, or better electrodes are in contact to subject body through non standard supports like clothes where they are integrated in.

Aiming at satisfying the specifications originated from this application, the recent progresses in the textile technology which yielded to the availability of conductive fibres. These yarns are being used to create textile sensors directly integrated in a garment, or also in furniture and mostly every other textile-covered object in the environment [18, 20]. In our prototypes, we used conductive yarns to create electrodes and conductive pathways. It is worth noting that the performances of these systems can also depend on the characteristics of the skin and the specific respiration rate, which can alter them.

Movement. The standard technologies for movement analysis are video and optoelectronic motion capture systems, widely used in clinical, domotics and research applications. Unfortunately these technologies can not satisfy our requirements in terms of portability, wearability and integration in the commercial devices. Although there are systems already introduced in the ambient, for our applications it is conceivable to look for smarter and more efficient solutions in the Micro-Electro-Mechanical Systems (MEMS) technology which provides enough precision and cost effective solutions. They can sense acceleration, in order to obtain indirect indication on subjects movement and posture [22].

Respiration. There are many techniques which can be used in order to assess respiratory activity. Discarding the optical ones, for the same reasons argued in the previous session, the acquisition can be made with different wearable systems:

- Impedance inductive plethysmography [23];
- Resistive or piezoelectric strain gauges;
- Direct measurement of the impedance of the thorax.
- Accelerometers on upper body
- Thermistor placed at the nostril entrance.

The latter two systems are not suitable for monitoring chest movement, but are suitable for breathing rate measure. The BioBelt system adopted a textile-extensimeter suitable for measuring chest dilatations.

5.1 The BioBelt

What are the technologies available to realize small, integrated and portable solutions in order to implement unobtrusive acquisition? Is it possible to realize processing

 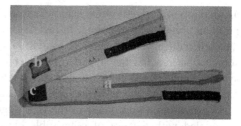

Fig. 1. The Belt prototype: The respiratory sensor (a), an electrode for ECG (b), and the pocket for the accelerometer (c) are shown

systems which can disappear in the surrounding environment? Many concrete ideas can be imagined and considered, but practically there are many specifications which have to be addressed [21]. The BioBelt is a wearable device functionally augmented with a set of sensors to be placed between the infant's chest and abdomen. Our prototype is made out of soft fabric (cotton – for bio-compatibility – plus lycra – for a best fitting of the sensors to the body), with biosensors directly integrated in the tissue (Fig. 1).

First of all, we searched the possibility to realize miniaturized systems, with a flexible architecture suitable for palpable applications. The measuring specifications for biosignals (see table 1) in terms of sampling rate, bandwidth, data throughput, filtering) can be met through a proper electronics design.

Table 1. Typical bandwidth of the proposed signals [24]

ECG Holter	0.05-55Hz
RESPIRATION	<1Hz
SKT	DC
MOVEMENT	DC-25Hz

We remind that in unobtrusive measurements are adopted sensors embedded in garments or in environment, and consequently the skin/electrode impedance dramatically increases [25-26]. The first stage of acquisition systems is the most critical for the following reasons:

1. It has to collect the signals from the sensors;
2. It is responsible of the first, most important amplification;
3. It has to reject common mode voltages;
4. It has to provide the rejection of the low frequencies drift and noise.

Moreover the possible instability of the contact between skin and sensors, particularly when the subject moves, becomes more critical. The consequent skin-motion artefacts caused by the subject movement might affect the low frequency components of the signal, increasing the possibility of saturation of the input front-ends [25, 27]. Considering the model of the skin proposed by Fowles [28], with the assumption of perfectly polarisable electrodes, it is possible to deeply understand the problem of electrical coupling. In fact the high resistance presented to the sensors by the cutis induces a poor signal transmission, reducing the coupling between the signal source (that reaches the hypodermal layer) and the input stage of the amplification system. Such sensors increase also the effects related to the instability of the contact, enhancing high frequency noise, which can corrupts the signals.

The high input impedance of the first stage of our biopotential amplifiers, when it is coupled with the use of polarisable electrodes and unstable contact, makes the circuit prone to collect the 50Hz external interferences producing an increase of the risk of output saturation. The adoption of wireless transmission (this solution allows to reduce the EMI coupling of the cable), ad-hoc printed circuits board (PCB) layouts and shielding, when possible, allowed us to provide solutions for the mentioned problems without requiring an hardware notch-filter, but only a first order, high-pass filter and a third order, low-pass filter. A low-cost, industrial microcontroller was used in this device, coupled with a 12-bits analogue to digital converter (ADC).

As wireless solution, we adopted a commercial class II Bluetooth® module (PAN1540, Panasonic: Matsushita Europe) able to transmit all the data with only 30mA of average current absorption. The transmission data rate was set in order to optimize the power consumption without affect signal quality (the higher is the sampling frequency, the lower will be the noise acquired by the ADC). The Bluetooth technology allows the systems to integrate itself with many other different devices. This feature is extremely useful in a dynamic "palpable" assembly: moreover the distributed, pervasive computing of PalCom architectures, allows for the distribution of rules and parameters for decision making and inspection processes can be shared between different devices. An example of data output from the BioBelt, is shown in Fig. 2.

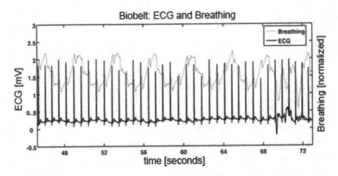

Fig. 2. ECG signal and breathing signal acquired through the Belt (adult people)

5.2 Pulse Oximeter

We have used a Masimo Radical Pulse Oximeter [29]. It permits monitoring of SpO_2 and Heartrate values (with timestamps) over a serial RS-232 line. The Pulse Oximeter is connected to a Palcom node utilizing this serial communication link.

5.3 Simulated Ventilator

As in the current state of development, we can not try this system on a real premature newborn we simulate the Ventilator with an accelerometer placed on the BioBelt. The solution to fully include a real Ventilator in the system is similar to the Pulse Oximeter, as has been described, is already implemented with the real hardware.

5.4 Palcom Nodes

The PalCom node is an I/O-device functioning as a bridge between non-palpable devices (existing technologies in the ward) and the PalCom technologies. This allows non-palpable equipment to take part in palpable assemblies [9].

PalCom architecture can exploit the resources available in "Palpable" devices to establish the connection between them and to manage the flow of information through the assembly. In the working scenario depicted in this paper, the three main devices (BioBelt, Pulse Oximeter and Ventilator) were introduced in the architecture through their available channels (Bluetooth, RS-232, Adapter). This transport allowed us to create different Palcom nodes and services regarding the specific information acquired from the instruments. More in detail, in this preliminary study we created the BioBelt Node, the Pulse Oximeter Node (Saturation) and the Ventilator Node. The signals coming from the first two nodes provide us with raw signals that PalCom services can process and convert in synthetic parameters like Heart rate (BioBelt and Pulse Oximeter), Breathing rate (BioBelt and Ventilator), SpO_2 (Pulse Oximeter) and Posture (BioBelt).

Other nodes can be represented by for example a Webcam and microphones, useful for more reliable inspections of the baby. In order to provide a complete vision of the whole scenario, different services have been deployed in the framework, extracting the parameters required by the clinicians.

The different clusters of information (HR, BR, Movement etc.) can be analyzed through real-time processing, compared with values of the same clusters (e.g. HR of the BioBelt vs. HR of the SpO_2). Through applying different, specific rules the assembly can show and indicate the reliability of the different data. The subsequent presentation of the raw data is another resource that is possible to show in order to help clinicians in the decision-making process of potential fault or babies' critical conditions. Such flexible solution is suitable not only for an inspection scenario, but also for the daily monitoring scenario, especially when coupled with the other technologies that are going to be develop d in PalCom project.

5.5 Assembly Browser

With the browser users can manage assemblies throughout the whole assembly lifecycle [30]. It allows the users to construct, initiate assemblies as well as reconfigure and turning off assemblies along the activity. The Assembly browser exists today as one version targeting developers. One intended for the end-users are now being under development [9]. An example of services running in the Assembly Browser can bee seen in Fig. 3.

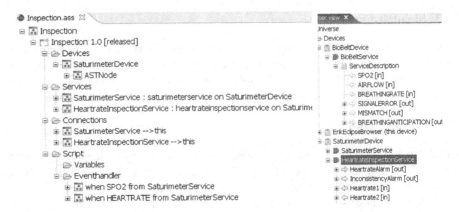

Fig. 3. Different Palcom nodes running, visualized in the Assembly Browser

6   Inspection Through the BioAssembly

The Incubator is a re-configurable system that can be adapted accordingly throughout the different treatments, thus allowing the medical staff to respond to the development of the baby more flexibly and sensitively. The palpable devices (e.g. the BioBelt) can be assembled in combination with the current equipment (e.g. the Pulse Oximeter) through the Assembly Browser and can result in a deeper understanding of the baby's conditions. Indeed in this way any failure in the functional connections among the assembly components can be easily detected, in particular those which directly affect the baby's conditions.

The Incubator assemblies described above define a system of different components that can allow novel forms of inspection by relying on the networking among the assembly components. This allows the medical staff to respond to the evolution of the baby conditions more flexibly and sensitively. In this system different assemblies can co-exist (e.g. the BioBelt, the Pulse Oximeter and the assembly browser in parallel with the BioBelt, the Pulse Oximeter and the Ventilator) integrating palpable applications with the existing equipment in the NICU.

This notion of assembly captures a very critical feature of the work the NICU. The use of the BioAssembly in this setting can significantly modify this situation by establishing novel connections among the incubator equipment and making it visible the functional relations among the assembly components.

6.1   Inspection Strategies

We have been designing technologies that can be used to create flexible incubator assemblies that can be adapted on-the-fly for different kinds of treatments and situations. This allows the staff members to manage events related to the baby care more flexibly and sensitively.

The neonatologist can combine the value of SpO_2, Heart Rate and Breathing Rate coming from the BioBelt, with the data from other machinery and sensors, currently

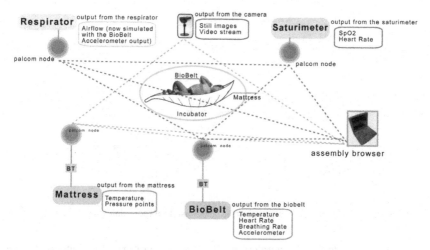

Fig. 4. Two possible concurrent assemblies running on the system

in use at the NICU, in order to get more detailed assessment of the baby conditions. A first BioAssembly configuration consists of the Pulse Oximeter and the biosensors Belt for monitoring of the Sp02 values (Fig. 4).

In the figure above, an exemplification of the notion of assembly is provided. In this application two assemblies co-exist and integrate data to monitor the baby's conditions, anticipate the occurrence of problems and allow for system's inspection by using the networking properties of the assemblies. In detail, the 'red assembly' reveals the functional interdependencies among the current respirator at the NICU, the Pulse Oximeter and the BioBelt in order to monitor the respiratory abnormalities and heart rate functions of the baby and to allow for the coupling of any failure at the level of one device with the baby's conditions and with the information coming from the other devices. In this way, the standard redundancy inspection method is combined with the networking strategy supported by the assembly [9].

Currently, when a variation in the SpO_2 value occurs, the process of understanding the baby conditions can be long and can generate misinterpretations, due to the difficulties of understanding if the values depend on the newborn condition or is they are generated by any malfunction of the machine.

The use of assemblies not only allow to connect PalCom devices with existing ones but its networking properties support the inspection of the system by checking the status of the functional connections among the different components of the assembly. To facilitate this task, the belt can transmit also the raw biosignals (ECG and the chest dilatation (respiratory movement)) thus facilitating the understanding of possible sensors' failures.

In the implemented system, it is possible to recognize two complementary strategies to allow inspection of the system behaviour. The first one is illustrated in Fig. 5. In this case a classical *redundant error handling strategy* is applied. The heart rate (HR) detected by the Pulse Oximeter (HR1) is continuously compared with the heart rate coming from the BioBelt (HR2) that the child wears. In this application an

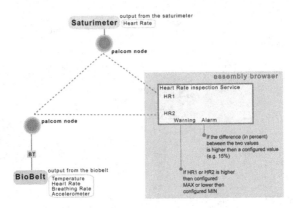

Fig. 5. Inspection strategies based on redundancy

"inconsistency alarm" is generated each time the compared values overcome a defined threshold, for a predefined number of pulses. This can indicate a fault in the setup providing a classical inspection strategy which compares the same value coming from different sources. Currently this comparison is done by the medical staff without any external support [9].

The "fault alarm" is different from the alarm regarding biological condition (i.e. HR go over or go under the thresholds set by the clinicians). In the complex scenario here investigated, also the possibility to discriminate between problems in health condition and the less critical instrument error.

In the scenario illustrated in Fig. 4, the Ventilator provides the child with oxygen, while the breathing rate, which correlates to the ventilator function, is monitored by the BioBelt; the SpO_2 values are monitored by the Pulse Oximeter. Whether any malfunction occurs in the ventilator the discovery protocols enabled by the PalCom nodes will propagate the information on the missing signal from the ventilator to the whole assembly. These inspection scenarios are developed to bridge current problems in the medical practice, where the different monitoring devices are not functional connected. Here the flexible, loosely coupled system approach provided by a palpable middleware can prove useful. This creates a novel inspection opportunity for the user who can understand what is going wrong and at which level of the system, showing the potential impact of "palpable" and "unobtrusive" technologies applied in the health care context. The scenario described here represents a first functional device and system implementation. This system has been developed with the actual users and responds to their specific requests. An experimental study conducted with the medical staff at the NICU will provide more insights on the use of assembly in this setting. An initial 1 month test-period of the system is going to be performed in order to assess the use of the BioBelt as an unobtrusive monitoring device and what diagnostic opportunities the notion of assemblies together with the different inspection strategies can offer for the neonatologists' daily practice.

7 Conclusion

The research has been strongly influenced by the critical setting of the NICU. An Intensive care situation provides a highly dynamic environment where a number of heterogeneous actors co-exist. This ongoing, dynamically changing situation provides very specific, but in the same time, continuously changing requirements. The BioAssembly prototype and the emerging framework of Palpable computing investigates on a functional, logical and activity level the notion of Ambient computing and what requirements needs to be fulfilled when applying ambient systems within such a critical setting as the NICU. Thus we have described visibility, construction and user control as key components for ambient systems design in dynamic and critical situations. Visibility emerges as an important property for the different users to understand the status of the system and potential error situations. By mean of the PalCom architecture, users can then construct assemblies of heterogeneous technologies as discussed in this paper. Differently from common ambient computing solutions, the palpable framework aim to provide awareness and control over the system for the users. Further studies and field trials have to be made, but these early results are coherent with outcomes from other studies in emergency and intensive care situations [31-32]. However, these changes have to be implemented both from a technical perspective (i.e. support implemented in the software architecture) and from an activity perspective (i.e. the way users do perceive these ambient systems and how they can interact with them). Initial results show the possibility to use redundancy inspection scenarios within this domain. We would now like to further investigate other inspection strategies (e.g. network-based inspection [9]) to understand how the user can make sense and perceive the assemblies, in particular in relation to breakdowns and failures in ambient computing systems.

Acknowledgments. Thanks to Prof. Bagnoli, Maria Grazia Burroni and the medical staff at the Neonatal Intensive Care Unit of the "Le Scotte" hospital, Siena, for their open-minded collaboration and continuous support. Furthermore, we would like to thank Patrizia Marti at the University of Siena, without her this work would not have been possible. The research was part of the EC IST PalCom project (www.ist-palcom.org).

References

1. Weiser, M.: The Computer for the Twenty-First Century, pp. 94–10. Scientific American (September 1991)
2. Schultz, U.P., Corry, E., Lund, K.E.: Virtual Machines for Ambient Computing: A Palpable Computing Perspective. In: Black, A.P. (ed.) ECOOP 2005. LNCS, vol. 3586, Springer, Heidelberg (2005)
3. Rullo, A., Marti, P., Grönvall, E., Pollini, A.: End-user composition and re-use of technologies in the Neonatal Intensive Care Unit. In: Proceedings of Pervasive Healthcare 2006, 29 November – 1 December, Innsbruck, Austria (2006)

4. Grönvall, E., Marti, P., Pollini, A., Rullo, A., Bertelesen, O.: Palpable time for heterogeneous care communities. In: Proceedings of Critical Computing between Sense and Sensibility, The Fourth Decennial Aarhus Conference, August 20-24, Aarhus, Denmark (2005)

5. Kyng, M.: Scandinavian Design: Users in Product Development. In: CHI 1994. Human Factors in Computing Systems, Celebrating Interdependence, Association for Computing Machinery, Boston, MA (1994)

6. Ehn, P., Kyng, M.: The collective resource approach to systems design. In: Bjerknes, G., Ehn, P., Kyng, M. (eds.) Computers and democracy - a Scandinavian challenge, Gower, Aldershot, UK (1987)

7. Höök, K.: Designing Familiar Open Surfaces. In: NordiCHI 2006, Oslo, Norway, ACM Press, New York (2006)

8. Gaver, B., Dunne, T., Pacenti, E.: Design: Cultural probes. Interactions 6(1), 21–29 (1999)

9. Marti, P., Grönvall, E., Pollini, A., Rullo, A.: Designing inspection strategies for palpable Assemblies, Designing for Palpability. In: Workshop at Pervasive 2007, May 13-17, Toronto, Canada (2007)

10. Grönvall, E., Marti, P., Pollini, A., Rullo, A.: Active surfaces: a novel concept for end user composition. In: NordiCHI 2006 (October 14-18, 2006)Oslo, Norway (2006)

11. Ingstrup, M., Hansen, K.M.: Palpable Assemblies: Dynamic Service Composition for Ubiquitous Computing. In: Proceedings of the Seventeenth International Conference on Software Engineering and Knowledge Engineering, Taipei, Taiwan, Republic of China (July 2005)

12. Brown, A., Johnston, S., Kelly, K.: Using Service Oriented Architecture and Component Based Development to Build Web Services Application. Rational-IBM White paper, 2003Brown, A.: Large-Scale, Component-Based Development. Prentice Hall, Englewood Cliffs (2000)

13. Büscher, M., Christensen, M., Hansen, K.M., Mogensen, P., Shapiro, D.: Bottom-up, top-down? Connecting software architecture design with use. In: Voss, A., Hartswood, M., Ho, K., Procter, R., Rouncefield, M., Slack, R., Büscher, M. (eds.) Configuring user-designer relations: Interdisciplinary perspectives, Springer, Heidelberg (2005) PalCom. PalCom External Report 31: Deliverable 32 (2.2.1): PalCom Open Architecture – first complete version of basic architecture. Technical report, PalCom Project IST-002057 (October 2005), http://www.ist-palcom.org/publications/deliverables/Deliverable-32-[2.2.1]-palcom-open-architecture.pdf

14. PalCom. PalCom External Report 50: Deliverable 39 (2.2.2): PalCom Open Architecture. Technical report, PalCom Project IST-002057 (December 2006), http://www.ist-palcom.org/publications/deliverables/Deliverable-39-[2.2.2]-Palcom-Open-Architecture.pdf

15. Di Rienzo, M., Andreoni, G., Piccini, L.: A Wearable system for the unobtrusive measure of ecg. In: Proceedings of Mediterranean Conference on Medical and Biological Engineering, Naples, Italy (July-August 2004)

16. Lymberis, D.d.R.A.: Wearable eHealth systems for personalised health management. IOS press, Amsterdam (2004)

17. Picard, R.W., Healey, J.: Affective Wearables. Personal Technologies. Personal and Ubiquitous Computing 1, 231–240 (1997)

18. Post, E., Orth, M.: Smart Fabric, or "wearable clothing". IEEE Computer Society Press, Los Alamitos (1997)

19. Piccini, L., Arnone, L., Beverina, F., Cucchi, A., Petrelli, L., Andreoni, G.: Wireless DSP architecture for biosignals recording. In: Proceedings of IEEE international Symposium on Signal Processing and Information Technology Conference, Rome, Italy (2004)
20. Veltink, P.H., Bussmann, H.B.J., de Vries, W., Martens, W.L.J., Van Lummel, R.C.: Detection of static and dynamic activities using uniaxial accelerometers. IEEE Tran. Rehabil. Eng. 4(4), 357–385 (1996)
21. Grossman, P., Wilhelm, F., Spoerle, M.: Respiratory sinus arrhytmia, cardiac vagal control, and daily activity
22. Webster, J.G.: Medical instrumentation: Application and Design. Wiley, Chichester (1997)
23. Webster, J.G.: Noise sources in surfaces electrodes. Innov. Tech. Biol. Med. 12(1), 39–45 (1991)
24. Jossinet, J., McAdams, E.T.: The skin/electrode interfaces impedance. Innov. Tech. Biol. Med. 12(1), 21–31 (1991)
25. Zinc, R.: Distortion and interference in the measurement of electric signals from the skin (ecg, emg, eeg). Innov. Tech. Biol. Med. 12(1), 46–57 (1991)
26. Fowles, D.C., Christie, M.J., Edelberg, R., Grings, W.W., Lykken, D.T., Venables, P.H.: Publication recommendations for electro-dermal measurements. Psychophysiology 18(3) (1981)
27. http://www.masimo.com/pulseOximeter/radical.htm
28. Svensson, D., Magnusson, B., Hedin, G.: Composing adhoc applications on ad-hoc networks using MUI. In: Proceedings of Net.ObjectDays, 6th Annual International Conference on Object-Oriented and Internet-based Technologies, Concepts, and Applications for a Networked World, Erfurt, Germany (September 2005)
29. Kristensen, M., Kyng, M., Palen, L.: Participatory design in emergency medical service: designing for future practice. In: Proceedings of the SIGCHI conference on Human Factors in computing systems, Montréal, Québec (2006)
30. Kyng, M., Toftdahl Nielsen, E.: Challenges in designing interactive systems for emergency response. In: Proceedings of the 6th ACM conference on Designing Interactive systems, University Park, PA, USA (2006)

Improving Mobile Solution Workflows and Usability Using Near Field Communication Technology

Päivi Jaring, Vili Törmänen, Erkki Siira, and Tapio Matinmikko

VTT Technical Research Center of Finland, 90571 Oulu, Finland
{paivi.jaring,vili.tormanen,erkki.siira,tapio.matinmikko}@vtt.fi

Abstract. Organisations want nowadays more controlled processes and easily usable solutions, but achieving them requires winning many challenges. Radio Frequency Identification (RFID) based technology has been proposed for improving mobile solution workflows and usability. NFC (Near Field Communication) technology is based on integrating RFID on mobile devices. This paper identifies how NFC based systems could be used to improve mobile solution workflows and usability. The results of this study are based on the implementation of six pilot cases in 2005-2007. This paper concludes that use of NFC provides both advantages and disadvantages and, therefore, to estimate the potential of NFC, its pros and cons have to be weighed up for each case in question. This paper also concludes that only a comprehensive solution achieves the full potential of NFC from users' point of view. Considering mobile solution usability, this paper concludes that NFC based solutions are easy to use, but the small and limited keyboard of mobile devices poses challenges to the design of these solutions. NFC use poses new organizational challenges like need for the rest of the system to catch up and feeling of distrust from the user side.

Keywords: NFC, RFID, mobile, workflow, usability.

1 Introduction

Organisations want nowadays more and more controlled workflows and easily usable systems, but achieving these requires winning obstacles caused for example by mobile/remote work and usability limitations of mobile devices.

Workers whose work has been somewhat mobile or remote, i.e. the worker works at customer site or some other location chosen by him [1][2], have partly caused difficulties in achieving controlled workflows. Mobile workers include for example travelling managers, field workers and emergency rescuers [3]. Mobile solution workflows are work processes realized by mobile workers using a mobile device. Common problems that organisations with mobile workers encounter include the following:

- limited access to information and data collection applications in the field,
- manual use of pen and paper in the field causes a lot of paperwork when the worker is back at the office,
- manual re-entry of the collected data enhances the risk of making errors,
- outdated client information/service history, and
- outdated site/product/service instructions. [4]

B. Schiele et al. (Eds.): AmI 2007, LNCS 4794, pp. 358–373, 2007.

Usability defines the extent to which specified goals defined by users can be achieved [5]. To gain user acceptance a solution has to:

- support user tasks and goals, which means that the actions offered should correspond to what they want to do;
- acknowledge the strengths and limitations of people and technologies, which means that the application keeps its users in charge of activities; and
- fit into the users' big picture, i.e. to the several aspects outside the immediate focus of the work [6].

Designing a user-friendly solution requires taking the following characteristics of contexts into account

- physical context, i.e. variable lighting conditions, noise, varying climate, physical moving of the user,
- social context, i.e. need to share information with others [7]
- tasks and organizational characteristics [5], and
- environment, which includes the physical context but also hardware, software and materials [5].

For improving mobile solution workflows and usability, Vuorinen [4] proposes using RFID based technology that along NFC is one of the most common technologies to implement the touching paradigm. In the touching paradigm the interaction in the environment is realized by bringing the mobile device into contact or very close to a smart object. Touching as an interaction method is natural to humans as we often touch things we want to use. [8, 9] Studies have shown that the touching paradigm is easy to learn and intuitive to use [8]. The basic idea behind RFID is that items are marked with tags that contain transponders that emit messages readable by specialized RFID readers. NFC is based on integrating already existing RFID technology [10] to mobile devices such as mobile phones. In this study RFID is defined as an underlying technology of NFC, i.e. use of the terms is very close to each other. NFC has been defined in standards [11, 12] as a short-range wireless technology that allows device communication in close proximity [13]. NFC is evolved from the earlier near-field RFID contactless identification and interconnection technologies such as ISO14443, MIFARE and FeliCa [14]. NFC-device can communicate with another NFC enabled device or communicate with a RFID/NFC-tag [15]. All tags have a 4 to 10 byte long unique ID number, which can effectively be used to identify the tag. As the IDs vary between different manufacturers and technologies, collisions may occur with multiple manufacturers.

The most interesting RFID applications include the ones for supply chain management, security, and tracking of objects and personnel [16]. The advantages of the RFID based systems are the following: 1) real time updating of data, 2) removal of human error, 3) integration of different modules, 4) ability to manage product's whole lifecycle, 5) ability to remote support [17], and 6) real-time access to information and applications.

RFID technology, though being used in logistics for decades, is a novel concept when used with mobile phones or other devices over a network connection. The main challenges of mobile devices targeted to non-technical users are limited input/output facilities, which include small screens, poor audio output, limited keyboard both in size and number of keys [18]. The mobile workers of today are familiar with mobile phones, but use of RFID enabled phones is an unknown territory for them. For example in the pilot 6, the maintenance men report, instead of using the traditional per and paper -method, their inspections several times a week via mobile phone by answering to the questions sent them by the back end system.

This paper illustrates how NFC can be used to improve mobile solution workflows and usability.

1.1 Scope of the Study

All the pilots presented in this study were done in the city of Oulu, Finland. Finland has been selected as the target country of the pilots, because of 1) the extensive coverage of mobile phones in the country [19] and 2) the potential of remote work due to long distances provide a good environment for NFC use. Table 1 explains the pilots in more detail.

Service provider means in this study a company that provides the service and service user a company that uses the service. In pilots 1-3 the service provider (SP) and -user is the same company; in pilots 4-6 the service user and -provider are different companies. In this study, the term user refers to both genders although we have used the terms he/his when referring to a user. The companies functioning as service providers and -users were selected to this study based on their 1) existing active involvement in use of mobile technologies in improving organizational issues, and 2) the need of solving existing real life problems by using NFC.

The specific pilots were selected into this study, because 1) we wanted to find various kinds of application areas where NFC could be used, and 2) each of the pilot cases involved organizational issues and problems that needed to be improved.

Experiences from the pilots were collected by interviewing the service users and managers of the service user organization. Users of each pilot -except the pilot 1- were interviewed face-to-face. In pilot 1, the two user groups were sent the questions beforehand by email and 2-3 representatives per user group replied them in an interview. The interviewees had to answer six open-ended questions concerning: 1) usefulness of the pilots, 2) advantages and disadvantages that occurred when using the pilots, 3) their feelings considering use of the touching paradigm, and 4) deficiencies/improvements in the pilot use. The interviewed managers represented the management level of each organization in the pilot implementation. The interviews of the managers were free-form, i.e. the interviewees analyzed in an open discussion the true causes and effects of NFC use. A freeform interview was chosen because the organizations were different and problems the NFC-based solutions tried to solve were different.

1.2 Goal and Outline

This paper aims to identify how NFC based systems could be used to improve the mobile solution workflows and usability. The experiences received from NFC use in this study are based on implementation of six pilot cases in 2005-2007. The presented pilots are categorized into two groups as presented in section 3.

This paper contributes RFID/NFC related research by presenting implementation of six real pilot cases for solving real organizational issues and problems in various application areas. As there is not much research available in this area, contributions presented in this paper are worthwhile for other researchers in the domain.

The paper is composed as follows. Section two presents the related research after which the pilot cases and their rationale are presented. Section four presents results received from applying NFC to the pilots. The paper is concluded by an outline to further research topics.

2 Related Research

Considering the impact of NFC on organization in general there is not too much research available. Most of the research considering RFID/NFC use is focused on the use of RFID in logistical solutions and supply chain management. The related research presented in this section focuses on RFID/NFC use from the viewpoint of mobile solution workflows and usability.

Michael and McCathie handle in their article [20] pros and cons of RFID in supply chain management. According to their research, RFID reduces labor and enhances visibility, but is on the other hand costly and lacks standardization.

Chuang and Shaw evaluate in their article [21] the impact of RFID on supply chain networks. According to them, RFID can improve operational efficiencies, increase visibility and eliminate errors, but is costly to implement.

Lefebvre et al. examine in their article [22] the potential of RFID in warehouse activities. They conclude that RFID eliminates inefficiencies, adds value to processes and increases electronic integration between supply chain members. According to them, RFID also poses several challenges to organizations including need for radical changes to existing business processes and strain on the capacity to manage all received data.

Yoon et al. show in their research [17] prototype of RFID enabled aircraft maintenance system that is integrated with part management system. According to their research, the implementation of their RFID pilot will have many advantages compared to the existing system, for example removal of human error, ability to manage whole product lifecycle.

Norman presents in his book [23] seven principles how to transform difficult tasks into easy ones. The presented principles help the designers to take user centerd design into account. According to Norman [23] designers should make sure "that the user can figure out what to do and the user can tell what is going on".

Belt et al. present in their paper [24] a study of user perceptions on mobile interaction with visual and RFID-tags. Most of the users of their study viewed RFID as being quick, taking less effort, and feeling natural compared to visual tags. The users of their study were not familiar with the concept of RFID and were surprised on unexpected access to networked data resources. The study also revealed potential usability risks with the mobile interaction with RFID and visual tags. The study also showed that there are no existing practises and mental models for the usage of the tags in the studied consumer domain.

Välkkynen and Tuomisto study in their research [25] physical browsing by using passive long-range RFID-tags. They concluded that from users' point of view invisibility of RFID-tags can cause problems such as: 1) how can a user know what action of functionality will follow from activating a link, and 2) how does a user know what part of the object the link is if he knows of its existence etc.

Salminen et al. compared in their study [26] a standard Bluetooth device and service discovery method with RFID based service selection by asking users to print a short note with application and printer service. Fourteen out of fifteen users of their study preferred the RFID enhanced method, because of the following reasons: 1) it was faster to use 2) there was no need for menu selections, and 3) it was easier or more pleasant to use. One user of the study preferred RFID based method, because it was seen as a less technical method. Some users of the study regarded the RFID based method unreliable or untrustworthy.

3 Pilot Cases

This section presents the six pilots of this study and rationale for the information gathered from the pilots. The pilots presented in this section are divided into two categories based on the information they gather. In the first category (pilots 1, 3 and 4) the pilots gather only location- and timestamp- information, i.e. the users report their location that is mapped with timestamp to gather log to know where he has been and when. In Figure 1 the process for gathering location- and timestamp-information is marked with number 1. In the second category (pilots 2, 5 and 6) the users report the location and timestamp, but also some additional information, so a user has to complete both processes 1 and 2 of Figure 1.

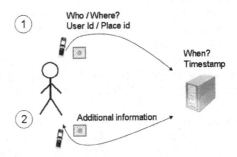

Fig. 1. Basic processes of the pilot applications

Implementation and deployment of the software of pilots 1, 2 and 4-6, all user training, mid-pilot oversights and gathering post-pilot information were done by VTT (The Technical Research Centre of Finland). The pilot 3 was implemented in cooperation with VTT and a RFID system integrator. The oversights included technical support for the users and overall surveillance on how the pilot was working.

Table 1 presents the six pilots of this study, their user amount, the category, aim of each pilot and the users involved. The duration of all the pilots was 8-12 weeks.

Table 1. Pilots of the study and their quality attributes

Pilot nr	Pilot name	User amount	Category	Aim of the pilot from users' point of view	Users involved
1	Work time management	16	Location- and timestamp information	Report work time accurately instead of pen/ paper	Library employees, swimming hall maintenance men
2	Driver's log	5	Location-, timestamp- and other information	Fill travel expenses forms for the compensation	Employees who used own car
3	Logistics	5	Location- and timestamp information	Provide timestamp information to the organization	Drivers who delivered the food
4	Cleaning	2	Location- and timestamp information	Report the time used for cleaning the conference rooms	Cleaner
5	Meter reading	1	Location-, timestamp- and other information	Report readings in electric form	Maintenance man
6	Maintenance	2	Location-, timestamp- and other information	Fill electronic service manual questions on the spot instead of doing it later on the control room	Maintenance men doing routine inspections

The pilots are presented in the following section in timely order based on their realization.

This following section presents the pilots in more detail.

3.1 Pilot 1: Work Time Management

The pilot was realized in the autumn 2005. All users of the pilot were employees of the service provider/user from two different administrative organizations. Of the pilot users, six were maintenance workers from the main swimming hall and 10 librarians from four different branch libraries. Before implementing the pilot the participants used the classic pen and paper -method for keeping track of their working times. The pilot users reported their work time by using the following process: 1) the user touches his individual ID-tag to confirm his identity as the current device user and 2) the user touches the location tag to confirm where he is. Phases 1 and 2 are realized when arriving to a work place and when leaving it.

3.2 Pilot 2: Driver's Log

The pilot was implemented in the autumn 2005 with five users who were employees of the SP. The users' work includes lots of driving with own car and thus they are entitled to compensations for each driven kilometer. To gain the compensations the users need to fill a travel expense form. Filling the expense form requires keeping a detailed log about the trips. The pilot application itself had not special features and its' ease of use made using it possible also for non-technical users. The process for using the pilot was the following: 1) the user touches his operational tag and the application is launched automatically, 2) the user fills appropriate fields, and 3) the data is sent to the backend system.

3.3 Pilot 3: Logistics

The pilot was implemented in the autumn 2006 as a part of NFC enabled catering service pilot. The participants of the pilot were five service provider/user's drivers, whose job is to distribute daily meals to elderly people. Before implementation of the pilot there was no formal control for tracking the realization of the delivery route. As tracking the delivery route is used for billing or route optimization, there is a need for the route control. In the NFC enabled process of the pilot, the route control was realized in the following way: 1) the user touches his individual ID-tag to confirm his identity, 2) when leaving for the route the user touches a correct "start route x" –tag on a kitchen wall, 3) when delivering a meal the user touches a tag in an elderly's house, and 4) when finishing the route the user touches the "end route" tag on a kitchen wall.

3.4 Pilot 4: Cleaning

The pilot was realized in the autumn 2006 with two users of the SP. The work of the users included cleaning meeting rooms and other premises. Before implementing the pilot, the time spent for cleaning each individual room was roughly estimated and the actual time was not traced. The pilot users reported cleaning time of each room by using the following process: 1) the user touches his individual ID-tag to confirm his identity, 2) when entering a room for cleaning the user touches a tag in that room, 3) when the cleaning has been finished and the user is leaving the room, he touches the same tag in a room, and 4) at the end of day, the user touches his ID-tag to end work shift.

3.5 Pilot 5: Meter Reading

The pilot was implemented in the autumn 2006 in the same project with pilot 4. The participant of the pilot was SP's maintenance man, who routinely reported electricity and water meter readings. Before implementing the pilot, the maintenance man used pen and paper-method for recording the meter id and its reading. Afterwards the readings were transferred to an excel-worksheet that was forwarded to the responsible person. With the help of a NFC enabled mobile phone, the maintenance man reported the meter readings in the following way: the user 1) touches the tag identifying the meter and 2) enters the meter reading in the phone. The phases 1 and 2 are repeated until all meters in the room are read.

3.6 Pilot 6: Maintenance

The pilot was implemented at the beginning of 2007. In the pilot, two maintenance men of the service user/provider reported their daily inspections in different parts of the facility. Before implementing the pilot, the reporting was done weekly via electric service manual. In the NFC based solution, the maintenance men reported their inspections several times a week via mobile phone by answering to the questions sent them by the back end system. The process for reporting the inspections in the pilot was the following: 1) at the beginning of the day the user touches his ID-tag to identify himself, 2) in each location the user touches the attached tag, 3) the user answers to the questions sent by the system, and 4) at the end of the work shift, the user touches his ID-tag. The phases 2 and 3 are repeated in every inspection location.

4 Results of Applying NFC to the Pilots

This section presents the advantages and disadvantages of NFC use for mobile solution workflows and usability based on the experiences received from the pilots. Additionally this section presents general challenges/problems of NFC use to the organisation and solving them in the pilot cases.

4.1 Advantages and Disadvantages of NFC Use for Mobile Solution Workflows

As an advantage of NFC use, based on the six pilot cases, are seen:

- Ability to decrease or eliminate duplicate work. The duplicate work was caused by an inefficient process where the data was first entered to paper and then moved into electronic form when user had access to a computer.
- Reducing users' memory payload. The payload was caused by several facts: 1) the pen/paper-bookkeeping was not always up to date, 2) there was not available right equipment for the bookkeeping or 3) there was no time for the bookkeeping. When the bookkeeping was not up to date, the user needed to memorize the facts until he had chance to update the files.
- Decreasing the amount of user made errors. Decreasing the amount of duplicate work decreased the user made errors, because the amount of opportunities to make errors was diminished.
- Increased capability of the system to verify user actions. Implementing the pilots enabled the system to verify that someone had been in a location at certain time and report accurately when the work was made.
- Increased demonstrability and verifiability that are important features in relationships between organisations. Contracts, laws, etc. give some prerequisites for the operations and in a case of disagreement it is good to have verifiable data to back up the claims of each party.

As disadvantages of NFC use were seen the following points:

- Shifting the bottleneck forward in the chain if information that is entered into the process in electronic form becomes unnecessarily manual in later phases.
- Investment needed for integrating the systems. To avoid shifting the bottleneck forward in the chain (see the previous point) all systems within the organization and between organizations has to be integrated and the data has to be turned into electronic form. Without integration, the advantages achieved in one spot will be eliminated in later phases.
- Limitations caused by the small user interface of the mobile device. Based on the pilot user experiences, the mobile device's keyboard seems to hinder the advantages of NFC. Although the touching based -interactions reduce the time needed for the task, the input via mobile device's keyboard is cumbersome. Thus from usability point of view the traditional pen/paper-method can be competitive, even if it means losing some other advantages like real time support.
- Investments needed for purchasing separate devices for reading the tags. As the selection of mobile phones that support reading RFID tags is limited, using NFC means additional investment from the SP on the phones that are able to read tags.

4.2   Advantages and Disadvantages of NFC Use for Mobile Solution Usability

Considering the user experience, in the pilot cases the most interesting points of view were:

1. How users experienced the touching paradigm, i.e. how touching by using a mobile phone feels. Users touched the tags for several reasons such as to launch the application, to identify themselves as users or to make time stamp.
2. How NFC-technology can advance use of mobile technology in work environment.

Table 2 summarizes the user experiences received from the pilots.

Table 2. Summary of the pilot user experiences

Gained usability advantage/disadvantage from users' point of view	Achieved in pilots
Touching paradigm (question 1)	
Easier usability: 1. touching the tags was experienced to be an easy way to get information from tags, 2. it was possible for the applications to start up with touching the tag, 3. there was no manual entry needed for identifying the user or place, 4. less need for textual input.	Points 1 and 2 realized in all pilots. Point 3 realized in pilots 1 and 3-6. The point 4 realized in pilot 4, where the users only needed to use checkboxes and check them to report that everything was ok; only if there was some problem the users needed to write a short textual commentary about the problem.

Table 2. (*continued*)

Advancing mobile technology in work environment (question 2)	
Improved accuracy	Pilot 1: more accurate time stamps for the working hour lists.
Reducing users' memory payload	Pilots 2 and 6: before implementation of the pilots, the users had to memorize their driving kilometres, places, amount of persons aboard and project numbers → now they can immediately fill the entries at the beginning and end of the trip.
Decreasing the phases in work flow by changing paper work into electronic form	All pilots: the users regarded transfer into an electronic way positively. Pilot 2: the acceptor of an expense form did not have to guess the handwriting as all the notes were printed.
Providing "electronic pipe" to deliver information.	Pilot 5: before implementing the pilot: 1) the reading was typed to the paper, 2) the correspondence between the figure on the paper, the figure of the meter and the ID of the meter was checked, and 3) the reading was transferred into electronic form → now the ID of the meter was read from the tag and the figure was checked simultaneously → removal of manual input.
Removing unnecessary driving from and to the office.	Pilot 6: some of the users liked the fact that they could enter the relevant information from their inspection route immediately as it 1) removed the need to visit PC (Personal Computer) after the route to fill the electronic service manual and 2) "forced to do the inspection with good care".
Using the system difficult due to hidden tags.	Pilot 4: the fact that the tags were hidden made them free from vandalism, but it also made the system 1) impossible to be used by temporary work force and 2) difficult to use at the beginning as the cleaners had difficulties to remember the tag locations.

Table 3 presents the realization of requirements for user friendliness in pilots.

Table 3 concludes that the goals for user friendliness and contexts were taken into account in the pilots, but they did always have impact on the user experience.

Table 3. Realization of user friendliness in pilots

Goal for a solution to gain user acceptance	Achieved in pilots
Support user tasks and goals	Yes/no. All pilots except 3 and 4 supported fully users' tasks and goals. Pilots 3 and 4 were not seen to be valuable to the end-users, but only to managers and supervisors.
Acknowledge the strengths and limitations of people and technologies	Yes. The pilot users were assumed to be novice mobile phone users, and therefore all applications were built as simple as possible. Small screen size and poor text input properties of mobile devices were taken into account when building the applications.

Table 3. (*continued*)

Fit into users' big picture	Yes. In pilot 1, the organizational culture was the key aspect that impacted the acceptance of accurate time stamping system in users' big picture. In pilots 2 and 5 no extra time was needed for handling the information several times. In pilots 3 and 4 the application did not improve the work processes, but the pilots were seen to be useful in assisting work planning. In Pilot 6 a mobile phone was a natural way for maintenance man to make reports on the inspection route.
Contexts that has to be taken into account	**Achieved in pilots**
Environment (software, hardware, materials, physical context)	Yes. In pilot 1 the requirement for an application to make a 'beep' when a tag is read, was inappropriate for the library employees, because they were used to the fact that beeping does not necessarily mean anything. The pilot 3 brought fourth phone for the use of the driver as he already had an own phone, a work phone and a car's phone. Thus carrying an additional phone generated negative feelings to use the application. The conclusion was that the work phone should have been NFC enabled to avoid carrying additional devices. In pilots 4-6 the working environment did not bother the use. The temperature of the working environment varied between +20°C and -20°C degrees and especially the cold temperature was taken into account by reducing the amount of keyboard use to minimum.
Tasks and organizational characteristics	Yes. In designing the pilots, the organizational needs and users' tasks were taken into account.

All in all based on the experiences received from the pilots, use of NFC has both advantages and disadvantages and, therefore, its pros and cons have to be weighed up for each case in question.

From pilot users' point of view, lessons learnt for the future solution design were the following:

1. *Place the tags carefully.* The tags should -based on the received experience- be in a visible location to avoid additional memory payload for the users and to help temporary workforce to use the system. For avoiding vandalism, the tags should be attached in such a way that they blend in with the environment or are protected. Tags can be protected with a plastic casing or attach them on hidden,

obvious and fixed locations (i.e. behind doorplate). Figure 2 demonstrates placing of tags on pilots 2, 4 and 6.

2. *Keep the amount of textual input information as minimum as possible for the task.* In some of the pilots the data input was done by using the keyboard of the mobile device, but the interviews revealed that even if entering numerical information into the system was regarded acceptable, the amount of textual input entered with mobile phone was very low. Because of the small keyboard, the textual input of data was made in the pilots rather with PC keyboard than with phone's keyboard. To facilitate entering textual input, for example PDA (Personal Digital Assistant) devices could be used in NFC solutions. In pilot 2, the users only typed at maximum the first letters of the route locations to indicate the place information; rest of the route information was entered afterwards by using a web interface. NFC helps the goal 2 for example by reducing the need to type login information.

3. *Enable interaction with other applications and systems.* In pilots, as a desirable feature it was seen possibility of the system to interact with other applications and systems. As NFC enables easy user and place identification, the services becomes easy to use for example by the aid of the place tag.

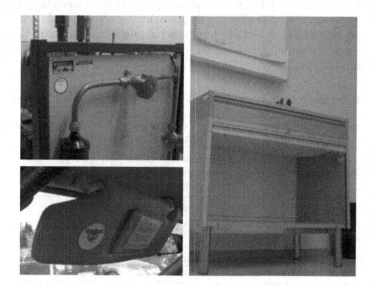

Fig. 2. Tag locations on pilots 2, 4 and 6: pilot 2 on bottom left, pilot 4 on the right and pilot 6 on upper left

4.3 Challenges of NFC Use to the Organization

When NFC enables a user to enter his data electronically into the organisation's information system, the *rest of the system must catch up*. Integration of various systems is challenging especially when the interaction occurs between several organizations [27]. Systems typically are characterized by different architectural solutions and implemented in various programming languages. These differences may cause problems when integrating systems in an inter-organizational context (as an example of potential problems see [28]). Before implementation of the pilots it seemed that the bottleneck of delivering information was the field worker and his slow reporting. Implementation of all the pilots showed that the rest of the organisation was not ready for the real time data input that NFC powered employees generate. The old processes, where paper reports from the field were circulated from desk to desk to get formal approvals, become new bottlenecks for information, if the whole process chain is not changed. The lesson learnt from the pilots was that once information is electronic, it should stay electronic to avoid possible bottlenecks later in the system.

As the information collected from the field became electronic in the pilots, a *need emerged to spread it across different parties' information systems*. For example when a cleaner reported that he had cleaned a conference room, the information was expected also to be passed to the room reservation-system. The possibilities for work-flow-optimisation and worker coordination were seen as an important feature and as an incentive for NFC based solutions.

Some users *considered NFC based real time systems as a surveillance and distrust of their work ethic* although some others regarded the system to be helpful and provide evidence of the hard work they had done. Feeling of distrust was bigger when the work was done within a same organisation; in inter-organizational activities tracking of activities is regarded as normal part of work. User acceptance of these kinds of systems needs to be taken into account when planning them. An even more extended form of control are under-the-skin RFID chips of which commercial solutions already exist [29, 30] .

Table 4 summarizes the organizational problems NFC could solve and their realization in the pilot cases.

Table 4. Potential problems that NFC could solve and their realization in the pilot cases

Problems NFC could solve	Advantage of NFC use	Problem solved in the pilots
Limited access to information and data collection applications in the field	Enable access to information and applications in the field	Partly
Manual use of pen and paper in the field causes a lot of paperwork when the worker is back at the office	Real time updating of data	Yes
Manual re-entry of the collected data enhances the risk of making errors	Removal of human errors	Yes
Outdated client information/service history	Enabling access to real-time information	Not implemented
Outdated site/product/ service instructions	Enabling access to real-time instructions	Partly
User has to keep the information in his head until he updates the files	Reducing users' memory payload	Yes
Verifying if someone has been in a certain location and when	Ability to verify someone's presence in certain location	Yes

As can be seen from Table 4, NFC could solve most of the problems that appeared before implementing the pilots.

5 Conclusions and Further Research

The aim of this paper was to identify how NFC technology could be used to improve mobile solution workflows and usability and summarize what advantages/disadvantages NFC was seen to have. In general NFC is seen to have lot of potential especially in supply chain management, security, and tracking of objects and personnel. This paper contributed in the area by presenting six pilot cases where NFC could be used.

Based on the results of this study it was found out that NFC can improve mobile workflows by solving various problems related to mobile/remote work. In the pilot cases use of NFC solved wholly/partially the following problems: 1) enabling access to real-time information, applications and instructions in the field, 2) real time updating of data, 3) removal of human errors, 4) reducing users' memory payload, and 5) creating ability to verify someone's presence in certain location. As a disadvantage of NFC use was seen the possible shifting of the bottleneck forward in the organization, limitations caused by the small user interface of mobile devices and investments into the devices and system integration.

Considering mobile solution usability, this paper concluded that NFC based solutions are easy to use, but the small and limited keyboard of mobile devices poses challenges to the design of these solutions. From usability and user experience point of view in NFC based solutions emphasis should be placed in the following aspects: placing the tags, easiness of the application use and amount of textual input of data. The contexts and requirements for user friendliness were taken into account in the pilots, but they did not always impact the user experience.

This paper concluded that only a comprehensive solution achieves the full potential of NFC from users' point of view; realizing small parts does not help. If the rest of the system does not catch up, the users can regard using NFC only as an additional burden, which for example increases the handling times of forms and amount of errors later in the process. Based on the experiences received from the pilots, NFC use poses the following challenges to the organization: 1) the rest of the information system must catch up to avoid possible bottlenecks later in the system, 2) need to spread the information across different parties' information system, and 3) feeling of some users that real-time systems are used for their surveillance because of distrust towards their work.

Experiences received from all the pilots of this study have in general been positive and all pilots will either be implemented in future or there is going on discussions about their future implementation.

Considering the 'big picture' of RFID/NFC use, it has to be remembered that some users will consider NFC based real time systems as a surveillance and distrust of their work ethic. An even more extended form of control is under-the-skin RFID chips of which commercial solutions already exist. Wide use of under-the-skin chips enables 'Big Brother' kind of real-time surveillance of individuals and their actions.

In further research it could be evaluated if the advantages/disadvantages of NFC are realized also in other application areas and/or when the user amount is bigger than the pilots presented in this study. In future research it would also be interesting to compare user experiences received from various NFC solutions and draw general guidelines for designing user-friendly NFC solutions. As the pilots presented in this study has been implemented, it would also be interesting to collect user experiences from longer time period to find out how the implementation has improved the total workflow of the company and its usability. Integration of the pilots with rest of the system also leaves space for further research considering user-friendliness of the whole use process from beginning until end. The challenges posed by NFC to organizations and solving them leave also space for further research. The economic benefits of NFC use vs. their expenses provide also an interesting further research topic.

References

[1] Higa, K., Wijayanayake, J.: Telework in Japan: perceptions and implementation. In: Thirty-First Hawaii International Conference on System Sciences (1998)

[2] Harroud, H., Karmouch, A.: A policy based context-aware agent framework to support users mobility. In: Advanced Industrial Conference on Telecommunications, 2005. Telecommunications/Service Assurance with Partial and Intermittent Resources Conference/ E-Learning on Telecommunications Workshop. AICT/SAPIR/ELETE (2005)

[3] Yufei, Y., Wuping, Z.: The Fit between Mobile Task and Mobile Work Support: A Theoretical Framework. In: ICMB 2006. International Conference on Mobile Business (2006)

[4] Vuorinen, P.: Applying the RFID technology for field force solution. In: The 2005 Joint Conference on Smart Objects and Ambient intelligence: innovative Context-Aware Services: Usages and Technologies -sOc-EUSAI, October 12-14, 2005, Grenoble, France (2005)

[5] ISO, ISO 13407: 1999 International standard on Human-centred design processes for interactive systems, p. 32 (1999)

[6] Miller, J.: The User Experience. IEEE Internet Computing 9, 90–92 (2005)

[7] Väänänen-Vainio-Mattila, K., Ruuska, S.: Designing mobile phones and communicators for consumer's needs at Nokia. In: Bergman, E. (ed.) Information appliances and beyond. Interaction design for consumer products, pp. 169–204. Morgan Kaufmann Publishers, San Francisco (2000)

[8] Välkkynen, P., Niemelä, M., Tuomisto, T.: Evaluating touching and pointing with a mobile terminal for physical browsing. In: 4th Nordic Conference on Human-Computer interaction: Changing Roles, October 14-18, 2006, Oslo, Norway (2006)

[9] Rukzio, E.K.L., Callaghan, V., Schmidt, A., Holleis, P., Chin, J.: An experimental comparison of physical mobile interaction techniques: Touching, pointing and scanning. In: Dourish, P., Friday, A. (eds.) UbiComp 2006. LNCS, vol. 4206, Springer, Heidelberg (2006)

[10] ISO/IEC, ISO/IEC 14443 Standard on Proximity Cards (PICCS) (2007)

[11] ECMA, Standard ECMA-340: Near Field Communication interface and Protocol-1 (NFCIP-1) p. 65 (2004)

[12] ECMA, Standard ECMA-352: Near Field Communication Interface and Protocol-2 (NFCIP-2), p. 12 (2003)

[13] Ortiz Jr., S.: Is near-field communication close to success? IEEE Computer 39, 18–20 (2006)

[14] Want, R.: An Introduction to RFID Technology. IEEE Pervasive Computing 5, 25–33 (2006)

[15] Jalkanen, J.: User-initiated Context Switching using NFC. In: IJCAI 2005 Workshop on Modelling and Re-trieval of Context, Edinburgh (July-August 2005)

[16] Weinstein, R.: RFID: a technical overview and its application to the enterprise. IT Professional 7, 27–33 (2005)

[17] Yoon, S.C., Chang, H.O., Yoon, S.W., Jae, J.L., Jang, A.K., Min, S.K., Jun, S.P., Ung, Y.P.: Development of RFID Enabled Aircraft Maintenance System. In: IEEE International Conference on Industrial Informatics, IEEE Computer Society Press, Los Alamitos (2006)

[18] Dunlop, M., Brewster, S.: The challenge of mobile devices for human-computer interaction. Personal and ubiquitous computing 6, 235–236 (2002)

[19] Tilastokeskus, Televiestintä 2003- Kiinteät liittymät ja matkapuhelinliittymät 100 asukasta kohti vuosina 1990 ja 1995-2003 (2004)

[20] Michael, K., McCathie, L.: The pros and cons of RFID in supply chain management. In: ICMB 2005 (2005)

[21] Chuang, M.-L., Shaw, W.H.: How RFID will impact supply chain networks. In: 2005 IEEE International Engineering Management Conference (2005)

[22] Lefebvre, L.A., Lefebvre, E., Bendavid, Y., Wamba, S.F., Boeck, H.: RFID as an Enabler of B-to-B e-Commerce and Its Impact on Business Processes: A Pilot Study of a Supply Chain in the Retail Industry. In: HICSS 2006. The 39th Annual Hawaii International Conference on System Sciences (2006)

[23] Norman, D.A.: The psychology of everyday things. Basic Books, New York (1988)

[24] Belt, S., Greenblatt, D., Häkkilä, J., Mäkelä, K.: User Perceptions on Mobile Interaction with Visual and RFID Tags. In: MIRW 2006, Workshop W5 @ MobileHCI 2006, Espoo, Finland (2006)

[25] Välkkynen, P., Tuomisto, T.: Physical Browsing Research. In: Pervasive Mobile Interaction Devices (PERMID 2005)- Mobile Devices as Pervasive User Interfaces and Interaction Devices (2005)

[26] Salminen, T., Hosio, S., Riekki, J.: Enhancing Bluetooth connectivity with RFID. In: PerCom 2006. Fourth Annual IEEE International Conference on Pervasive Computing and Communications, IEEE Computer Society Press, Los Alamitos (2006)

[27] Hasselbring, W.: Information system integration. Communications of the ACM archive 43, 32–38 (2000)

[28] Garlan, D., Allen, R., Ockerbloom, J.: Architectural mismatch or why it's hard to build systems out of existing parts. In: 17th international conference on Software engineering, Seattle, Washington, United States (1995)

[29] Kanellos, M.: Under-the-skin ID chips move toward U.S. hospitals. CNET New.com (2004)

[30] VeriChip, Homepage of VeriChip (2007)

Author Index

Lecture Notes in Computer Science

Sublibrary 3: Information Systems and Application, incl. Internet/Web and HCI

For information about Vols. 1– 4365
please contact your bookseller or Springer

Vol. 4601: S. Spaccapietra, P. Atzeni, F. Fages, M.-S. Hacid, M. Kifer, J. Mylopoulos, B. Pernici, P. Shvaiko, J. Trujillo, I. Zaihrayeu (Eds.), Journal on Data Semantics IX. XV, 197 pages. 2007.

Vol. 4592: Z. Kedad, N. Lammari, E. Métais, F. Meziane, Y. Rezgui (Eds.), Natural Language Processing and Information Systems. XIV, 442 pages. 2007.

Vol. 4587: R. Cooper, J. Kennedy (Eds.), Data Management. XIII, 259 pages. 2007.

Vol. 4577: N. Sebe, Y. Liu, Y.-t. Zhuang, T.S. Huang (Eds.), Multimedia Content Analysis and Mining. XIII, 513 pages. 2007.

Vol. 4568: T. Ishida, S. R. Fussell, P. T. J. M. Vossen (Eds.), Intercultural Collaboration. XIII, 395 pages. 2007.

Vol. 4566: M.J. Dainoff (Ed.), Ergonomics and Health Aspects of Work with Computers. XVIII, 390 pages. 2007.

Vol. 4564: D. Schuler (Ed.), Online Communities and Social Computing. XVII, 520 pages. 2007.

Vol. 4563: R. Shumaker (Ed.), Virtual Reality. XXII, 762 pages. 2007.

Vol. 4561: V.G. Duffy (Ed.), Digital Human Modeling. XXIII, 1068 pages. 2007.

Vol. 4560: N. Aykin (Ed.), Usability and Internationalization, Part II. XVIII, 576 pages. 2007.

Vol. 4559: N. Aykin (Ed.), Usability and Internationalization, Part I. XVIII, 661 pages. 2007.

Vol. 4558: M.J. Smith, G. Salvendy (Eds.), Human Interface and the Management of Information, Part II. XXIII, 1162 pages. 2007.

Vol. 4557: M.J. Smith, G. Salvendy (Eds.), Human Interface and the Management of Information, Part I. XXII, 1030 pages. 2007.

Vol. 4541: T. Okadome, T. Yamazaki, M. Makhtari (Eds.), Pervasive Computing for Quality of Life Enhancement. IX, 248 pages. 2007.

Vol. 4537: K.C.-C. Chang, W. Wang, L. Chen, C.A. Ellis, C.-H. Hsu, A.C. Tsoi, H. Wang (Eds.), Advances in Web and Network Technologies, and Information Management. XXIII, 707 pages. 2007.

Vol. 4531: J. Indulska, K. Raymond (Eds.), Distributed Applications and Interoperable Systems. XI, 337 pages. 2007.

Vol. 4526: M. Malek, M. Reitenspieß, A. van Moorsel (Eds.), Service Availability. X, 155 pages. 2007.

Vol. 4524: M. Marchiori, J.Z. Pan, C.d.S. Marie (Eds.), Web Reasoning and Rule Systems. XI, 382 pages. 2007.

Vol. 4519: E. Franconi, M. Kifer, W. May (Eds.), The Semantic Web: Research and Applications. XVIII, 830 pages. 2007.

Vol. 4518: N. Fuhr, M. Lalmas, A. Trotman (Eds.), Comparative Evaluation of XML Information Retrieval Systems. XII, 554 pages. 2007.

Vol. 4508: M.-Y. Kao, X.-Y. Li (Eds.), Algorithmic Aspects in Information and Management. VIII, 428 pages. 2007.

Vol. 4506: D. Zeng, I. Gotham, K. Komatsu, C. Lynch, M. Thurmond, D. Madigan, B. Lober, J. Kvach, H. Chen (Eds.), Intelligence and Security Informatics: Biosurveillance. XI, 234 pages. 2007.

Vol. 4505: G. Dong, X. Lin, W. Wang, Y. Yang, J.X. Yu (Eds.), Advances in Data and Web Management. XXII, 896 pages. 2007.

Vol. 4504: J. Huang, R. Kowalczyk, Z. Maamar, D. Martin, I. Müller, S. Stoutenburg, K.P. Sycara (Eds.), Service-Oriented Computing: Agents, Semantics, and Engineering. X, 175 pages. 2007.

Vol. 4500: N.A. Streitz, A.D. Kameas, I. Mavrommati (Eds.), The Disappearing Computer. XVIII, 304 pages. 2007.

Vol. 4495: J. Krogstie, A. Opdahl, G. Sindre (Eds.), Advanced Information Systems Engineering. XVI, 606 pages. 2007.

Vol. 4480: A. LaMarca, M. Langheinrich, K.N. Truong (Eds.), Pervasive Computing. XIII, 369 pages. 2007.

Vol. 4473: D. Draheim, G. Weber (Eds.), Trends in Enterprise Application Architecture. X, 355 pages. 2007.

Vol. 4471: P. Cesar, K. Chorianopoulos, J.F. Jensen (Eds.), Interactive TV: A Shared Experience. XIII, 236 pages. 2007.

Vol. 4469: K.-c. Hui, Z. Pan, R.C.-k. Chung, C.C.L. Wang, X. Jin, S. Göbel, E.C.-L. Li (Eds.), Technologies for E-Learning and Digital Entertainment. XVIII, 974 pages. 2007.

Vol. 4443: R. Kotagiri, P. Radha Krishna, M. Mohania, E. Nantajeewarawat (Eds.), Advances in Databases: Concepts, Systems and Applications. XXI, 1126 pages. 2007.

Vol. 4439: W. Abramowicz (Ed.), Business Information Systems. XV, 654 pages. 2007.

Vol. 4430: C.C. Yang, D. Zeng, M. Chau, K. Chang, Q. Yang, X. Cheng, J. Wang, F.-Y. Wang, H. Chen (Eds.), Intelligence and Security Informatics. XII, 330 pages. 2007.

Vol. 4425: G. Amati, C. Carpineto, G. Romano (Eds.), Advances in Information Retrieval. XIX, 759 pages. 2007.

Vol. 4412: F. Stajano, H.J. Kim, J.-S. Chae, S.-D. Kim (Eds.), Ubiquitous Convergence Technology. XI, 302 pages. 2007.

Vol. 4402: W. Shen, J.-Z. Luo, Z. Lin, J.-P.A. Barthès, Q. Hao (Eds.), Computer Supported Cooperative Work in Design III. XV, 763 pages. 2007.

Vol. 4398: S. Marchand-Maillet, E. Bruno, A. Nürnberger, M. Detyniecki (Eds.), Adaptive Multimedia Retrieval: User, Context, and Feedback. XI, 269 pages. 2007.

Vol. 4397: C. Stephanidis, M. Pieper (Eds.), Universal Access in Ambient Intelligence Environments. XV, 467 pages. 2007.

Vol. 4380: S. Spaccapietra, P. Atzeni, F. Fages, M.-S. Hacid, M. Kifer, J. Mylopoulos, B. Pernici, P. Shvaiko, J. Trujillo, I. Zaihrayeu (Eds.), Journal on Data Semantics VIII. XV, 219 pages. 2007.